California Heritage Continues

Books by The Junior League of Pasadena

PASADENA PREFERS, VOLUMES I AND II
THE CALIFORNIA HERITAGE COOKBOOK
CALIFORNIA HERITAGE CONTINUES

California Heritage Continues

A COOKBOOK

The Junior League of Pasadena

PHOTOGRAPHY BY
Robin S. Muller

DOUBLEDAY & COMPANY, INC.
GARDEN CITY, NEW YORK

PUBLISHED BY DOUBLEDAY
a division of Bantam Doubleday Dell Publishing Group, Inc.
666 Fifth Avenue, New York, New York 10103

DOUBLEDAY and the portrayal of an anchor with a dolphin
are registered trademarks of Doubleday,
a division of Bantam Doubleday Dell Publishing Group, Inc.

The Junior League of Pasadena, Inc., is an organization of women committed to promoting voluntarism and to improving the community through the effective action and leadership of trained volunteers. Its purpose is exclusively educational and charitable.

The profit realized by The Junior League of Pasadena, Inc., from the sale of *California Heritage Continues* will be used for projects which we sponsor in the community, and it is to this community program that we dedicate our book.

DESIGN BY M FRANKLIN-PLYMPTON

Food Styling by Helene Tsukasa

Library of Congress Cataloging-in-Publication Data
California heritage continues.
    Includes index.
    I. Cookery, American—California style.
1. Junior League of Pasadena.
TX715.C15148   1987   641.59794   86-29175
ISBN 0-385-41759-4

Preface

California's proud heritage continues. From the Americans who have settled in California bringing regional cooking from all over our United States, to our south-of-the-border neighbors, to the new Californians of Asian, European, and Middle Eastern countries—all are influencing California cuisine today. The California style is distinctive, imaginative, fresh, and sophisticated.

Exquisite produce, wide varieties of fresh herbs from lemon thyme to cinnamon basil, fresh fruits, and vegetables of all sorts abound in markets everywhere. The freshest fish and seafood, straight from the seas and streams, beautiful meats, poultry, and game are readily available, and all are having a profound effect on everyday as well as special-occasion cooking. Not to be forgotten are the creative young chefs who are giving everyone the confidence to explore the new ingredients and lighter techniques.

The photographs in the book illustrate California's diverse and imaginative cooking. Four cities, Pasadena, San Diego, San Francisco, and Los Angeles, showcase four very different menus. Each represents a unique occasion for culinary enjoyment. The Pasadena New Year's Eve Dinner is a traditional but spectacular feast for a very special time of year in the City of Roses. A relaxing summer evening in San Diego is the theme of Southwestern with Style. To highlight San Francisco, what could be more appropriate than a lovely seafood luncheon? A lavish Oscar Night buffet featuring delectable appetizers and desserts celebrates Los Angeles.

We wish to thank Robin Muller, Photographer, and Helene Tsukasa, Food Stylist, for their talent, guidance, and patience with the photography. To all of the members and friends of The Junior League of Pasadena who submitted, tested, and tasted the recipes, we are very grateful. We especially thank Mr. Stanley Anderson of S. Anderson Wines, the author of our wine chapter; Nancy Smith, our talented graphic artist and Junior League member; Susan Kranwinkle and Peggy Rahn of Inner Gourmet Cooking School, Pasadena, California, who provided inspiration and support throughout the development of the book. We also appreciate the contributions of Jerry di Vecchio of *Sunset* Magazine, David Bean of KitchenAid, and Chef Lori Tannenbaum.

Mary Anne Borovicka—Chairman
Christine Benter—Assistant Chairman
Cynthia Yost—Sustaining Advisor

The California Heritage Continues Committee

Committee 1984–1985

Hilary Clark	Deborah Hollingsworth	Deborah Perkins
Tink Cheney	Vicki Hough	Donna Poulson
Nancy Cole	Kathleen LeRoy	Christine Reeder
Nadine Danz	Betsy Livadary	Nancy Smith
Patricia Ellison	Debby Mielke	Beth Stevens
Mary Kay Gilmour	Deborah Moore	Suzanne Wilcox
Parme Giuntini		

Committee 1985–1986

Hilary Clark	Deborah Hollingsworth	Lorraine Reaume
Nancy Cole	Vicki Hough	Nancy Smith
Nadine Danz	Kathleen LeRoy	Mary Thomas
Patricia Ellison	Betsy Livadary	Jo Anne Thompson
Mary Kay Gilmour	Deborah Moore	Beth Stevens
Parme Giuntini	Donna Poulson	Suzanne Wilcox

Committee 1986–1987

Hilary Clark	Deborah Moore	Nancy Smith
Nancy Cole	Donna Poulson	Jo Anne Thompson
Nadine Danz	Lorraine Reaume	Cyndia Wheeler

Editorial Committee

Nancy Cole	Donna Poulson
Nadine Danz	Nancy Smith
Deborah Moore	

Photography Committee

Deborah Moore
Donna Poulson
Nancy Smith

Computer Committee

Lorraine Reaume
Beth Stevens
JoAnne Thompson

Contents

I   *A Taste of Wine*   *1*

II   *Appetizers*   *9*

III   *Soup*   *49*

IV   *Salads*   *71*

V   *Pasta, Pizza and Rice*   *103*

VI   *Fish*   *131*

VII   *Poultry and Game*   *165*

VIII   *Meat*   *205*

IX   *Vegetables*   *243*

X   *Brunch and Lunch*   *275*

XI   *Breads*   *297*

XII   *Desserts*   *309*

XIII   *Menus*   *365*

Index   *373*

Whenever the name of a recipe is capitalized, the recipe is included elsewhere in the book and may be found by consulting the Index.

I

A Taste of Wine

It is a cool spring afternoon. A picnic table is set in the shade of a large wisteria, overlooking the vineyard's sea of green foliage. Thirty wineglasses, on a pristine white cloth are arranged in a semicircle at each place setting. Also on the table are blank cards for tasting notes and a basket of thinly sliced sourdough bread—to clear the palate. Awaiting nearby are the wines and culinary delights—the wines and cheeses coming to an even temperature, ready to offer themselves up to the arriving guests. Such is the setting for a wine tasting.

If we could listen to the comments an hour later, we might hear the tasters bandying wine vocabulary about. The appearance and color described in ruby reds to butterscotch gold; the brilliance against the white cloth. Some of the guests have a particularly keen sense of smell and would like to describe the bottle bouquet for as long as the aroma lingers in the glass. Full, fruity, pineapple, grapefruit, perhaps a hint of vanilla and berries or pepper in the "bigger" reds. Being lost in the noses for some time, (somewhat like a delectable tray of appetizers) the taste is really the main course. One swirls the glass again, takes a sip, and lets it roll over his tongue, slowly aerating the wine.

There is a sequential consideration to tasting wine: a beginning, a middle and a finish, during which one assesses balance, acid, fruit, and complexity, but most important, pleasure!

After several of the wines have been tasted, favorites will emerge. So now is the time to fill the glasses and explore tasting with the local chèvre, softened Brie, vegetable pâtés, a salmon mousse, and tarts of fresh fruit. The California wine adventure begins.

The cultivation of grapes and the art of wine making was introduced to California over two hundred years ago by the Spanish padres who built the missions throughout the state. Although wild grapes already grew along the river banks and hills near the missions, they were not suitable for the making of wine. It was Father Junipero Serra who first brought the Vitus vinifera, a vine of European origin, to California. The church maintained a monopoly on the wine making until 1833, when the Mexican Government ordered the secularization of the vast mission lands. As a result, most of the vineyards were abandoned and died from lack of care.

About the same time, in 1824, the first commercial winegrowers came from Europe to establish vineyards in California. They imported cuttings of different varieties of European grapes. The new cuttings made possible a greater variety of wines. With names like Haraszthy, Concannon, Beringer, Masson, Wente, and Korbel, immigrants brought their viticultural skills to the West. During the late 1800s and early 1900s, wine making came of age in California.

The Prohibition laws of 1919 put wine making in California and the United States on hold until repeal in 1933. It was not until the early 1960s that a renewed interest created a renaissance for California wine. The reality that there was an insufficient supply of quality grapes for wine sent the scientific experts and oenological prospectors to valleys throughout California to seek and develop additional plantings. As a consequence of this viticultural explosion, the number of wineries has grown from some two hundred wineries in 1960 to over seven hundred today.

With the diversity of plantings in new viticultural areas, the wine industry and the government sought to bring an element of constancy and control to the production of wine. The development of labeling laws provides the wine buyer with specific information including the appellation of origin, the variety of grape, alcohol content, grower and winery locale, and the year of production, if vintage dated. Reading the label, one can then glean the brand name and know something of the origin of the grapes. For instance, if the label boasts Napa Valley, one knows that 85 percent of the wine comes from this established viticultural area. Vintage dating, though optional, tells the buyer that at least 95 percent of the grapes used for the wine's production came from that year's harvest. If a grape variety is named, such as Chardonnay, it means that the wine contains at least 75 percent of that variety. Generic wines, where no specific grape variety is claimed, are considered a blend of different grapes and are usually red, white, or rosé. Interesting to the consumer is the "estate bottled" notation, which mandates that the wine must be produced entirely on that winery's premises from grapes grown on its own vineyards, all from within the same viticultural area.

Most wines state the alcohol content in percent by volume, however, a table wine is synonymous with an alcohol content under 14 percent. Other terms such as *private reserve* or *proprietor's selection,* though they have no legal meaning, are often used to indicate special lots.

Befitting any definitive cooking text is a mention of the complementation of wine and food. The possibilities and permutations are as endless as one's creativity. The traditional approach of red wine with red meats and white wine with fish or poultry offer the hostess a reliable guideline . . . but why restrict the gourmet? The current cooking trend is more imaginative and one can be as creative with wine as with nouvelle cuisine. In order to be creative with wine, though, one must have the confidence to experiment.

Before joining in the creative process though, you may find that a short description of several important varietals and conventional culinary complementation provides a helpful foundation.

Chardonnay

The queen of the full-bodied dry white wines is Chardonnay. The wine with its complex and unmistakable aroma and bouquet suggests many varieties of fruit, including green apples, citrus fruits, and melons. The caress of lingering buttery flavors on the palate and the fruity nuances when blended with the California style of fermentation and barrel aging provide a vinous balance that will complement the lighter fish, crab, scallops, veal, and poultry meats, yet stand up well to the sauce and spice of any nouvelle entree, including salmon, grilled pork—even lamb with chutney.

Chardonnay is produced in a range of styles from the very dry, flinty, and crisp style to the oaky and buttery "blockbusters" which will continue to develop for three to six years past their vintage date. The more than three hundred available Chardonnays produced in the United States allows this wine to sit at table with some of the finest culinary delights that can be designed. Chardonnay is most often at its very best when served at cellar temperature (58 degrees).

Sauvignon Blanc

The dramatic rebirth of Sauvignon Blanc as a stylish complement to a broad range of foods must certainly be attributed to the wine makers' enthusiastic efforts and imagination. A white grape with an intensely aromatic bouquet that seems best described as herbaceous or "grassy" has been created to complement poached, grilled, or creamed fish, chicken or lobster dishes as well as quiches, crepes, soufflés, and of course, salads. Sauvignon Blanc is produced in a vast profusion of styles, ranging from dry, crisp, lean, fruity, through the fuller oaky, smoky *fumés* to the dessert wines often married with Semillion grapes to give luscious, late-harvest, honey flavors. Most of these wines are at their best when served chilled.

Riesling

The Riesling wine represents the California wine maker's approach to the principal wine grape of Germany. Possessing an abundance of floral to rich stone fruit bouquet in the nose, the equally full varietal flavors may be tart and spicy, berrylike to honeyed fruit or pineapples on the palate. When produced in the dry style, the various menu directions of the wine serve most to complement lighter fish, stir-fry vegetables, shellfish, onion tarts, and crab salad.

Desserts, pastries, and pound cake are enhanced by the late harvest and botrytised offerings, many with slightly higher alcohols and residual sugar of up to 9 percent, giving these luscious wines a generous peach and apricot nuance on the finish. Riesling should be served chilled, but not colder than 50 degrees.

Cabernet Sauvignon

The king of red wines in California is considered by most to be the deep garnet product of the Cabernet Sauvignon grape. The "nose" can be an extraordinary combination of currants, chocolate, eucalyptus, cranberries, cherries, bell peppers, and even damp earth. The taste components, often minty, tannic, and berrylike when young, will mature to incredible softness and roundness of balance, at approximately four to six years of bottle age. A wine "not to be rushed" to the glass, Cabernet Sauvignon is a perfect partner with roasted, grilled, or sautéed beef as well as game or duck. A well-aged Cabernet Sauvignon is a fitting complement for cheese after any great meal. It is a grape often blended with merlot or cabernet franc for earlier consumption.

Cabernet Sauvignon, as with all red wines, should be served anywhere from cellar to room temperature, approximately 58 to 65 degrees.

Pinot Noir

A grape of two directions and purposes in California wine making is the Pinot Noir. Most recently it serves as the backbone of most sparkling wine cuvées. The greater quantity produces a medium to deep brilliant red wine. The nose can have qualities of rich musk, peppermint, and raspberries with overtones of crab apples and roses. This majestic wine can be robust with great berries, pepper, and spices exploding on the tongue, or a reserved one with velvety touches of fresh fruit in the Beaujolais style for picnic sipping. The classic Pinot Noir is best with beef, lamb, game fowl and venison, even eggs. Following the meal, it pairs wonderfully with nuts and cheeses.

Zinfandel

Quite probably the most "truly Californian" of any grape is the Zinfandel. Local history indicates substantial plantings of Zinfandel in the foothills of

Pasadena, La Canada, and Glendale in the grape boomlet of the 1880s. Alas, the land developers and Prohibition put an end to this viticulture. The plantings of Napa, Sonoma, and the "Mother Lode" counties now provide California and the world with this excellent grape. Zinfandel, with its aromas of ripe berries, sweet vanilla, spiced plums, and mint, has captured the loyalty of many wine lovers. The palate will often reveal chocolate, cinnamon, raspberries, vanilla, and pepper over a glycerine viscosity to give it the traditional "legs" in the glass. A moderate to big red wine, it may accompany red meat, barbecue, and even some Mexican dishes in its traditional style, but the recently popular white or "blush" Zinfandel has yet to capture a specific cuisine.

Red Zinfandel should be served at room temperature and white Zinfandel may be served chilled, but not colder than 50 degrees.

Sparkling Wines

A discussion of California wines would not be complete without some commentary on Champagne, or as it is more properly called outside of the Champagne district in France, sparkling wine. By strict definition, it is any wine containing dissolved carbon dioxide gas. But to the producer of sparkling wine and to those who find it pleasing to the palate, it is much more. There has been a tenfold increase in the consumption of sparkling wine in the last twenty years. This greater consumption parallels an increase in production across the oenological strata from the major producers of sparkling wine with their European influence and economic partners to the smaller boutique producers of small lots of a high-quality handmade product.

Reflected in the product outcome is the manner in which the sparkling wine was produced. The bulk technique or Charmat process involves fermenting the wine in a steel tank and then bottling; the transfer process describes a wine fermented in the bottle, removed from the bottle, clarified, and rebottled without loss of pressure; in the traditional *méthode champenoise* technique, the wine is shepherded through its development in the same bottle and may rest on the yeast several years in its riddling-board home in a stone cavern.

Sparkling wines can provide the perfect beginning or ending to an evening or enjoyed throughout the meal. They range in sweetness from the French classifications *brut,* with almost no perceptible sweetness, to *doux,* which is very sweet with 8–10 percent sugar content.

The drier creations complement such appetizers as oysters on the half shell, caviar, fois gras, seafood mousse, and delicate cheeses. As an accompaniment to desserts, sweeter wines are a wonderful choice. Sparkling wines are at their best served well chilled, about 40 degrees.

So, raise a glass and toast the full-bodied and complex Chardonnay, the aromatic Sauvignon Blanc, the royal Cabernet Sauvignon and the versatile California sparkling wines. Above all, have confidence, explore, and enjoy! Wine can be a wonderful social blender of and by itself but when used to complement lovingly planned and prepared cuisine, the real pleasure of life begins as the California heritage continues.

Stan Anderson

In an effort to develop an active lifestyle for his retirement years, Stanley Anderson and his wife, Carol, have created much more. As producers of Estate Chardonnay and fine sparkling wine, they are S. Anderson, Napa Valley, California.

The Andersons purchased thirty acres in the Napa Valley in 1971. For fifteen years, while continuing to practice dentistry in Pasadena, California, Stan and Carol commuted weekends, driving the four hundred miles to the Napa Valley to transform an old dairy farm into a productive winery. They were rewarded in 1980, when their first release of sparkling wine garnered a three-star rating from a prestigious California wine newsletter. The awards have been forthcoming ever since and after a thirty-two-year career in dentistry, Stan Anderson is a full-time vintner. The Andersons are now leading the energetic retirement they so desired, with their greatest reward being the excitement that comes from the knowledge that others are sharing in the enjoyment of their wine.

II

Appetizers

Crab and Asparagus Dijonnaise

MAKES ABOUT 24

2 1/4 teaspoons vegetable oil
2 1/4 teaspoons fresh lemon juice
1 teaspoon fresh minced
    tarragon *or* 1/4 teaspoon dried
    tarragon
1 1/2 teaspoons minced shallots
1/4 teaspoon salt
1/2 pound fresh crabmeat, cooked
    and shredded

2–3 heads Belgian endive,
    carefully separated, rinsed,
    and chilled
12 or more asparagus spears
    steamed, chilled, and split
    lengthwise
Dijon Sauce (below)

Combine the oil, lemon juice, tarragon, shallots, and salt. Toss with the crab. Place in a covered container and refrigerate for several hours to let flavors blend.

To serve, place an asparagus spear-half on each leaf of endive. Top with approximately 2–3 teaspoons Dijon Sauce and sprinkle with crab.

DIJON SAUCE

2 egg yolks, room temperature
1 tablespoon rice wine vinegar
2 teaspoons fresh lemon juice
5 teaspoons Dijon mustard
1/2 teaspoon sugar

1/4 teaspoon salt
Dash of white pepper
1/2 cup vegetable oil
1/2 cup Crème Fraîche

Place the egg yolks, vinegar, lemon juice, mustard, sugar, salt, and pepper in a blender. Blend for a few seconds. With the motor still running, add the oil in a slow steady stream until well incorporated. Remove the sauce to a bowl and whisk in the Crème Fraîche. Cover and refrigerate. This can be made several days in advance and kept in the refrigerator. Leftover sauce is wonderful with chilled artichokes.

Cold Mussels with Red Pepper Relish

SERVES 6

Succulent mussels brightened with red peppers epitomize the flavors of the new California cooking.

2 pounds mussels, unshelled
1/2 cup dry white wine
3 tablespoons unsalted butter
2/3 cup finely chopped red onions
1/4 cup minced green onions
2 cups finely chopped red bell
    peppers

1 tablespoon cider vinegar
4 teaspoons sugar
1/4 teaspoon freshly ground
    black pepper
1/8 teaspoon cayenne pepper

Place the mussels and wine in a large shallow pan with a lid. Cook, covered, over high heat for 5–8 minutes, or until the shells open. Shake the pan during cooking to prevent scorching. Using a slotted spoon, transfer the mussels to a jelly-roll pan, discarding any unopened shells. Discard the top shells and release the mussels from the bottom shells, leaving them in the shells. Chill the mussels, loosely covered with damp paper towels, at least 2 hours or overnight.

Melt the butter in a skillet. Add the red and green onions and cook until limp, about 5 minutes. Add the red peppers, cover the pan with a round of waxed paper, and steam for 3 minutes. Remove the paper and add the vinegar and sugar. Cook 1 minute. Add the black and cayenne peppers, stir, and cook 1 more minute. Remove from the heat and chill the mixture until ready to serve.

To serve, arrange mussels on a large platter or divide among 6 plates. Carefully spoon 1 teaspoon of the relish on each mussel.

Grilled Oysters

SERVES 6

A wonderful way to serve large Pacific oysters.

Rock salt
1 pound andouille sausage,
   grilled and sliced in 1/4-inch
   slices *or* 6 bacon slices,
   cooked and crumbled
2 dozen fresh oysters in the
   shell

Worcestershire Sauce
Tabasco sauce
6 green onion tops, finely sliced
2 lemons sliced in wedges, for
   garnish
Tomatillo Salsa (below)

Heat a large ovenproof platter spread with 1/2 inch of rock salt in a 450-degree oven for 15 minutes.

On a barbecue, grill the sausages until done. Remove. Place the oysters curved side down directly on the grill. When the shells open slightly (2–4 minutes), remove the oysters from the fire. Finish opening them with an oyster knife and discard the flat top shell. Arrange the oysters on the hot rock salt. Place a dash each of Worcestershire and Tabasco sauce on each oyster, top with a slice of sausage, and garnish with green onions. Serve with lemon wedges and Tomatillo Salsa.

TOMATILLO SALSA

3/4 pound tomatillos, husks
   removed *or* 1 cup canned,
   drained tomatillos
1/4 cup fresh cilantro leaves
2 tablespoons chopped green
   onions

1 small garlic clove
1/2–1 tablespoon seeded and
   chopped jalapeño chile, or to
   taste
1 tablespoon fresh lime juice
1/2 teaspoon salt

Combine all ingredients in food processor and process until almost smooth. Chill before serving.

Tangerine Scallops

MAKES 40

This colorful appetizer looks beautiful when presented on a black platter.

1 pound fresh scallops
8 tablespoons fresh lime juice
4 tangerines
1 garlic clove, minced
2 teaspoons peeled and minced
  fresh ginger
2 tablespoons honey

1 green onion, minced
1 teaspoon dried red pepper
  flakes
1/4 teaspoon black pepper
30 snow peas
1 (11-ounce) can mandarin
  oranges, drained

Cut the scallops in half. Place them in a glass bowl with the lime juice and marinate, refrigerated, 2 hours to "cook" them. Drain. Finely grate the peel of 2 of the tangerines. Squeeze the juice from these tangerines and the other 2 tangerines into a bowl. Add the grated tangerine peel, garlic, ginger, honey, onions, red pepper flakes and black pepper. Add the scallops and marinate, refrigerated, for at least 6 hours.

Before serving, blanch the snow peas in boiling water for 15 seconds. Drain and immediately refresh in cold water. Remove the ends and strings from the snow peas. Skewer an end of a snow pea on a toothpick, then a scallop half (or quarter if they are very large), and a mandarin orange slice; then wrap the remaining end of the snow pea around the scallop and orange and skewer onto the toothpick.

Dilled Shrimp on Cucumbers

MAKES 36

The shrimp's delicate pink against the deep green of the cucumber and dill makes this dish a striking beauty.

8 ounces cream cheese, softened
1/4 teaspoon cayenne pepper
3 anchovies, finely minced
2 green onions, minced
1 tablespoon peeled and minced
  fresh ginger
1 teaspoon finely grated lemon
  peel

2 tablespoons fresh dill
3 tablespoons capers
1 pound cooked bay shrimp,
  coarsely chopped
2 seedless cucumbers (English or
  hothouse), unpeeled
Salt and pepper
Fresh dill for garnish

Blend the cream cheese, cayenne, anchovies, green onions, ginger, lemon peel and dill until smooth. Gently mix in the capers and shrimp. Score the cucumbers lengthwise with a fork, cut into 1/4-inch slices, and salt and pepper lightly. Mound each cucumber slice with 1 1/2 teaspoons of the shrimp mixture. Garnish with a fresh dill sprig.

Shrimp Rémoulade

SERVES 6

1/2 cup chopped onions
3/4 cup vegetable oil
1/2 cup brown creole or any
  grainy spicy mustard
2 teaspoons paprika
3/4 teaspoon cayenne pepper
1/2 teaspoon salt

2 garlic cloves, minced
1/2 cup chopped green onions
2 pounds shrimp prepared with
  New Orleans Shrimp Boil
1 recipe New Orleans Shrimp
  Boil (below)

In a food processor, combine all of the ingredients except the green onions and shrimp. Process 5 seconds. Stir. Process for another 5 seconds. Add the green onions and process for 2 more seconds. Do not purée! Chill overnight. Serve the shrimp that have been prepared in the New Orleans Shrimp Boil on a platter of shredded lettuce. Either pour the sauce over the shrimp or use as a dip. Makes 2 cups sauce.

NEW ORLEANS SHRIMP BOIL
6 cups water
2 bay leaves
1 teaspoon dried basil
1 teaspoon dried thyme
2 teaspoons minced garlic
1 teaspoon salt

1 teaspoon dried mustard
1/2 teaspoon cayenne pepper
1/2 teaspoon black pepper
2 pounds medium shrimp,
  unpeeled

Place the water and spices in a large pot and bring to a boil. Reduce heat and simmer 5 minutes. Return to boiling and add the shrimp. Cook, uncovered over high heat 3–5 minutes or until pink. Drain the shrimp and cool. Peel and devein the shrimp. Chill well.

Solvang Caraway Cheese Spread

MAKES I ¼ CUPS

Especially good as spread on toasted black bread.

6 ounces cheese such as Gruyère
   or Jarlsberg, cut in chunks
1 teaspoon caraway seeds
2 tablespoons coarse-grained
   mustard

2 tablespoons mayonnaise
2 tablespoons unsalted butter,
   softened

Using a food processor, blend all the ingredients until smooth. Refrigerate several hours before serving for flavors to blend. This can be prepared several days ahead and refrigerated. Bring to room temperature before serving.

Parmesan French Toast

MAKES 32

1 egg
½ cup milk
Pinch cayenne pepper
12 slices very thin white bread,
   crusts removed

½ cup butter, melted
1 cup freshly grated imported
   Parmesan cheese

Preheat the oven to 450 degrees. Beat the egg and milk together with cayenne. Pour into a shallow baking dish and soak 4 slices of the bread, turning once. When the bread has absorbed most of the milk mixture, remove. Stack the bread slices in threes with the soaked bread in the center of each stack. Cut the bread stacks into quarters and dip all sides in the butter and then into the Parmesan cheese. Bake for 10 minutes or until browned. Cut each appetizer in half before serving. These can be assembled and refrigerated several hours ahead. Adjust cooking time for cold sandwiches.

Red Pepper Cheese Ball

SERVES 10–12

1 red bell pepper, seeded
1 pound sharp Cheddar cheese at
   room temperature
8 ounces cream cheese, softened

1 garlic clove, minced
1/4 teaspoon salt
Chili powder
Melba crackers

Combine the pepper, cheeses, garlic, and salt in a food processor and blend until smooth. Form into a ball and chill several hours until firm. Before serving, roll in chili powder. Serve with melba crackers.

Tomato Cheese Crostini

MAKES 2 DOZEN

1 narrow French bread baguette,
   frozen
Olive oil
8 ounces goat cheese with herbs
8 ounces ricotta cheese

8 ounces mozzarella cheese,
   grated
1 medium garlic clove, minced
White pepper to taste
24 sun-dried tomato halves

Preheat the oven to 300 degrees. Slice bread in 1/4-inch slices. Arrange on cookie sheet and brush tops with olive oil. Bake until golden brown. Increase oven temperature to 350 degrees. Combine the cheeses with garlic and pepper in a mixing bowl. Blend well. Spread each bread slice with some of the topping. Top with a sun-dried tomato half, and return to oven. Bake until cheese begins to melt.

ALTERNATE TOPPING FOR CROSTINI
8 ounces mascarpone or basil torta cheese
4 tablespoons fresh basil, finely chopped.

Use the cheese as a topping for crostini. Bake as directed above. Sprinkle with chopped basil before serving.

Brie with Apricot Sauce

SERVES 12

4 (10-ounce) cans whole peeled
    apricots, pitted
1/4 cup Grand Marnier, apricot
    brandy, or other fruit liqueur

1/4 cup slivered almonds
1 (10-inch) round Brie
Mild crackers

Preheat the oven to 275 degrees. Strain the apricots, reserving the syrup in a saucepan. Boil the syrup over high heat for 12–15 minutes, or until reduced by half. Cool. Add the liqueur and 16 of the apricots (use remainder for another purpose). On a cookie sheet, lightly brown almonds by baking for 10–15 minutes, watching them carefully. To serve, place the Brie on a serving plate, pour the sauce over, and top with almonds. Accompany with crackers.

Bread Round with Melted Brie

SERVES 10–12

Also very good with Camembert or St. André cheese.

1 (1-pound) round or oval loaf of
    day-old French bread
2 garlic cloves, minced

1/3 cup olive oil or melted butter
1 1/2 pounds Brie

Preheat the oven to 350 degrees. Cut off the top of the bread a quarter way down. Reserve the top. Carefully scoop out the inside, leaving a 1-inch shell and cut the bread in 1 1/2-inch cubes. Mix the garlic with oil. Brush the inside of the bread shell with half the mixture and the bread cubes with the remainder. Place the cheese with or without rind in bread shell, cutting to fit as needed. Replace the top.

    Place filled shell and bread pieces in a single layer on a 10 × 15-inch pan. Bake in the oven for 10 minutes. Remove the bread cubes to a rack and cool. Continue baking cheese-filled bread until the cheese melts, about 10 minutes longer. Serve with bread cubes for dipping.

Goat Cheese Mold

SERVES 10

Make this in a heart mold for Valentine's Day or a tree-shaped mold for Christmas.

16 ounces cream cheese,
  softened
8 ounces goat cheese, softened
2 tablespoons drained and
  chopped, bottled roasted red
  peppers

1/4 cup chopped fresh parsley
1/4 cup minced fresh chives
French bread rounds or water
  crackers

In a food processor, blend the cream cheese and the goat cheese until smooth. Line a 1 1/2- to 2-cup mold with damp cheesecloth. Spoon half the cheese mixture into the mold and top with the red peppers. Top with the remaining cheese. Tap the pan lightly to remove any air bubbles. Refrigerate covered, several hours or overnight. Turn onto a serving plate and peel away the cheesecloth. Press the parsley and chives around the molded cheese and serve with bread or crackers.

Gorgonzola Walnut Rounds

MAKES 2–3 DOZEN

1 narrow French bread baguette,
  frozen
1/2 cup olive oil
2 tablespoons chopped fresh
  basil, *or* 2 teaspoons dried
  basil

3 garlic cloves, minced
1/4 pound walnuts
1/3 pound Gorgonzola cheese,
  crumbled
Fresh basil leaves for garnish

Preheat the oven to 300 degrees. Slice the bread in 1/4-inch slices. Combine the olive oil, basil, and 2 of the garlic cloves. Reserving 1 tablespoon, brush this mixture on one side of each bread round. Bake until golden brown. Increase oven temperature to 350 degrees. In a food processor, blend walnuts, 1 garlic clove, and reserved oil until it reaches a pastelike consistency. Spread 2 teaspoons on the untoasted side of each bread round and top with crumbled cheese. Place in oven and bake until the cheese bubbles. Sprinkle with chopped basil.

Gruyère Puffs

MAKES 20

4 extra-large egg whites
7 ounces Gruyère cheese, grated

1 cup very fine day-old bread
   crumbs
Peanut oil

Beat the egg whites to soft peaks. Gently fold in the cheese. Form in 1-inch balls and roll in the bread crumbs. In a deep skillet or electric frying pan, heat 1 1/2 inches of oil to 425 degrees, and fry cheese balls until lightly browned, about 2 minutes per side. Drain well on paper towels. Serve immediately.

Layered Salmon Mold

SERVES 10–12

The combination of parsley and cornichons or fresh dill and capers make delightfully different creations.

1 pound cream cheese, softened
3 tablespoons minced fresh
   parsley or fresh dill
4 1/2 teaspoons minced onions
3 tablespoons minced cornichons
   or capers

8 ounces smoked salmon or lox,
   thinly sliced
Dill, for garnish
Tomato rose, for garnish
Cocktail rye rounds

Divide the cream cheese in 4 equal parts. Mix together the parsley or dill, onions, and cornichons or capers. Line a 6-inch round bowl or small fish mold with clear plastic wrap. Put one fourth of the cheese in the bottom of the bowl. Top with one third of the salmon. Sprinkle with one third of the onion mixture. Repeat this procedure twice more. Top with the remaining cheese. Cover with plastic wrap and press down on mold to even the mixture. Chill. To serve, unmold on a platter and garnish with a sprig of dill and a tomato rose. Serve with cocktail rye rounds.

Stilton Cheese Puffs

MAKES 32

1 pound Stilton or other blue-veined cheese, crumbled
2 tablespoons chopped fresh chives
1 (17-ounce) package frozen puff pastry, thawed according to package
instructions (or 1 pound of your own recipe)

Preheat the oven to 400 degrees. Combine the cheese and chives. Shape in
1-inch balls and freeze.

Roll out the puff pastry and cut out 2-inch rounds. Place a frozen cheese
ball on half the rounds. Top with a second circle and pinch dough together at
edges. Refreeze. Bake frozen pastries on an ungreased cookie sheet for 20
minutes. Serve hot.

Smoked Salmon with Wild Rice Pancakes

MAKES ABOUT 3 DOZEN

2 eggs
2 cups buttermilk
2 cups sifted flour
1 teaspoon baking soda
1 teaspoon salt
1/4 cup melted unsalted butter
2 cups cooked wild rice

1/2–3/4 pound smoked salmon,
  thinly sliced
2–3 medium avocados, peeled
  and sliced
1 cup sour cream
1 (2-ounce) jar caviar (optional)

Beat the eggs until thickened. Stir in the buttermilk and set aside. Sift together
the flour, soda, and salt. Gradually add the flour mixture to liquid, beating
constantly. Add the butter and wild rice. Let stand for 10 minutes. Heat a
heavy griddle or skillet, brush with butter, and pour the batter into 2-inch
pancakes. Turn when bubbles appear and edges are dry. Remove to a warm
platter. Can be made ahead and reheated in foil.

To assemble, cover each pancake with salmon slices. Top with 2–3 avocado
slices and 1 teaspoon sour cream. Garnish with caviar, if desired. Pancakes
should be served warm.

Gravlax with Mustard Sauce

SERVES 10

A superb alternative to smoked salmon.

1/2 cup sugar
1/4 cup coarse salt
1 tablespoon freshly ground
  pepper
2 pounds center-cut salmon
  fillets with skin on

2 bunches fresh dill, coarsely
  chopped
Mustard Sauce (below)
1 French bread baguette, thinly
  sliced and toasted

Combine the sugar, salt, and pepper. Place 1 salmon fillet skin side down in a ceramic or glass dish. Rub half the sugar mixture on the exposed side. Cover with dill. Rub the remaining sugar mixture into the second fillet. Place skin side up on top of first fillet and cover with dill. Cover the fish with plastic wrap, sealing the sides. Place a board on top and weight the salmon. Refrigerate for at least 2 days, turning and basting 3 times a day with the accumulated juices.

To serve, scrape away the dill and spices and thinly slice the salmon fillets diagonally to the skin, but not through the skin. Accompany with Mustard Sauce and French bread toasts.

MUSTARD SAUCE
1/4 cup chopped fresh dill
1 cup olive oil
6 tablespoons Dijon mustard
1/4 cup white vinegar

2 tablespoons sugar
1 teaspoon prepared horseradish
Salt and freshly ground pepper
  to taste

Combine all ingredients in a blender or food processor and blend until smooth. Refrigerate overnight to blend the flavors.

Roasted Pepper Spread

MAKES I CUP

1 (7-ounce) jar roasted red
    peppers, drained
1–2 jalapeño chiles, seeded
4 large green olives, pitted
1 tablespoon fresh parsley

2 teaspoons olive oil
1 1/2 teaspoons fresh lemon juice
Salt and pepper
French bread or sesame crackers

In a food processor, finely chop the peppers, olives, and parsley. Add the olive oil and lemon juice and process just until mixed. Add salt and pepper to taste. Spread on French bread slices or sesame crackers.

Layered California Guacamole

SERVES 8

4 ripe avocados, mashed
1/2 cup sour cream
1–2 drops Tabasco sauce
1 garlic clove, minced
1/2 teaspoon salt
1/4 cup fresh lemon juice
4 ounces sharp Cheddar cheese,
    grated

4 ounces Jack cheese, grated
4 medium tomatoes, diced
1/2 cup chopped green onions
3/4 cup sliced pitted black olives
3/4 cup sour cream
1 cup Salsa
1/4 cup chopped fresh cilantro
Tortilla chips

Combine the avocados with the 1/2 cup sour cream, Tabasco, garlic, salt, and lemon juice. On a serving platter, layer ingredients in the following order: avocado mixture, cheeses, tomatoes, green onions, olives, sour cream, Salsa, cilantro. Serve with tortilla chips.

Salsa

MAKES ABOUT 2 CUPS

3–4 long green chiles, *or* 1
  (4-ounce) can green chiles,
  chopped
1 jalapeño chile, chopped
1/2 cup sliced green onions
1/3 cup minced fresh cilantro
1/2 cup minced red onions

3 garlic cloves, minced
1/8 cup lime juice
2 tablespoons salad oil
1 teaspoon salt
3 tomatoes, chopped
2 medium avocados, (optional)
Tortilla chips

If using fresh chiles, roast and peel by the following method: Using a long-handled fork, char the chiles over an open flame, turning them for 2–3 minutes, or until the skins are blackened. Or, place the chiles on a broiler pan and broil about 2 inches from the heat until the skins are blackened, turning frequently. This will take approximately 15 minutes. (Use care when handling fresh chiles, wearing gloves if necessary.) Transfer the chiles to a plastic bag, close tightly, and let them steam until they are cool enough to handle. Peel, seed, and chop into small dice. If using canned chiles, drain thoroughly.

In a bowl, combine the chiles with the green onions, cilantro, red onions, garlic, lime juice, oil, and salt. Add the tomatoes and chill. At serving time, peel and chop the avocados, if desired and add to the Salsa. Serve with tortilla chips at room temperature.

Moroccan Dip

MAKES 1 1/2 CUPS

3 large garlic cloves
1/3 cup olive oil
2 (15-ounce) cans garbanzo
  beans
1/3 cup fresh lemon juice

2 drops Tabasco sauce
1/4 teaspoon salt
Chopped fresh parsley
Paprika
Pita bread or crudités

In a food processor, mince the garlic. Slowly add the oil. Drain the garbanzo beans, reserving 1/4 cup liquid. Add the beans, reserved bean liquid, lemon juice, Tabasco, and salt to the food processor and blend until puréed. Serve at room temperature, garnished with parsley and paprika. Use as a dip for pita bread or crudités.

Beet Dip

MAKES 3/4 CUP

1 green onion
1/4 pound raw beets, peeled and
  quartered
4 tablespoons chopped
  watercress
6 ounces cream cheese, softened
1 teaspoon fresh lemon juice

1 eggplant or green cabbage
Crudités such as jícama,
  cauliflower, snow peas,
  zucchini, cucumbers, green
  beans, radish roses, white
  carrots, baby corn

Chop the onion in a food processor. Add the beets and process until finely chopped. Add the watercress and process 5 seconds. Add the cream cheese and lemon juice and process until the mixture is well blended. Slice a wedge off the bottom of the eggplant or cabbage so that it will stand up straight. Hollow out the inside and fill it with the beet mixture. To serve place the eggplant or cabbage on a serving tray and surround with the crudités.

Herb Cheese

MAKES 3 CUPS

Make this in the summertime when fresh herbs are bountiful.

1 1/2 pounds small-curd creamed
  cottage cheese
1 tablespoon sour cream
1 pound cream cheese
3 garlic cloves, finely minced
1 shallot, finely minced
1/2 teaspoon salt
1 teaspoon finely chopped fresh
  basil
1/2 teaspoon finely chopped fresh
  tarragon

1/2 teaspoon finely chopped fresh
  thyme
1/2 teaspoon finely chopped fresh
  sage
1/2 teaspoon ground white pepper
2 tablespoons chopped fresh
  chives
2 tablespoons finely chopped
  fresh parsley
Crackers, bread, or crudités

In a food processor or blender, process cottage cheese until smooth. Add the remaining ingredients and beat until creamy. Let stand 24 hours in refrigerator, covered. Serve with crackers, bread, or crudités.

Indian Dip

MAKES 4 CUPS

1 (9-ounce) bottle Major Grey
   chutney
1 cup chunky peanut butter
3/4 cup refried beans
2 tablespoons canned chopped
   green chiles

5 drops Tabasco sauce
2 teaspoons ground coriander
1 teaspoon ground cumin
1/4 teaspoon cayenne pepper
1/2–1 cup Chicken Stock
Curried Cracker Bread (below)

Using a food processor, purée the chutney. In a saucepan bring to a boil the
peanut butter, refried beans, chiles, Tabasco, and spices. Add the hot mixture
to the chutney and blend until smooth, using Chicken Stock to thin to desired
consistency. Taste and adjust seasoning. May be kept refrigerated up to 1
week. Serve warm or at room temperature with Curried Cracker Bread.

CURRIED CRACKER BREAD
1/2 cup butter
1 teaspoon curry powder
1 large round cracker bread (Lahvosh)

Preheat the oven to 275 degrees. Melt the butter, and add the curry. Brush
both sides of the cracker bread with the mixture. Place on a buttered cookie
sheet and bake about 20 minutes, or until lightly browned. Remove from oven.
When cool, break in pieces.

Pâté with Green Peppercorns

MAKES 2 CUPS

6 cups water
1 bay leaf
1/4 cup chopped celery
1/4 cup peeled and chopped
   carrots
8 black peppercorns
1 pound chicken livers
6 tablespoons unsalted butter
1/2 cup minced red onions
2 garlic cloves, minced

1 1/2 teaspoons marjoram
2 tablespoons brandy
1/2 teaspoon salt
1/2 teaspoon ground allspice
1 teaspoon Dijon mustard
1/4 cup heavy cream
3 tablespoons water-packed
   green peppercorns, drained
French bread

In a large pan, bring the water, bay leaf, celery, carrots, and black peppercorns to a boil. Reduce heat and simmer 10 minutes. Add the livers and simmer 10 minutes. Drain the livers and set them aside. Discard vegetables. Melt the butter in a medium skillet and add the onions, garlic, and marjoram, and cook over medium heat until the onion is tender, but not browned. Combine the onion mixture, cooked livers, brandy, salt, allspice, and mustard in a food processor and process until smooth. Add the cream and process a few more seconds. Remove to a 2-cup crock and gently stir in the green peppercorns. Refrigerate 4 hours or overnight. Serve with thinly sliced French bread.

Carpaccio

SERVES 8–12

Those who favor steak tartare will delight in this appetizer introduced to California from the cuisine of Italy.

3/4 **pound very fresh top sirloin or top round**
1 **teaspoon salt**
2 **teaspoons freshly ground pepper**
1/2 **cup capers, rinsed and drained**
3–4 **garlic cloves, finely chopped**
1 **medium onion, minced**
1/2 **cup chopped fresh parsley**
1/2 **cup finely chopped green onions**

2 **teaspoons finely grated lemon peel**
3/4 **cup olive oil**
4–6 **tablespoons red wine vinegar**
4 **ounces imported Parmesan cheese, thinly sliced**
1 **hard-boiled egg, chopped**
1 **French bread baguette, sliced**

Trim the fat from meat and slice in wafer-thin slices. (This is easier if the meat has been placed in the freezer just long enough for ice crystals to form, but not long enough to freeze solid.) Arrange the meat on a large platter so that it overlaps slightly. Season with salt and pepper. Sprinkle with capers, garlic, onions, parsley, green onions, and lemon peel. Mix together oil and vinegar and drizzle over meat. Refrigerate 30 minutes. Before serving arrange cheese slices and egg on top. Serve with lightly toasted sliced French bread.

Veal and Pork Terrine

SERVES 10–12

Like a French charcuterie's country pâté, this will reward your extra effort with compliments.

1/2 cup brandy
8 medium pitted prunes
1 pound pork stew meat, finely ground
1 pound veal stew meat, finely ground
1/4 pound pork fat, ground
4 medium shallots, finely chopped
2 garlic cloves, minced
1/4 cup flour
2 eggs
1/3 cup heavy cream
1/2 cup chopped fresh parsley

1/4 pound chicken livers, ground
1 1/2 teaspoons salt
1/2 teaspoon finely ground pepper
1/2 teaspoon dried savory
1 teaspoon dried thyme
1 teaspoon ground allspice
1 teaspoon cinnamon
1 teaspoon nutmeg
1/4 cup pistachios
1/2 pound bacon
1 bay leaf
Fresh parsley sprigs, for garnish

Heat the brandy in a small saucepan over medium heat. Remove from the heat, add the prunes, and let stand 30 minutes to plump. Preheat oven to 300 degrees. In a large bowl, combine the pork, veal, and pork fat and blend well. Add the shallots, garlic, and flour. Strain the brandy into this mixture, reserving prunes. Blend the meat mixture well. Add eggs, cream, and parsley and blend. Add the chicken livers and seasonings and mix until ingredients are well combined. Add the pistachios and blend again.

Completely line the bottom and sides of a large (11 1/2 × 5 1/2 × 4-inch) terrine or loaf pan with bacon strips, allowing 2–3 inches of strips to overhang pan sides. Put half of the meat mixture in the pan. Arrange the reserved prunes along the center of meat and top with remaining meat mixture, carefully patting down to remove air bubbles. Cover the top with overhanging bacon and place the bay leaf in the center. Cover with aluminum foil. Place the terrine in a larger pan and add enough water to come halfway up terrine. Bake at 300 degrees for 3 1/2 hours. Remove from oven and place cooking weights or a brick over the foil. (A weighted terrine is denser and easier to serve.) Drain off accumulated fat. Cool 1 hour at room temperature. Place in refrigerator and cool completely. When terrine is cool, wrap in aluminum foil and refrigerate until serving. This terrine is best if prepared 2 days in advance.

Gorgonzola-Pistachio Loaf

MAKES I LOAF

1 pound cream cheese, softened
1/2 pound Gorgonzola cheese,
    softened
1 cup unsalted butter, softened

1 cup chopped fresh parsley
1 cup shelled, chopped pistachios
French bread slices or crackers

Line an 8 × 4-inch loaf pan with two moistened 18-inch cheesecloth squares, or plastic wrap, draping the excess over the sides. Combine the cream cheese, Gorgonzola, and butter and blend well. Spread one third of cheese mixture into the prepared pan. Sprinkle with parsley. Cover with half of the remaining cheese mixture. Sprinkle with the pistachios. Top with the remaining cheese mixture. Fold the ends of cloth over top and press down lightly. Refrigerate until firm, about 1 hour. Invert onto a serving plate and carefully remove cheesecloth. Serve at room temperature with sliced French bread or crackers.

Indian Meatballs with Mint Chutney

MAKES 4 DOZEN

1/2 cup golden raisins, plumped
    in hot water for 15 minutes,
    drained, and chopped
1/4 cup minced green onions
1/2 cup coarsely chopped pine
    nuts, lightly toasted
1 teaspoon ground allspice

1 teaspoon cinnamon
1/2 teaspoon salt
2 garlic cloves, minced
1 pound ground lamb
1/3 cup olive oil
Mint Chutney

In a large bowl, combine the raisins, green onions, pine nuts, spices, garlic, and lamb. Mix well. Using a rounded tablespoon of mixture, form into balls. In a large heavy skillet, heat the oil over moderately high heat until hot but not smoking. Brown the meatballs for 7–8 minutes, turning frequently. Drain on paper towels. Serve hot with Mint Chutney.

Sausage in Brioche

SERVES 10

A sophisticated appetizer for an important cocktail buffet.

1/2 cup milk
2 packages dry yeast
Pinch of sugar
2 cups unbleached white flour
1 teaspoon salt
1 tablespoon sugar
4 large eggs

1/2 cup unsalted butter, melted
Coarse grained mustard
2 spicy smoked Polish Kielbasa
   sausages, about 1/2 pound each
   cooked saucisson d'lail
2 tablespoons milk

Preheat the oven to 400 degrees. Warm the 1/2 cup of milk to 110 degrees. Combine the milk, yeast, and pinch of sugar. Let stand for 10 minutes. Combine the flour, salt, and sugar in a large mixing bowl. Add the yeast mixture and 3 of the eggs. Mix well. Add the butter and mix well. Knead the dough for a few minutes in the bowl. Pick up a handful and slap it against the side of the bowl. The dough should be moist but hold together well. If too moist, add a bit more flour. Sprinkle a board lightly with flour. Turn the dough out and continue kneading by lifting and slapping the dough onto the bread board for 3 minutes. When the dough is smooth and elastic, place it in a buttered mixing bowl. Cover the bowl with plastic wrap and put in a warm place to rise for 1 hour. Punch down the risen dough and divide in half. On floured surface, roll or pat each of the two pieces into rectangular shapes a little longer than the sausages. Spread with a thin layer of mustard; enclose a sausage in each dough rectangle. Place the brioche on a buttered cookie sheet, cover and let rise in a warm place for 1 hour. Lightly beat together the remaining egg with the 2 tablespoons of milk. Brush the surface of the brioche and bake for 30 minutes or until the tops are golden brown. Slice and serve with mustard.

These freeze well. Reheat in a slow oven.

Spicy Chicken Wings

MAKES 24 PIECES

24 chicken wings (disjointed,
   tips discarded)
Garlic salt

Onion salt
Freshly ground pepper
Peanut Sauce (below)

Preheat broiler or barbecue. Sprinkle the chicken with garlic salt, onion salt, and pepper. Broil on a rack 4–6 inches from heat source until crisp and brown, about 3–5 minutes per side. Serve hot or at room temperature with Peanut Sauce.

PEANUT SAUCE

1/3 cup apricot preserves
1/3 cup half-and-half
1/3 cup peanut butter

2 tablespoons soy sauce
1 tablespoon fresh lemon juice

Combine all of the ingredients in a blender or food processor and blend until smooth. Serve at room temperature.

Beef Satay

MAKES 60

2 pounds flank steak, slightly frozen
1 large garlic clove, minced
1/2 cup minced onions
1 teaspoon ground coriander
1 tablespoon sugar
1/4 cup soy sauce
1/4 cup fresh lemon juice

1 teaspoon salt
1/4 teaspoon pepper
1/4 teaspoon dried red pepper flakes
60 long wooden skewers
Indonesian Dipping Sauce (below)

Slice the steak against the grain into 1/4-inch strips. In a large glass bowl, combine the garlic, onions, coriander, sugar, soy sauce, lemon juice, and seasonings. Add the meat and marinate for 6 hours or overnight. Soak the skewers in water for 1 hour. Thread each strip of meat on a skewer and grill over hot coals for 10 minutes, turning frequently. The meat may also be broiled.

INDONESIAN DIPPING SAUCE

2 large garlic cloves, minced
1 1/2 cups unsweetened coconut milk
2/3 cup peanut butter
4 teaspoons sugar
1/4 teaspoon cayenne pepper
1 tablespoon soy sauce

2 tablespoons fresh lemon juice
1/2 teaspoon dried red pepper flakes
1/2 cup heavy cream
1/2 teaspoon ground coriander
1/4 teaspoon ground cumin

Mix all of the ingredients in a blender or food processor and blend until smooth.

Escargot and Prosciutto Stuffed Mushrooms

MAKES 24

6 tablespoons unsalted butter
24 medium mushrooms, stems
  removed
2 shallots, minced
1/2 cup chopped prosciutto
4 garlic cloves, minced
1/2 teaspoon thyme

3 tablespoons minced fresh
  parsley
1/4 cup peeled, finely chopped,
  tomato
3 tablespoons dry vermouth
1 (7 1/2-ounce) can snails, rinsed,
  drained, and chopped

In a large skillet, melt 4 tablespoons of the butter and sauté mushrooms until soft, about 5 minutes. Remove the mushrooms and drain on paper towels. In another pan sauté the shallots, prosciutto, and garlic in the remaining 2 tablespoons of butter until soft. Add thyme, parsley, tomato, and vermouth and cook over medium heat for 10 minutes. Add the snails and heat through. Fill the mushroom caps with the snail mixture. Place in a shallow baking dish and broil until hot, about 3 minutes.

Mushrooms Stuffed with Smoked Oysters

MAKES 30

6 tablespoons butter
30 medium mushrooms, stems
  removed
2 tablespoons brandy
1/4 cup minced fresh chives

1/4 pound salted cashews,
  chopped
6 ounces cream cheese
3 ounces smoked oysters,
  drained and halved

In a large skillet, melt 4 tablespoons of the butter and sauté mushrooms until tender, about 5 minutes. Add the brandy. Heat and ignite. Swirl the pan until the flame dies. Remove the mushrooms and drain on paper towels. In another pan, sauté the chives and cashews in the remaining 2 tablespoons of butter for 1 minute. Remove from heat and add cream cheese, blending well. Fill the mushroom caps with the cheese mixture and top each with an oyster half. Arrange in a baking dish and broil 2–4 minutes until hot.

Chinese Wontons

SERVES 8–10

These can be frozen after cooking and reheated for 30 minutes in a 300-degree oven.

1 pound ground pork
1 tablespoon salad oil
1 (5-ounce) can water chestnuts, finely chopped
2 green onions, thinly sliced
2 tablespoons soy sauce
1 garlic clove, minced

1 tablespoon sherry
1 teaspoon cornstarch
1 package wonton skins
2 eggs, beaten
Cooking oil
Currant Mustard Sauce (below)

Fry the pork in the oil until just brown and crumbly. Add the chestnuts, green onions, soy sauce, garlic, sherry and cornstarch. Cook 1 minute and remove from heat. Put 1 heaping teaspoon of the pork mixture in the center of a wonton skin. Moisten two edges of skin with beaten egg. Fold the corners in to form a square pouch and press edges to seal. Repeat with remaining wonton skins. Heat 2 inches of oil in a large skillet. Fry 6 wontons at a time for 1–2 minutes until light golden brown. Turn to cook evenly. Serve immediately or keep warm in a 200-degree oven. Serve with Currant Mustard Sauce.

CURRANT MUSTARD SAUCE   MAKES 1 ½ CUPS

1 cup currant jelly
1/2 cup Dijon mustard
1/2 cup dried currants

In a small saucepan, heat the jelly, mustard, and currants. Simmer for 5 minutes.

Indian Wontons

SERVES 8–10

2 tablespoons peeled and minced
 fresh ginger
1/4 cup chopped green onions
1 tablespoon corn oil
1 teaspoon chili powder
1 teaspoon turmeric
2 teaspoons Garam Masala
 (below)

1 teaspoon salt
1 pound ground lamb
1 cup hot water
2 tablespoons chopped fresh
 cilantro
1 package wonton skins
1 egg, beaten

In a medium skillet, sauté the ginger and onions in the oil. Add the spices and sauté for 2 minutes. Add the lamb and cook, stirring occasionally, for 5 minutes. Add 1 cup hot water and cook over low heat until liquid is absorbed. Add cilantro. Remove from heat and cool. Put 1 heaping teaspoon of lamb mixture in the center of a wonton skin. Moisten two edges of skin with beaten egg. Fold corners in to form a square pouch and press edges to seal. Repeat with remaining wonton skins. Heat 2 inches of oil in a large skillet. Deep-fry 6 wontons at a time for 1–2 minutes until light golden brown. Turn to cook evenly. Serve immediately or keep warm in a 200-degree oven. (These freeze well. Reheat for 30 minutes in a 300-degree oven.)

GARAM MASALA

MAKES 1 CUP

Garam Masala is used in most Indian dishes, giving an extra taste and fragrance to food.

20 large black cardamom seeds
1/4 cup coriander seeds
4 tablespoons cumin seeds

2 tablespoons cloves
2 tablespoons ground cinnamon

Remove the skins from the cardamom seeds. Mix together coriander, cumin and cloves and finely grind in a coffee grinder. Add the cinnamon. Keep in an airtight jar.

Thai Lamb in Lettuce Leaves

SERVES 6–8

2 heads Boston or Bibb lettuce
2 tablespoons olive oil
1 2-inch piece fresh ginger,
   peeled and minced
3 garlic cloves, minced
1 pound ground lamb

1/2 cup chopped fresh mint
1 teaspoon sesame seeds
1/2 teaspoon dried rosemary
1/4–1/2 teaspoon dried red pepper
   flakes
1/4 cup fresh lime juice

Rinse and separate lettuce leaves into cups. Chill. Heat the oil in a skillet. Sauté the ginger and garlic until golden. Add the lamb and fry over medium heat until brown and crumbly, 5–10 minutes. Stir in mint, sesame seeds, rosemary, red pepper, and lime juice. Transfer to a heated serving dish. To serve, spoon a generous tablespoon of hot lamb into each chilled lettuce cup.

Minced Chicken in Lettuce

SERVES 6–8

Sometimes made with squab, this is a popular first course at some of California's finest Chinese restaurants.

2 heads Boston or Bibb lettuce
3 tablespoons vegetable oil
1 (1-inch) piece fresh ginger,
   peeled and minced
1 whole large chicken breast,
   boned, skinned, and diced
1/4 cup chopped mushrooms
1/4 cup chopped water chestnuts
1 tablespoon chopped bamboo
   shoots

1/4 cup chopped green onions
1/4 cup minced pine nuts
1 teaspoon dried red pepper
   flakes, or less, to taste
1 teaspoon dark soy sauce
1/2 teaspoon sugar
1 teaspoon sesame oil

Rinse and separate lettuce leaves into cups. Chill. Heat the oil in a wok. Brown the ginger in the oil to flavor it. Remove ginger and discard. Add the chicken to the oil and stir-fry for 1 minute. Add the mushrooms, water chestnuts, bamboo shoots, onions, pine nuts, red pepper flakes, soy sauce, and sugar. Cook for 15 minutes, and add the sesame oil. Transfer to a heated serving dish. To serve, spoon a generous tablespoon of hot chicken into a chilled lettuce cup.

Quesadilla

MAKES 24

12 medium flour tortillas
1/4 cup unsalted butter, melted
3/4 cup Tomatillo Sauce (fresh or bottled)

1 pound Jack cheese, grated
1/2 cup chopped fresh cilantro
1/4 cup finely grated Parmesan cheese

Preheat the oven to 350 degrees. Place 1 tortilla on a buttered cookie sheet and brush it with butter. Top with some sauce, Jack cheese, and cilantro. Repeat for 2 more layers. Top with a tortilla, brush with butter, and sprinkle with Parmesan cheese. Repeat the entire procedure using the remaining tortillas to make 3 stacks. Bake for 10 minutes, or until lightly browned. Cut each stack in 8 wedges and serve immediately.

Chile Bites

MAKES 20

These mild chiles are filled with spicy tuna. Also try them with Horseradish Beef Filling or Smoked Salmon Filling (below).

4 fresh long green chiles, about 6 inches long
6 ounces cream cheese, softened
1 (9-ounce) can water-packed tuna, drained
1/2 teaspoon ground cumin

2 tablespoons chopped fresh cilantro
2 green onions, finely chopped
2 tablespoons canned, chopped green chiles

Carefully slit the chiles lengthwise. Under running water, remove the seeds, being careful to retain the chiles' shape. Set aside. Combine the cream cheese, tuna, and cumin. Add the cilantro, green onions, and chiles. Fill the chiles with the tuna mixture. Refrigerate several hours or overnight. Before serving, slice the chiles in 1/2-inch rounds.

HORSERADISH BEEF FILLING
4 ounces roast beef, minced
6 ounces cream cheese, softened
1 tablespoon prepared horseradish

Combine all of the ingredients and blend well. Use as a filling for Chile Bites.

SMOKED SALMON FILLING

6 ounces smoked salmon, minced
6 ounces cream cheese, softened
3 tablespoons fresh lime juice

1 tablespoon minced onions
3 tablespoons minced fresh dill
or 1/2 tablespoon dried dill

Combine all the ingredients and blend well. This is best if flavors are allowed to blend 2–3 hours before serving. Use as a filling for Chile Bites.

Radicchio Cups with Smoked Chicken

SERVES 10–12

1 celery root
2 tablespoons fresh lime juice
2 heads radicchio
2 cups shredded Smoked
  Chicken

Red Chile Mayonnaise (below)
Minced fresh cilantro, for
  garnish

Peel and shred the celery root. Toss with lime juice to prevent discoloration. Cut off root end of radicchio to facilitate separating leaves. Rinse leaves and pat dry. Cut leaves in half if they are large. Fill each radicchio cup with shredded chicken, 1 tablespoon Red Chile Mayonnaise, and shredded celery root. Sprinkle with minced cilantro.

RED CHILE MAYONNAISE   MAKES 1 CUP

1/2–1 dried red chile, minced
1 large garlic clove, minced
3 egg yolks, room temperature
1 teaspoon fresh lime juice

1/4 teaspoon ground cumin
1/4 teaspoon sugar
1/4 teaspoon salt
3/4–1 cup mild olive oil

In a blender, place the chile, garlic, egg yolks, lime juice, cumin, sugar, and salt. Blend well. With the machine running, slowly pour in the oil in a fine stream until the mayonnaise is thick and smooth and the oil is well incorporated. Cover and refrigerate until ready to use.

California Rolls

MAKES 20

1 recipe Sushi Rice
2 teaspoons wasabi powder
   (Japanese horseradish)
1 tablespoon water
1 medium-size ripe avocado
4 whole sheets nori (toasted
   seaweed)

6 ounces cooked fresh crabmeat
1/2 hothouse cucumber, cut into
   1/4-inch julienne strips
2 teaspoons sesame seeds
Soy sauce for dipping

Prepare Sushi Rice and cool to room temperature.

In a small bowl, mix the wasabi powder and water. Cut the avocados in 1/2-inch slices. Lay 1 sheet of seaweed on a work surface. With dampened hands, spread 1 cup of rice evenly over the seaweed, leaving a 1-inch strip along top edge free. Using one fourth of the wasabi mixture, "paint" a stripe on the rice 1 inch above bottom edge. Arrange one fourth of the crab over the stripe. Arrange one fourth of the avocado slices next to the crab, and then a fourth of the cucumber slices next to the avocado. Sprinkle with 1/2 teaspoon of the sesame seeds. Beginning at bottom edge, carefully roll the seaweed and its contents jelly-roll style. Moisten the top free seaweed edge to seal. Make other 3 seaweed-and-rice rolls in the same way. Using a very sharp knife, slice each roll into 2-inch segments. Serve accompanied by a bowl of soy sauce for dipping.

Tortilla Rolls with Mustard

MAKES 50

Also try these with Salsa or Tomatillo Sauce.

1 pound cream cheese
1 pound ham, chopped
8 ounces canned, chopped green
   chiles

8 ounces chopped black olives
1 package of 12 medium flour
   tortillas
Mustard Dip (below)

Blend the cream cheese, ham, chiles, and olives together. Spread evenly on the tortillas. Roll the tortillas jelly-roll style and refrigerate for 4 hours covered with plastic wrap and a damp cloth. Before serving, cut in 1/2-inch slices and serve with Mustard Dip.

MUSTARD DIP
1 cup malt vinegar   1 cup sugar
1/4 cup dry mustard   3 eggs

Combine all ingredients in a blender and mix well. Pour into the top of double
boiler and cook 8–10 minutes over boiling water, stirring constantly. Refrigerate. The sauce will thicken as it cools.

Mexican Sandwiches

MAKES 32

8 fresh long green chiles   5 whole cloves
1/2 cup olive or salad oil   2 bay leaves
1/4 cup wine vinegar   3/4 pound dry Kassari cheese
2 tablespoons brown sugar   1/2 pound Parmesan cheese
5 black peppercorns   French bread, thinly sliced

Steam the chiles in 1/2 inch of water for 5 minutes. Remove from water. Split,
remove seeds, drain and dry the chiles. Flatten chiles and place in a flat dish.
Combine the oil, vinegar, sugar, peppercorns, cloves, and bay leaves in a small
bowl. Cover chiles with the marinade and let stand 1 hour. Grate and combine
cheeses and set aside. Remove the chiles from the marinade, drain them, and
cut in quarters. Remove the peppercorns, cloves, and bay leaves from the
marinade and add the cheeses, stirring to mix thoroughly. Cut slices of French
bread to the size of the chiles. Place a chile on the bread and top with a
generous amount of the cheese mixture.

Stuffed Cherry Tomatoes

MAKES 24

1 pint cherry tomatoes   1/4 cup sour cream
1 pound bacon, cut in 1-inch   2 green onions, finely chopped
   pieces   1 tablespoon chopped fresh
1/4 cup mayonnaise   parsley

Cut a thin slice off the tops of the tomatoes. With a small spoon, scoop out the
centers and invert the tomatoes on paper towels to drain. Fry the bacon, drain

well, and crumble. Combine the mayonnaise and sour cream; add the onions and parsley and stir well. Stir in the bacon. Stuff the tomatoes with the bacon mixture.

Sliced Figs with Ricotta

MAKES 16

For an al fresco supper, follow these with a creamy pasta and chilled Soave.

8 ripe figs, peeled and cut in half lengthwise
1/4 pound prosciutto, sliced paper thin

1/2 cup ricotta cheese
Freshly ground black pepper

On a serving platter, arrange the figs cut sides up. Top (or wrap) each fig half with a slice of prosciutto. Top with a heaping teaspoon of ricotta and sprinkle liberally with ground pepper.

Foccacio

SERVES 10–12

This is a seasoned Italian bread with various toppings.

2 loaves frozen white bread dough
10 tablespoons olive oil
1/4 cup grated Parmesan cheese

Eggplant and Pepper Topping (below)
Spinach, Ricotta, and Feta Topping (below)

Defrost the dough according to package instructions. Knead 1 tablespoon olive oil into each loaf. Grease 2 jelly-roll pans with 2 tablespoons oil each. Roll and stretch each loaf until it fits the pan. Let the dough rise until doubled, about 2–3 hours. Preheat the oven to 350 degrees. Sprinkle each loaf with an additional 2 tablespoons of oil and 2 tablespoons of Parmesan cheese. Bake for 10 minutes, or until lightly browned. This can be made up to this point several days ahead. Increase the oven temperature to 400 degrees. Top with Eggplant and Pepper Topping or Spinach, Ricotta, and Feta Topping and bake for 10 minutes or until hot. To serve, cut in squares.

EGGPLANT AND PEPPER TOPPING

1 eggplant
1 red bell pepper
1 yellow bell pepper
1/4 cup olive oil

1 cup Pesto Sauce
1 cup shredded mozzarella
   cheese

Preheat the oven to 350 degrees. Peel and slice the eggplant and cut into 1/2-inch strips. Seed the peppers and cut them into 1/4-inch slices. Coat a jelly-roll pan with 2 tablespoons oil. Place the eggplant and peppers on the pan and sprinkle with the remaining 2 tablespoons of oil, or enough to coat them well. Bake for 20 minutes or until vegetables are soft. Drain on paper towels. Spread the Foccacio with Pesto Sauce. Evenly top with eggplant and peppers. Sprinkle with the cheese and bake, as directed.

SPINACH, RICOTTA, AND FETA TOPPING

1/2 cup chopped fresh spinach
   leaves
1/2 cup ricotta cheese
1/2 teaspoon dried basil
1/2 teaspoon pepper

1/2 cup thinly sliced green onions
1 cup crumbled feta cheese
1/2 cup sun-dried tomatoes
   (optional)

In a medium bowl, combine the spinach, ricotta, basil, and pepper. Spread on the Foccacio. Top with the onions, feta, and tomatoes. Bake as directed.

Gingered Kumquats

MAKES 20

1/4 cup cream cheese, softened
4 teaspoons minced crystallized
   ginger

20 kumquats
Fresh mint

Combine the cream cheese and ginger. Slice the top off the kumquats and hollow out the centers to form small cups. Stuff the fruit with the cream-cheese mixture. Decorate each cup with a mint sprig.

Belgian Endive with Two Fillings

MAKES 36

1/2 pound (4–5 small heads)
    Belgian endive, carefully
    separated, rinsed, and chilled

Salmon Tartare (below)
Smoked Turkey Rémoulade
    (below)

Place 2 teaspoons of filling on each leaf and arrange on a serving platter.

SALMON TARTARE

1 pound very fresh salmon fillet
1/4 cup fresh lemon juice
2 teaspoons mayonnaise
2 tablespoons grainy mustard
2 tablespoons finely chopped
    fresh parsley

1 tablespoon capers, rinsed and
    drained
1 tablespoon Tabasco sauce
1/4 teaspoon white pepper

Using a food processor, coarsely chop the salmon. Remove to a medium bowl. Add the lemon juice, mayonnaise, mustard, and parsley. Blend well. Gently stir in the capers. Season with Tabasco and pepper. Refrigerate for 2 hours.

SMOKED TURKEY RÉMOULADE

2 garlic cloves
1/2 onion
3/4 cup vegetable oil
1/4 cup tarragon vinegar
1/2 cup brown creole or any
    grainy, spicy mustard

2 teaspoons paprika
3/4 teaspoon cayenne pepper
1/4–1/2 teaspoon salt
1/2 pound smoked turkey,
    chicken, or ham, julienned
1/2 cup chopped green onions

In a food processor with the motor running, drop the garlic through the feed tube and mince. Add the onion and process until chopped. Add the oil, vinegar, mustard, paprika, cayenne, and salt. Process until just mixed. Pour into a small bowl, cover and refrigerate. To serve, place a portion of the turkey on each endive leaf, top with a dollop of the sauce, and sprinkle with onions.

Brioche with Tomatoes and Brie

SERVES 8

This brioche, sometimes called a *flamiche,* can be baked up to 6 hours in advance, wrapped in foil, and reheated at 350 degrees for 10–15 minutes.

1/2 cup milk
2 packages dry yeast
Pinch of sugar
2 cups unbleached white flour
1 teaspoon salt
5 eggs
1/2 cup butter, melted
3/4 pound ripe Brie cheese

2 medium tomatoes, sliced
2 tablespoons butter, softened
2/3 cup whipping cream
1/2 teaspoon each of chopped
  fresh parsley, fresh tarragon,
  and fresh chives
Salt and pepper
1 egg yolk

Warm the milk to 110 degrees. Combine the milk, yeast, and pinch of sugar. Let stand for 10 minutes. Combine the flour and salt in a large mixing bowl. Add the yeast mixture and 3 of the eggs. Mix well. Add the butter and mix well. Knead the dough for a few minutes in the bowl. Pick up a handful and slap it against the side of the bowl. The dough, although moist, should hold together well. If too moist, add a bit more flour. Sprinkle a board lightly with flour. Turn the dough out and continue kneading by lifting and slapping the dough onto the bread board for 3 minutes. When the dough is smooth and elastic, place it in a buttered mixing bowl. Cover the bowl with plastic wrap and put it in a warm place to rise for one hour. Punch down the risen dough. Lightly knead the dough on floured surface. Butter a 10-inch springform pan. Roll the dough in a circle 5 inches larger than pan. Line the pan with dough draping over the rim.

Preheat the oven to 400 degrees. Remove the rind from the cheese and cut cheese in 1/4-inch slices. Cover the dough with the cheese and layer the tomato slices on top. Dot with the butter. Beat the remaining 2 eggs with the cream and herbs. Season to taste with salt and pepper. Pour the egg mixture over the cheese and tomatoes. Fold the dough overlapping the pan rim in to form a border covering half the filling. Beat the egg yolk with 1/2 teaspoon salt, and brush the dough rim with half this mixture. Allow the dough to rise 15 minutes. Brush again with the remaining egg. Bake until the crust is browned and the custard is set, 45–60 minutes. If the top browns too quickly, cover with foil.

Tortellini with Sour Cream Gorgonzola Sauce

SERVES 6–8

This is a great appetizer for a cocktail party or a buffet. It may easily be doubled.

1/2 pound spinach tortellini,
  cooked and drained
1 tablespoon walnut oil
3 ounces Gorgonzola cheese
1/4 cup milk

1/2 cup sour cream
2 teaspoons minced garlic
1 teaspoon fresh lemon juice
1/4 teaspoon salt
1/2 cup chopped walnuts, toasted

Toss the cooked tortellini with the walnut oil and chill. Blend together the Gorgonzola, milk, sour cream, garlic, lemon juice, and salt. Just before serving stir in the walnuts and pour into a serving dish. Place the sauce on a large platter and surround with the tortellini. Provide skewers or toothpicks for dipping.

Tarte Provençale

SERVES 8

1/2 (17-ounce) package frozen
  puff pastry
1 egg white
3 egg yolks
1/4 cup fresh lemon juice
1 garlic clove
1 anchovy fillet, rinsed

1 1/2 cups olive oil
1/2 cup minced red onions
2 tablespoons capers, drained
1 teaspoon dried oregano
2 ripe tomatoes, sliced
1 cup crumbled feta cheese
Niçoise olives, for garnish

Preheat the oven to 375 degrees. Thaw the pastry for 20 minutes and roll out on a floured surface into a 15 × 10-inch rectangle. Cut in half to form two 7 1/2 × 10-inch pieces. Cut strips of pastry 3/4 inch wide from each side. Place the pastry rectangles on an ungreased cookie sheet and place the pastry strips along the edges on top of the rectangles to make a border. Combine the egg white with 1 teaspoon water and brush this mixture over all pastry surfaces. Bake for 10 minutes. Remove and let cool before assembling the tarte. Reduce oven temperature to 350 degrees.

    Place the egg yolks in a food processor and beat until pale. Add the lemon juice, garlic, and anchovy and process until smooth, about 5 seconds. With the machine running, slowly pour in the oil in a fine steady stream. Add the red onions, capers, and oregano and switch the machine on and off until just mixed.

Place the tomato slices on the cooked pastry and crumble the feta cheese over them. Spread the mayonnaise sauce evenly over the top. Bake for 12–15 minutes or until golden and bubbly. With a very sharp knife, cut each tarte into quarters, and serve as a first course garnished with Niçoise olives.

Appetizer Baked Potatoes

MAKES 24

Sour cream with caviar or smoked salmon make equally delightful fillings for these bite-size morsels.

12 small red potatoes
1 pound bacon, cut in 1-inch
pieces
1 cup sour cream

1/4 cup chopped fresh cilantro
1 avocado, diced
1 large tomato, diced

Preheat oven to 425 degrees. Clean and prick the potatoes. Bake for 40 minutes or until tender. When cool enough to handle, cut the potatoes in half and scoop out the centers with a spoon or melon baller, leaving 1/4 inch of potato to form a shell. Set aside. Cook the bacon until crisp and drain well on paper towels. Combine bacon, sour cream, cilantro, avocado, and tomatoes and fill the potato shells with the mixture. Serve warm or at room temperature.

New Potatoes with Wasabi Mayonnaise

MAKES 24–30

6 small red new potatoes
Wasabi Mayonnaise (below)

Boil the potatoes for 20–25 minutes until cooked through. Drain and add cold water to the potatoes in the pan. Drain again. Place the potatoes on paper towels until cool enough to handle. Slice each potato into 4 or 5 rounds, depending on the size. Top the potato slices with a dollop of Wasabi Mayonnaise and serve.

WASABI MAYONNAISE

2 extra-large egg yolks

2 tablespoons wasabi powder
(Japanese horseradish)

1 tablespoon rice wine vinegar

1/4 teaspoon salt

2 tablespoons fresh lime juice

1 cup vegetable oil

In a food processor, combine the egg yolks, wasabi, vinegar, salt, and lime juice and process until thickened and well blended, about 10 seconds. With the machine running, slowly pour in the oil in a fine stream until the mayonnaise is thick and smooth. Taste for seasoning, adding more salt or lime juice if necessary.

San Diego Spuds

MAKES 18

9 small red potatoes

3 tablespoons butter, melted

3/4 teaspoon chili powder

1/4 teaspoon salt

1/2 cup Tomatillo Salsa

1/2 cup chopped ripe olives

1/2 cup chopped green onions

1 cup grated Jack cheese

Sour cream, for garnish

Preheat the oven to 425 degrees. Clean and prick the potatoes. Bake for 40 minutes or until tender. When they are cool enough to handle, cut the potatoes in half and scoop out the centers with a spoon or melon baller, leaving 1/4 inch of potato to form a shell. Place skin sides up on a cookie sheet. Brush the skins with the butter and sprinkle with chili powder and salt. Bake an additional 5 minutes. Remove from the oven and turn the potatoes over. Fill the centers with the Tomatillo Salsa, olives, onions, and cheese. Broil 2–3 minutes, or until the cheese is melted. Top with sour cream before serving.

Melba Hearts

MAKES 20

3/4 cup unsalted butter
3 garlic cloves, minced (optional)
1 of the following: Parmesan

cheese, dill, chopped fresh
parsley
1 loaf firm white bread, sliced

Preheat the oven to 250 degrees. Melt the butter with the garlic and cheese or herb. With a heart-shaped cookie cutter, cut the bread into hearts. Dip each heart into the butter so that it is fully covered. Place the hearts on a greased cookie sheet and bake, turning once, for 40–50 minutes or until lightly browned. Turn the oven off, open the door slightly, and allow the hearts to dry for 1 hour. Store in an airtight container.

Soufflé Crackers

MAKES 3 DOZEN

Ice water
36 2-inch soda crackers
1/2 cup butter, melted
1/2– 3/4 teaspoon of one of the

following: poppy seeds,
caraway seeds, sesame seeds,
curry powder, dillweed, garlic,
Parmesan cheese

Preheat the oven to 400 degrees. Fill a large shallow pan with ice water. Add the crackers and allow them to absorb as much water as possible without breaking (about 30 seconds). Transfer the crackers with a slotted spoon to a buttered cookie sheet. Brush the crackers with the melted butter. If you choose an herb, add it to the butter before brushing. Otherwise, butter the crackers, and then sprinkle them with the seeds or cheese. Bake for 15 minutes. Reduce temperature to 300 and continue to bake for 10 minutes more or until brown. Turn off the oven. Open the door slightly and allow the crackers to dry completely, about 2 hours.

Feta Crisps

MAKES 2–3 DOZEN

1/2 cup butter, room temperature
1/2 pound feta cheese, room
   temperature

1 cup flour
1/2 teaspoon cayenne pepper

Preheat the oven to 400 degrees. Beat all the ingredients together until well combined. Form into 2 rolls 1 1/2 inches in diameter. Wrap in waxed paper and refrigerate for at least 3 hours or until firm. Slice in 1/4-inch wafers. *Or* pipe the dough through a cookie press, using the largest star or the running tip. Cut in 1 1/2-inch pieces. Bake on an ungreased cookie sheet for 8 minutes or until lightly browned. Store in an airtight container.

Sesame Cheese Twists

MAKES ABOUT 24

1 pound puff pastry
3/4 cup grated Parmesan cheese
4 tablespoons toasted sesame seeds

Preheat the oven to 350 degrees. On a lightly floured board, roll out the puff pastry dough to approximately 20 × 24 inches. Sprinkle half the cheese and sesame seeds on the dough. Press gently with the rolling pin. Fold the dough in half crosswise, making a rectangle 20 × 12 inches. Roll it out once more to 20 × 24 inches. Sprinkle the remaining cheese and sesame seeds on the dough and press gently with the rolling pin.

Cut the dough into 1/3-inch strips. Twist each strip into a corkscrew and place on an ungreased baking sheet. Strips should be placed very close together to prevent untwisting during baking.

Place the cheese twists in the middle of the oven and bake 15 to 20 minutes or until they are golden brown and crisp. Remove from the oven and allow to cool 5 minutes. Cut the twists apart with a sharp knife. Cool on racks and store in an airtight container or plastic bag.

III

Soup

Yellow Pepper Gazpacho

SERVES 6

This colorful soup is spectacular when served in pepper shells, but make sure that the peppers are level by slicing off some of the bottom end.

6 yellow bell peppers, chopped
2 hothouse cucumbers, chopped
3/4 cup chopped red onions
I garlic clove, minced
4 ripe tomatoes, chopped

2 cups Chicken Stock
1/4 cup white wine vinegar
2 tablespoons drained capers
Salt and pepper to taste

Place all of the vegetables in a large bowl. Add the stock, vinegar, and capers. Season to taste with salt and pepper. Cover and chill several hours.

Sunshine Soup

SERVES 6

The bright green mint garnish contrasts beautifully with this rich golden soup.

2 tablespoons butter
1/2 teaspoon peeled and minced
    fresh ginger
I pound carrots, peeled and
    thinly sliced
1/2 cup thinly sliced leeks, white
    part only

3 cups Chicken Stock
I 1/2 cups fresh orange juice
Salt and white pepper
Fresh mint, for garnish

Melt the butter in a large saucepan. Add the ginger, carrots, and leeks. Sauté until the leeks are soft. Add 2 cups of the Chicken Stock, cover, and simmer until the carrots are cooked, about 30 minutes. Purée in a blender or food processor. Return to the saucepan and stir in the remaining Chicken Stock and orange juice. Season with salt and pepper to taste. Chill for several hours. Garnish with a sprig of fresh mint.

Cold Tomato Yogurt Soup

SERVES 6

1 cup plain yogurt
2 1/2 cups tomato juice
1 1/2 teaspoons fresh lemon juice
4 1/2 teaspoons white vinegar
1/2 teaspoon curry powder
4 1/2 teaspoons finely chopped
  onions

2 tablespoons chopped fresh
  parsley
Salt and pepper to taste
6 slices cucumber, for garnish

Place all of the ingredients except the cucumber slices in a blender. Whirl until smooth, about 10–15 seconds. Chill for several hours. Serve in chilled bowls and garnish with cucumber slices.

Purée of Sweet Pepper Soup

SERVES 6

5 large red bell peppers
6 cups Chicken Stock
1 medium red onion, cut in
  1-inch cubes
1 large boiling potato, peeled
  and cut in 1-inch cubes

1/2 teaspoon crumbled dried
  thyme
2 bay leaves
1 whole clove
Salt and freshly ground pepper,
  to taste
Sour cream, for garnish

Seed the peppers and cut in 1-inch pieces. In a heavy saucepan, combine the peppers, Chicken Stock, onion and potato. Cover and simmer 45 minutes over medium heat. Strain the vegetables, reserving stock. Place the vegetables in a blender or food processor with 1 cup of the stock. Purée until smooth and return to saucepan. Wrap and tie in a cheesecloth the thyme, bay leaves, and clove. Add to the saucepan with the remaining stock. Season with salt and pepper. Simmer 25 minutes, stirring occasionally. Discard the bag of herbs and chill the soup for several hours. Serve garnished with a dollop of sour cream.

California Cucumber Soup

SERVES 8

3 medium cucumbers, peeled, seeded, and diced
2 large garlic cloves, diced
2 cups Chicken Stock
3 cups sour cream
1/4 cup lemon juice
Salt to taste

1/8 teaspoon of cayenne pepper

Condiments Toasted pine nuts; cilantro, finely chopped; green onions, green part only, thinly sliced; red bell pepper, cut into small julienne strips

Purée the cucumbers and garlic in a blender or food processor. Add the Chicken Stock and blend until smooth. Transfer to a large bowl. Whisk in the sour cream, lemon juice, salt, and pepper. Chill several hours and serve with assorted condiments.

Classic Cucumber Soup

SERVES 6–8

1/4 cup butter
2 onions, chopped
2 leeks, white part only, chopped
2 cucumbers, peeled, seeded and chopped
2 cups Vegetable Stock
2 tablespoons dry white wine
Salt and pepper to taste
1 teaspoon butter
1 teaspoon flour
1/2 cup heavy cream

1 teaspoon minced fresh dill *or* 1 1/2 teaspoons chopped fresh mint
1/2 teaspoon lemon juice
3–5 drops Tabasco sauce
1 cup peeled, seeded, and finely chopped cucumbers
6–8 small fresh dill sprigs *or* 6–8 fresh mint sprigs, for garnish
Sour cream

Melt the butter in a large saucepan. Add the onions, leeks, and the 2 cucumbers and sauté about 10 minutes until soft. Stir in the Vegetable Stock, white wine, salt, and pepper. Bring to a boil. Combine the butter and flour and whisk in bit by bit. Simmer for 1 hour. Purée the mixture in batches in a blender or food processor. Strain through a fine sieve into a bowl and whisk in the cream, the dill or mint, lemon juice, Tabasco, and the 1 cup chopped cucumbers. Chill, covered, for several hours. Ladle into chilled bowls and garnish with a dollop of sour cream and a sprig of dill or a sprig of mint.

Sweet Potato Vichyssoise

SERVES 6

2 tablespoons butter
1 medium onion, sliced
1 celery stalk, sliced
1 tablespoon flour
6 cups Beef Stock

1 1/2 pounds sweet potatoes,
   peeled and thinly sliced
Salt and pepper to taste
1 cup heavy cream

Melt the butter in large saucepan. Add the onions and celery and cook until soft. Blend in the flour and slowly add the Beef Stock, stirring well. Add the potatoes and cook until very tender, about 15 minutes. Place the vegetables in the blender or food processor with 1 cup of the stock and purée. Remove to a large bowl and add remaining stock and blend well. Season with salt and pepper. Chill several hours. Just before serving, whisk in the heavy cream until well blended.

Cold Clam Bisque

SERVES 8–10

3 tablespoons butter
4 leeks, white part only, sliced
1/2 cup minced shallots
1 garlic clove, minced
3 cups peeled and diced red
   potatoes
3 cups Chicken Stock

2 (7-ounce) cans minced clams,
   undrained
1 cup milk
2 cups half-and-half
Salt and white pepper to taste
Fresh chives, minced, for garnish

Melt the butter in a large saucepan. Sauté the leeks, shallots, and garlic until soft. Add the potatoes and Chicken Stock. Cover and simmer until potatoes are soft. Add the clams and clam juice and purée the mixture in a blender or food processor, in batches if necessary. Add the milk and half-and-half and season to taste with salt and pepper. Chill several hours. Garnish each serving with minced chives.

Chilled Curried Pea Soup

SERVES 4

1 ¼ cups Chicken Stock
1 (10-ounce) package frozen peas
1 tablespoon fresh chives
1 teaspoon fresh lemon juice
1 teaspoon curry powder, or to
   taste

Salt and pepper to taste
½ cup half-and-half
4 sprigs mint, for garnish

Bring the stock to a boil. Reduce heat so that the stock continues to gently boil. Add the peas and simmer for 10 minutes, covered. Cool slightly and add the chives, lemon juice, curry powder, salt, and pepper. Purée in a blender or a food processor. Chill for several hours. Strain through a fine sieve. Add the half-and-half, whisking until well blended. Adjust seasonings if necessary. Serve in well-chilled bowls. Garnish each serving with a mint sprig.

Chilled Banana Soup Indienne

SERVES 6–8

This exotic blend is a unique addition to a summer menu that might include Tandoori Chicken with Punjabi Sauce.

2 tablespoons butter
1 onion, finely chopped
1 garlic clove, minced
2 teaspoons curry powder
¼ cup raw rice
5 cups Chicken Stock

1 ½ cups half-and-half
½ cup whipping cream
2 ripe bananas, sliced
2 tablespoons fresh lemon juice
Salt and white pepper
Lime slices, for garnish

Melt the butter in a large saucepan. Add the onions and garlic and sauté about 5 minutes until soft. Add the curry powder and continue cooking 2 more minutes. Stir in the rice and Chicken Stock. Bring to a boil. Cover and cook over medium-low heat until the rice is cooked, about 25 minutes. Purée in a blender or food processor with half-and-half, cream, bananas, and lemon juice, in batches, if necessary. Season with salt and pepper to taste. Chill several hours. Just before serving, stir the soup well and garnish with slices of lime.

Wild Mushroom Soup

SERVES 4–6

1/2–3/4 cup thinly sliced dried
  oyster mushrooms
1/2–3/4 cup thinly sliced dried
  shiitake mushrooms
2 tablespoons unsalted butter

2–3 tablespoons minced shallots
1 1/2 cups thinly sliced fresh
  domestic mushrooms
6 cups Chicken Stock
2 teaspoons fresh lemon juice

Soak dried mushrooms in enough hot water to cover, for 30 minutes or until soft. Melt the butter in a large saucepan. Add the shallots, cooking until they are soft, about 3 minutes. Add the mushrooms and cook for 5 minutes more, stirring occasionally. Add the Chicken Stock and bring to a boil. Reduce heat. Simmer, uncovered, for 30 minutes. Add the lemon juice and serve.

Note   If a clear mushroom broth is desired, use 2 1/2–3 cups of fresh domestic mushrooms. Follow the above directions. After simmering for 30 minutes, cool, and then strain soup through a coarse sieve, pressing the mushrooms firmly to extract all the liquid. Add 1 teaspoon of lemon juice and garnish with lemon slices.

Italian Vegetable Soup

SERVES 4–6

Serve this soup with Beer Bread and assorted cheeses for a quick winter supper.

1 (16-ounce) can stewed
  tomatoes
2 tablespoons butter
1 large green onion, chopped
1 large garlic clove, minced
3 1/2 cups Chicken Stock or Beef
  Stock
1/2 teaspoon dried basil

1/8 teaspoon freshly ground
  black pepper
1/2 teaspoon dried thyme
1/8 teaspoon dried oregano
1 cup sliced carrots
1 cup sliced celery
1 cup finely chopped cabbage
Freshly grated Parmesan cheese

Purée the tomatoes in a blender or food processor and set aside. Melt the butter in a large saucepan, and sauté the onions and garlic for 3 minutes. Add the stock, pureed tomatoes, basil, pepper, thyme, oregano, and vegetables. Simmer for 45 minutes. Serve with Parmesan cheese.

Oriental Soup with Shrimp and Pineapple

SERVES 6–8

8 cups Chicken Stock
1 tablespoon peeled and minced
  fresh ginger
1 1/2 cups chopped watercress
2 tablespoons oriental sesame oil
3 green onions including some of
  the green sliced diagonally
1 pound raw shrimp, shelled and
  deveined

1 1/4 cups crushed pineapple,
  fresh or canned
3 tablespoons ñuoc mam fish
  sauce, available in oriental
  markets
1 tablespoon sugar
2 tablespoons red wine vinegar
1/2 teaspoon freshly ground
  black pepper

Combine the stock and ginger. Boil, covered, for 10 minutes. Add the watercress to the stock. Cover and cook 20 minutes. Heat the sesame oil in a pan and sauté the onions and shrimp for 2 minutes. Add to the broth with the rest of the ingredients. Simmer for 6 minutes.

Chinese Ginger-Meatball and Watercress Soup

SERVES 6

Serve as the first course of a traditional Chinese dinner or alone as a light, nutritious supper.

MEATBALLS
1 (8-ounce) can water chestnuts
1 pound finely ground lean pork
4 1/2 teaspoons peeled and
  minced fresh ginger

Ground white pepper, to taste
1 1/2 teaspoons soy sauce
2 1/8 teaspoons cornstarch
Salt to taste

Finely chop 12 of the water chestnuts. Reserve the remaining ones for garnish. Combine the pork, ginger, chopped water chestnuts, soy sauce, cornstarch, salt, and pepper. Mix well and form into balls 3/4 inch in diameter. These may be made in advance and frozen. Be sure to thaw completely in refrigerator before poaching.

SOUP

5 cups Vegetable Stock

5 cups Chicken Stock

Salt

Freshly ground black pepper

2 bunches watercress, chopped

3 green onions, finely chopped

Bring the Vegetable Stock and Chicken Stock to a simmer in a large pot. Put a fourth of the meatballs in the broth and poach until they rise to the top. Remove and keep warm. Repeat with the remaining meatballs. About 20 minutes prior to serving, return stock to a boil and add the meatballs. Cook 10–15 minutes. *(Note* Meatballs will be slightly pink in the center even after the second cooking.) Season with salt and black pepper to taste. Turn heat to medium low. Add the watercress and green onions. Cook, uncovered, for a few minutes until watercress is slightly wilted and bright green in color. Add the remaining water chestnuts and cook for 1 minute so that they remain crisp. Serve immediately.

Mexican Corn Chowder

SERVES 4–6

2 tablespoons butter

1 large onion, chopped

2–3 garlic cloves, minced

2 tablespoons flour

2 (12-ounce) cans whole kernel corn, undrained

1 1/3 cups Chicken Stock

1/4 cup chopped fresh parsley

2 cups half-and-half

1 teaspoon salt

1/2 teaspoon freshly ground black pepper

1/4 teaspoon dried oregano

1–2 jalapeño chiles, seeded and finely chopped

Condiments

1–2 cups shredded Cheddar and Jack cheese

1 cup peeled, seeded, and diced tomatoes

1 avocado, diced

1 chicken breast, cooked, cut in julienne strips

6 slices bacon, fried crisp, drained, and crumbled

Tortilla strips

Melt the butter in a large saucepan and sauté the onions and garlic until the onions are soft, about 3–5 minutes. Blend in the flour and cook until bubbly. Remove from heat. Blend in half of the corn, the Chicken Stock, and parsley. Pour the mixture into a blender or food processor and process until just blended, the mixture should not be smooth. Return the mixture to the pan.

Add the half-and-half, remaining corn, salt, pepper, and oregano. Bring to a boil over medium heat. Add the chiles, reduce heat, and simmer 5 minutes, stirring to prevent scorching. Serve with assorted condiments.

Tortilla Soup

SERVES 4–6

1 1/2 tablespoons olive oil
1 large onion, chopped
2 garlic cloves, minced
1 (28-ounce) can Italian plum tomatoes, undrained
1/4 cup diced green chiles
3 tablespoons chopped red bell pepper
4 cups Chicken Stock

1 teaspoon dried oregano
2 tablespoons chili powder
1 tablespoon ground cumin
Salt and pepper
6 corn tortillas cut in 1/4-inch strips
Oil for frying tortillas
2 cups shredded Jack cheese

In a large saucepan, heat the olive oil and sauté the onion and garlic until soft. Process the tomatoes in a blender or food processor until smooth. Add the tomatoes, chiles, red pepper, Chicken Stock, and seasonings to pan. Simmer 30 minutes. While the soup is cooking, fry tortilla strips in oil until crisp. Drain well on paper towels. Preheat the broiler. Place the tortilla strips in ovenproof bowls. Ladle the soup over tortillas. Top with the grated cheese. Broil until cheese is bubbly and lightly browned.

Mexican Vegetable Soup

SERVES 6

2 1/2 cups Chicken Stock
2 1/2 cups Beef Stock
1/2 teaspoon chili powder
1/2 cup julienned carrots
1/4 cup thinly sliced green onions
1/4 cup julienned yellow bell pepper

1 cup stewed tomatoes
1/4 teaspoon ground cumin
1/4 teaspoon ground coriander
Salt and freshly ground black pepper
Lemon slices, for garnish

Heat the Chicken Stock and Beef Stock with chili powder, over medium-low heat. Add the carrots, onions, peppers, tomatoes, cumin, and coriander. Simmer for 10 minutes. Season with salt and pepper to taste. Garnish with lemon slices.

Cajun Bean Soup

SERVES 6

A great initiation to the rich, spicy flavors of Louisiana cooking. Cajun fans hope for rare leftovers of this soup to serve cold with a dollop of sour cream.

1/2 pound dried black beans
3 tablespoons olive oil
2 ounces salt pork, cut into
    small cubes
2 ounces prosciutto, julienned
2 onions, finely chopped
2 garlic cloves, minced
1/2 cup chopped celery, including
    leaves
6 cups Beef Stock
4 1/2 teaspoons concentrated
    liquid beef bouillon

1/8 teaspoon cayenne pepper
1 teaspoon ground cumin
Salt and black pepper, to taste
1 tablespoon red wine vinegar
2 tablespoons dry sherry

Condiments: Chopped onions;
    lemons or limes, very thinly
    sliced; cooked ham, finely
    chopped; hard-cooked eggs,
    chopped and sprinkled with
    paprika; cooked rice

Place the beans in a large pan and cover with water. Let them soak overnight. The next day, bring the beans to a boil, remove from heat immediately, and drain. Set aside. Heat the oil in a large pan. Add the salt pork, prosciutto, onions, garlic, and celery. Sauté about 5 minutes until the onions are soft and the salt pork has been rendered of its fat. Add the beans, Beef Stock, and liquid beef bouillon. Bring to a boil. Add the cayenne and cumin. Partially cover, and simmer about 4 hours, stirring occasionally. Add salt and pepper. Purée in small batches in a blender or food processor. Return to the pan. Blend in the vinegar and the sherry. Serve with condiments.

Vegetable Soup with Orzo and Pesto

SERVES 8–10

1 cup white beans
1 tablespoon butter
1 tablespoon olive oil
1 cup chopped leeks, white part
  only
2 garlic cloves, minced
1 cup peeled and chopped
  carrots
8 cups Chicken Stock
1 cup boiling potatoes, peeled
  and cubed
1/2 cup chopped celery
1/4 cup orzo (small, rice-shaped
  pasta)

1/2 head cabbage, finely grated
1 cup fresh green beans, cut in
  thin diagonal slices
1/2 cup fresh green peas (or
  frozen defrosted)
1 1/2 cups peeled, seeded, and
  chopped tomatoes
1 bunch fresh spinach, stems
  removed
1 cup finely chopped fresh
  parsley
Salt and white pepper to taste
Pesto (below)

Place the beans in a large pan and cover with water. Let soak overnight. The next day, drain the beans and set aside. Melt the butter and oil in a large saucepan. Add the leeks and garlic, cooking until soft. Add the carrots and cook for several minutes. Stir in the Chicken Stock, potatoes, and beans. Bring to a boil, reduce heat, and simmer 20 minutes. Add the celery, orzo, and cabbage, and simmer 10 minutes. Add green beans, peas, and tomatoes and simmer until the peas and beans are tender. Add the spinach and parsley. Cover and simmer until spinach and parsley have wilted. Season to taste with salt and pepper. Serve, swirling 1 tablespoon of Pesto into each bowl of soup.

PESTO
1/2 cup pine nuts
4 garlic cloves, coarsely chopped
1 teaspoon freshly ground black
  pepper
3–4 cups fresh basil leaves
1/4 pound freshly grated
  Parmesan cheese

1/4 pound freshly grated Romano
  cheese
1 1/2–2 cups olive oil
1 teaspoon salt

In a blender or food processor, place all of the ingredients except oil and salt. Process until well blended with 1/2 cup of the olive oil. Add the remaining oil and process until smooth. Season to taste with salt.

Creamy Leek Soup with Shallots and Bacon

SERVES 8–10

1/2 pound bacon, cut in 1/2-inch
   pieces
8 leeks, white parts only,
   julienned
3 tablespoons minced shallots
1/4 teaspoon freshly grated
   nutmeg
1 bay leaf

1 cup dry white wine
2 cups heavy cream
1/2 cup unsalted butter
1/2 cup flour
8 cups Chicken Stock
Chopped fresh parsley, for
   garnish

In a large saucepan, fry the bacon until crisp and drain. Add the leeks, shallots, nutmeg, and bay leaf. Cook, covered, over moderate heat for 10 minutes or until the leeks are tender, stirring occasionally. Add the wine and cream and bring to a boil. Reduce heat and simmer for 10 minutes. Remove the bay leaf, and purée the leek mixture in batches in a blender or food processor. In a large saucepan, melt the butter over low heat. Add the flour and cook, stirring constantly, for 3 minutes. Slowly add the Chicken Stock. Continue cooking until the mixture has thickened. Add the leek mixture and simmer for 20 minutes, stirring occasionally. Garnish with parsley.

Country Corn Chowder

SERVES 6

This soup is best made one day ahead and reheated slowly to develop flavors.

3 slices bacon, cut in 1/2-inch
   pieces
3/4 cup finely chopped onions
3/4 cup finely chopped celery
4 cups Chicken Stock
4 cups whole kernel corn, fresh
   or canned
2 cups peeled and diced red
   potatoes

1/2 teaspoon salt
1 cup heavy cream
2 tablespoons fresh chopped
   parsley
1/8 teaspoon white pepper
1 pound boned chicken breast,
   poached, cut into 1/2-inch
   cubes

In a large saucepan, fry bacon until crisp. Remove from the pan and pour off all but 2 tablespoons of the bacon drippings. Add the onions and celery. Cook 10–15 minutes, stirring frequently. Meanwhile in a blender, combine 1 cup of the stock and 2 cups of the corn, blending until smooth. Add to the saucepan with remaining corn, potatoes, remaining stock, and salt. Bring to a boil, reduce heat to simmer, cover partially and cook for 20 minutes or until potatoes are tender. Whisk in the cream, parsley, and pepper. Add the chicken and simmer 3 minutes. Stir in bacon.

White Bean Soup with Swiss Chard

SERVES 6–8

If Swiss chard is unavailable, this soup is wonderful with spinach.

1 cup Great Northern beans
3 tablespoons olive oil
2 large onions, chopped
2 carrots, peeled and finely chopped
1/2 pound red or white Swiss chard, ribs and leaves, coarsely chopped
5 cups Chicken Stock
3 garlic cloves, minced
1 bay leaf
1 1/2 teaspoons salt
1/2 teaspoon ground black pepper
3 tablespoons freshly chopped parsley
Grated Parmesan cheese

Place the beans in a large pan and cover with water. Let them soak overnight. The next day, drain the beans, reserving 2 cups liquid. In a large pan, heat the oil. Add the onions and sauté until tender, about 5 minutes, stirring occasionally. Add the carrots and sauté for an additional 3 minutes. Add the chard to pan. Cook until wilted, about 3 minutes. Add the Chicken Stock, bean water, beans, garlic, and bay leaf. Partially cover and simmer for 1 hour, until beans are tender. Remove the bay leaf. Purée half of the soup in the blender or food processor. Return to the pan with remaining soup. Add the salt, pepper, and parsley. Serve with Parmesan cheese.

Wild Rice and Mushroom Soup

SERVES 6–8

A truly elegant soup suitable for Thanksgiving or Christmas dinner.

2/3 cup wild rice
3 cups water
I teaspoon salt
3 medium-size leeks, white and a
  little green, diced
1/2 pound fresh mushrooms,
  diced

1/2 cup butter
1/2 cup flour
6 cups Chicken Stock
Salt and white pepper to taste
1/2–3/4 cup half-and-half
  (optional)

Place the wild rice in a strainer and rinse carefully under running water. Place in a saucepan with the water and salt. Bring to a boil. Reduce heat, cover, and simmer for 45 minutes until tender. Fluff with a fork, then drain all excess liquid. Set aside. Sauté the leeks and mushrooms in melted butter until tender. Sprinkle with flour and cook for 1 minute. Add the Chicken Stock and stir until thickened. Cool slightly. Purée in batches in blender or food processor. Return to the pan and add the rice, salt, and pepper if desired. Heat slowly. If a thicker consistency is desired, stir in up to 3/4 cup half-and-half.

Tomato Ginger Soup

SERVES 4

2–3 tablespoons peeled and
  minced fresh ginger
I medium white onion
4 large tomatoes, peeled and
  seeded, *or* 14–16 ounces
  canned tomatoes, undrained

1/2 cup unsalted butter
1/2 cup Chicken Stock
2 tablespoons sugar
Salt and white pepper
I cup heavy cream

Purée the ginger and onion in a food processor and set aside. Purée the tomatoes and set aside. Melt the butter in a saucepan over medium heat and add the puréed ginger and onion. Cook over medium heat about 3 minutes. Add the puréed tomatoes, stock, sugar, salt, and pepper to taste. Bring to a boil. Add the cream. Reduce heat and simmer 30 minutes.

Apple Broccoli Soup

SERVES 4

This beautiful and versatile soup is delicious served hot or very refreshing served chilled as a prelude to a summer dinner.

2 tablespoons butter
1 small onion, thinly sliced
1 large Golden Delicious apple,
    peeled, cored, and chopped

3/4 pound broccoli
2 cups Chicken Stock
Salt and white pepper to taste
Plain yogurt, for garnish

Melt the butter in a medium saucepan. Add the onions and apples. Cover and cook until soft, about 5–7 minutes. Peel and chop the broccoli, separating flowerets. Add the stock and broccoli to the saucepan and bring to a boil. Reduce heat and simmer, uncovered, until broccoli is tender. Cool slightly. Purée in a blender or food processor until smooth. Reheat over low heat and season to taste. Garnish with dollop of yogurt. Can be served cold. May also be served as a vegetable purée if stock is reduced to 1 cup.

Winter Ham Soup with Blue Cheese

SERVES 6

Simple and delicious. This rich soup gives holiday ham a praiseworthy encore.

1/4 cup butter
1/2 cup chopped onions
2 cups peeled and diced potatoes
1/4 cup water
1/4 cup flour
3 cups milk

1 (10-ounce) package frozen peas
1 1/2 cups chopped ham
1/4 teaspoon dried marjoram
1/4 teaspoon salt
1/4 teaspoon white pepper
2 ounces blue cheese, crumbled

In a large saucepan, melt the butter. Add the onions, potatoes, and water. Cover and cook over low heat until the potatoes are tender, about 20 minutes. Stir in the flour and slowly add the milk. Cook until thickened. Stir in the peas, ham, marjoram, salt, and pepper. Cook until the peas are tender. Garnish with blue cheese.

California Onion Soup

SERVES 6

1/4 pound butter
4 white onions, thinly sliced
6 shallots, minced
1 teaspoon sugar
3 tablespoons flour
6 cups Beef Stock

1/3 cup dry sherry
Salt and freshly ground pepper
  to taste
1/2 cup heavy cream
1/4 cup grated Parmesan cheese

Melt the butter in a large saucepan, and add the onions. Cook slowly until golden brown, about 5 minutes. Stir in shallots and sugar. Cook 2 more minutes, remove from heat, and stir in flour, blending well. Slowly add 2 cups of the Beef Stock and return to heat for 5 minutes, stirring frequently. Purée in a blender or food processor. Deglaze the saucepan with remaining stock. Add puréed mixture and bring to a boil. Reduce to a simmer and cook for 15 minutes. Add sherry and cook 5 minutes more. Season to taste with salt and pepper. Pour the soup into ovenproof bowls. Top with cream that has been whipped with Parmesan cheese. Brown slightly under broiler.

Tomato Dill Soup in Puff Pastry

SERVES 8

An impressive beginning for a special dinner.

3 tablespoons butter
2 yellow onions, sliced
2 pounds very ripe tomatoes *or*
  32 ounces canned tomatoes,
  drained
2 garlic cloves, chopped
1 teaspoon salt
1/2 teaspoon sugar
1/4 teaspoon white pepper

3 tablespoons tomato paste
4 tablespoons flour
1 1/2 cups half-and-half
1/2 cup heavy cream
2 tablespoons fresh chopped dill
2 (8-ounce) packages frozen puff
  pastry (defrosted according to
  directions)
2 egg yolks, beaten

Preheat oven to 400 degrees. Melt the butter in a (4-quart) saucepan and sauté the onions until they are soft. Add the tomatoes, garlic, 1 1/2 cups water, salt, sugar, and pepper. Cover and cook slowly until tomatoes are very soft, about 20 minutes. Stir in the tomato paste.

Dissolve flour in 1/2 cup water. Add 2 1/2 cups of water and blend again until smooth. Add this mixture to the tomatoes and bring to a boil, stirring constantly. Strain the soup and add the half-and-half, cream, and dill. Ladle the warm soup into 8 straight-sided soup bowls, filling them two-thirds to three-quarters full.

Cut rounds from defrosted puff pastry 1 inch larger than the diameter of the soup bowls. Paint around the edge of the bowls with the beaten egg yolk. Then, place a pastry round over the top of each bowl, slightly stretching it and pressing to secure. Cut out miniature hearts, stars, etc., from the remaining dough and adhere them to the tops with the egg yolk.

Place the bowls on a cookie sheet and bake about 15 minutes, or until lightly browned. Serve immediately.

Pumpkin Soup with Ginger

SERVES 6

3 tablespoons butter
1 onion, chopped
1 1/2 tablespoons flour
1 tablespoon curry powder
4 cups Chicken Stock
4 1/2 teaspoons chopped
    crystallized ginger

1 tablespoon fresh lemon juice
1 1/2 cups pumpkin purée
3 tart apples, peeled, cored, and
    chopped
1/8 teaspoon cinnamon
1–2 tablespoons brown sugar

Melt the butter in a large saucepan. Sauté the onions until soft. Add flour and curry powder, and cook for 2 minutes. Slowly add 2 cups of the Chicken Stock, stirring constantly. Blend in the ginger, lemon juice, pumpkin purée, apples, and cinnamon. Simmer, uncovered, for 10 minutes. Purée in small batches in blender or food processor. Return to saucepan and slowly add remaining stock until desired thickness is attained. Add brown sugar to taste.

Beef Stock

YIELD 2 ½ QUARTS

Keep a good supply of beef stock in your freezer for soups and sauces.

5 pounds beef shin or soup bones with meat

1–2 pounds marrow bones, cracked

3 quarts cold water

2 celery stalks, including leaves, diced

2 onions, quartered

2 carrots, peeled, sliced

1 turnip, peeled, quartered

1 or 2 leeks, white part only, cut in pieces

2 garlic cloves

8 black peppercorns, slightly crushed

¼ teaspoon dried thyme

1 bay leaf

2 whole cloves

1 tablespoon chopped fresh parsley

1 tablespoon salt

Preheat oven to 450 degrees. Remove any meat from the shinbones and cut in 1-inch cubes. Crack the bones with a hammer or have the butcher cut them into 2–3-inch lengths. Place the bones and meat in a shallow pan in the preheated oven. Roast for 30 minutes. Turn all the pieces and roast for 30 minutes more or until they are all well browned. Browning the meat first gives the stock a rich brown color. Place all the meat and bones in an 8-quart kettle and add the water. Bring to a boil over medium heat, occasionally skimming off the fat that forms. Add the remaining ingredients and cover the kettle loosely, adding more water if necessary to cover the ingredients. Reduce the heat and simmer the mixture for 2 ½–3 hours, occasionally skimming the fat from the surface. Remove the bones and meat with a slotted spoon and discard them. Strain the rest of the stock through a fine sieve or cheesecloth. Refrigerate the stock overnight or until cold, and then remove the hardened fat from the surface. The stock may then be refrigerated for 2–3 days. Or, place the cooled stock in quart containers and freeze.

Chicken Stock

YIELD 2 ½ QUARTS

1 large stewing chicken, cut up
3 quarts cold water
2 leeks, white part only, cut in
   pieces
1 bay leaf
2 tablespoons chopped fresh
   parsley
2 celery stalks, including leaves,
   cut in 1-inch pieces

1 teaspoon dried thyme
2 whole cloves
1 medium carrot, peeled,
   quartered
1 large onion, quartered
6 peppercorns, slightly crushed
2 teaspoons salt

Place the chicken in an 8-quart stockpot and add the cold water. Bring the mixture to a boil over medium heat. Skim the surface with a spoon. Add the remaining ingredients, cover the kettle loosely, and reduce the heat to simmer. Simmer the mixture for 2 ½–3 hours. Remove all the chicken pieces with a slotted spoon and discard. Strain the stock through a fine sieve or a piece of cheesecloth. Refrigerate the stock overnight or until cold. Remove the hardened fat from the surface. The stock may then be refrigerated for 2–3 days. Or, place cooled stock in quart containers and freeze.

Fish Stock

YIELD 2 QUARTS

2 tablespoons butter
1 onion, thinly sliced
16–18 parsley stems
1 celery stalk, quartered
1/4 cup peeled and diced carrots
4 pounds fish bones and
   trimmings (white fish
   preferred)

3 tablespoons fresh lemon juice
2 cups dry white wine or
   vermouth
2 quarts cold water
2 teaspoons salt
4 black peppercorns

In a heavy 4–6-quart stockpot, melt the butter. Add the onions, parsley, celery, and carrots and sauté over low heat until soft but not brown, about 3–4 minutes, stirring frequently. Add fish bones, trimmings, and lemon juice and cook for 5 minutes. Add the wine and simmer uncovered 20 minutes. Add water, salt, and peppercorns, raise heat, and bring to a boil. Boil slowly at moderately low heat for 45 minutes or until reduced by half. Strain. This stock may be kept frozen up to 2 months.

Quick Fish Stock

MAKES ABOUT 2 ½ CUPS

2 cups clam juice

1 ¼ cups water

1 ¼ cups dry white wine

1 onion, thinly sliced

¼ cup chopped parsley

Place all of the ingredients in a large saucepan and simmer for 30 minutes. Allow the liquid to reduce to about 2 ½ cups. Strain the stock before using.

Vegetable Stock

YIELD ABOUT 2 QUARTS

Other vegetables may be added or substituted for zucchini, red pepper, and tomatoes. Be careful to avoid vegetables that may add too strong a taste of their own.

2 quarts water

2 onions, quartered

4 stalks celery, including leaves, cut in 1-inch pieces

4 carrots, unpeeled, cut in ½-inch pieces

2 leeks, white part only, cut in ½-inch pieces

1 zucchini, ends trimmed, cut in thick slices

1 red bell pepper, seeded, cut in chunks

4 tomatoes, seeded and chopped

3 whole garlic cloves, peeled

3 bay leaves

3 sprigs fresh parsley

10 whole peppercorns

1 tablespoon fresh thyme

Bring all ingredients to a boil in a large stockpot. Reduce heat and simmer, uncovered, for 2 hours. Strain to remove all solids. Cool to room temperature. Refrigerate for 2–3 days or freeze stock for use at another time.

IV

Salads

Asparagus with Raspberry Cream

SERVES 6

The essence of spring accentuated with a delicate pink sauce.

1 1/2–2 pounds asparagus
1 (10-ounce) package frozen
  raspberries, thawed and well
  drained
6 tablespoons olive oil

1/4 cup heavy cream
2 tablespoons sherry wine
  vinegar
1/2 teaspoon salt

Trim the asparagus and place in a large saucepan of boiling water. Cook for 3–6 minutes until just tender. Immediately drain and rinse under cold water until cool. Pat dry and chill.

Purée the raspberries in a blender or a food processor. Press through a fine sieve with the back of a spoon to remove the seeds. Combine the olive oil, cream, vinegar, salt, and raspberry purée in the food processor and blend. Chill. Serve sauce over asparagus.

Cold Asparagus with Mustard Vinaigrette

SERVES 8

When asparagus season is over, try this with green beans.

2 1/2–3 pounds fresh asparagus
1/2 cup rice wine vinegar
1/2 cup Dijon mustard
3/4 cup olive oil

3/4 cup vegetable oil
2–3 tablespoons honey
Salt and pepper to taste
2 shallots, finely minced

Trim the asparagus and place in a large saucepan of boiling water. Cook 3–6 minutes until just tender. Immediately drain and rinse under cold water until cool. Pat dry and chill.

Whisk the vinegar and mustard together. Add the olive oil and the vegetable oil bit by bit, whisking vigorously. Add the honey, salt, pepper, and shallots. Blend well. The dressing may be made in advance.

To serve, arrange asparagus spears on serving plates, drizzle each serving with 2 tablespoons of the dressing, and serve the rest on the side.

Green Pea and Apple Salad

SERVES 4–6

Easy to make early in the day for a buffet or barbecue.

1 (10-ounce) package frozen
petits pois
1 tart green apple, unpeeled and
chopped
3 green onions, including some
of the tops, thinly sliced

Horseradish Cream Dressing
(below)
4–5 slices of bacon, cut into
1/2-inch pieces

Place the frozen peas in a colander and rinse under hot running water until just thawed. Drain thoroughly. Combine the peas, apples, and onions. Toss lightly with Horseradish Cream Dressing. Chill well. Fry the bacon until crisp, and drain well. At serving time, garnish the salad with the bacon.

HORSERADISH CREAM DRESSING
1/2 cup sour cream
1/2–1 teaspoon horseradish (or to
taste)
1/4 teaspoon salt

1/8 teaspoon freshly ground
pepper
2 teaspoons fresh lemon juice

Combine all ingredients and mix well.

Green Bean, Walnut, and Feta Salad

SERVES 6

1 1/2 pounds green beans, halved
1 cup chopped toasted walnuts
1 cup diced red onions

1 cup crumbled feta cheese
Mint Dressing (below)

Place the beans in a large saucepan of boiling water and cook for 4 minutes. Drain immediately and rinse under cold water until cool. Pat dry and chill. To serve, arrange the beans on a platter. Sprinkle with the nuts, onions, and cheese. Just before serving, add the dressing and toss.

MINT DRESSING

3/4 cup olive oil

1/2 cup chopped mint

1/4 cup white wine vinegar

3/4 teaspoon salt

1/2 teaspoon minced garlic

1/4 teaspoon pepper

Combine all of the ingredients and blend well.

Mediterranean Eggplant Salad

SERVES 8–10

This delectable dinner side dish becomes a dramatic luncheon entree when served stuffed in an artichoke.

1 onion, chopped

1 1/2 pounds eggplant, diced

2 large garlic cloves, minced

1/4 cup olive oil

3–4 tomatoes, peeled, seeded, and diced

4 anchovy fillets

15–20 stuffed green olives or Kalamatra olives, chopped

1/2–3/4 cup toasted pine nuts (or slivered almonds)

2 tablespoons capers

Champagne Vinaigrette (below)

Sauté the onions, eggplant, and garlic in hot oil for 10–12 minutes. Add the tomatoes and anchovies. Cook 5–8 minutes more until anchovies are dissolved and vegetables are soft. Cool. Add olives, pine nuts, capers, and Champagne Vinaigrette. Chill.

CHAMPAGNE VINAIGRETTE

1/4 cup champagne vinegar

1/2 cup olive oil

1/4 teaspoon paprika

1 teaspoon cracked pepper

Combine the above ingredients and blend well.

Potato Salad with Roquefort

SERVES 6

2 pounds small new potatoes
Tarragon Vinaigrette (below)
1/2 cup Roquefort cheese,
  crumbled
1/2–3/4 cup heavy cream

10 slices bacon, fried crisp,
  drained, and crumbled
2 tablespoons finely chopped
  fresh chives
Watercress for garnish

Cook potatoes until just tender, about 20 minutes. Peel and slice the potatoes while still warm. Place in a bowl and toss gently with half the Tarragon Vinaigrette. Set aside. Add the Roquefort and cream to the remaining vinaigrette. Mix well. Sprinkle the potatoes with bacon and place on a platter. Top with the Roquefort-cream mixture, vinaigrette, and chives. Garnish with watercress and serve at room temperature.

TARRAGON VINAIGRETTE
2 teaspoons dried tarragon
3 tablespoons tarragon-flavored
  vinegar
3/4 teaspoon salt
1/2 teaspoon cracked pepper

2 teaspoons Dijon mustard
1/2 cup olive oil
2 tablespoons finely minced
  fresh parsley

In a blender or food processor, combine all ingredients except the oil. Slowly add oil, processing until well blended.

Warm Mushroom Salad

SERVES 6

1 bunch fresh parsley, stems
  removed
1 (7-ounce) can pitted black
  olives
1 tin anchovy fillets, rinsed and
  drained
Juice of half a lemon
2 garlic cloves

1/2 teaspoon coarse black pepper
2–3 tablespoons capers
2 pounds mushrooms
2 tablespoons butter
1 tablespoon oil
Lettuce
2 ounces Gorgonzola cheese,
  crumbled

In a blender or food processor, combine parsley, olives, anchovy fillets, lemon juice, garlic, and pepper until finely minced. Stir in the capers and set aside. Slice the mushrooms and sauté in the butter and oil over low heat for 5 minutes. Add the parsley mixture and bring to a simmer. Serve warm on a bed of lettuce topped with the Gorgonzola cheese.

Center Stage Salad

SERVES 8

This is a delightful salad with many variations. Try adding crumbled bacon or substituting Stilton or Maytag Bleu cheese for the Roquefort.

2 heads Boston lettuce
4–6 ounces Roquefort cheese, crumbled
1/2 red onion, thinly sliced

3 green onions, thinly sliced
Cayenne Nuts (below)
Center Stage Vinaigrette (below)

Combine the lettuce, cheese, and onions. Add Cayenne Nuts, and toss with vinaigrette dressing.

CAYENNE NUTS
1/3 cup sugar
1/4 cup unsalted butter
1/4 cup fresh orange juice
1 1/2 teaspoons salt

1 1/4 teaspoons cinnamon
1/4–1/2 teaspoon cayenne pepper
1/4 teaspoon ground mace
1 pound pecan halves

Position rack in center of oven and preheat to 250 degrees. Line a jelly-roll pan with aluminum foil. Heat the sugar, butter, orange juice, salt, cinnamon, cayenne and mace in heavy skillet over low heat until butter melts and sugar is dissolved. Increase heat to medium. Add nuts and toss until coated. Spread in a single layer on foil-lined pan. Bake 1 hour, stirring every 15 minutes. Transfer the nuts to large sheet of foil. Separate the nuts with a fork. Cool completely. Store in an airtight container up to 5 days. Can be frozen one month. Bring to room temperature before serving. If sticky, bake on foil-lined pan at 250 degrees until crisp, about 20 minutes.

CENTER STAGE VINAIGRETTE
1/2 cup olive oil
3 tablespoons raspberry vinegar
1 tablespoon minced shallots

1/4 teaspoon salt
1/8 teaspoon white pepper

Combine all ingredients and blend well.

Parsley and Tomato Salad

SERVES 8

2 cups fresh parsley, stems
  removed
1/2 cup chopped green onions
1 cup drained sweet pickles
2 large garlic cloves
1/2 cup olive oil

1/2 cup white wine vinegar
1/4 cup tarragon vinegar
1/2 teaspoon dried tarragon
Salt and pepper
4 large beefsteak tomatoes
Boston lettuce

In a food processor, place the parsley, onions, pickles, and garlic. Process until finely chopped. Add the olive oil, the vinegars, tarragon, and salt and pepper to taste. Chill. May be made several days in advance.

At serving time, peel and slice the tomatoes. Arrange the lettuce on a serving plate. Top with the tomatoes and the dressing.

Pepper and Tomato Salad

SERVES 8

3 large beefsteak tomatoes
1 red bell pepper, seeded
1 green bell pepper, seeded
8–10 mushrooms
1 white onion

4 hard-cooked eggs, cut in
  wedges
8 slices bacon, fried crisp,
  drained, and crumbled

Cut the tomatoes in large chunks, removing seeds. Cut the red and green peppers in large chunks. Slice the mushrooms. Cut the onion in 1/2-inch pieces. Place the tomatoes, peppers, mushrooms, and onions in a salad bowl. Toss with the dressing and garnish with the egg and bacon.

PAPRIKA DRESSING
1 tablespoon sugar
1 tablespoon water
1/4 cup champagne vinegar
2/3 cup vegetable oil

1/2 teaspoon paprika
1 tablespoon ketchup
Freshly ground pepper

Heat 1 tablespoon of sugar and 1 tablespoon of water over low heat until sugar is dissolved. Combine all of the remaining ingredients and blend well. This is best if made at least 4 hours in advance.

Napa Cabbage Salad

SERVES 6

1 large Napa cabbage (Chinese)
Walnut Dressing (below)
1/4 pound prosciutto or smoked ham, slivered

Slice the cabbage as though for slaw. Toss with the dressing. Add the ham and toss again lightly. Chill before serving.

WALNUT DRESSING
1/4 cup minced walnuts
1/2 cup olive oil
1/2 cup champagne vinegar

Combine the walnuts and oil and set aside for 1 hour. Add the vinegar to the walnuts and oil at serving time and mix well.

Cauliflower and Olive Salad

SERVES 6

1 head cauliflower
20 pitted ripe black olives
3 tablespoons capers, rinsed and
    drained

Anchovy Mayonnaise (below)

Cut the cauliflower into flowerets and steam until just barely tender. Rinse under cold water, drain, and chill. When ready to serve, toss cauliflower, olives, and capers with the Anchovy Mayonnaise.

ANCHOVY MAYONNAISE
1/2 teaspoon Dijon mustard
1 egg
1 tablespoon fresh lemon juice

1 anchovy fillet
1/8 teaspoon salt
1/2–1 cup vegetable oil

Blend the mustard, egg, lemon juice, anchovy, and salt in a blender or a food processor. While the machine is running, slowly add 1/2 cup of oil. Taste for seasoning and add more lemon juice if necessary. If mixture is too thick, continue to add oil until proper consistency is reached.

Italian Marinated Vegetable Salad

SERVES 8

Italian Marinade (below)
1 red bell pepper, cut in 1/2-inch
　strips
1 yellow bell pepper, cut in
　1/2-inch strips
2 carrots, cut in matchsticks
1 (16-ounce) can artichoke
　hearts, drained and cut in half

5 green onions, chopped
1 cup small ripe black olives
2 cups broccoli flowerets
1 pint cherry tomatoes
1/2 pound fresh mushrooms
Fresh parsley, chopped, for
　garnish

Pour marinade over peppers, carrots, artichoke hearts, onions, and olives and marinate several hours at room temperature or longer in the refrigerator. Place the broccoli in boiling water for 2 minutes. Drain, rinse under cold water, and chill several hours.

Just before serving, add broccoli, tomatoes and mushrooms to marinated vegetables and toss gently. Garnish with parsley.

ITALIAN MARINADE
3/4 cup champagne vinegar
1/2 teaspoon sugar
3/4 teaspoon salt (optional)
1/4 teaspoon pepper

1 teaspoon dried oregano
1/2 cup vegetable oil
1/2 cup olive oil

Heat the vinegar, then add the sugar and seasonings and cool slightly. Place in a blender or food processor and add oils slowly. Blend until well mixed.

Brie Salad with Pecans

SERVES 12

1 large green apple
1 large red apple
Orange Vinaigrette (below)
2 large heads Boston lettuce

1 large red onion
1 pound Brie cheese, sliced in 12
　pieces
1/2–3/4 cup chopped pecans

Cut each apple in 12 thin slices and coat with some of the Orange Vinaigrette. Thinly slice the lettuce and onion and toss with the remaining dressing. Arrange the lettuce and onions on salad plates and top with the apple slices. Place the Brie on top of the salad and sprinkle with pecans.

ORANGE VINAIGRETTE

1/2 cup vegetable oil

1/2 cup walnut oil

1/3 cup balsamic vinegar

2 tablespoons Dijon mustard

Zest of 1 orange

1 tablespoon minced garlic

Salt and freshly ground pepper

Combine all ingredients and blend well.

Baked Goat Cheese Salad

SERVES 6

8 ounces goat cheese

1/4 cup olive oil

1 tablespoon chopped fresh
thyme

6 slices day-old bread

1/2 cup butter

3 garlic cloves, minced

1 cup fine bread crumbs

1 teaspoon dried thyme

Salt and pepper

3 small heads lettuce (red leaf,
Boston, Limestone, or a
combination) washed and
dried well

Balsamic and Thyme Vinaigrette
(below)

Cut the cheese into twelve rounds. Marinate overnight in the olive oil and fresh thyme. Slice bread into cubes, removing crusts. Melt the butter in a medium skillet, add garlic, and sauté until soft. Add bread cubes and sauté until lightly brown. Set aside.

Preheat oven to 350 degrees. Remove the cheese rounds from the marinade with a slotted spoon, reserving the marinade.

In a small bowl, mix the bread crumbs, the dried thyme, and salt and pepper to taste. Coat the cheese rounds with the bread crumbs and place in a shallow baking dish. Bake 8–10 minutes until lightly browned.

Add the reserved marinade to the vinaigrette and toss with the greens. Arrange on salad plates and toss with croutons. Place 2 cheese rounds in center of each salad and serve immediately.

BALSAMIC AND THYME VINAIGRETTE

1/4 cup balsamic vinegar

1/2 cup olive oil

Salt and pepper

1 teaspoon dried thyme

Combine the vinegar, olive oil, salt and pepper and thyme. Mix well and set aside.

California Greek Salad

SERVES 6–8

3 large avocados, diced
Juice of 2 lemons
2 large tomatoes, chopped
2 cups diced jícama

8 ounces feta cheese, crumbled
4 ounces pitted ripe black olives,
  sliced
4 tablespoons olive oil

Arrange the avocados on a serving platter in a single layer. Sprinkle a third of the lemon juice over the avocados. Arrange the tomatoes on top of the avocados. Layer the jícama over the tomatoes. Sprinkle with half of the remaining lemon juice. Crumble the cheese over all. Top with the olives and sprinkle the remaining lemon juice over the olives and drizzle with olive oil. May be made 4–6 hours ahead and refrigerated.

Green Salad with Artichoke Hearts and Hearts of Palm

SERVES 6

1 head Boston lettuce
1 head romaine lettuce
1 (14-ounce) can artichoke
  hearts
1 (14-ounce) can hearts of palm

2 medium tomatoes, peeled and
  chopped
Lemon Mustard Vinaigrette
  (below)

Thoroughly chill the greens and tear in bite-size pieces. Rinse and drain the artichokes and cut in half. Rinse and drain the hearts of palm and slice. Toss tomatoes, lettuce, artichoke hearts and hearts of palm, add Mustard Vinaigrette and toss again.

LEMON MUSTARD VINAIGRETTE
6 tablespoons oil
2 tablespoons fresh lemon juice
1 teaspoon sugar
1 teaspoon salt
1 teaspoon freshly ground
  pepper

2 teaspoons Dijon mustard
1 garlic clove, crushed
1 teaspoon Worcestershire sauce

Combine all ingredients and blend well.

Green Salad with Fennel

SERVES 6–8

Fennel, long a favorite among French and Italian chefs, has a delicate flavor that creates an uncommonly good salad.

1/2 head red leaf lettuce
1/2 head romaine lettuce
1/2 head Boston lettuce
1/2 cup thinly sliced fennel stalks
2 tablespoons fresh minced
　chives

2 tablespoons fresh chopped
　parsley
1 1/2 cups small shrimp, cooked
　(optional)
Sour Cream Mustard Dressing
　(below)

Thoroughly wash and chill greens. Tear in bite-size pieces and combine with fennel, chives, parsley, and shrimp. Toss with just enough dressing to lightly coat.

SOUR CREAM MUSTARD DRESSING
1 teaspoon Dijon mustard
1 teaspoon salt
1 egg
Juice of 1 large lemon
1/2 cup salad oil

1/2 cup sour cream
1/8 teaspoon hot pepper sauce
Freshly ground black pepper to
　taste

Combine the mustard, salt, egg, and lemon juice in a blender or food processor. Slowly add the oil while the machine is running until well blended. Add sour cream, hot pepper sauce, and pepper and blend about 30 seconds.

Gruyère and Walnut Salad

SERVES 4

The dressing for this dinner salad is compatible with the finest red wines.

1 head Boston lettuce
Watercress to taste
1/4 to 1/2 cup chopped walnuts

4 ounces Gruyère cheese, cut in
　matchsticks
Red Wine Vinaigrette (below)

Tear lettuce into bite-sized pieces and combine with watercress, walnuts, and cheese. Toss with Red Wine Vinaigrette.

RED WINE VINAIGRETTE

1/4 cup olive oil
1 tablespoon red wine
1 tablespoon red wine vinegar

1 tablespoon Dijon mustard
1/2 teaspoon salt or to taste
1/2 teaspoon pepper

Combine all ingredients and blend well.

Boston Lettuce with Avocado, Hazelnuts, and Raspberry Vinaigrette

SERVES 6–8

The subtle flavor of the avocado oil is a perfect complement to the hazelnuts.

2 heads Boston lettuce
2 ounces hazelnuts (filberts)
2 ripe avocados

Creamy Raspberry Vinaigrette
(below)

Wash lettuce, tear in bite-size pieces, and chill.

Place the hazelnuts on a cookie sheet and bake them in a 350-degree oven for 15 minutes. Wrap nuts in a tea towel and let cool. Rub the nuts in the towel to remove the skins. Chop the nuts coarsely in a food processor.

At serving time, peel and slice the avocados. Combine the lettuce, avocado slices, and hazelnuts in a salad bowl and toss with Raspberry Vinaigrette.

CREAMY RASPBERRY VINAIGRETTE

1 tablespoon Dijon mustard
4 tablespoons raspberry vinegar
Salt and pepper to taste

1 cup avocado oil (peanut oil
   may be substituted)
1 tablespoon heavy cream

Combine the mustard, vinegar, salt, and pepper in a blender or food processor. Slowly add the oil and cream and blend again for about 30 seconds.

Spinach Salad with Chutney Mustard Dressing

SERVES 4

1 bunch fresh spinach
4–5 pieces bacon, fried crisp,
    drained, and crumbled
2 hard-cooked eggs, chopped
5 mushrooms, sliced

1 ripe avocado, chopped
1/2 cup diced red onions
Chutney Mustard Dressing
    (below)

Wash the spinach well, discard stems, and tear in small pieces. Add the bacon, eggs, mushrooms, avocado, and onions, and toss with the dressing.

CHUTNEY MUSTARD DRESSING
2 teaspoons sugar
1/4 cup white wine vinegar
1 garlic clove, minced

3 tablespoons chutney
2 teaspoons dry mustard
1/3–1/2 cup olive oil

Combine all ingredients except oil in blender or food processor. With motor running, add the oil a little at a time until smooth.

Spinach Antipasto Salad

SERVES 6

1 large red bell pepper, cut in
    bite-size pieces
5 ounces pepperoni, peeled and
    thinly sliced
1 red onion, thinly sliced
6 ounces provolone cheese, cut
    in 2-inch strips

1 medium zucchini, thinly sliced
Antipasto Dressing (below)
1–2 bunches fresh spinach, torn
    into bite-size pieces
7 ounces black olives, pitted

Combine the red bell pepper, pepperoni, onions, cheese, and zucchini. Toss with the Antipasto Dressing. Add spinach. Toss again. Garnish with olives.

ANTIPASTO DRESSING

2 teaspoons minced fresh basil
　　or 1/2 teaspoon dried basil
1/3 cup minced fresh parsley
2 teaspoons minced fresh
　　oregano *or* 1/2 teaspoon dried
　　oregano

2 medium garlic cloves, minced
1/4 cup balsamic vinegar
1/4 cup safflower oil
2 tablespoons olive oil
Salt and pepper to taste

Combine all ingredients and blend well.

Spinach Salad with Three Dressings

SERVES 6

3 bunches fresh spinach (or 1–2
　　heads romaine lettuce)
1 cup sliced celery (optional)
6 green onions, thinly sliced

3 large firm Red Delicious
　　apples, diced
1 cup dry-roasted peanuts
1/2 cup raisins

Wash the spinach well, discard stems, and tear into small pieces. Combine with the celery, onions, apples, peanuts, and raisins and toss with one of the following dressings.

CURRIED DRESSING

2 tablespoons toasted sesame
　　seeds
2/3 cup salad oil
1 tablespoon finely chopped
　　chutney

1 teaspoon curry
1 teaspoon salt
1 teaspoon dry mustard
1/4 teaspoon liquid hot pepper
　　seasoning

Combine all ingredients in a jar, and mix well. This should be prepared 2 hours in advance and refrigerated. Shake again before using.

WARM BACON DRESSING

6 slices bacon, cut in 1/4-inch
　　pieces
1/3 cup vinegar
2 tablespoons water
2 teaspoons sugar
1 teaspoon salt

1 teaspoon mixed dried Italian
　　herbs
1/2 teaspoon dried basil
1/2 teaspoon pepper
1/2 teaspoon dry mustard

Sauté bacon until crisp. Drain and save 1/3 cup of the drippings. If necessary, add oil to make 1/3 cup. Add all other ingredients and blend. Pour over salad, toss, and serve immediately while dressing is still warm.

CREAMY MUSTARD DRESSING

4 eggs	2 teaspoons salt
4 tablespoons dry mustard	2 cups heavy cream
1/2 cup sugar	2/3 cup white wine vinegar

Beat the eggs well in a large bowl. Add the mustard, sugar, and salt and beat again. Slowly add 1 cup of the heavy cream and all of the vinegar to the egg-mustard mixture. Stir well. Pour into a heavy saucepan and cook over low heat until thickened. Remove from heat and add the remaining cup of cream, whisking until well combined. This dressing should be served at room temperature.

Note For a delicious mustard, omit the second cup of cream.

Cold Beef and Artichoke Salad

SERVES 6

8 ounces marinated artichoke hearts, drained	1 cup thinly sliced red onions
8 ounces Gouda cheese, julienned	Red Wine Vinegar and Lime Dressing (below)
1 pound flank steak, fillet, or top sirloin, cooked and sliced in thin strips	

Combine the artichoke hearts, cheese, steak and onions. Toss with the dressing 1 hour before serving and chill.

RED WINE VINEGAR AND LIME DRESSING

1 teaspoon Dijon mustard	1 garlic clove, minced
1/3 cup olive oil	1 tablespoon sour cream
1 tablespoon fresh lime juice	1 1/2 teaspoons red wine vinegar

Mix together all of the ingredients and blend well.

Salade de Canard

SERVES 4 AS A MAIN COURSE

Versions of this popular French salad appear on menus throughout California. Ours uses duck breast only, for ease of preparation.

1 large red onion, sliced	2 tablespoons unsalted butter
6 tablespoons olive oil	2 whole duck breasts, boned but
1/4 pound mushrooms, sliced	not skinned, and cut in half
2 cups sliced Boston lettuce	4 tablespoons sherry wine
2 cups sliced red leaf lettuce	vinegar
4 small tomatoes, chopped	Salt and pepper

In a large skillet, sauté the onions in 2 tablespoons of the olive oil until just lightly browned. Add the mushrooms, and sauté 2 minutes longer. In a large bowl, combine the onions, mushrooms, lettuce, and tomatoes. Set aside.

In the same skillet, melt the butter with 2 tablespoons of the oil. Add duck breasts, skin side down. Sauté for 8 minutes, turn, and sauté for about 7 minutes more. The timing will depend on the size of the duck breast. The meat should be moist and the juices clear. Remove the duck from the pan, cool, and skin. Cut the skin into small pieces. Return to same pan, and sauté until all fat is rendered and pieces are very crisp. Drain on paper towels. Slice the duck in bite-size pieces and add with the duck skin to salad. Discard the fat from skillet and deglaze with 2 tablespoons of the vinegar. Scrape up browned bits from the skillet and pour over the salad. Blend the remaining 2 tablespoons vinegar, salt and pepper to taste, and remaining 2 tablespoons oil. Pour over salad and toss. Serve immediately.

Chicken Salad with Stilton Cheese

SERVES 6 AS A MAIN COURSE

If Stilton is unavailable, Gorgonzola may be substituted.

2 whole chicken breasts, cooked, skinned and boned	3 hard-cooked eggs, chopped
1 pound bacon	1/2 pound Stilton or Gorgonzola cheese, crumbled
2 bunches fresh spinach	4 green onions, chopped
4 ounces slivered almonds, toasted	Curry Cream Dressing (below)

Slice the chicken in strips, and set aside. Fry the bacon, drain, and crumble. Wash spinach well, discard stems, and tear into bite-size pieces. In a large salad bowl, combine the chicken, bacon, almonds, eggs, cheese, onions, and spinach. Toss with dressing.

CURRY CREAM DRESSING
1/2 cup sour cream
1/2 cup mayonnaise
1 teaspoon curry powder or to taste

Combine all ingredients and blend well.

Sonoran Chicken Salad

SERVES 8 AS A MAIN COURSE

1 1/2 cups diced cooked chicken breast
1/4 cup mayonnaise
1/2 cup finely chopped celery
2 tablespoons finely chopped jalapeño chiles
1 tablespoon finely chopped onions
1 tablespoon finely chopped carrots

1 tablespoon finely chopped parsley
Salt and pepper to taste
4 ripe avocados
8 lettuce leaves
Creamy Cilantro Dressing (below)

Combine the chicken, mayonnaise, celery, peppers, onions, carrots, and parsley and mix well. Season with salt and pepper to taste. Peel and halve the avocados. Fill the avocados with the chicken mixture and turn upside down on a lettuce leaf. Top with 1 teaspoon of the dressing and serve immediately. Serve rest of dressing on the side.

CREAMY CILANTRO DRESSING
1/2 cup mayonnaise
1/2 cup sour cream
2 tablespoons chopped fresh cilantro

1/2 teaspoon ground cumin

Combine the ingredients and mix well.

Cajun Chicken Salad

SERVES 6 AS A MAIN COURSE

2 tablespoons olive oil
1 tablespoon Cajun Seasoning
  (below)
1 1/2 pounds boneless chicken
  breast, sliced in 2-inch strips
8 ounces spicy Italian sausage,
  cooked and sliced (optional)
2 tablespoons minced garlic
2 cups finely chopped green
  onions

2 tablespoons chopped hazelnuts
  (filberts)
1/2 cup julienned fresh spinach
1/2 cup julienned red cabbage
1 cup julienned romaine lettuce
Balsamic Vinaigrette (below)
Radicchio cups (optional)

In a large skillet heat the olive oil. Mix in the Cajun Seasoning. Then add chicken, sausage, garlic, onions, and nuts and sauté for approximately 5 minutes. Add the spinach and cabbage and sauté until wilted. Add more seasoning if desired. Toss romaine with Balsamic Vinaigrette to lightly coat, add chicken mixture, and toss. Serve in radicchio cups.

CAJUN SEASONING
1 tablespoon paprika
2 tablespoons salt
1 teaspoon each: onion powder,
  garlic powder, and cayenne

3/4 teaspoon each white and
  black pepper
1/2 teaspoon each dried thyme
  and dried oregano

Mix all ingredients together.

BALSAMIC VINAIGRETTE
1 cup olive oil
1/2 cup balsamic vinegar
1/2 teaspoon salt

Combine all ingredients and blend well.

Mandarin Chicken Salad

SERVES 6–8 AS A MAIN COURSE

The combination of the orange juice and cilantro makes this salad truly distinctive.

1 (6-ounce) can frozen orange-juice concentrate

1 cup pineapple juice

6 ounces soy sauce

2 garlic cloves, minced

1/2 teaspoon peeled and minced fresh ginger

2 whole chicken breasts

1/2 package wonton skins

Vegetable oil or peanut oil

4 ounces slivered almonds, toasted

1 bunch green onions, julienned

1 cup fresh cilantro leaves

Mandarin Dressing (below)

In a small bowl combine the orange juice, pineapple juice, soy sauce, garlic, and ginger. Pour over the chicken and marinate for several hours or overnight. Bake the chicken in the marinade at 350 degrees for 25 minutes or until just springy to the touch. Turn once during cooking. When cool, remove the chicken and reserve marinade. Discard skin and bones and shred. Set aside. Cut the wonton skins in 1/2-inch strips and fry in the oil until crisp. Toss the chicken, wontons, almonds, onions and cilantro together just before serving. Add the dressing and toss again.

MANDARIN DRESSING

Reserved chicken marinade

2 tablespoons hoisin sauce

1 teaspoon oriental sesame oil

2 tablespoons lemon juice

1 teaspoon dry mustard

Skim the fat from the marinade. Simmer all ingredients gently to blend flavors. Cool. Pour over salad and toss.

Shrimp Salad Guadalajara

SERVES 6–8

1 medium red onion
1 red bell pepper
1 green bell pepper
3 medium tomatoes, peeled and
   seeded
1 1/2 pounds medium raw shrimp,
   shelled and deveined

1/2 cup pitted ripe black olives,
   drained
1/2 cup stuffed green olives
Jalapeño Dressing (below)
2 lemons

Slice the onion, red and green peppers, and tomatoes in julienne strips. Place the shrimp in boiling water and cook just until they turn pink, about 2 minutes. Cut the black and green olives in half. Combine all ingredients, except lemons, in a serving bowl and toss with the dressing. Slice the lemons thinly and use for garnish.

JALAPEÑO DRESSING
1 garlic clove
3 fresh or canned jalapeño chiles
1/2 cup olive oil
1/3 cup lemon juice

1 teaspoon cumin
1 bay leaf
Salt and freshly ground black
   pepper

Mince the garlic and peppers and combine with other ingredients. Mix well. Remove the bay leaf before using.

Shrimp and Jícama Salad

SERVES 4

A lovely salad with an oil-free dressing.

1 pound medium shrimp, cooked
2 cups jícama, peeled and cut in
   julienne strips

4 tomatillos, husked and sliced
Cilantro Vinaigrette (below)
Cilantro sprigs for garnish

In a large bowl, combine the shrimp, jícama and tomatillos. Add the vinaigrette and marinate at least 1 hour in refrigerator before serving. Garnish with cilantro sprigs.

CILANTRO VINAIGRETTE

2/3 cup white wine vinegar
1/8 cup sugar
3 tablespoons seeded and minced
  jalapeño chiles

4 tablespoons chopped fresh
  cilantro

Mix all of the ingredients together in a small bowl.

Spring Seafood Salad

SERVES 8 AS A MAIN COURSE
SERVES 12 AS A BUFFET COURSE

16 thin asparagus spears,
  trimmed
2 pounds bay scallops
1 pound medium shrimp, shelled
  and deveined
1/2 pound crab, cooked
1/3 cup olive oil
3 tablespoons white wine vinegar

3 tablespoons sherry wine
  vinegar
1 garlic clove, minced
2 green onions, minced
1 pound spinach, washed and
  stemmed
1 pint cherry tomatoes
Creamy Basil Dressing (below)

Place the asparagus in boiling salted water, uncovered, for 3–5 minutes until crisp-tender. Refresh under cold water, drain, and chill. Bring 2 quarts water to a boil. Reduce heat to a simmer. Poach the scallops for 2 minutes until just opaque. Do not overcook. Remove scallops to a large bowl. Poach the shrimp in same manner as scallops just until they turn pink. Rinse with cold water. Add shrimp and crab to scallops. Combine the olive oil, vinegars, garlic, and onions. Toss with seafood and chill. To serve, arrange spinach leaves around edge of a platter. Mound the seafood in center. Garnish with tomatoes and asparagus. Accompany with Creamy Basil Dressing.

CREAMY BASIL DRESSING

3 tablespoons white wine vinegar
1 tablespoon Dijon mustard
1/3 cup fresh basil
1 large garlic clove
3 tablespoons vegetable oil

1/2 cup sour cream
1/4 cup heavy cream
3 tablespoons minced fresh
  parsley
Salt and white pepper to taste

Combine vinegar, mustard, basil, and garlic in blender or food processor and mix until almost smooth. With machine running, drizzle in oil. Add sour cream, heavy cream, and parsley and purée until smooth. Season with salt and pepper and chill. Stir well before serving.

Pasta Salad with Tomatoes, Basil, and Sherry Vinegar

SERVES 6

1/2 cup olive oil
1/4 cup sherry wine vinegar
3 large garlic cloves
2 tablespoons minced fresh parsley
1 cup julienned fresh basil leaves
1/2 teaspoon salt
1 (28-ounce) can tomatoes, with juice

1 pound rotelle or small shell pasta, cooked and drained
1 cup fresh grated Parmesan cheese
1/4 cup Niçoise olives
1 cup cubed Jack cheese (optional)

In a food processor, combine the olive oil, vinegar, and garlic until garlic is minced. Add the parsley, basil, salt, and tomatoes and process quickly, until well mixed and the tomatoes are finely chopped. Do not purée. Combine with pasta, Parmesan cheese, olives, and Jack cheese. Chill for several hours before serving.

Oriental Pasta Salad with Dried Mushrooms

SERVES 4–6 AS A MAIN COURSE

4 ounces oriental dried mushrooms (shiitake or oyster)
8 ounces lo mein noodles *or* 8 ounces thin spaghetti
1/4 cup oriental sesame oil
1/4 cup soy sauce

1/4 cup rice wine vinegar
1/8 teaspoon cracked black pepper
2–3 cups cooked, diced chicken or crab
2 tablespoons chopped fresh cilantro

Soak the mushrooms in water for 30 minutes or until soft. Cook the lo mein noodles or spaghetti according to package directions. Rinse in cold water and drain well. Blend together the oil, soy sauce, vinegar, and pepper. Pour over the noodles. Drain the mushrooms, pat dry, and add to the noodles with the chicken or crab. Chill for several hours. Toss with cilantro just before serving.

Chicken Pasta Salad

SERVES 10–12 AS A MAIN COURSE

4 whole chicken breasts, cooked, skinned and boned
2 pounds fettucine, cooked and drained
Rosemary Marinade (below)
4 zucchini, thinly sliced

1 cup chopped green onions
1 1/2 cups snow peas, blanched and refreshed
1 1/2 cups chopped parsley
1/2 cup freshly grated Parmesan cheese

Slice the chicken in thin strips. Combine with the fettucine. Reserve 1/3 cup of the marinade for later use and pour the rest over the chicken and fettucine. Toss and chill overnight for the flavors to blend. Two hours before serving, add the zucchini, onions, and snow peas to the chicken and noodles. Toss well with the reserved marinade. Toss with the parsley and cheese just before serving.

ROSEMARY MARINADE
1 1/2 cups oil
3/4 cup fresh lemon juice
2 garlic cloves, minced
5 teaspoons sugar (or to taste)
2 1/2 teaspoons dry mustard

3 tablespoons minced fresh rosemary *or* 3 teaspoons dried rosemary
1 1/4 teaspoons salt

Combine all marinade ingredients and mix well.

California Riviera Salad

SERVES 8–10

This is a salad with many variations. With the shrimp it becomes a delightful first course for a lovely spring or summer dinner. The addition of artichokes makes it an outstanding side dish.

1 pound fettucine, preferably tomato

2 cups petits pois

1 cup chopped green onions

3/4 cup sliced ripe olives

2 cups halved cherry tomatoes

2 avocados, diced

1 1/2 pounds cooked shrimp (optional)

1 cup artichoke hearts, quartered (optional)

Riviera Dressing (below)

1 cup freshly grated Parmesan cheese

In a large salad bowl, gently blend all salad ingredients. Toss with dressing and sprinkle with Parmesan cheese.

RIVIERA DRESSING

3 tablespoons chopped onions

4 garlic cloves

1 1/2 teaspoons dry mustard

1 1/2 teaspoons salt

3 tablespoons sugar

3/4 teaspoon white pepper

3/4 cup salad oil

1/2 cup olive oil

1/2 cup cider vinegar

3 tablespoons water

1/2 teaspoon dried basil

1/4 teaspoon dried oregano

In a food processor, place the onions and garlic and process until smooth. Add the mustard, salt, sugar, and pepper and process again. With the machine running, slowly add the salad oil and olive oil. Add the vinegar, 1 tablespoon at a time, processing after each addition. Add the water, basil and oregano and process briefly. Refrigerate at least 2 hours before serving.

Shrimp and Pasta Salad

SERVES 6

2 cups small shell pasta
Tarragon Mayonnaise (below)
1/2 pound medium cooked shrimp
1–2 teaspoons lemon juice
Romaine lettuce leaves

1 lemon, sliced
Fresh parsley, chopped, for
  garnish
1 pint cherry tomatoes, halved,
  for garnish

Cook the pasta al dente. Drain and mix immediately with enough of the mayonnaise to moisten, and set aside. Stir the shrimp into the pasta, adding more mayonnaise or lemon juice if necessary. Line a salad bowl with the whole lettuce leaves, and add the shrimp-and-pasta mixture. Garnish with the lemon slices, parsley, and cherry tomatoes.

TARRAGON MAYONNAISE

1 egg
1/2–1 cup vegetable oil
Juice of 1 lemon

2 anchovy fillets
1/2 teaspoon dried tarragon
2 tablespoons capers

Process the egg briefly in a food processor or blender. Slowly add the oil until mixture begins to thicken. Add the lemon juice, anchovies, and tarragon and blend until smooth. Stir in capers and chill.

Wild Rice and Raisin Salad

SERVES 6

To serve as a pretty side dish salad, omit the ham and add half a cup of cooked peas.

1/2 cup wild rice
1/2 cup (or 20 large) pecan
  halves
1/2 pound lean ham
3/4 cup golden raisins

1/2 cup green onions, thinly
  sliced
Rice Wine Vinaigrette (below)
Lettuce cups

Place the rice in a 3-quart saucepan filled with water. Pour into a strainer. Repeat several times to wash the rice thoroughly. Return the rice to the saucepan and add 2 quarts water. Bring to a boil. Cover, and boil gently, without stirring, until tender and each grain has opened, about 40–50 minutes. Have extra boiling water on hand to add toward the end of the cooking so that the rice is always covered with boiling water. Rinse under hot water, draining well. In a small shallow baking pan, spread pecan halves in a single layer. Bake in a preheated 350-degree oven until toasted, about 10 minutes. Slice the ham in 1/4-inch × 1-inch strips. Place the raisins in a small bowl and cover with hot water until plumped. Drain well. Combine rice, ham, raisins, and onions in a serving bowl. Toss salad with dressing. Cover, and chill. At serving time, place in lettuce cups and garnish with pecans.

RICE WINE VINAIGRETTE
1/3 cup olive oil
1/4 cup rice wine vinegar
1/4 teaspoon pepper

Combine all ingredients together and mix well.

Wild Rice and Shrimp Salad

SERVES 8

3/4 pound mushrooms, sliced
4 tablespoons olive oil
2 pounds shrimp, shelled and
    deveined

6 ounces wild and brown rice
    mix
1 1/2 cups sliced celery
Curry Dressing (below)

Sauté the mushrooms in the olive oil until soft. Add the shrimp and sauté until cooked, about 3–4 minutes. Set aside. Prepare rice according to package instructions. Blend in the shrimp mixture and add the celery. Toss with just enough dressing to moisten. Chill. At serving time pass additional dressing.

CURRY DRESSING
1 cup sour cream
1 cup mayonnaise
8 green onions, sliced
1 garlic clove, minced
1/2 teaspoon oregano

1/2 teaspoon thyme
1–2 teaspoons curry powder
4 tablespoons fresh lemon juice
1/2 teaspoon salt
White pepper

In a small bowl, combine the sour cream, mayonnaise, onions, garlic, oregano, thyme, and curry powder. Stir in the lemon juice and season to taste with salt and white pepper.

Note   As a variation, make this salad with chicken. Cook the chicken breasts ahead of time and add to rice with sautéed mushrooms.

California Niçoise Salad

SERVES 8–10

1 pound Great Northern beans
3 carrots, quartered
1 bay leaf
1 teaspoon thyme
1 tablespoon salt
1/2 cup chopped green onions
1 1/2 cups sliced celery
1/4 cup chopped parsley
Red Wine and Coriander
    Vinaigrette (below)

1 head romaine lettuce
3 (6 1/2-ounce) cans water-
    packed tuna, chilled
1 medium cucumber, scored,
    sliced, and chilled
3 medium tomatoes, sliced and
    chilled
24 ripe black olives, pitted

Rinse the beans and soak in just enough water to cover for 4–5 hours. Drain. Place the beans in a large saucepan with 1 quart of water to cover. Add the carrots, bay leaf, thyme, and salt. Simmer 1 1/2 hours over medium heat. Drain and slice the carrots and discard bay leaf. Combine the warm beans, onions, celery, parsley, carrots, and dressing. Toss and chill several hours or overnight.

To serve, line a platter with romaine, mound the beans in the center. Arrange the tuna, cucumbers and tomatoes around beans. Garnish with olives.

RED WINE AND CORIANDER VINAIGRETTE

1 1/2 cups salad oil
1/2 cup red wine vinegar
3 teaspoons dry mustard
2 garlic cloves, crushed

2 teaspoons salt
2 teaspoons ground coriander
1/2 teaspoon pepper

Combine all ingredients and blend well.

Pear and Raspberry Salad

SERVES 8

4 pears, peeled or unpeeled
Juice of 1 lemon
Bibb lettuce
8 ounces semisoft mild cheese,
  such as Bel Paese or
  Camembert

2 cups raspberries
8 watercress leaves
Raspberry Orange Vinaigrette
  (below)

Halve the pears and sprinkle with lemon juice. Arrange the pears on lettuce leaves. Shred the cheese and sprinkle over the pears. Garnish with raspberries and watercress leaves and pour 2 tablespoons of dressing over each salad.

Note Cheese may be cut into decorative shape as illustrated on cover.

RASPBERRY ORANGE VINAIGRETTE
2 tablespoons orange zest
1/4 cup raspberry vinegar

3/4 cup vegetable oil
Vanilla extract

Grate the orange zest and combine with the vinegar and oil. Mix well. Add vanilla to taste.

Blue Cheese and Nectarine Salad

SERVES 8

Excellent with Roquefort. Or try a fine Maytag blue.

4 nectarines, peeled
1 head radicchio

8 ounces blue cheese
Raspberry Vinaigrette (below)

Slice the nectarines and arrange in 8 individual radicchio leaves. Crumble blue cheese over nectarines. Pour 2 tablespoons of the dressing over each salad.

RASPBERRY VINAIGRETTE
1/4 cup raspberry vinegar
3/4 cup vegetable oil
Salt and pepper

Combine all ingredients and mix well.

Spring Green Salad with Strawberries, Avocado, and Kiwi

SERVES 6

This beautiful salad is extremely light and colorful.

12 strawberries, sliced
3 kiwi, peeled and sliced
1 head Boston lettuce or mixture
    of greens

1 avocado, cut into cubes
Orange Dressing (below)

Combine all ingredients except avocado and dressing and chill. Just before serving add avocado and toss with dressing.

ORANGE DRESSING
1/3 cup olive oil
3 tablespoons raspberry vinegar
3 tablespoons fresh orange juice

1/2 teaspoon salt
1/8 teaspoon cracked pepper

Combine all ingredients and mix well.

Roquefort or Stilton Dressing

MAKES ABOUT 2 CUPS

4 ounces Roquefort or Stilton
    cheese
1/2 cup mayonnaise
1 teaspoon lemon juice

1 cup sour cream
1/4 teaspoon Worcestershire
    sauce
Salt to taste

Mash half the cheese with a fork. Add the mayonnaise, lemon juice, sour cream, and Worcestershire sauce and mix well. Crumble the remaining cheese and add to mixture. Season to taste with salt. Chill. Thin with milk or cream, if desired. This dressing can be made several days ahead and refrigerated.

Mustard Dill Dressing

MAKES ABOUT 3 1/4 CUPS

1/2 cup Dijon mustard
1/2 cup cider vinegar
1 1/2 teaspoons dried tarragon
1 1/2 teaspoons dried dillweed

2 cups safflower oil
2 tablespoons grated Parmesan
  cheese
2 tablespoons half-and-half

Combine the mustard, vinegar, and herbs and let stand 10 minutes. Slowly add oil, whisking constantly until thickened. Blend in Parmesan and half-and-half.

Garlic Egg Salad Dressing

MAKES ABOUT 1 CUP

1 garlic clove
1 teaspoon salt
1 teaspoon sugar
1/2 teaspoon Dijon mustard

3 tablespoons cider vinegar
3/4 cup salad oil
1 egg, room temperature

In a blender or food processor, mix garlic, salt, sugar, and mustard to a paste. Slowly add vinegar, then slowly add the oil with processor running. Add egg and blend briefly. This dressing is delicious served over warm new potatoes.

Tarragon Dressing

MAKES ABOUT 1 1/2 CUPS

1 tablespoon minced fresh
  tarragon
1/2 teaspoon Dijon mustard
2 teaspoons minced fresh basil

1 teaspoon lemon juice
1/4 cup sherry wine vinegar
1/2 cup soy oil
1/2 cup olive oil

In a food processor or blender, combine the tarragon, mustard, basil, lemon juice, and vinegar until well blended. With motor running, slowly drip in oils until combined. This dressing is wonderful drizzled over papaya and avocado or cantaloupe slices.

V

Pasta, Pizza and Rice

Basic Pasta Cooking Directions

One pound of pasta is the maximum amount that should be cooked in one pot, so that the pasta is never crowded. In a large kettle, bring 6–8 quarts of cold water to a full rolling boil; 1–2 teaspoons of salt may be added to the water, but this is not necessary if the sauce that you will be serving with the pasta contains salt. Add 1 tablespoon of olive oil or salad oil. Add the pasta all at once and stir gently with a fork or pronged pasta server to separate it. Cook at a full boil until the pasta is al dente (still firm to the bite). Dried pasta cooks more slowly than fresh pasta. There is no absolute measure of time. Fresh pasta usually cooks in 3–4 minutes, dried in about 8–10 minutes. Cut pasta (rigatoni, shells, bowties, or rotelle) takes a few minutes longer than strand pasta.

When the pasta is done, immediately drain it into a colander but do not rinse if the pasta is to be served hot. If it needs to be held for any period of time, simply toss the pasta with a few tablespoons of oil or butter to prevent it from sticking.

Fresh Pasta

2 cups semolina flour or all-purpose flour
3 eggs, slightly beaten
1 tablespoon olive oil

MANUAL METHOD
Place the flour in a bowl and make a well in the center. Add the eggs and slowly mix in the flour, working from the center of the well out to the sides. When all of the flour is incorporated add the oil and mix well. Knead the dough on a floured board for 10 minutes, or until smooth.

FOOD PROCESSOR METHOD
Place the flour in a food processor. With the machine running, drop in the eggs and add the oil. Continue processing until the dough just begins to form a ball. If the dough seems too sticky, add 1–2 tablespoons more flour. If the dough is too dry, add a few drops of water. Turn the dough out onto a floured board and knead for 3–5 minutes or until smooth.

To shape the pasta, break off a piece of the dough that is approximately the size of an egg. Use a pasta machine to shape the dough, following manufacturer's instructions, or roll by hand to desired thickness and cut into strips or shapes. Repeat with remaining dough. Follow Basic Pasta Cooking Directions.

Artichoke Linguine

SERVES 6 AS A FIRST COURSE
SERVES 4 AS A MAIN COURSE

1/4 cup butter
1/4 cup olive oil
1 tablespoon flour
1 cup Chicken Stock
1 garlic clove, minced
1 tablespoon minced fresh
    parsley
1 tablespoon fresh lemon juice
Salt and white pepper to taste
2 cups canned or frozen
    artichoke hearts, drained and
    sliced

2 tablespoons freshly grated
    Parmesan cheese
2 teaspoons capers, drained and
    rinsed
1 tablespoon unsalted butter
2 tablespoons olive oil
1 tablespoon freshly grated
    Parmesan cheese
1/4 teaspoon salt
1 pound linguine, cooked and
    drained

Melt the 1/4 cup of butter with the 1/4 cup of oil in a small saucepan over medium heat. Add the flour and stir until smooth, about 3 minutes. Blend in the stock, stirring until thickened, about 1 minute. Reduce the heat to low. Add the garlic, parsley, lemon juice, salt, and pepper. Cook 5 minutes, stirring constantly. Blend in the artichokes, the 2 tablespoons of Parmesan cheese and capers. Cover and simmer over low heat 8 minutes. Melt the remaining butter in large skillet over medium heat. Stir in remaining oil, cheese, and salt. Add linguine and toss lightly. Arrange pasta on platter and pour sauce over all. Serve immediately.

Cappellini with Butter and Spices

SERVES 4–6

1/2 cup unsalted butter, softened
1/2 teaspoon cinnamon
1/2 teaspoon nutmeg
Dash cayenne pepper
1 pound cooked and drained
    cappellini

1/2 cup reserved cooking water
    from the pasta
3/4 cup freshly grated Parmesan
    cheese
Black pepper to taste

In a small bowl, blend together the butter, cinnamon, nutmeg, and cayenne.

Toss with the hot pasta and 1/4 cup of the reserved water. Add additional water, if needed, to coat all pasta. Toss with the cheese and black pepper to taste. Serve immediately.

Cappellini with Fresh Tomato and Basil Sauce

SERVES 4–6 AS A MAIN COURSE

1 pound very ripe fresh plum tomatoes, peeled, seeded, and chopped

1 cup coarsely chopped fresh basil

3 tablespoons sherry vinegar

1 (3 1/4-ounce) jar capers, drained and rinsed

Salt and pepper to taste

1 pound cappellini or angel hair pasta, cooked and drained

3/4 cup olive oil

Combine the tomatoes and basil and let stand at room temperature 1–2 hours or overnight in refrigerator. Mix the vinegar, capers, salt, and pepper into tomato mixture. Toss the hot pasta with the oil and blend in tomato sauce. Serve immediately.

Pasta with Lemon Lime Sauce

SERVES 4 AS A FIRST COURSE
SERVES 6 AS A SIDE DISH

It is important to use a fine champagne in this dish in order to achieve the best results; however a dry white wine will give a different but still delicate flavor.

2 large shallots, minced

1 cup champagne or dry white wine

1 cup unsalted butter

2 tablespoons fresh lemon juice

1 teaspoon fresh lime juice

zest from 1 lemon

zest from 1 1/2 limes

Salt to taste

1/2 pound angel hair pasta, cooked and drained

In a large saucepan, place the shallots and champagne. Bring to a boil over moderate heat and cook until liquid is reduced to about 1/2 cup. Reduce the heat to low and add the butter, 1 teaspoon at a time, whisking constantly. Stir in the juices and zest of lemon and limes. Season to taste with salt and keep warm. When ready to serve toss the hot pasta with sauce and garnish with slivers of lime peel.

Pasta Twists with Porcini and Cream Sauce

SERVES 6–8 AS A FIRST COURSE

Porcini mushrooms from Italy are noted for their rich, complex flavor. Although they are expensive, few are needed to capture this unique quality. This recipe is worthy of a very special occasion.

1 cup dried porcini mushrooms, approximately 1/4 pound
2 tablespoons unsalted butter
3 cups heavy cream
Salt and freshly ground pepper to taste

1 pound pasta twists, cooked and drained
1 cup freshly grated Parmesan cheese

Soak the porcini in hot water for 30 minutes. Drain and mince. In a skillet, melt the butter and sauté the porcini over medium heat until soft. In a small heavy saucepan, cook the cream over medium heat until reduced by one third. Add the porcini and simmer for 20 minutes. Season with salt and pepper to taste.

Toss the hot pasta with the sauce and the Parmesan cheese. Serve immediately.

Tomato Basil Cream with Linguine

SERVES 6–8 AS A FIRST COURSE

3 tablespoons olive oil
1 pound fresh plum tomatoes, peeled, seeded, and coarsely chopped
2 garlic cloves, minced
1/2 cup heavy cream

Salt and white pepper to taste
2 cups coarsely chopped fresh basil
1 pound linguine, cooked and drained

In a medium-size skillet, heat the olive oil over low heat. Add the tomatoes and garlic and sauté until tomatoes are soft. Stir in the cream and cook until slightly thickened, about 5 minutes. Season with salt and white pepper to taste. Just before serving, stir in basil and toss with the hot pasta.

Summer Tomato Sauce with Spaghettini

SERVES 6

This simple, uncooked sauce should be at room temperature when tossed with the pasta. For variety, add small cubes of mozzarella or Jack cheese to the hot pasta before tossing with the sauce.

2 pounds very ripe tomatoes
1 teaspoon salt
1/3 cup olive oil
1/3 cup fresh chopped basil
Juice of 1 lemon

Black pepper
1 pound of spaghettini, cooked
  and drained
Freshly grated Parmesan cheese

In a food processor, chop the tomatoes. Add the salt, oil, basil, and lemon juice. Process until well combined but still chunky. Add pepper to taste.
   Toss the hot pasta with the sauce. Pass the freshly grated Parmesan cheese.

Pasta, Sage, Rosemary, and Thyme

SERVES 4–6

3 garlic cloves, peeled
1 tablespoon fresh rosemary *or*
  1 1/2 teaspoons dried rosemary
1 1/2 teaspoons fresh thyme *or* 1
  teaspoon dried thyme
1/4 teaspoon fresh sage *or* 1/8
  teaspoon dried sage
1–2 small dried red chile peppers
1/4 cup olive oil

4 cups chopped and seeded
  tomatoes *or* 1 (1-pound,
  12-ounce) can whole plum
  tomatoes, drained
Salt and pepper to taste
1 pound spaghetti or vermicelli,
  cooked and drained
1 cup freshly grated Parmesan
  cheese

In a saucepan, sauté the garlic, rosemary, thyme, sage and chiles in the olive oil over medium heat for 2–3 minutes. Add the tomatoes and cook over medium heat for 15–20 minutes until the sauce thickens slightly. Add salt and pepper to taste. Place the hot pasta in a serving bowl. Strain the sauce over the pasta, pushing with a large spoon to extract all liquid. Sauce will be thin. Immediately toss the pasta with the cheese. Pass additional cheese.

Sweet Red Pepper Sauce with Linguine

SERVES 6 AS A FIRST COURSE

This versatile sauce is also a perfect accompaniment to broiled steak or chicken.

1 1/2 pounds red bell peppers
2 tablespoons olive oil
1 cup chopped onions
1/4 cup chopped celery, with leaves
1 teaspoon minced garlic
1 1/2 cups peeled, seeded, and chopped tomatoes

1/2 teaspoon thyme
Salt and freshly ground pepper to taste
1 pound linguine, cooked and drained

Using a long-handled fork, char the peppers over an open flame, turning them for 2–3 minutes, or until the skins are blackened. Or, place the peppers on a broiler pan and broil about 2 inches from the heat until the skins are blackened, turning frequently. This will take approximately 15 minutes. Transfer the peppers to a plastic bag, close tightly, and let them steam until they are cool enough to handle and peel. Cut into strips.

In a medium saucepan, heat the oil. Sauté the onions, celery, and garlic until soft but not brown. Add the peppers, tomatoes and thyme and simmer, uncovered, 20–30 minutes or until very thick. Purée in food processor until smooth. Season to taste with salt and pepper. Toss the hot pasta with the sauce.

Shells with Double Tomato Sauce

SERVES 6 AS A FIRST COURSE OR SIDE DISH

Sun-dried tomatoes contribute their distinctive flavor to this very rich sauce.

4 tablespoons unsalted butter
1/3 cup sun-dried tomatoes,
 slivered
4 cups peeled, seeded, and
 chopped fresh tomatoes *or* 1
 (1-pound, 12-ounce) can
 chopped tomatoes, drained

1/2 cup sour cream
Salt and pepper to taste
1 pound small pasta shells,
 cooked and drained
1/4 cup freshly grated Parmesan
 cheese

In a medium saucepan, melt the butter over low heat. Stir in the sun-dried tomatoes, fresh tomatoes, and sour cream. Without letting the sauce come to a boil, cook over medium heat, stirring constantly, until heated through. Season to taste with salt and pepper. Toss with hot pasta and Parmesan cheese. Serve immediately.

Pasta with Baked Tomato Sauce

SERVES 4–6

2 pounds very ripe tomatoes
1 teaspoon sugar
1 teaspoon salt
1/3 cup olive oil
Pepper to taste

1 pound rotelle, cooked and
 drained
1/3 cup chopped fresh basil
 leaves
Freshly grated Parmesan cheese

Preheat oven to 325 degrees. In a large pot of boiling water, blanch the tomatoes for 15 seconds. Drain them in a colander and refresh them under cold running water. Peel, core, seed, and coarsely chop the tomatoes. Combine them with the sugar, salt, oil, and pepper to taste. Place the mixture in a 13 × 9-inch baking dish and place in the oven for 40 minutes. Stir the sauce mixture well and place in a heated serving bowl. Add the hot pasta, and basil. Toss. Serve immediately. Pass freshly grated Parmesan cheese.

Pasta with Four Cheeses

SERVES 6 AS A FIRST COURSE

5 tablespoons unsalted butter
1 tablespoon olive oil
1 medium onion, chopped
1 garlic clove, minced
1 (28-ounce) can whole plum
    tomatoes in purée
1/2 teaspoon salt
1/4 teaspoon freshly ground
    pepper
1 1/2 cups heavy cream
1/2 cup freshly grated Parmesan
    cheese

1/2 cup grated Bel Paese or
    Fontina cheese
3/4 cup Gorgonzola cheese,
    crumbled
1/4 cup ricotta cheese
1 pound pasta rigatoni, penne, or
    shells, cooked and drained
2 tablespoons minced fresh
    parsley

In a large heavy saucepan, melt 1 tablespoon of the butter with the oil over medium-low heat. Add the onions and garlic and cook until soft, stirring occasionally. Blend in the tomatoes and increase the heat to medium high. Simmer, uncovered, until thickened, stirring occasionally, for about 10 minutes. Season with salt and pepper to taste. In a heavy skillet, bring the cream to a boil. Reduce heat and simmer until thickened, about 5 minutes. Stir in the tomato sauce and cheeses and keep warm.

    Toss the hot pasta with the remaining 4 tablespoons butter and the sauce. Garnish with chopped parsley and serve immediately in heated bowls.

Pasta with Gruyère Cheese

SERVES 4–6

2 cups Crème Fraîche
1 cup finely grated Gruyère
    cheese
1/4 teaspoon freshly grated
    nutmeg

1/4 teaspoon salt
White pepper to taste
1 garlic clove, halved
1 pound fettucine, cooked and
    drained

Preheat the oven to 400 degrees. In a large bowl, combine the Crème Fraîche, 1/2 cup of the grated Gruyère cheese, the nutmeg, salt, and white pepper to taste. Toss the hot pasta, with the sauce and add additional nutmeg and salt if desired. Rub an 11-inch gratin dish with the garlic and butter it well. Add the pasta and sprinkle it with the remaining Gruyère. Bake for 15 minutes or until cheese is bubbly and golden.

Manicotti with Lemon Tomato Sauce

SERVES 6 AS A FIRST COURSE

1/2 pound Jack cheese, grated
1 cup ricotta cheese
1 cup feta cheese
1/2 cup freshly grated Parmesan cheese
3 cups chopped fresh spinach leaves
1/2 cup finely chopped green onions, including some of the green part
1 teaspoon chopped fresh mint
1/4 cup chopped fresh parsley
1/2 cup finely chopped fresh mushrooms
1 teaspoon salt
1 egg
1 (6-ounce) package manicotti noodles (12 pieces), cooked, drained and tossed with 3 tablespoons olive oil
Lemon Tomato Sauce (below)

Preheat the oven to 350 degrees. In a large bowl mix together the 4 cheeses, spinach, onions, mint, parsley, mushrooms, salt, and egg.

To stuff the noodles, split one side of the noodle lengthwise. Fill with 3 tablespoons of cheese mixture and close shell. Place seam side down in a baking pan lightly coated with Lemon Tomato Sauce. Pour the remaining sauce over the manicotti. This dish may be prepared ahead of time to this point and refrigerated. When ready to serve, bring to room temperature and bake covered for 20 minutes until heated through.

LEMON TOMATO SAUCE
3 tablespoons olive oil
3 cups very ripe seeded and chopped tomatoes or 1 (28-ounce) can tomatoes
1/3 cup chopped fresh basil or 1 tablespoon dried basil
1 teaspoon salt
Pepper to taste
2 tablespoons tomato paste
Juice of 1 lemon

Place the olive oil and tomatoes in a medium saucepan. Bring to a boil over high heat. Add basil, salt, and pepper and simmer until juices are reduced and sauce is starting to thicken, about 20 minutes. Add the tomato paste and simmer for 5 minutes more. Add lemon juice to sauce and purée mixture in food processor or food mill. Taste for seasonings.

Fettucine with Gorgonzola, Bell Peppers, and Basil

SERVES 4 AS A MAIN COURSE
SERVES 6 AS A FIRST COURSE

5 tablespoons unsalted butter
1 medium red bell pepper, julienned
1 medium yellow bell pepper, julienned
1 garlic clove, minced
1/2 teaspoon salt
1/4 teaspoon freshly ground black pepper
1 medium zucchini, julienned

1 1/2 cups heavy cream
1/2 cup Gorgonzola cheese
1 teaspoon flour
1/2 cup freshly grated Parmesan cheese
1/4 cup chopped fresh basil leaves
1 pound fettucine (spinach fettucine, if possible), cooked and drained

In a large skillet, melt 2 tablespoons of the butter over moderate-low heat. Add the peppers, garlic, salt, and ground pepper and blend well. Cover and cook until peppers are just tender, about 5 minutes. Add the zucchini and cook 1–2 minutes longer.

In a blender or food processor, combine 1/4 cup of the cream and the Gorgonzola. Purée until smooth and set aside. In a medium saucepan, melt the remaining 3 tablespoons butter over moderate heat. Add the flour and cook, stirring, for 1 minute. Do not let the mixture brown. Stir in the remaining 1 1/4 cups cream, reduce heat to medium-low, and simmer until the mixture reduces slightly—about 5 minutes. Whisk in the cheese mixture. Add 1/4 cup of the Parmesan cheese, the pepper-zucchini mixture, and the basil. Season with salt and pepper to taste. Keep warm.

Toss the hot pasta with the sauce and top with the additional Parmesan cheese. Serve immediately.

Shells with Peas and Basil

SERVES 6 AS A SIDE DISH

6 tablespoons unsalted butter
1 cup chopped green onions
1 1/2 cups dry vermouth *or* dry
   white wine
6 tablespoons finely chopped
   fresh basil *or* 1 1/2 teaspoons
   dried basil

1 cup cooked peas
1 pound small pasta shells,
   cooked and drained
Salt and pepper

In a medium saucepan, heat the butter until foaming and add the onions and vermouth or white wine. Cook over medium heat until onions are soft and the wine thickens. Add the basil and peas and cook over high heat for 2 minutes. Immediately pour sauce over the hot pasta. Season with salt and pepper to taste. Toss and serve immediately.

Confetti Pasta

SERVES 4 AS A MAIN COURSE
SERVES 6 AS A SIDE DISH

This imaginative and colorful pasta exemplifies the spirit of California cuisine.

3 large ears of grilled corn *or* 1
   (16-ounce) can corn kernels,
   drained
3 tablespoons olive oil
1 large red bell pepper, chopped
1 large yellow bell pepper,
   chopped
3/4 cup chopped red onions

1 cup heavy cream
1 tablespoon chili powder
Salt and pepper
1 pound tricolor shell pasta,
   cooked and drained
2 tomatoes, peeled, seeded and
   chopped
1/4 cup chopped fresh cilantro

If using fresh corn, remove the kernels from the ears. In a large skillet, heat the olive oil and sauté the peppers, corn, and onions until the onions are soft. Add the cream and chili powder. Season to taste with salt and pepper. Cook 3–5 minutes until cream has slightly thickened. Toss with hot pasta. Serve on warm plates with a tablespoon of the chopped tomatoes and a sprinkling of the cilantro.

Shells Genovese

SERVES 6 AS A FIRST COURSE
SERVES 4 AS A MAIN COURSE

4 tablespoons unsalted butter
8–10 slices smoked ham or
  prosciutto, cut in thin strips
1 1/4 cups heavy cream
1 cup ricotta cheese
1/2 cup freshly grated Parmesan
  cheese

1/2 teaspoon marjoram
1/4 teaspoon nutmeg
1 (10-ounce) package frozen
  peas, thawed
Salt and pepper to taste
1 pound medium shells, cooked
  and drained

In a skillet, melt the butter and lightly brown the ham. Set aside. In a medium saucepan, combine the cream, ricotta, Parmesan, marjoram, and nutmeg and heat until the cheeses are melted. Add the ham and peas and heat. Season with salt and pepper to taste. Toss the hot pasta with the sauce and serve immediately.

Linguine with Ham and Tomato Sauce

SERVES 6 AS A MAIN COURSE

1/4 cup unsalted butter
2 cups diced ham
1 cup diced celery
1 cup diced carrots
2 tablespoons chopped onions
2 teaspoons minced garlic
2 (16-ounce) cans plum
  tomatoes, drained and
  chopped

1/2–1 teaspoon (or to taste) red
  pepper flakes
Salt and pepper
1 pound linguine, cooked and
  drained
Freshly grated Parmesan cheese

In a large skillet, melt the butter and add the ham, celery, carrots, onions, and garlic. Cook until the vegetables are tender. Add the tomatoes and simmer gently, until thickened, about 20–30 minutes. Add the red pepper flakes and season to taste with salt and pepper. Toss the hot pasta with the sauce and serve with Parmesan cheese.

Noodles with Sautéed Cabbage and Caraway Seeds

SERVES 6 AS A SIDE DISH

2 teaspoons salt
8 cups shredded cabbage
1/2 cup butter
4 teaspoons sugar
1 1/4 teaspoons caraway seeds

1/2 teaspoon freshly ground
   black pepper
8 ounces medium noodles,
   cooked and drained

Sprinkle the salt over the cabbage, toss lightly, and let stand 30 minutes. Squeeze the cabbage in paper towels to dry. In a large skillet over medium-high heat, melt the butter. Add the cabbage, sugar, caraway seeds, and pepper. Cook, stirring occasionally, until the cabbage is just tender (about 4–5 minutes). Add the hot cooked noodles and toss with the cabbage mixture.

Cappellini with Smoked Salmon and Black Caviar

SERVES 6 AS A FIRST COURSE

1/4 cup unsalted butter
6–7 green onions, finely chopped
1/4 pound fresh mushrooms,
   thinly sliced
3 tablespoons fresh lemon juice
Salt and white pepper
1/2 cup dry white wine
3 cups heavy cream
1 pound cappellini (or other very
   thin pasta), cooked and
   drained

6 ounces smoked salmon, thinly
   sliced and cut in 1/4-inch
   strips about 2 inches long
2 tablespoons green peppercorns
3 tablespoons finely chopped
   fresh parsley (flat leaf if
   possible)
2 ounces red or black caviar,
   rinsed and drained

In a large skillet, melt the butter. Add the onions and cook for 2–3 minutes. Add the mushrooms and lemon juice and season with salt and pepper to taste. Sauté for 5 minutes. Add the wine and reduce over high heat until about 2 tablespoons of liquid remain, about 5 minutes. Add the cream and reduce by half, or until cream is quite thick, about 10 minutes.

Add pasta to sauce in the skillet. Add salmon and peppercorns, toss and heat, but do not boil.

To serve divide on 6 plates and sprinkle each with parsley and top with the caviar.

Lemon Pasta with Mussels

SERVES 4–6 AS A MAIN COURSE

3 pounds mussels, in the shell
2 tablespoons flour
4 tablespoons water
1 1/2 cups dry white wine
8 tablespoons unsalted butter
2 tablespoons olive oil
4 garlic cloves, minced
4 tablespoons minced fresh
    parsley, (flat-leaf variety, if

possible), plus additional, for
    garnish
Freshly ground black pepper
1 cup heavy cream
1 cup strained broth from the
    steaming mussels
1 recipe Lemon Pasta (below) *or*
    1 pound fettucine, cooked and
    drained

Scrub the mussels well with a rough brush under running water. Scrape off beards with a knife. Mix the flour and water thoroughly. Fill a large bowl with several quarts of water and stir in the flour-and-water mixture. Place the mussels in a bowl and soak for 30 minutes in refrigerator and then drain. Place mussels in a large sauté pan or stockpot with the wine. Cover and cook over high heat until the mussels open. Remove the mussels from the pot with a slotted spoon, leaving as much broth as possible. Discard any mussels that have not opened. Remove the mussels from shells, saving a few for garnish if desired. Chop the mussels coarsely, and set aside. Strain the broth through several thicknesses of cheesecloth and set aside.

In a large skillet heat 6 tablespoons of the butter with the olive oil and add the garlic. Cook the garlic until it is soft and add the 4 tablespoons of the parsley, pepper, cream, and reserved broth. Let the mixture boil 1–2 minutes until slightly thickened. Add the mussels and just heat through. Toss the pasta with the sauce and add the remaining butter. Season to taste with salt and serve immediately. Garnish the dish with reserved mussels and chopped parsley.

LEMON PASTA
3 eggs, room temperature
2 tablespoons lemon juice
Rind of 2 large lemons, grated
    (about 2 tablespoons)

1/2 teaspoon salt
2–2 1/4 cups flour

For an electric pasta machine make according to machine directions.

For a manual pasta machine, combine all ingredients in food processor or by hand until mixture resembles cornmeal. Remove and knead until mixture holds together (if too dry add a couple of drops of water). Put through the widest blades and run through machine several times until pasta is very smooth. Cut into desired widths and cook in salted boiling water until done, about 4–5 minutes.

Shrimp Vermicelli

SERVES 6–8 AS A MAIN COURSE

1/2 cup butter
1 cup sliced green onions
5 tablespoons flour
3 cups Chicken Stock
1/2 cup heavy cream
1/4 cup dry white wine
1 teaspoon dried oregano,
   crumbled
1/2 cup freshly grated Parmesan
   cheese

2 garlic cloves, minced
1/4 cup slivered sun-dried
   tomatoes
1/2 pound sliced mushrooms
1 pound vermicelli, cooked and
   drained
4 cups cooked medium shrimp

Melt 1/4 cup of the butter in skillet and sauté the onions until soft but not browned. Blend in the flour to form a roux. With a whisk blend in the stock, cream, and wine. Cook over medium-low heat for 3 minutes, stirring constantly until sauce thickens. Add the oregano and 1/4 cup of the cheese. Set sauce aside.

Melt the remaining butter and sauté the garlic, tomatoes, and mushrooms for about 2 minutes.

Combine the sauce, mushroom mixture, vermicelli, and shrimp in an oven-proof baking dish. Sprinkle with additional cheese and bake at 375 degrees for 20 minutes.

Pizza or Calzone Dough

1 package yeast
1 teaspoon sugar
1 cup warm water
3 tablespoons milk
2 tablespoons olive oil (more
   may be needed)

2 teaspoons salt
2 3/4 cups all-purpose flour (more
   may be needed)

Dissolve the yeast and sugar in 1/4 cup warm water (115 degrees) and set aside until it foams, about 10 minutes. This proofs the yeast and assures you of a live culture. Stir in the milk, olive oil, remaining 3/4 cup water, and salt. Add the flour and stir until the dough becomes very stiff.

Turn the dough out onto a lightly floured work surface and knead by hand until it is smooth and elastic, about 10 minutes. Place the dough in an oiled bowl. Turn the dough to coat it. Cover loosely with plastic wrap and let rise in a warm, draft-free place until it has doubled in bulk and an indentation remains when the dough is pressed gently. Use for calzone or pizza.

For a quicker pizza dough: preheat oven to 200 degrees and turn off. If you have a gas pilot light, the pilot may be left on to warm the oven. Cover the dough tightly with plastic wrap and place in the warmed oven for 30 minutes. Punch dough down and roll out for calzone or pizza. The texture of the dough will be somewhat different but still delicious.

Pizza Dough, Food-processor Method

1 package active dry yeast	3/4 teaspoon salt
1 teaspoon sugar	2 teaspoons olive oil
2/3 cup warm water (120 degrees)	1 1/2 tablespoons cornmeal
1 2/3 cups flour	

Dissolve the yeast and sugar in the warm water and set aside until it foams, about 10 minutes. This proofs the yeast and assures you of a live culture. Place the flour and salt in a food processor. Turn the machine on and pour in the yeast mixture through the feed tube. Process for about 45 seconds, until the dough pulls away from the sides of the bowl. Add the oil and process for about 60 seconds. If the dough sticks to the sides of the bowl, add 1 tablespoon of flour at a time, processing for 10 seconds after each addition. The dough should leave the sides of the work bowl but still remain soft.

Place the dough in a lightly oiled bowl and turn to coat completely with oil. Let the dough rest for 5 minutes. Roll into 1 large pizza, 15 inches in diameter, or 4 small pizzas or calzones. Oil a pizza pan or cookie sheet and sprinkle with the cornmeal. Place the dough on the prepared pan. The crust is now ready to fill and bake.

Three-Cheese Pizza with Sausage, Olives, and Peppers

1 recipe Pizza Dough
1 pound sweet Italian sausage
1 tablespoon butter
1 medium onion, thinly sliced
1/3 cup olive oil
1 garlic clove, minced
1/4 teaspoon red pepper flakes
1/2 cup coarsely chopped black
   olives

1 red bell pepper, julienned
1/4 cup chopped fresh basil
1/4 cup minced fresh Italian
   parsley
1 cup freshly grated Parmesan
   cheese
2 cups grated Italian Fontina
   cheese
2 cups grated mozzarella cheese

Preheat oven to 450 degrees. Prepare the Pizza Dough for a 14–15-inch pizza and set aside to rise. In a medium skillet, fry the sausage over moderate heat until brown and completely cooked, about 15 minutes. Drain well, cool, and thinly slice.

In a small skillet over low heat, melt the butter. Add the onions and sauté until soft, about 10 minutes. Remove from the skillet and set aside.

Blend together the olive oil, garlic, and pepper flakes. Roll out the pizza dough and brush with the oil mixture. Top evenly with the sausage, then the onions, olives, bell pepper slices, basil, parsley, and cheeses. Bake 20–25 minutes.

Calzone with Black Forest Ham and Ricotta

MAKES 8

1/3 cup olive oil
1 garlic clove, minced
1/4 teaspoon dried red pepper
   flakes
2 recipes Pizza Dough
2 cups chopped Black Forest
   ham or other smoked ham
1 cup chopped green onions,

   including some of the green
   part
1 1/2 cups ricotta cheese
1 cup shredded mozzarella
   cheese
1/2 cup freshly grated Parmesan
   cheese
Freshly ground black pepper

Preheat oven to 425 degrees. Combine the olive oil, garlic, and pepper flakes in a small bowl. Divide dough into 8 equal portions. On a flour-covered surface, roll each portion in an 8-inch circle. Brush dough with olive oil, being careful to leave at least a 1/2-inch border around the edges free of oil.

Combine the ham, onions, and cheeses. Add black pepper to taste. Mound 2/3 cup filling on each dough circle. Fold dough over as for a turnover and press the edges to seal. Crimp with a fork all around edges. Lightly brush with more oil. Bake for 20 minutes or until brown.

The calzone may be made ahead and refrigerated or individually wrapped and frozen. If frozen, an additional 5–8 minutes time may be required in baking.

Calzone with Smoked Chicken and Goat Cheese

MAKES 8

1/3 cup olive oil
1 garlic clove, minced
1/4 teaspoon dried red pepper
  flakes
2 recipes Pizza Dough
2 cups shredded smoked chicken
1 cup chopped fresh basil
1 cup shredded mozzarella
  cheese

1/2 cup freshly grated Parmesan
  cheese
2/3 cup crumbled goat cheese
1 cup chopped green onions,
  including some of the green
  part
Salt and pepper

Preheat the oven to 425 degrees. In a small bowl, combine the olive oil, garlic, and pepper flakes. Divide dough into 8 equal portions. On a flour-covered surface, roll each portion in an 8-inch circle. Brush dough with olive oil, being careful to leave at least a 1/2-inch border around the edges free of oil.

Combine the chicken, basil, cheeses, green onions, salt and pepper to taste. Mound 2/3 cup filling on each dough circle. Fold dough over as for a turnover and press edges to seal. Crimp with a fork all around edges. Lightly brush with more oil. Bake for 20–25 minutes until brown.

Calzone may be made ahead and refrigerated or individually wrapped and frozen. If frozen, an additional 5–8 minutes cooking time may be required in baking.

Orzo with Lemon Pesto

SERVES 8

Serve this delightful side dish in avocado halves or lemon shells.

1 pound orzo (small, rice-shaped
    pasta)
2 teaspoons salt
2 garlic cloves
2 cups tightly packed fresh basil

1 cup olive oil
1/2 cup lemon juice
1 cup freshly grated Parmesan
    cheese
Pepper to taste

Cook the orzo in boiling water with 1 teaspoon of the salt until al dente. Drain and refresh with cold water.

In a food processor, process the garlic and basil. Gradually add the olive oil, using only as much as is necessary to produce a thick sauce.

Transfer the basil mixture to a large mixing bowl. Add the lemon juice and remaining teaspoon of salt. Combine the orzo and the basil mixture and stir in the Parmesan cheese. Season with additional salt and pepper to taste. Chill for several hours.

If prepared in advance, additional lemon juice, oil, and salt may be needed.

Couscous

SERVES 6

This recipe will lend distinction to a menu including grilled beef or lamb.

1/2 cup currants
1/3 cup dry sherry
2 tablespoons unsalted butter
2 cups Chicken Stock
1 teaspoon cinnamon
1 teaspoon paprika
1/4 teaspoon salt

1 cup couscous
1/2 cup finely diced carrots
4 green onions, sliced thinly,
    both white and green part
1 tablespoon fresh lime juice
1/3 cup toasted pine nuts
1/2 cup fresh orange juice

Preheat oven to 350 degrees. In a small bowl, plump the currants in the sherry for 30 minutes. Drain, reserving the currants. In a medium saucepan combine the butter, stock, cinnamon, paprika, and salt and heat to boiling. Add the couscous, stirring constantly. Cook until all of the liquid is absorbed, about

I–2 minutes. Remove from heat and add the reserved currants. Cover, and let stand for 10–15 minutes. Stir in the carrots, onions, lime juice, and pine nuts. Gradually add the orange juice, a tablespoon at a time, until it is absorbed. Fluff the couscous with a fork. Season with salt and pepper. Cover with foil and heat in oven for 30 minutes.

Gorgonzola Polenta

SERVES 6

3 cups milk
2 tablespoons unsalted butter
3/4 cup cornmeal
3 tablespoons heavy cream
1/3 cup freshly grated Parmesan
  cheese

1/2 cup crumbled Gorgonzola
  cheese
1/2 teaspoon salt
1/8 teaspoon freshly grated
  nutmeg

In a heavy saucepan, bring the milk and butter to a boil. Gradually stir in the cornmeal, whisking constantly, and bring back to a boil. Continue to stir constantly until the mixture is very thick and smooth, about 5 minutes. Add the cream, cheeses, salt, and nutmeg and beat until smooth. Taste for seasoning and add more salt if necessary.

Butter 6 timbales or half-cup ramekins. Divide the mixture evenly, smoothing tops with spatula. Refrigerate 1 hour. When ready to bake, preheat the oven to 450 degrees. Unmold on a well-buttered baking dish and bake for 10–12 minutes. Place under broiler until lightly golden.

Herbed Rice with Tomatoes and Onion

SERVES 6

1 onion, finely chopped
2 tablespoons olive oil
1 cup long-grain rice
2 cups Chicken Stock
1 tomato, peeled, seeded, and
  chopped

2 tablespoons chopped fresh
  chives
2 tablespoons chopped fresh
  parsley
Salt and pepper to taste
1/8 teaspoon dried thyme

Sauté the onions in oil until they are soft and clear. Add the rice and sauté until rice is just beginning to color. Stir in the remaining ingredients and cover. Simmer the rice for 20 minutes or until liquid is absorbed and rice is tender.

Brown Rice with Raisins and Mint

SERVES 4

2 tablespoons unsalted butter
1 cup chopped onions
1 cup brown rice
1 cup shredded carrot
2 cups Chicken Stock

1/2 cup raisins
1 tablespoon chopped fresh mint
1/4 cup chopped fresh parsley
1 teaspoon ground cumin

In a large skillet, melt the butter and sauté the onions until soft, about 5 minutes. Add the rice and carrots and cook, stirring, for 2–3 minutes. Add stock, raisins, mint, parsley, and cumin. Cover and simmer for 25 minutes until liquid is all absorbed and rice is tender.

Greek Spinach Rice

SERVES 6

3 tablespoons olive oil
3/4 cup thinly sliced leeks,
    including some of the green
    part
1 garlic clove, minced
1 cup white rice

4 cups chopped fresh spinach
    leaves
2 cups Chicken Stock
1 teaspoon grated lemon peel
1/2 cup lightly toasted pine nuts
    (optional)

In a medium saucepan heat the olive oil. Add the leeks and garlic, cooking until soft, about 8 minutes. Mix in the rice and stir until well coated. Add the spinach leaves and stir until the spinach is wilted. Add Chicken Stock and bring to a boil. Cover pan and simmer over low heat for 20 minutes or until all liquid is absorbed and the rice is tender. Stir in the lemon peel and pine nuts just before serving.

Sushi Rice

SERVES 4–6

This is authentic "sticky" rice that is also a flavorful side dish.

1 1/2 cups short-grained white
   rice
1 3/4 cups cold water
1/4 cup rice wine vinegar

2 tablespoons sugar
1 1/2 teaspoons salt
1 tablespoon mirin (sweet sake),
   or dry sherry

Rinse the rice. In a saucepan with a tight-fitting lid, add the rice and cold water. Let stand for 15 minutes. Over high heat bring the water and rice to a boil, cover, and reduce the heat and cook until the water is absorbed, 10 minutes. Reduce heat to its lowest point and simmer another 5 minutes. Do not remove lid during cooking. Remove from heat and let the rice stand, covered, for at least 5 minutes. Transfer the rice to large nonmetallic platter. Mix together the vinegar, sugar, salt, and mirin and pour over rice, mixing with a fork. Cool to room temperature.

Pricey Rice

SERVES 6 AS A SIDE DISH

2 ounces dried imported
   mushrooms, such as porcini,
   chanterelles, or shiitake
1 cup water
1 medium onion, finely chopped
5 tablespoons olive oil
1 1/2 cups long-grain rice

1 1/3 cups Chicken Stock
1 teaspoon salt
1/8 teaspoon cayenne pepper
2/3 cup dry white wine
1/2 cup freshly grated Parmesan
   cheese

Soak mushrooms in hot water for 30 minutes. Chop finely and set aside, reserving liquid.

In a large pan, sauté the onions in oil until they are soft and clear. Add the rice to the onions and stir until well coated. Add the Chicken Stock, salt, cayenne, mushrooms, reserved liquid, and wine. Cover and simmer for 20–25 minutes or until all liquid is absorbed and the rice is tender. Add the cheese just before serving.

Pilaf with Snow Peas, Pine Nuts, and Roasted Peppers

SERVES 4–6

This is excellent with grilled Italian sausages.

1 red bell pepper
1 yellow bell pepper
3 tablespoons olive oil
1 small garlic clove, minced
1/2 teaspoon salt
1/4 cup pine nuts, lightly toasted
4 ounces snow peas, blanched
    for 1 minute, then refreshed
    under cold water

1 tablespoon unsalted butter
1 cup chopped onions
1/2 teaspoon salt
1 cup long-grain rice
1 1/2 cups Chicken Stock
1/2 cup dry white vermouth or
    white wine
1 tablespoon minced fresh
    parsley

Using a long-handled fork, char the peppers over an open flame, turning them for 2–3 minutes or until the skins are blackened. Or, place the peppers on a broiler pan and broil about 2 inches from the heat until the skins are blackened, turning frequently. This will take approximately 15 minutes. Slice in thin strips. Transfer the peppers to a plastic bag, close tightly, and let them steam until they are cool enough to handle and peel.

In a medium skillet, heat 1 tablespoon of the oil over low heat. Add the garlic, roasted pepper strips, and salt to skillet and sauté slowly for 3–5 minutes. Add the pine nuts and snow peas to the pan. Stir, off heat, until nuts and peas are coated with garlic oil. The vegetables can be made ahead to this point.

In a large skillet, heat the remaining oil and butter over medium heat. Add the onions, and 1/2 teaspoon salt to the skillet and sauté until the onions are soft. Add the rice and continue sautéing until the rice begins to color. Heat the stock and vermouth, until mixture comes to boil.

Add the heated broth to the rice. Bring to a boil and cover. Simmer the rice over low heat 20–25 minutes or until the liquid is absorbed and the rice is tender. Fluff rice with a fork and carefully stir in the vegetables. Heat through. Sprinkle with parsley before serving.

Scallop and Sausage Fried Rice

SERVES 4 AS A MAIN COURSE
SERVES 6 AS A SIDE DISH

This is an excellent light entree as well as a unique Oriental side dish. Increase the ground pork and scallops to a pound each when serving as a main course.

1/2 cup fresh snow peas
1/2 pound lean ground pork
3 teaspoons soy sauce
3 teaspoons dry sherry
3 tablespoons oyster sauce
4 tablespoons peanut oil
1/2 pound scallops, rinsed and
   halved

2 cups chilled cooked rice
1 egg, lightly beaten
6 green onions, chopped,
   including some of the green
   part
1/2 cup bean sprouts

Add the pea pods to boiling water for 1 minute. Drain and refresh in cold water. Drain again and pat dry on paper towels.

Combine the ground pork with 1 teaspoon of the soy sauce and 1 teaspoon of the sherry. Cover and refrigerate for half an hour. Mix the remaining 2 teaspoons of soy souce and 2 teaspoons sherry with the oyster sauce and reserve. In a wok or large skillet, heat 2 tablespoons of the peanut oil over high heat. Add the scallops and cook for 1–2 minutes or until scallops are opaque and just cooked through. Remove the scallops with a slotted spoon and keep warm. Add the ground pork and stir-fry until light brown and crumbly. Remove the pork and pour out oil. Add the remaining oil to the wok. Add the rice, stirring, until heated through. Oil a small skillet and lightly scramble the egg. Add the egg, scallops, pork, onions, bean sprouts, snow peas, and the reserved sauce mixture and stir-fry for 2–3 minutes until heated through. Serve immediately.

Parmesan Rice with Walnuts

SERVES 4

2 tablespoons fresh parsley
2 garlic cloves, peeled
1/4 cup walnuts
1/2 cup freshly grated Parmesan
   cheese

4 tablespoons olive oil
1 cup long-grain rice
2 cups Chicken Stock
1/2 teaspoon salt
Juice of half a lemon

In a blender or food processor, blend the parsley, garlic, and walnuts. Add the cheese and mix well. With the motor running, slowly add 3 tablespoons of the olive oil. In a sauté pan, heat the remaining oil. Add the rice and stir until well coated. Add the Chicken Stock, salt, and lemon juice. Bring to a boil, cover, and simmer for 20 minutes or until all liquid is absorbed and the rice is tender. Stir the cheese mixture into the hot rice and serve.

Wild, Wild Rice

SERVES 6

3 cups Beef Stock
1 cup wild rice, rinsed well
2 tablespoons butter
3 ounces shiitake mushrooms,
   sliced
3 ounces oyster mushrooms,
   sliced

1/4 cup chopped green onions,
   including some of the green
   part
1/4 cup pale dry sherry

In a medium saucepan, bring the stock to a boil and stir in wild rice. Cover and simmer for 40–50 minutes or until rice is tender. In a medium-size skillet melt butter and sauté the mushrooms and onions for 3–5 minutes. Add mushrooms, onions, and sherry to wild rice and cook until heated through.

VI

Fish

Barbecued Albacore with Red Pepper Sauce

SERVES 6

When fresh albacore is unavailable, try this with any firm-fleshed fish.

1/4 cup olive oil
2 tablespoons fresh lemon juice
2 tablespoons minced fresh
  cilantro
1 garlic clove, minced

1/4 teaspoon salt
2 pounds of albacore fillets 1 1/2
  inches thick
Red Pepper Sauce (below)

In a small bowl, combine the olive oil, lemon juice, cilantro, garlic, and salt. Blend with a whisk until thickened and well combined. Pour over the fillets and marinate 3–6 hours. Barbecue over hot coals for 10 minutes for each inch of thickness, turning midway through the cooking time. Serve with Red Pepper Sauce.

RED PEPPER SAUCE
1 red bell pepper, seeded and cut
  in eighths
1 jalapeño pepper, seeded
3 large garlic cloves
2 egg yolks

1 tablespoon fresh lemon juice
1/2 teaspoon salt
1 cup olive oil
2–3 tablespoons fresh bread
  crumbs (optional)

In a food processor, combine the red pepper, jalapeño pepper, garlic, egg yolks, lemon juice, and salt. Process until very smooth. Slowly pour in the olive oil in a steady stream. If a thicker consistency is desired, add bread crumbs and process until thickened.

Fish Fillets with Orange Ginger Cream

SERVES 4

1 1/3 cups heavy cream
1 teaspoon grated orange rind
3/4–1 teaspoon peeled and
   minced fresh ginger
1 tablespoon unsalted butter
1/4 cup fresh orange juice
1/3 cup dry white vermouth or
   dry white wine

1 1/2 pounds fish fillets (red
   snapper, orange roughy, lotte)
Salt and pepper
Flour
Peel of half an orange, julienned

In a small saucepan, combine the cream, grated orange rind, and ginger and simmer over low heat for about 20 minutes until the mixture is reduced by half. Remove from the heat and set aside.

In a large skillet, combine the butter, orange juice, and vermouth and bring the mixture to a simmer. Season the fish fillets with salt and pepper and dust lightly with flour. Place the fillets in the skillet, cover and cook for 3 minutes. Turn the fillets over and continue cooking for 3–4 minutes more. Remove the fish with a slotted spoon and keep warm. Reduce the liquid in the pan until thick and syrupy. Add the cream mixture and simmer, stirring constantly for 1–2 minutes. Strain the sauce through a fine sieve and pour over the fish. Garnish with the julienned orange peel.

Sonoma Style Fillets with Chèvre

SERVES 4

Chèvre is a variety of goat cheese produced in France and now in California. The tangy flavor is surprising and delicious.

2 tablespoons minced shallots
1 teaspoon chopped fresh
   tarragon
1 tablespoon chopped fresh
   parsley
3 tablespoons unsalted butter,
   melted
1/2 cup heavy cream
5 ounces chèvre, crumbled

2 bunches fresh spinach leaves,
   chopped
1/2 cup chopped green onions,
   including some of the green
   part
4 fillets of snapper, cod, or
   orange roughy
Salt and white pepper

Sauté shallots, tarragon, and parsley in 1 tablespoon of the butter until soft. Add the cream and simmer for about 5 minutes or until slightly thickened. Add the chèvre and heat, stirring constantly, until cheese is melted and sauce is smooth. Remove from heat and cover.

Bring a large pot of water to a boil. Drop the spinach leaves into the water. Bring the water back to a boil and then drain the spinach immediately, pressing out excess water.

Preheat the oven to 400 degrees. In a small pan, add the second tablespoon of butter and sauté the onions 2 minutes. Combine the spinach and onions and spread over the bottom of a lightly buttered baking dish. Arrange the fillets on top of the spinach. Brush with the remaining melted butter and season with salt and white pepper. Cover with foil and bake for 15 minutes. Remove from oven and mask the fillets with the chèvre sauce. Broil for 2–3 minutes until sauce is bubbly.

Marathon Snapper

SERVES 4

This recipe is fast, healthful, and low in calories; hence the name.

1 1/2 pounds red snapper fillets
1/2 cup plain yogurt
1/2 cup thinly sliced red onions
1 cup Fresh Salsa (below)

Freshly ground pepper
1/3 cup chopped fresh cilantro, for garnish
Lime slices, for garnish

Marinate the fish in the yogurt at room temperature for 1 hour.

Preheat the oven to 450 degrees. Place each fillet on a square of foil and top with equal amounts of the onions and Fresh Salsa. Sprinkle with the pepper. Fold the foil over the fish and seal tightly. Bake for 10–12 minutes. Garnish with cilantro and lime slices.

FRESH SALSA
3/4 cup tomatillos, fresh or canned
2 cups chopped tomatoes
1/2 cup chopped red onions

1/4 cup chopped fresh cilantro
1/2 cup chopped long green chiles, fresh or canned
3 tablespoons fresh lime juice

If using fresh tomatillos, remove the husks. If using canned ones, drain them. Place all ingredients in a food processor and process just until well-combined but not puréed. Refrigerate until ready to use.

Poisson Printemps

SERVES 4

I 1/2 pounds firm white fish
    fillets (snapper, sole, cod)
2 tablespoons vegetable oil
1/2 cup chopped onions
1/2 cup fresh green beans, thinly
    sliced lengthwise
1/2 cup sliced carrots
I cup seeded and chopped
    tomatoes
1/2 cup frozen peas, thawed

1/2 cup seedless grapes
3–4 medium garlic cloves,
    minced
I teaspoon cumin seed
1/2 teaspoon salt
1/8 teaspoon pepper
1/2 cup dry sherry
1/2 cup water
2 tablespoons chopped fresh
    parsley

Preheat the oven to 350 degrees. Place the fish fillets in a single layer in a lightly oiled baking dish. Sauté the onions in oil until tender. Add the beans and carrots and sauté 5 minutes more. Add the tomatoes, peas, grapes, garlic, cumin, and salt and pepper. Mix well and add the sherry and water. Stir, and pour over the fish fillets. Cover the dish with foil and bake for 20 minutes. Remove fish and vegetables with a slotted spoon and sprinkle with chopped parsley.

Poached Fillets with Wild Mushroom Cream Sauce

SERVES 6

The combination of wild mushrooms such as shiitake, oyster, or chanterelles and domestic mushrooms gives this dish its rich and unique flavor.

I 1/2 cups dry white wine
1/4 cup fresh lemon juice
2 pounds fish fillets, such as
    snapper, orange roughy, or
    sole
2 tablespoons unsalted butter
2 tablespoons minced shallots
1/2 pound mixed wild and
    domestic mushrooms, sliced

2 tablespoons flour
1/2 cup heavy cream
1/4 teaspoon white pepper
I teaspoon salt
2 tablespoons chopped fresh
    parsley

In a large skillet over medium heat, bring the wine and lemon juice to a boil. Add the fillets and simmer for 2–3 minutes on each side, carefully turning the fish. Transfer the fish to a platter and keep warm. Reserve 1 cup of the wine mixture.

In a skillet over medium-low heat, melt the butter and sauté the shallots for 2–3 minutes. Add the mushrooms and sauté for 4–5 minutes more until they are soft. Add the flour and cook, stirring, about 1 minute. Add the reserved wine mixture, cream, pepper, and salt and cook, for about 5 minutes, stirring constantly, until sauce thickens slightly. Spoon the sauce over the fish and sprinkle with chopped parsley.

Fish Stew Normande

SERVES 6

4 tablespoons unsalted butter, softened
4–6 medium onions, sliced
2 (8–10-ounce) cans whole clams, drained, with juice reserved
1 (8-ounce) bottle clam juice
1–1 1/2 cups apple cider
1 1/2 pounds turbot or halibut, cut in large cubes

Salt and pepper
2–3 tablespoons flour
1/2 pound cooked tiny bay shrimp
1/4 cup chopped fresh parsley
Lemon juice

In a large deep saucepan or Dutch oven, melt 2 tablespoons of the butter and sauté the onions over medium heat for 5–8 minutes until soft. Stir in the reserved clam liquid, clam juice, and 1 cup of the apple cider. Bring the mixture to a simmer and add the fish, with more cider if needed to cover the fish. Simmer gently 8–10 minutes until the fish is firm to the touch. Season with salt and pepper to taste. Remove the fish with a slotted spoon and keep warm. Combine the remaining butter with the flour and whisk into the cider mixture. Cook for 3–4 minutes until thickened. Add the fish, clams, shrimp and parsley to the pan. Season to taste with lemon juice. Cook at high heat for 1 minute until heated through. Serve immediately.

Seafood Boudin with Lobster and Watercress Cream Sauce

SERVES 8 AS A FIRST COURSE
SERVES 4 AS A MAIN COURSE

An incredibly easy recipe for such an elegant and delicate entree. It also makes a spectacular first course.

1/2 pound sole	1/8 teaspoon nutmeg
1/4 pound scallops	Small pinch of cayenne pepper
2 egg whites	1/4 cup heavy cream
1 teaspoon minced shallots	1 small bunch spinach, stemmed
1 tablespoon vermouth	and chopped
1 tablespoon tomato paste	1/2 cup diced cooked lobster
1/2 teaspoon grated lemon rind	3/4 cup heavy cream, whipped
1/2 teaspoon salt	Watercress Cream Sauce (below)

In a food processor, process the sole and scallops for 2 minutes until well puréed. With the motor running, add the egg whites, shallots, vermouth, tomato paste, lemon rind, salt, nutmeg, cayenne, and the 1/4 cup of cream. Process for 2 minutes more and then refrigerate the mixture.

Drop the spinach into boiling water, return to a boil, and immediately drain and refresh under cold water. Press the excess liquid out of spinach until almost dry. Combine the fish mixture with the spinach and diced lobster. Fold the whipped cream into the mixture. Refrigerate until ready to assemble.

Assembly and Cooking
8–10 pieces of plastic wrap, 12 × 12 inches
Aluminum foil
2 quarts boiling water with slices of 1 lemon

Place 1/8 of the mixture in the center of a piece of plastic wrap and roll and twist ends forming it into a log, 1 1/2 inches in diameter. Twist the ends tightly and then wrap securely in foil. Repeat with the remaining mixture. Place the foil-wrapped pieces in a large kettle of simmering water and poach for 12–15 minutes, turning them occasionally as they come to the surface. They will look and feel firm to the touch when done. Remove from the pan and unwrap. Place on paper towels to absorb excess liquid. Spoon some Watercress Cream Sauce on heated plates and top with sliced boudin.

WATERCRESS CREAM SAUCE

3/4 cup white vermouth
8 ounces bottled clam juice
1 tablespoon fresh lemon juice

1 cup heavy cream
1/2 cup stemmed and coarsely
   chopped watercress

In a small saucepan, combine the vermouth, clam juice, and lemon juice. Boil over high heat until reduced to 3/4 cup. Add the cream and boil rapidly for 10–20 minutes or until the sauce is reduced and thickened. Just before serving, stir in the watercress cooking until it is slightly wilted.

Cioppino

SERVES 8–10

STOCK

1/2 cup olive oil
1 cup finely chopped onions
1 cup thinly sliced leeks, white
   part only
1/2 cup thinly sliced carrots
1/2 cup thinly sliced celery
2 pounds tomatoes, peeled and
   chopped, *or* 1 (28-ounce) can
   plum tomatoes, including juice
Grated peel of half an orange *or*
   1 teaspoon dried orange peel
1 teaspoon crushed fennel seeds

1/2 teaspoon dried thyme
2 tablespoons minced garlic
2 bay leaves
1/8 teaspoon dried red pepper
   flakes
3 1/2 cups Fish Stock or bottled
   clam juice
1 1/2 cups red wine such as
   Zinfandel
3 tablespoons fresh lemon juice
Salt and pepper

In a large pot, heat the olive oil and add the onions, leeks, carrots, and celery and sauté, stirring occasionally, for about 8 minutes. Add the tomatoes, orange peel, fennel seeds, thyme, garlic, bay leaves and red pepper. Cook for 2–3 minutes and then add the Fish Stock or clam juice, wine, and lemon juice. Cover and simmer the mixture for 30–40 minutes. Season with salt and pepper to taste.

FISH

14 clams or mussels, or both if
  desired, scrubbed
2 tablespoons flour
3/4 pound of halibut or bass, cut
  in bite-size pieces
3/4 pound snapper, sole, or
  orange roughy, cut in bite-size
  pieces

1 pound scallops
1 pound of shrimp, peeled and
  deveined
Crab or lobster (optional)

Scrub the mussels well with a rough brush under running water and scrape off
the beards with a knife. Mix the flour thoroughly with 4 tablespoons water.
Fill a large bowl with cold water and stir in the flour-water mixture. Place the
mussels in the bowl and soak for 30 minutes; then drain in a colander.

Add the halibut to the simmering stock and cook 2 minutes. Add the snapper and clams or mussels and cook 2 minutes more. Discard any unopened
clams or mussels. Then add the scallops, shrimp (crab/lobster) and cook for
2–3 minutes. Remove the bay leaves. For an authentic presentation and richer
flavor, leave the shellfish in their shells.

Seafood Risotto with Goat Cheese
and Sun-dried Tomatoes

SERVES 6

1/2 pound bay scallops
1 1/2 pounds mussels
2 tablespoons flour
1 pound raw shrimp, peeled and
  deveined, shells reserved for
  the stock
1 small onion, quartered
1/2 cup dry white wine
2 tablespoons tomato paste
1/2 teaspoon salt
Freshly ground pepper to taste

3 tablespoons olive oil
1 small onion, finely chopped
2 garlic cloves, minced
1 1/2 cups Arborio rice or
  imported Italian rice
1 (8-ounce) bottle clam juice
8 ounces goat cheese, preferably
  Montrachet
1/2 cup julienned sun-dried
  tomatoes
1/4 cup minced fresh parsley

Rinse the scallops under cold water and pat dry. Scrub the mussels well with a
rough brush under running water and scrape off the beards with a knife.
Thoroughly mix the flour with 4 tablespoons water. Fill a large bowl with cold

water and stir in the flour-water mixture. Place the mussels in the bowl and soak for 30 minutes; then drain in a colander.

In a medium saucepan, place the shrimp shells and the quartered onion in 4 cups of water and simmer for 30 minutes. Strain and discard the shells and onion. Reserve the broth. In a pan large enough to hold the mussels, combine 1 cup of water with the wine and bring to a simmer. Place the mussels in the pan, cover, and steam about 4–6 minutes or until the shells open. Shake the pan occasionally during the steaming. Remove the mussels with a slotted spoon and refrigerate. Discard any unopened ones. Strain the mussel broth through a fine sieve and add it to the shrimp-shell broth. Add the tomato paste and salt and pepper and bring the broth to a simmer.

Heat the olive oil in a heavy 4–6 quart saucepan. Add the chopped onions and garlic and sauté until soft. Add the rice and stir to coat it with the oil. Over medium-high heat begin adding the seafood stock 1/2 cup at a time, stirring constantly, until all the liquid is absorbed. Continue cooking, adding more stock until all is used and rice is barely tender. Use bottled clam juice if more liquid is needed.

Stir in the shrimp and scallops and cook for 3 minutes. Add the mussels in their shells and cook 1–2 minutes longer. Crumble the goat cheese and add it with the dried tomatoes to the risotto. Sprinkle with parsley.

Note   1 1/2 pounds shrimp and 2 pounds clams may be substituted for the shrimp, mussels, and scallops. Clean and soak the clams in the same manner as the mussels.

Grilled Halibut with Pine Nut Butter

SERVES 4

4 halibut steaks
Olive oil
1 lemon
1/2 cup butter, softened

1/2 cup chopped fresh basil
2–3 tablespoons lightly toasted
  pine nuts
1 small garlic clove, minced

Brush the halibut steaks with olive oil and sprinkle with lemon juice. In a food processor, combine the butter, basil, pine nuts, and garlic and mix until smooth. It is best to let mixture stand at least 1 hour. Grill the halibut steaks over medium-hot coals or under a broiler 6 inches from the source of heat 10 minutes for each inch of thickness, turning midway through the cooking time. After turning, place about 1 teaspoon of the pine-nut butter on the fish. Serve topped with additional pine nut butter.

Baked Oriental Halibut Steaks

SERVES 6

2 pounds halibut steaks, 1 1/2
  inches thick
1/4 cup orange juice
1/4 cup soy sauce
2 tablespoons ketchup
2 tablespoons minced fresh
  parsley

2 tablespoons oil
1 tablespoon fresh lemon juice
1/2 teaspoon dried oregano
1/2 teaspoon pepper
1 large garlic clove, crushed

Preheat the oven to 350 degrees. Cut the halibut in serving pieces and place in a single layer in a lightly oiled baking dish. Combine the orange juice, soy sauce, ketchup, parsley, oil, lemon juice, oregano, pepper, and garlic and pour over the fish. Bake the fish for 20–25 minutes or until firm to the touch.

Note To broil or barbecue the fish, allow the steaks to marinate in the refrigerator for 1 hour or longer, turning them once. Reserve the marinade for basting. Barbecue over hot coals or broil about 6 inches from the source of heat 10 minutes for each inch of thickness, turning midway through the cooking time, basting frequently.

Scandinavian Baked Halibut Steaks

SERVES 4

This is a colorful and delicious way to serve halibut. As an added convenience, it is baked and served in the same dish. A paella pan is the perfect choice.

1 1/2 pounds halibut steaks, 1 1/2
  inches thick
Flour
Freshly ground pepper
2 tablespoons peanut oil
1/4 cup dry white wine

12 cherry tomatoes
12 small new potatoes, steamed
1/4 cup minced fresh dill
2 tablespoons unsalted butter,
  melted
Lemon wedges, for garnish

Preheat the oven to 425 degrees. Lightly dust the fish with flour and season with pepper. In a large ovenproof skillet or paella pan, heat the oil until very hot. Sauté the fish for about 2 minutes on each side. Pour in the wine and surround the fish with tomatoes and potatoes. Sprinkle with 3 tablespoons of the fresh dill (reserve 1 tablespoon for garnish). Bake for 12 minutes or until the fish is firm to the touch. Remove from the oven and drizzle the melted butter over the potatoes. Garnish with remaining dill and serve with lemon wedges.

Note Tuna, salmon, or swordfish steaks may be substituted for the halibut.

Thai Fish with Pickled Red Ginger

SERVES 6

In recent years, Thai cooking has become very popular in California. This simple-to-prepare fish represents the best of the new influence.

2 pounds fish fillets, such as red
   snapper, orange roughy, or
   cod
Flour
Salt and pepper
12 dried oriental mushrooms or
   12 fresh mushrooms
3 tablespoons peanut oil
8 tablespoons vinegar

3 tablespoons soy sauce
8 tablespoons sugar
1 cup water
8 tablespoons pickled red ginger,
   chopped
3 green onions, chopped
2 tablespoons cornstarch
1/2 red bell pepper, thinly sliced

Season the fillets with salt and pepper and flour them lightly. If using dried mushrooms, soak them in hot water for 20 minutes, then drain and remove stems. In a large skillet, heat the oil until it is very hot and sauté the fillets for 2 minutes on each side. Remove the fish and keep warm. In a medium saucepan, combine the mushrooms, vinegar, soy sauce, sugar, the 1 cup of water, ginger, and onions. Simmer for 5 minutes. Mix the cornstarch with 2 tablespoons of water and add to the simmering mixture. Cook until thickened and clear. Pour over the fillets and garnish with the red-pepper slices.

Poached Lotte (Monkfish) with Red Pepper Cream

SERVES 6

Lotte is often called "poor man's lobster" because its taste and texture are so similar to lobster. The Red Pepper Cream is extremely delicious and complements any fish. Try it with poached bay scallops as a first course.

2 1/2 pounds lotte
Salt and white pepper
2 tablespoons unsalted butter
1 cup white wine
1/4 cup dry sherry

1 cup heavy cream
1/2 cup Red Pepper Purée (below)
2 tablespoons minced fresh chives, for garnish

Cut the lotte into medallions approximately 1–1 1/2 inches thick and sprinkle them with salt and pepper. In a large skillet melt the butter. Add the wine and sherry and bring to a simmer. Place the medallions in the simmering liquid but do not crowd them; cook in batches if necessary. Simmer for 2 minutes on each side or until firm to the touch. Remove the fish with a slotted spoon to a bowl and keep warm. Over medium-high heat reduce the wine until it is syrupy, about 8 minutes, and add the cream and any juices that have accumulated around the fish. Boil for 5 minutes. Add the Red Pepper Purée and heat through. To serve, ladle several spoonfuls of sauce on each plate and place the lotte medallions on top of the sauce. Sprinkle lightly with minced chives.

RED PEPPER PURÉE

1/4 cup unsalted butter
2 pounds red bell peppers, seeded and diced
2 tablespoons sugar
2 tablespoons white wine vinegar

1 1/4 teaspoons paprika, preferably Hungarian sweet paprika
1/8 teaspoon dried red pepper flakes

In a heavy saucepan, melt the butter. Add all other ingredients, cover, and cook over low heat for 1 hour, stirring occasionally. Uncover the pan and increase heat, stirring constantly, until all of the liquid evaporates. Purée in the food processor and strain through a sieve. Yields approximately 1 1/2 cups. This purée may be stored in the refrigerator for 1 week or frozen.

Note   Red snapper or orange roughy fillets may be substituted for the lotte. Leave the fillets whole and poach them in the liquid for 2–3 minutes on each side.

Orange Roughy with Balsamic Vinegar and Capers

SERVES 4

Cooking the capers in hot oil until they burst gives them the appearance of small flowers.

1 1/2 pounds orange roughy
    fillets (sole or red snapper
    fillets may be substituted)
Flour
2 tablespoons vegetable oil

9 tablespoons unsalted butter
1/3 cup olive oil
1/3 cup capers
2 tablespoons balsamic vinegar

Lightly flour the fillets. In a large skillet, heat the vegetable oil and 3 table-spoons of the butter. Sauté the fish for 2–3 minutes on each side, or until firm and golden. Remove the fish to a heated platter and keep warm. In a small skillet, heat the olive oil until very hot. Drop in the capers and cook until they open or flower. Drain well. In a small saucepan, melt the remaining butter over medium heat until it just starts to change color. Add the vinegar and capers and combine well. Pour sauce over the fish.

Spicy Baked Fish

SERVES 6

2 whole fish (1 1/2–2 pounds
    each) or 1 (3–4-pound) fish
    (snapper, trout), cleaned
1/4 cup chopped fresh cilantro
1 tablespoon peeled fresh ginger
3 green onions, including some
    of green
1 teaspoon dried red pepper
    flakes

1/2 teaspoon turmeric
1/2 teaspoon salt
1/4 cup peanut oil
1/2 teaspoon sugar
1 tablespoon oriental sesame oil
3 tablespoons soy sauce
2 tablespoons dry sherry
Lime slices, for garnish

Preheat the oven to 400 degrees. Rinse the fish, pat dry, and place in an oiled baking pan. Process all other ingredients except the soy sauce and sherry in a blender or food processor until the ginger and onions are finely minced. Brush liberally over all of the fish, inside and out. Combine the soy sauce and sherry and drizzle over the fish. Bake, uncovered, for 20 minutes. Garnish with the lime slices.

Salmon with Tomato Basil Beurre Blanc

SERVES 4

1 medium garlic clove
4 medium shallots
1 cup dry white wine
1 tablespoon white wine vinegar
1/4 teaspoon salt
1 small tomato, peeled, seeded, and chopped

1 cup hot melted butter
3–4 tablespoons sliced fresh basil leaves
4 salmon fillets or steaks
2 tablespoons olive oil

Process the garlic and shallots in a food processor until minced. In a saucepan, simmer the garlic mixture with the wine until reduced to 1/4 cup. Stir in vinegar and salt. Add more vinegar to taste as needed. Add tomatoes to saucepan and heat to simmering. The sauce may be made ahead to this point. Just before serving, return the tomato-wine mixture to a simmer and transfer to processor. With machine running, add hot butter in a steady stream. Process until tomato is puréed. Stir in basil leaves.

Brush salmon with oil. Grill over medium coals for 10 minutes for each inch of thickness, turning midway through cooking time. Serve the salmon with the sauce and garnish with a whole basil leaf.

Grilled Whole Salmon with Spinach Mint Sauce

SERVES 8

1 whole salmon, about 6 pounds, cleaned and boned
1/2 teaspoon salt and cracked pepper
2 green onions, split lengthwise in thirds

1 lemon, thinly sliced
4 parsley sprigs
Vegetable oil
Spinach Mint Sauce (below)

Rinse the fish with cold water and pat dry. Open flat and place on a double thickness of aluminum foil, skin side down. Sprinkle with salt and pepper. Arrange the onions, lemon slices, and parsley on the fish. Drizzle with the oil. Grill over hot coals for 10 minutes for each inch of thickness (measured at the salmon's thickest point). The fish should be firm to the touch. To serve, remove the lemons, onions and parsley. Cut in serving pieces, and with a spatula ease the fish away from the skin. The skin will stick to the foil. Serve with Spinach Mint Sauce.

SPINACH MINT SAUCE

$1/2$ cup dry white wine

1 cup heavy cream

1 tablespoon unsalted butter

2 green onions, chopped,
    including some of the green

1 bunch spinach leaves, chopped

$1/3$ cup fresh mint leaves

1 teaspoon fresh lemon juice

$1/4$ teaspoon salt

In a small saucepan, bring the wine to a boil until it is reduced to 1 tablespoon. Add $1/4$ cup of the cream and boil until it is reduced to about 2 tablespoons. Stir in the remaining cream and set aside.

In a large skillet, melt the butter. Add the onions and sauté just until they turn a bright green. Add the spinach and cook for 2 minutes, stirring constantly. Add the mint leaves and cook for 30 seconds more. Drain the spinach mixture and press out all the moisture. Place in a food processor and with the machine running, pour in the remaining cream. Process the mixture until it is very smooth. Add the lemon juice and salt and taste for seasoning. The sauce may be served warm or at room temperature.

Summer Salmon

SERVES 4

4 salmon steaks

Olive oil

$1/4$ cup fresh dill, chopped

1 tablespoon crushed fennel seed

Tomato Red Pepper Sauce
    (below)

Brush the salmon with olive oil. Combine dill and fennel seed and coat both sides of the salmon with the mixture. Let the salmon stand, covered, in the refrigerator for 3–6 hours. Broil over hot coals for 10 minutes for each inch of thickness, turning midway through the cooking time. Serve with Tomato Red Pepper Sauce.

TOMATO RED PEPPER SAUCE

1 red bell pepper

2 large garlic cloves

$1/2$ cup cream

$1/4$ cup butter

2 tablespoons tomato paste

$1/2$ teaspoon sweet paprika

1 teaspoon vinegar

$1/2$ teaspoon salt

Using a long-handled fork, char the pepper over an open flame, turning it for 2–3 minutes, or until the skin is blackened. Or, place the pepper on a broiler pan and broil about 2 inches from the heat until the skin is blackened, turning frequently. This will take about 15 minutes. Transfer the pepper to a plastic bag, close tightly, and let it steam until it is cool enough to handle and peel. Chop and place in a food processor with the garlic and cream. Process until smooth.

Melt the butter in a saucepan. Add the tomato paste, paprika, vinegar, and red pepper mixture. Season to taste with salt and whisk until smooth over low heat. Do not allow to boil. This sauce may be served warm or at room temperature.

Southwest Snapper with Cilantro Cream

SERVES 4

1/2 cup fresh lime juice	1 1/2 pounds red snapper fillets,
1/2 cup dry red wine	or any firm fish fillets
1 small onion, sliced	1 tablespoon peanut oil
1/2 teaspoon curry powder	Cilantro Cream (below)
1/2 teaspoon dried oregano	4 sprigs cilantro
1 tablespoon chili powder	1 tablespoon sliced black olives

Combine the lime juice, wine, onions, curry powder, oregano, and chili powder. Pour over fish fillets, and marinate, refrigerated, for 1–3 hours. Remove the fillets and pat dry. In a large skillet, heat the oil until very hot and cook the fillets for 2 minutes on each side. Or broil them 6 inches from the source of heat for 4–5 minutes, turning once. Transfer the fillets to hot plates, mask with Cilantro Cream, and garnish each plate with a cilantro sprig and sliced black olives.

CILANTRO CREAM

1 cup clam juice	1/2 bay leaf
1/2 cup water	2 tablespoons fresh lemon juice
1 small stalk celery including	1 cup heavy cream
leaves	1/2 teaspoon salt
1 sprig parsley	1/4 cup chopped fresh cilantro

In a small saucepan combine the clam juice, water, celery, parsley, bay leaf, and lemon juice. Bring to a boil and continue boiling until liquid is reduced to

1/3 cup. Remove the celery, parsley, and bay leaf. Add the cream and simmer the mixture for 8–10 minutes until it is thickened. Add the salt and more lemon juice if needed. Stir in cilantro just before serving.

Pacific Snapper

SERVES 4

6 tablespoons olive oil
3 cups sliced onions
1/2 teaspoon paprika
I teaspoon sugar
I 1/2 pounds red snapper fillets
2 tablespoons lemon juice
I teaspoon salt
1/4 teaspoon pepper

1/8 teaspoon cayenne pepper
1/2 pound mushrooms, sliced
5 green onions, chopped,
    including some of the green
2 large tomatoes, sliced
1/4 cup dry sherry
1/2 cup buttered fresh bread
    crumbs (optional)

Preheat the oven to 400 degrees. In a medium skillet, heat 4 tablespoons of the olive oil and sauté the onions. Add the paprika and sugar and cook for I minute. Spread the onion mixture in the bottom of a buttered baking dish. Sprinkle the fish fillets with the lemon juice and place on top of the onions. Season with salt, pepper, and cayenne.

In the remaining olive oil, sauté the mushrooms and green onions until tender. Spread the mushroom mixture over the fish fillets and top with tomato slices. Pour sherry over the fish and vegetables; cover with buttered waxed paper and bake for 10 minutes. Uncover, and top with the bread crumbs, if desired. Bake for 10 minutes longer.

Snapper Piccata

SERVES 4

1/4 cup unsalted butter, melted
I tablespoon fresh lemon juice
I teaspoon grated lemon peel
1/4 teaspoon salt
2 tablespoons capers

I 1/2 pounds fish fillets, such as
    snapper, orange roughy, or
    sole
Fresh parsley, chopped, for
    garnish

Preheat the oven to 350 degrees. Combine butter, lemon juice, lemon peel, salt, and capers. Brush the fillets on one side with the mixture. Place fillets buttered side down in a baking dish. Pour on the remaining butter. Bake for 15–20 minutes, until firm to the touch. Garnish with the parsley.

Chinatown Snapper

SERVES 4–6

1/2 pound snow peas, trimmed
1/4 cup peanut oil
4 green onions, including 2 inches of the green, sliced diagonally
1 tablespoon peeled and minced fresh ginger

2 tomatoes, peeled, seeded, and chopped
1 1/2 pounds red snapper fillets, sliced in 3-inch strips
Salt and pepper
1/2 cup fresh cilantro leaves
2 teaspoons red wine vinegar

In a medium saucepan, blanch the snow peas in boiling water for 1 minute. Drain and refresh under cold water. Heat the oil in a wok or a heavy skillet. Add the onions and ginger and toss for 2 minutes over high heat. Add the tomatoes and stir-fry for 1 minute. Reduce the heat to medium high and add the fillets. Cover and cook about 3–4 minutes, until the fish is firm. Season to taste with salt and pepper. Add the cilantro, snow peas, and vinegar and cook, stirring gently, until heated through. Serve immediately.

Sole with Jade Butter

SERVES 4

4 sole fillets
Salt and pepper
4 tablespoons butter
3 tablespoons chopped fresh parsley

1 1/2 teaspoons peeled and minced fresh ginger
3 tablespoons fresh lime juice
2 teaspoons capers

Preheat the oven to 350 degrees. Place the fillets in a buttered baking dish and season lightly with salt and pepper. In a saucepan, melt the butter and add the parsley, ginger, and lime juice. Pour the mixture over the fillets and cover the baking dish with foil. Bake for 10–15 minutes, depending on the thickness of the fillets. Top with the capers before serving.

Sole Curry

SERVES 4–6

2 pounds sole fillets
1/4 cup unsalted butter
3 tablespoons minced shallots
3/4 teaspoon curry powder
1 tablespoon green peppercorns,
    rinsed and drained

1 tablespoon fresh lemon juice
1 cup Crème Fraîche or
    whipping cream

Cut the fillets in 1/2-inch-wide strips. In a large skillet, melt the butter. Add the shallots and curry powder and cook over medium heat for 1–2 minutes. Add the fillet strips and cook, uncovered, over high heat for 2–3 minutes on each side. Turn the fish strips gently with a spatula, being careful not to break them. Remove the fish and keep warm. Add to the pan the peppercorns, lemon juice, and Crème Fraîche and bring to a boil. Continue cooking, stirring constantly, until the sauce thickens slightly. Return the fish to the pan and cover with the sauce. Heat gently and serve.

Swordfish au Poivre Rose

SERVES 4

2 pounds swordfish (4 small or 2
    large steaks)
Salt
4 tablespoons crushed pink
    peppercorns
2 tablespoons unsalted butter
2 tablespoons vegetable oil

1/4 cup pale dry sherry
1 cup heavy cream
1/2 teaspoon salt
1 tablespoon fresh lemon juice
    or more to taste
3 tablespoons minced fresh
    parsley

Season swordfish steaks lightly with salt and then press crushed peppercorns into both sides of the fish. Cover and refrigerate for at least 1 hour.

In a large skillet, heat the butter and oil. Add the fish and cook 10 minutes for each inch of thickness, turning midway through the cooking time. Remove from the pan and keep warm. Deglaze the pan with the sherry and bring to a boil. Add the cream, salt, and lemon juice and simmer for 2–3 minutes, stirring constantly. Taste for seasoning and add more lemon juice if desired. Stir in the parsley and serve the fish masked with the sauce.

Sake Swordfish with Japanese Cucumber Salad

SERVES 4

1 teaspoon brown sugar
1/4 cup soy sauce
1/4 cup sake or dry white vermouth
1/4 cup mirin or dry sherry
2 medium garlic cloves, minced

1 tablespoon peeled and minced fresh ginger
1 1/2 pounds swordfish steaks, or tuna
Japanese Cucumber Salad (below)

Combine the brown sugar, soy sauce, sake, mirin, garlic, and ginger. Place the fish in a shallow dish and pour the marinade over it. Cover and marinate the fish in the refrigerator for 3–6 hours or overnight. Grill the fish over hot coals for 10 minutes for each inch of thickness, turning midway through the cooking time. Serve with Japanese Cucumber Salad.

JAPANESE CUCUMBER SALAD
1 hot house cucumber, shredded
2 tablespoons thinly sliced pickled ginger
2 green onions, thinly sliced, including part of the green

3 tablespoons rice vinegar
3 tablespoons sugar
1 teaspoon soy sauce
1 teaspoon salt

Combine all ingredients and chill well.

Grilled Swordfish

SERVES 6

6 swordfish steaks
2/3 cup vegetable oil
1/3 cup virgin olive oil
1 tablespoon minced fresh
    cilantro
1 tablespoon minced fresh
    parsley
2 teaspoons minced fresh
    oregano *or* 1 teaspoon dried
    oregano

1 large garlic clove, minced
1/4 teaspoon salt
1/4 teaspoon freshly ground
    pepper
Lemon and lime wedges

Place the swordfish in a single layer in a shallow dish. Combine all remaining ingredients except lemon and lime wedges and pour over the fish. Marinate, covered, in the refrigerator, for 3–6 hours or overnight. Grill the fish over hot coals or under a broiler 6 inches from the source of heat 10 minutes for each inch of thickness, turning midway through the cooking time. Baste frequently with marinade. Serve with lemon and lime wedges.

Grilled Swordfish with Wasabi Marinade

SERVES 6

1 cup soy sauce
2 tablespoons minced garlic
2 tablespoons peeled and minced
    fresh ginger
2 tablespoons minced green
    onions, including part of the
    green

1 tablespoon fresh lime juice
1 tablespoon wasabi powder or
    paste
6 swordfish steaks
Lime wedges

Combine the soy sauce, garlic, ginger, onions, lime juice, and wasabi powder or paste until well mixed. Pour over swordfish and marinate, covered, in the refrigerator for at least 3–6 hours or overnight. Grill over hot coals or under the broiler 6 inches from the source of heat 10 minutes for each inch of thickness, turning midway through the cooking time. Serve with lime wedges.

Mussels Provençal

SERVES 6 AS A FIRST COURSE
SERVES 4 AS A MAIN COURSE

3 dozen mussels (clams may be
  substituted)
2 tablespoons flour
6 shallots, minced
1 large garlic clove, minced
2 tablespoons olive oil
2 medium tomatoes, chopped *or*

1 (16-ounce) can tomatoes,
  well drained
4–6 tablespoons chopped fresh
  basil *or* 1 1/2 teaspoons dried
  basil
2 tablespoons Cognac
1/4 cup chopped fresh parsley

Scrub the mussels well with a rough brush under running water and scrape off
beards with a knife. Mix the flour thoroughly with 4 tablespoons water. Fill a
large bowl with cold water and stir in the flour-water mixture. Place the
mussels in the bowl and soak for 30 minutes; then drain in a colander.

In a large heavy pan with a lid or in a Dutch oven, sauté the shallots and
garlic in the olive oil until soft. Add the tomatoes and basil and simmer for
2–3 minutes. Add the mussels and cover the pan. Steam the mussels over
medium heat for 4 minutes, shaking the pan occasionally. Remove the mussels
with a slotted spoon to individual bowls and keep warm. Discard any unopened ones. Add the Cognac to the pan and bring to a boil. Pour over the
mussels and sprinkle with chopped parsley.

Apple Cider Steamed Mussels

SERVES 8 AS A FIRST COURSE
SERVES 4 AS A MAIN COURSE

3 dozen mussels
2 tablespoons flour
1 cup thinly sliced onions
1 cup apple cider

1/4 cup Applejack brandy, or
  brandy
2 cups heavy cream
1/4 cup minced fresh parsley

Scrub the mussels well with a rough brush under running water and scrape off
beards with a small knife. Mix the flour thoroughly with 4 tablespoons water.
Fill a large bowl with cold water and stir in the flour-water mixture. Place the
mussels in the bowl and soak for 30 minutes; then drain in a colander.

In a large pan with a tight-fitting lid, combine the onions, cider, and 1/4 cup
water and bring to a boil. Add the mussels and cook, covered, for 3–4 minutes

until they are opened. Discard any unopened ones. Transfer the mussels with a slotted spoon to a serving dish and cover with damp paper towels. Add the Applejack brandy to the pan and cook over high heat until the liquid is reduced to 1/2 cup. Add the cream and bring to a simmer. Cook for about 5 minutes until the sauce has reduced somewhat and has started to thicken. Pour the sauce over the mussels and garnish with parsley. The sauce may be strained for a more elegant presentation.

Punjab Crab with Cold Cucumber Relish

SERVES 6

3 tablespoons unsalted butter
1 cup minced shallots
1/2 teaspoon turmeric
1/4 teaspoon ground cloves
Pinch of cayenne pepper
1/2 teaspoon ground coriander

1 tablespoon flour
1/2 cup bottled clam juice
1 tablespoon fresh lemon juice
1 1/2 pounds crabmeat or any
    other cooked shellfish: shrimp,
    scallops, or lobster

In a heavy skillet, melt the butter. Add shallots and cook for 3 minutes. Add turmeric, cloves, cayenne, and coriander. Cook 2 minutes more. Add flour and stir until well mixed. Add the clam juice and lemon juice. Stir until smooth and thickened. Simmer for 3 minutes. Add the crab and cook until warmed through. Serve very hot with 1/2 tablespoon Cold Cucumber Relish for each serving.

COLD CUCUMBER RELISH

2 cups peeled grated hothouse
    cucumbers
1 teaspoon sugar
2 tablespoons rice vinegar

1 heaping teaspoon minced fresh
    cilantro
1/2 teaspoon salt
Pepper to taste

Drain cucumbers well and combine with the sugar, rice vinegar, cilantro, salt, and pepper and chill until very cold.

Baked Crab Stuffed Trout with Macadamia Butter Sauce

SERVES 4

4 trout, cleaned
Salt
1 cup shredded crabmeat
1 teaspoon Dijon mustard
1/4 cup minced fresh chives

2 tablespoons dry sherry
1/4 cup mayonnaise
Macadamia Butter Sauce
    (below)

Preheat the oven to 325 degrees. Sprinkle trout lightly with salt. Combine the crab, mustard, chives, sherry, and enough mayonnaise to lightly moisten mixture. Stuff the trout with equal amounts of crab stuffing. Place the trout in a buttered baking dish. Spoon 1–2 tablespoons Macadamia Butter Sauce over each trout. Bake for 20 minutes. Serve with the remaining sauce.

MACADAMIA BUTTER SAUCE
1/2 cup unsalted butter
1/2 cup chopped macadamia nuts
1 tablespoon fresh lemon juice or more to taste

In a medium-size saucepan, melt the butter and add the nuts, sautéing for 3–4 minutes. Add lemon juice and mix well.

Baked Oysters with Lime and Shallots

SERVES 4

2 dozen oysters *or* 1 1/2 pounds
    scallops
1 cup white wine
1/3 cup fresh lime juice
3 tablespoons minced shallots

1 tablespoon grated fresh ginger
3/4 cup unsalted butter, softened
4 tablespoons heavy cream
1/2 teaspoon salt

Preheat the oven to 375 degrees. Place the oysters or scallops in a baking dish. In a small saucepan, combine the wine, lime juice, shallots, and ginger. Bring to a boil and cook until reduced to about 1/4 cup. Remove from the heat and whisk in the butter 1 teaspoon at a time. Whisk the cream and season with salt, if desired. Pour over the oysters or scallops and bake in the oven for 6–7 minutes or until edges of oysters begin to curl or scallops are opaque.

Scallops in Cream with Kiwi

SERVES 6 AS A FIRST COURSE
SERVES 4 AS A MAIN COURSE

The delicate and smooth texture of this classic, rich sauce makes indulging in the extra calories worthwhile.

6 tablespoons unsalted butter, softened
2 tablespoons minced shallots
1 cup dry white wine
2 pounds scallops

Salt and white pepper
2 cups heavy cream
2 kiwi fruit, peeled and sliced, for garnish

In a large saucepan, over medium heat, melt 2 tablespoons of the butter and add the shallots. Cook for 2–3 minutes. Add the wine and simmer until reduced by half. Add the scallops and season with the salt and pepper. Cover with a piece of buttered waxed paper. Simmer gently for about 3 minutes for bay scallops and 4–5 minutes for larger scallops. Remove the scallops with a slotted spoon and place in a bowl to keep warm.

Reduce the juices to 2 tablespoons. Add the cream and simmer slowly for about 20–25 minutes until thickened. Whisk in the remaining 4 tablespoons of butter 1 teaspoon at a time and taste for seasoning. Add scallops to reheat. Serve garnished with the slices of kiwi.

Scallops with Parmesan Croustades

SERVES 6

2 tablespoons flour
Salt and pepper
2 pounds bay scallops or large scallops sliced in thirds
3 tablespoons olive oil
1 1/2–2 tablespoons minced garlic
1/2 cup minced fresh parsley

1 bay leaf
1/2 cup white wine or vermouth
1 tablespoon fresh lemon juice
3 cups fresh chopped tomatoes or canned tomatoes, well drained
Parmesan Croustades (below)

Season the flour with salt and pepper. Lightly dust the scallops with the seasoned flour. Heat the olive oil in a sauté pan and cook the garlic in it until it is just fragrant. Add the scallops and cook 1 minute, stirring and turning them continuously. Add the parsley, bay leaf, wine, lemon juice, and tomatoes and bring to a simmer for 2 minutes. Remove the bay leaf and discard. Serve over Parmesan Croustades.

PARMESAN CROUSTADES
1/4 cup unsalted butter, softened
1/4 cup freshly grated Parmesan cheese
6 pieces sourdough bread

Combine the butter and Parmesan cheese. Spread on the bread slices and toast until browned.

Martini Scallops

SERVES 4

1/4 cup olive oil
2 pounds scallops
1 tablespoon minced shallots
2 large garlic cloves, minced
1/4 cup dry white vermouth
1/4 cup vodka or gin

1/8 teaspoon cayenne pepper
1/2 cup sun-dried tomatoes,
    drained and cut in strips
1 cup heavy cream
1/2 teaspoon salt
White pepper

In a large heavy sauté pan, heat the olive oil. Add the scallops and sauté until just opaque, 2–3 minutes depending on their size. Remove the scallops and set aside. Add the shallots and garlic and sauté for 3 minutes. Add the vermouth, vodka, cayenne, and tomatoes and cook over high heat 5–10 minutes or until slightly reduced and syrupy. Add the cream, salt, and pepper and cook for 5 minutes until thickened and smooth. With a slotted spoon, return the scallops to the pan and cook 1 minute to reheat.

Baked Shrimp with Goat Cheese

SERVES 6

1 cup thinly sliced onions
1/2 cup olive oil
2 pounds tomatoes, seeded and
 chopped *or* 1 (28-ounce) can
 whole tomatoes, undrained
2 large garlic cloves, crushed
1/2 teaspoon salt
3/4 teaspoon dried oregano

1/8 teaspoon dried red pepper
 flakes
2 pounds raw shrimp, peeled and
 deveined
1/2 cup minced fresh parsley
8 ounces goat cheese, preferably
 Montrachet

In a heavy pan over medium heat, sauté the onions in the oil until soft and clear, about 5 minutes. Add the tomatoes, garlic, salt, oregano, and red pepper flakes and bring to a simmer. Cook over low heat for 15–20 minutes, stirring occasionally.

Preheat the oven to 325 degrees. Add the shrimp and parsley to the tomato mixture and cook until just pink, about 1–2 minutes. Place the shrimp in a shallow baking dish and top with the crumbled goat cheese. Bake for 15–20 minutes until cheese is melted and bubbly.

Thai Shrimp

SERVES 4

This makes an eye-catching presentation when the shrimp is mounded on a platter and surrounded with steamed rice. The sauce may be made ahead of time and reheated before cooking the shrimp.

1 red bell pepper
1 yellow bell pepper
2 serrano chiles
3 tablespoons peanut oil
1 cup minced onions
1 cup pineapple juice
1/2 cup coconut milk (liquid
 inside coconut)*

1 teaspoon ground cumin
1 teaspoon chili powder
1 teaspoon turmeric
1/2 teaspoon salt
1 pound large raw shrimp,
 peeled and deveined
2–3 tablespoons minced fresh
 cilantro

Remove the seeds from the peppers and chiles and slice in thin strips. Heat the oil in a pan and sauté the onions and peppers until onions are soft and clear.

Add the pineapple juice, coconut milk, cumin, chili powder, turmeric, and salt. Simmer the mixture for 3–4 minutes. Add the shrimp and simmer for 3 minutes until shrimp are just cooked through. Stir in the cilantro just before serving.

Note   If fresh coconut is not available, soak 1 cup of unsweetened coconut in 1 cup water for 1/2 hour. Strain 1/2 cup of the water for this recipe. Do not use canned coconut milk, unless it is unsweetened.

Cajun Barbecued Shrimp

SERVES 4

1 teaspoon cayenne pepper
1 teaspoon freshly ground black
  pepper
1 teaspoon salt
1/4 teaspoon dried crumbled red
  pepper flakes
1 teaspoon paprika
1 teaspoon crushed dried
  rosemary

1/2 teaspoon dried thyme
1/2 cup unsalted butter
1 pound raw shrimp, shelled and
  deveined (shells reserved for
  stock)
1 cup beer
1/2 cup Shrimp Stock (below) or
  bottled clam juice
2 teaspoons fresh lemon juice

Combine the cayenne, black pepper, salt, red pepper, paprika, rosemary, and thyme. Set aside. In a large skillet, melt the butter, and add the seasonings. Cook until bubbly. Add the shrimp and coat with the butter mixture. Cook 1 minute. Add the beer and Shrimp Stock and cook for 2–4 minutes depending on size of shrimp. Add the lemon juice and cook for 1 minute more. Serve in bowls.

SHRIMP STOCK
Shells from shrimp
2 quarts water
1 large garlic clove, halved

1 celery stalk
7 black peppercorns

Simmer all ingredients together for at least 2 hours. Strain and refrigerate. Leftover stock may be frozen.

Sautéed Shrimp with Pink Grapefruit and Vodka Glaze

SERVES 4–6

2 tablespoons unsalted butter
1 tablespoon olive oil
2 pounds raw shrimp, shelled
   and deveined
1 teaspoon dried thyme
1/4 teaspoon freshly ground
   pepper

1/3 cup vodka
1/2 cup fresh pink grapefruit
   juice
1 pink grapefruit, peeled,
   sectioned, pith removed
Fresh thyme, for garnish
   (optional)

In a large skillet, melt the butter with the oil. Add the shrimp and cook about 2 minutes on each side, sprinkling with the thyme and pepper as they cook. Remove the shrimp to a bowl and keep warm. Add the vodka to the pan and boil rapidly for about 1 minute. Add the grapefruit juice and continue to boil until the sauce is reduced by a third and slightly thickened. Return the shrimp to the pan along with the grapefruit sections and cook over medium heat until warmed through. Garnish with fresh thyme, if desired.

Summer Shrimp Curry

SERVES 3–4

This is a very mild curry. The use of cream and sour cream gives it a silky texture.

3 tablespoons unsalted butter
1/3 cup chopped green onions,
   including some of the green
2 teaspoons curry powder
3 tablespoons flour
1/2 cup Chicken Stock
1 pound cooked shrimp

1 cup peeled, seeded and
   chopped tomatoes
1 cup heavy cream
1/4 cup sour cream
1 ripe avocado, peeled and diced
2 tablespoons fresh lime juice

In a large skillet, over medium heat, melt the butter and sauté the onions with the curry powder until soft and clear, about 5 minutes. Stir in the flour and cook 1 minute. Add the stock and stir until thickened. Add the shrimp, tomatoes, cream, and sour cream. Heat for 5–7 minutes without letting mixture come to a boil. Fold in the avocado and lime juice.

Orange Szechuan Shrimp with Spinach

SERVES 4

3 tablespoons soy sauce
1 tablespoon rice wine vinegar
3 tablespoons grated orange peel
Juice of 1 orange
2 tablespoons honey
2 tablespoons chile oil
1/4 cup plus 2 tablespoons peanut
  oil

1 pound raw shrimp, peeled and
  deveined
1 tablespoon cornstarch
2 cups fresh spinach leaves, cut
  into 1-inch strips
1/3 cup halved water chestnuts

In a large bowl, combine the soy sauce, vinegar, orange peel, orange juice, honey, chile oil, and 1/4 cup of the peanut oil. Add the shrimp and marinate for at least 20 minutes. Remove the shrimp, reserving marinade. Pat the shrimp dry. Mix the cornstarch into the marinade until it is dissolved. Heat 2 tablespoons peanut oil in wok or large skillet. Add the shrimp to the wok and quickly stir-fry just until the shrimp begins to turn pink. Add the marinade and stir until it starts to thicken. Add the spinach and water chestnuts and cook for 30 seconds more.

Shrimp with Tarragon

SERVES 6

1/4 cup butter
1/2 cup olive oil
1/2 cup fresh lemon juice
1 cup thinly sliced green onions
1 cup chopped fresh parsley
3 medium garlic cloves, crushed
2–3 tablespoons fresh tarragon
  or 1 tablespoon dried tarragon

2 pounds raw shrimp, shelled
  and deveined
3 tablespoons heavy cream
6 slices sourdough bread
2 tablespoons olive oil

In a small saucepan, heat the butter and olive oil together until butter is melted. Add the lemon juice and let mixture cool slightly. Combine the green onions, parsley, garlic, and tarragon and toss with the shrimp. Pour the olive-oil mixture over the shrimp and marinate refrigerated for 1–2 hours.

Place shrimp and marinade in a large skillet. Bring to a simmer and cook 2 minutes. Turn the shrimp and continue to cook for 2 minutes more. Add the cream and boil for 1 minute. Serve on sourdough toast or croustades.

Note To prepare croustades, trim the crust from white or sourdough bread. In a sauté pan, heat 2 tablespoons of olive oil and add pieces of bread. Fry on both sides until well browned and crisp. These may be prepared ahead and quickly reheated in a 350-degree oven for a few minutes.

Lobster with Flavored Butters

3 tablespoons salt
1 live (1 1/2-pound) lobster per person
Flavored Butters (below)

To boil: Fill stockpot with water to within a few inches of top and add salt. Bring to a rolling boil. Grab the lobster from behind the head and drop it in head first. Cover the pan and let the lobster cook for 5 minutes for the first pound and 3 minutes more for each additional pound. Remove the lobster from the water and place it on its back. With a heavy, sharp knife or poultry shears, cut the lobster in half starting at the head. Remove the stomach and intestinal vein. The green tomalley and coral roe found in a female lobster are considered a great delicacy. You may wish to add the roe to the sauce accompanying the lobster.

To broil: Ask your local fish seller to split and clean the lobster for you. Brush the lobster generously with one of the butter sauces. To barbecue, place on the grill over medium coals, meat side down, for about 7–8 minutes. Turn, baste with more butter, and continue cooking for about 5 minutes more. To broil, brush with one of the butter sauces and place meat side up, 6 inches from the source of heat. Broil for 6–7 minutes, baste again and turn, cooking for 4–5 minutes more.

Precooked lobster: Brush the lobster with butter and broil meat side down for 3 minutes. Turn, basting again and cook for another 2 minutes until heated through.

Flavored Butter Sauces

SHERRY BUTTER SAUCE
6 tablespoons unsalted butter   **1/8 teaspoon cracked black**
1 teaspoon finely minced shallots   **pepper**
1/2 tablespoon sherry vinegar

Melt the butter with all other ingredients and use for basting and dipping.

CAYENNE BUTTER SAUCE

1/2 cup unsalted butter

2 tablespoons fresh lemon juice

1/2 teaspoon cayenne pepper

1/4 teaspoon paprika

1 tablespoon chopped fresh
   cilantro

Melt the butter and add lemon juice, cayenne, and paprika. Stir in cilantro. Use for basting and dipping.

Lobster Ragoût

Accompany with Ginger Corn Muffins and Pear and Raspberry Salad for a very special occasion.

3 tablespoons unsalted butter

2 cups mushrooms, thinly sliced

2 shallots, minced

2–2 1/2 cups cooked lobster meat

1/4 cup brandy

6 tablespoons tawny port

2 cups heavy cream

In a skillet, melt the butter and sauté the mushrooms and shallots for 3–4 minutes, until they have softened. Add the lobster meat and stir until it is lightly coated with the butter. Remove the mushrooms, shallots, and lobster to a bowl. Add the brandy and port to the pan and bring to a boil, stirring to scrape up any drippings. Add the cream and reduce by half over moderate heat, about 20 minutes. Add the lobster mixture to cream and stir until heated through.

VII

Poultry and Game

Chicken and Plum Tomatoes in Port

SERVES 4

4 chicken breast halves, boned
    and skinned
Salt and pepper
8 whole garlic cloves
2 teaspoons butter
1 tablespoon chopped shallots

1/4 cup port wine
3/4 pound plum tomatoes, cored
    and quartered
1/4 pound small mushrooms,
    sliced

Sprinkle the chicken with salt and pepper. Drop the garlic into a saucepan of boiling water and cook for 5 minutes. Drain and set aside to cool slightly. Peel and slice the garlic. In a large skillet, melt the butter over moderately high heat. Add the chicken and sauté 1 minute on each side. Sprinkle with the shallots and sliced garlic. Add the port, tomatoes, and mushrooms. Season to taste with salt and pepper. Cover and simmer for 10 minutes. Transfer the chicken to a warmed platter and arrange the tomatoes around the chicken. Cover and set aside. Bring the sauce to a boil and simmer until slightly thickened. Spoon the sauce over the chicken and tomatoes to serve.

Coronado Chicken

SERVES 4–6

6 chicken breast halves, boned
    but not skinned
1/3 cup fresh lime juice
1/2 cup butter, room temperature

1/3 cup chopped fresh cilantro
2 medium garlic cloves, minced
2 jalapeño chiles, seeded and
    minced

Marinate the breast halves in lime juice for about 30 minutes. Remove the chicken from the lime juice, reserving the juice.

With a fork, mix together the butter, cilantro, garlic, and chiles. Set aside. Starting at the top of each chicken breast, gently lift the skin to make a pocket, being careful not to tear the skin or membrane. Pat 1 tablespoon of the flavored butter under the skin of each breast. Melt the remaining chile butter. To grill, place the breasts skin side down over medium coals. Cook for 8–10 minutes, turn, and cook 8–10 minutes more or until springy to the touch. The chicken can also be prepared in the broiler. Baste with the reserved lime juice during cooking. Salt lightly and brush with melted chile butter before serving.

Chicken Breasts with Basil Butter

SERVES 8

The chicken can be stuffed the night before and refrigerated.

1/2 cup butter, sliced in several
  pieces
2 large garlic cloves
2 large shallots
1/2 cup chopped fresh basil
1 tablespoon minced fresh dill *or*
  1 teaspoon dried dill

1 tablespoon minced fresh
  oregano *or* 1 teaspoon dried
  oregano
4 large whole chicken breasts
  with skins, boned
Salt and freshly ground pepper

In a food processor, combine the butter, garlic, shallots, basil, dill, and oregano. Process until well blended. Place in an airtight container and refrigerate several hours for flavors to blend.

Preheat the broiler. Place the chicken on a work surface, skin side up. Starting at the top of each breast, gently lift the skin to make a pocket, being careful not to tear the skin or membrane. Pat 2 tablespoons of the basil butter under the skin and tuck flap over back side to secure. Place the breasts skin side down on a broiler pan. Broil 6 inches from the heat source for 8–10 minutes. Turn chicken, season with salt and pepper, and broil 8–10 minutes longer. Slice across the grain and brush with melted basil butter before serving.

Breast of Chicken Piccata

SERVES 8

8 large chicken breast halves,
  boned and skinned
1/2 cup flour
1 1/2 teaspoons salt
1/4 teaspoon pepper
Dash of paprika
4 tablespoons unsalted butter
1 tablespoon oil

1/4 cup dry white wine or
  vermouth
3 tablespoons fresh lemon juice
3–4 tablespoons capers, rinsed
  and drained
Lemon slices and minced fresh
  parsley, for garnish

Place the chicken breasts between two sheets of waxed paper. Flatten the breasts to a thickness of 1/4–1/2 inch by pounding them with a kitchen mallet.

In a small bowl mix the flour, salt, pepper and paprika. Lay the flattened breasts on a work surface. Sprinkle each side with the seasoned flour.

Heat the butter and oil in a 12-inch skillet over moderately high heat. When the foam subsides, add the chicken a few pieces at a time and sauté for 2–3 minutes a side. Blot on paper towels, set on a platter, and keep warm.

Pour off all but 2 tablespoons of the fat from the pan. Over moderately high heat, stir in the wine and deglaze the pan, scraping up the brown bits from the bottom. Add the lemon juice and simmer for 2 minutes. Return chicken to the skillet and add the capers. Glaze the chicken with the lemon sauce and arrange on a warm serving platter. Garnish with the lemon slices and parsley.

Breast of Chicken in Parmesan Cream

SERVES 4

Fresh oregano and imported Parmesan cheese give this superb dish its character.

2 tablespoons unsalted butter
2 large whole chicken breasts, boned, skinned, and cut in strips 1 × 3 inches
1 tablespoon minced fresh oregano *or* 1 teaspoon dried oregano
3/4 cup dry white vermouth
2 garlic cloves, minced
1 cup heavy cream

1 teaspoon freshly grated nutmeg
4–5 ounces imported Parmesan cheese, freshly grated
2 tablespoons chopped fresh Italian parsley plus additional, for garnish
1 tablespoon fresh lemon juice
Salt and pepper to taste

In a 10–12-inch skillet, heat the butter over moderately high heat. When the butter begins to foam, add the chicken and oregano. Do not crowd the chicken or it will not brown. Sauté for 3–5 minutes until chicken is lightly browned but not cooked all the way through. Be careful to regulate the heat so that the butter does not burn. Remove the chicken to a warm platter and tent it with foil. Add the vermouth to the skillet. Over high heat, deglaze the pan, stirring well, scraping up the drippings. Add the garlic and boil over moderately high heat until the liquid is reduced by half. Add the cream, reduce the heat, and simmer until cream has thickened slightly to a saucelike consistency. Add the nutmeg, cheese, parsley, and lemon juice. Stir until the cheese is melted.

Return the chicken to the sauce to finish cooking and heat through. Season to taste with salt and pepper. Sprinkle with parsley. Serve with rice or buttered pasta.

Garlic Chicken Breasts

SERVES 4

1 small head of garlic, unpeeled
1/4 cup chopped fresh Italian
  parsley
Salt and pepper

4 chicken breast halves, boned
  but not skinned
2 tablespoons unsalted butter
1/4 cup fresh lemon juice

In a small saucepan, place the garlic head in water to cover. Bring to a boil
and drain. Peel the garlic and slice very thinly. In a small bowl combine the
garlic and parsley. Season with salt and pepper to taste. Reserve half the
mixture for the sauce. Gently lift the skin of each chicken breast half to form a
small pocket. Stuff each pocket with a quarter of the remaining garlic mixture.
Grill or broil chicken breasts 8–10 minutes on each side or until springy to the
touch. Do not overcook. Heat the butter in a small skillet and add the remaining garlic mixture. Sauté for a few seconds, add lemon juice, and heat through.
Place the chicken on a warmed platter. Spoon the garlic-parsley sauce over the
chicken and serve.

Mediterranean Chicken Breasts

SERVES 8

2 lemons
4 large garlic cloves
1 teaspoon dried oregano
1/2 cup olive oil
1 teaspoon salt
8 chicken breast halves, boned
  and skinned
2 cups Chicken Stock
1 head of garlic
1 cup finely grated Parmesan
  cheese

1 cup fine fresh sourdough bread
  crumbs
2 tablespoons butter, melted
1 cup dry white wine
1/3 cup chopped fresh parsley
1–2 tablespoons fresh lemon
  juice to taste
Salt and pepper to taste

With a vegetable peeler remove the peel from both lemons. Juice the lemons
and set the juice aside. In a food processor, add the 4 garlic cloves and lemon
peel. Process until finely minced. Add the lemon juice, oregano, olive oil, and
salt. Process until well combined. Marinate the breasts in the lemon mixture
several hours or overnight.

Preheat the oven to 400 degrees. Bring the Chicken Stock to a boil with the head of garlic. Simmer for 10 minutes or until the garlic is soft. Remove the garlic with a slotted spoon. Reserve the stock. Peel the garlic and set it aside.

Remove the chicken from the marinade and drain. Combine the cheese and bread crumbs. Roll the chicken in the cheese mixture and place in a large baking dish. Drizzle with the melted butter and sprinkle with the cooked garlic. Bake for 20 minutes or until springy to the touch. Remove the chicken to serving plates.

While the chicken is baking, boil the stock over high heat until it is reduced to about 1 1/2 cups. Add the wine and boil over high heat until the liquid is reduced to 1 cup. Add the parsley, lemon juice, salt and pepper to taste. Spoon the sauce over each serving.

Szechuan Chicken with Peanuts

SERVES 4

1 egg white
1 tablespoon cornstarch
1 tablespoon dry sherry
1 tablespoon oriental sesame oil
2 teaspoons sugar
1 1/2 pounds chicken breasts, skinned, boned, and cut in 1-inch pieces
2 tablespoons soy sauce
1/3 cup water
1 teaspoon cornstarch

1 tablespoon oil
1/2 teaspoon–1 tablespoon dried red pepper flakes (to taste)
2 large garlic cloves, crushed
2 tablespoons peeled and minced fresh ginger
1 cup chopped onions
1/2 cup salted peanuts
1/4–1/2 pound snow peas
1/2 red bell pepper, julienned
4 cups hot cooked rice

In a medium mixing bowl, whisk together the egg white, the tablespoon of cornstarch, sherry, sesame oil, and sugar. Stir in the chicken pieces and coat the chicken well. In a small dish, stir together the soy sauce, water, and the teaspoon of cornstarch.

Heat a wok or large skillet over high heat. Add the oil. Stir-fry the pepper flakes, garlic, ginger, and onions for 30 seconds. Add the chicken mixture and sauté for 1 minute, stirring constantly. Whisk the soy-sauce mixture to recombine it and add it to the chicken. Continue cooking, stirring constantly, for 2 minutes or until the mixture coats the chicken. Add the peanuts, snow peas, and bell pepper. Cook, stirring, until chicken is springy to the touch and the vegetables are just heated through. Serve immediately over hot rice.

Chicken Cilantro with Tomatillo Sauce

SERVES 4–6

Poblano or pasilla chiles vary in size and in degree of hotness, which is not necessarily related to their size. In this recipe you should use poblano chiles that are about 3–4 inches in length. After roasting, peeling, and seeding the chiles, taste for hotness. They should be pleasantly hot but not overpowering. Use fewer chiles if you have extra-hot ones. If poblano are unavailable, fresh long green chiles can be substituted. They are similar in taste; however, their flavor does not have quite the same character.

4 poblano or pasilla chiles, cut in 1/4-inch strips
1 tablespoon oil
1 tablespoon butter
1/2 large onion, sliced
1 large garlic clove, minced
2 large whole chicken breasts, boned, skinned, and cut into 1/2 × 2-inch strips
Juice of 1 lime
Salt to taste
1 tablespoon minced fresh oregano *or* 1 teaspoon dried oregano

1 tablespoon minced fresh cilantro
Corn tortillas, steamed or fried, *or* fried corn-tortilla baskets
Tomatillo Sauce (below)

Condiments Sour cream, chopped tomatoes, sliced ripe olives, guacamole, shredded Cheddar and Jack cheese, shredded lettuce, lime wedges

Using a long-handled fork, char the chiles over an open flame, turning them for 2–3 minutes, or until the skins are blackened. Or, place the chiles on a broiler pan and broil about 2 inches from the heat until the skins are blackened, turning frequently. This will take approximately 15 minutes. Transfer the chiles to a plastic bag, close tightly, and let them steam until they are cool enough to handle. Wash, peel, seed and cut into 1/4-inch strips. In a 12-inch skillet, heat the oil and butter over a low flame. Add the chiles, onions, and garlic to the skillet and sauté very slowly for 10–15 minutes. Increase the heat to moderately high, add the chicken, and sauté quickly until chicken is no longer pink and just springy to the touch. Add the lime juice, salt, oregano, and cilantro. Reduce the heat to low and continue cooking for 5 minutes. Serve immediately in the corn tortillas with Tomatillo Sauce and condiments.

TOMATILLO SAUCE

3/4 pound fresh tomatillos, husks removed

2 garlic cloves, minced

1/2 large onion, chopped

1/2 cup Chicken Stock

1/2 teaspoon sugar

1/2 teaspoon salt

1 jalapeño chile, seeded and diced

1 cup fresh cilantro leaves

3 tablespoons vegetable oil

Wash the tomatillos and remove the stems. In the bowl of a food processor, place the tomatillos, garlic, onions, stock, sugar, salt, jalapeño chile, and cilantro. Process until well blended. Heat the oil in a 10–12-inch skillet over moderate flame. Add the tomatillo mixture, reduce heat and simmer at a low boil for 10 minutes. Remove from heat. Serve either heated or at room temperature. May be made the day ahead and refrigerated until ready to use, or can be prepared several days ahead and frozen.

Glazed Chicken Breasts Stuffed with Goat Cheese

SERVES 4

4 chicken breast halves, boned but not skinned

4 ounces goat cheese, mixed with 4 teaspoons fresh rosemary or 1 1/2 teaspoons dried rosemary (or oregano, tarragon, thyme)

1/4 cup butter, melted

4 ounces red jalapeño jelly, melted

Preheat the oven to 375 degrees. Place the chicken on a work surface, skin side up. Gently loosen the skin to open a pocket large enough for 1 ounce of cheese, being careful not to tear the skin or surrounding membrane. Using a spoon or fingers, stuff the cheese under the skin of each breast.

Place the breasts in a baking dish skin side up. Pour the melted butter over the chicken. Bake for 10 minutes. Remove from the oven and pour the melted jelly over the breasts. Return to the oven and bake for 15 minutes more or until springy to the touch. Spoon the sauce over each breast before serving.

Chicken with Lemon and Basil

SERVES 4

4 chicken breast halves, boned
  and skinned
2 tablespoons flour
2 tablespoons butter
1 cup Chicken Stock

1 tablespoon grated lemon peel
3 tablespoons fresh lemon juice
3 tablespoons chopped fresh
  basil

Place the chicken breasts on a cutting board and flatten slightly. Lightly flour both sides. Melt the butter in a large skillet over medium-high heat until bubbly. Sauté the breasts 3 minutes on each side until lightly browned. Add the stock, lemon peel, lemon juice, and basil. Cover and simmer 10 minutes. Remove the breasts to a warm platter with a slotted spoon. Cover loosely and keep warm. Boil the poaching liquid, uncovered, over high heat until reduced to a scant 1/2 cup. Spoon over breasts and serve.

Breast of Chicken and
Pear Slices with Port and Stilton Cream

SERVES 6

A traditional marriage of Stilton and pears brings sophistication to sautéed chicken.

6 chicken breast halves, boned
  and skinned
Flour
6 tablespoons clarified butter
Salt and pepper
3/4 cup unsalted Chicken Stock
3/4 cup port

1 1/2 cups heavy cream
3 pears, peeled, cored, and cut
  into sixths
1–2 tablespoons Stilton cheese
2 tablespoons minced fresh
  parsley

Flatten the chicken breasts slightly. Sprinkle lightly with flour. In a 10–12-inch skillet, heat 4 tablespoons of the clarified butter over a moderately high flame. When the butter begins to color slightly, add the chicken. After 4 minutes, turn the chicken and sauté until springy to the touch. Remove to a warm platter. Sprinkle the breasts with salt and pepper, tent with foil, and set in a 200-degree oven.

Add the stock and port to the same skillet and boil, reducing by half. Add the cream and boil until it is reduced to a saucelike consistency. Meanwhile, in a small skillet, sauté the pear slices for 5 minutes in the remaining 2 tablespoons of the clarified butter. Set aside. Add 1 tablespoon of the Stilton to the port sauce and stir until melted. Taste the sauce and add additional Stilton if desired.

Place the chicken on 6 serving plates and top each with 3 pear slices, some of the sauce, and minced parsley.

Chicken with Raspberry Vinegar

SERVES 8

2 cups Beef Stock
8 chicken breast halves
Salt and pepper
2 tablespoons butter
1/2 cup raspberry vinegar
2 tablespoons minced garlic
1/2 cup red wine vinegar

2 plum tomatoes, peeled, seeded, and finely chopped
1 tablespoon chopped fresh parsley
2 tablespoons chopped fresh tarragon

In a small saucepan, boil the Beef Stock over high heat until it is reduced to 1 cup. Sprinkle chicken with salt and pepper. In a large skillet melt the butter over moderately high heat. Sauté the chicken for 4–5 minutes on each side, or until golden brown. Add the raspberry vinegar and 1/2 cup of the reduced stock. Cover and simmer for 30 minutes until the chicken juices run clear when the chicken is pierced with a fork. Remove the chicken from the cooking liquid. Place on a warm platter, cover and keep warm.

Add the garlic to the cooking liquid and simmer for 1 minute over low heat. Add the wine vinegar, tomatoes, and remaining Beef Stock. Bring to a boil and simmer until slightly thickened. Add salt and pepper to taste. Spoon over the chicken and sprinkle with the parsley and tarragon.

Chicken Chile Relleno

SERVES 8–10

This south of the border specialty is ideal for casual entertaining as it may be prepared up to 24 hours in advance. Olé!

6 large chicken breast halves
1 small onion, sliced
1 carrot, sliced
2 stalks celery, sliced
4 sprigs parsley, chopped
1 bay leaf
4 whole black peppercorns
2 cups canned chicken broth
3 tablespoons butter
2 garlic cloves, minced
5 tablespoons flour
1 cup milk, heated
Reserved poaching stock, heated
1 cup sour cream
1 cup lightly packed fresh
   cilantro leaves
2 eggs, lightly beaten
1 1/2 teaspoons dried oregano

1 teaspoon ground cumin
1 tablespoon chili powder
Salt and pepper to taste

10–12 fresh long green chiles *or*
   14 ounces canned green chiles,
   seeded and opened flat
6 cups slightly crushed corn
   tortilla chips
2 cups chopped green onions,
   including 3 inches of the
   green
3/4 pound Monterey Jack cheese,
   shredded
3/4 pound medium sharp Cheddar
   cheese, shredded
2 large tomatoes, sliced

Arrange the chicken breasts concentrically in a 14-inch skillet. Cover with the onions, carrots, celery, parsley, bay leaf, peppercorns, and broth. Bring to a boil, cover, and reduce the heat. Simmer for approximately 20 minutes or until the chicken juices run clear when the thickest portion is pierced with a fork. Remove the chicken to cool. Over high heat, boil the poaching liquid, uncovered, until reduced to 1 cup. Strain and set aside. Remove the chicken from the bones and shred.

Melt the butter in a saucepan. Sauté the garlic in the butter over low heat until slightly golden. Gradually stir in the flour. Whisk in the heated milk and stock and stir constantly until thickened. Set aside.

Preheat the oven to 350 degrees. In a food processor, combine the sour cream, cilantro, eggs, oregano, cumin, and chili powder. Add the cream sauce. Process until well combined. Season to taste with salt and pepper.

If you are using fresh long green chiles, they must be roasted before adding to the recipe. Using a long-handled fork, char the chiles over an open flame, turning them for 2–3 minutes, or until the skins are blackened. Or, place the chiles on a broiler pan and broil about 2 inches from the heat until the skins are blackened, turning frequently. This will take approximately 15 minutes. Transfer the chiles to a plastic bag, close tightly, and let them steam until they are cool enough to handle and peel. Wash, peel, seed, and open the chiles flat.

In a 13 × 9 × 3-inch casserole, layer half each of the chips, chicken, green onions, chiles, sauce, and cheeses. Press to compact. Cover with the remaining half of the chips, chicken, green onions, and chiles. Top with the tomatoes, and remaining sauce and cheese. May be prepared ahead to this point. Bring to room temperature before baking. Bake for 50 minutes–1 hour or until bubbly and heated through.

Southwestern Grilled Chicken

SERVES 8–10

2 medium tomatoes, quartered
2 cups chopped onions
1/2 cup chopped red bell pepper
4 garlic cloves
1/4 cup fresh cilantro leaves, packed
2/3 cup soy sauce
6 tablespoons oil

2 tablespoons fresh lime juice
1 1/2 teaspoons black pepper
4–5 large whole chicken breasts, split, rib bones removed (boneless breasts can also be used)
Chopped fresh parsley, for garnish

Place the tomatoes, onions, pepper, garlic, cilantro, soy sauce, oil, lime juice, and black pepper in a blender or food processor and process for 30 seconds. Pour the marinade over the chicken breasts and marinate, covered and refrigerated, for at least 4 hours, turning frequently. Remove the chicken from the marinade and grill over medium coals for 20–30 minutes, turning frequently and basting with the marinade. Sprinkle the breasts with parsley before serving. Serve with California Black Beans.

Cheddar-crusted Chicken Pie
with Sausage and Apple

SERVES 6–8

For a fireside dinner, try baking this in individual serving dishes.

CHICKEN AND STOCK

3 1/2 pounds skinned chicken
  pieces
1 small onion, sliced
1 carrot, sliced
1 cup chopped celery tops
4 sprigs parsley
1/2 bay leaf

Pinch of dried thyme
4 whole black peppercorns
5 teaspoons instant chicken
  bouillon or 1 teaspoon for
  each cup of water
5 cups water, or just enough to
  cover chicken

In a covered stockpot, layer the chicken pieces meat side down. Top with the vegetables, spices, and instant bouillon. Add just enough water to cover. Bring to a boil, cover, and gently simmer for 20 minutes. Remove the chicken to a work surface to cool. Continue simmering the liquid, covered. Remove the meat from the bones and shred. This should make 4 generous cups. Reserve chicken. Return chicken carcasses to the liquid and continue simmering partially covered for 30–45 minutes. Strain the liquid through a sieve, pressing the vegetables and bones to extract the juices. Discard the vegetables and bones. With a large spoon, skim off accumulated fat, reserving 2 teaspoons. Return the liquid to the pot and boil over high heat until reduced to 2 cups.

FILLING

1/4 cup butter
5 tablespoons flour
2 cups reserved stock, heated
1 cup heavy cream, heated
12 ounces bulk pork sausage
2 teaspoons reserved chicken fat
1/2 cup chopped onions
1 teaspoon dried sage

1 teaspoon dried marjoram
1 cup unpeeled and shredded
  McIntosh apples, stirred with
  1 teaspoon fresh lemon juice
  to prevent discoloration
1 cup sliced celery
1 cup sliced carrots, parboiled
1 recipe Cheddar Crust (below)

In a 6-cup saucepan, melt the butter over low heat. Stir in the flour and cook slowly for 2 minutes, stirring constantly. Remove from heat. Pour in the heated liquid and cream and beat with a wire whisk to blend. Return to moderate heat and continue cooking and stirring for a few minutes until thickened. Remove from heat and set aside.

In a 6–8-inch skillet, crumble the sausage and sauté until no longer pink. Drain off fat and place the sausage on paper towels to remove any remaining grease. Wipe the skillet dry. Heat the reserved chicken fat over low heat in the same skillet. Stir in the onions, sage, marjoram, and slowly sauté until the onions are tender. Squeeze the apples dry in a clean cloth to remove excess moisture.

In a large mixing bowl, combine the chicken, cream sauce, sausage, onions, apples, celery, and carrots. Pour into a deep-dish casserole, approximately 10 inches in diameter. Cover with Cheddar Crust. (For day-ahead preparation, cover and refrigerate. Prepare crust just prior to baking.)

CHEDDAR CRUST

1/2 cup unsalted butter, softened

2 cups grated sharp Cheddar cheese

2 cups flour

1/4 teaspoon baking powder

1/4 teaspoon dry mustard

1/2 teaspoon salt

Preheat the oven to 425 degrees. In a food processor combine butter and cheese. Process the butter and cheese for 2–3 minutes, or until creamy and completely blended. Chill briefly. Sift together the flour, baking powder, mustard, and salt. Turn the butter and cheese into a mixing bowl. Blend in the flour mixture with hands (do not use a food processor) until it clings together. Form into a ball and wrap in plastic until ready to use.

On a work surface, roll the dough to extend 1/2 inch beyond the edge of the casserole dish. Carefully fit the pastry over the filling in the casserole, pressing the edges to seal. Prick well with a fork. Bake 10 minutes. Reduce the heat to 350 degrees and continue baking for 25–30 minutes, or until heated through.

Curry Glazed Chicken with Honey and Mustard

SERVES 4

2 tablespoons butter
2 tablespoons fresh lime juice
1 garlic clove, minced
1/2 teaspoon salt
2 teaspoons curry powder
3 tablespoons Dijon mustard

1/2 cup honey
2 1/2 pounds chicken, cut in
    serving pieces
1/2 cup dry white vermouth
1/2 cup Chicken Stock
1/2 cup sour cream

Preheat the oven to 375 degrees. Place the butter in a flameproof casserole and heat in the oven until melted. Stir in the lime juice, garlic, salt, curry powder, mustard, and honey. Arrange the chicken in the casserole, turning to coat. Bake, uncovered, for 20 minutes. Turn the chicken over and brush with sauce. Continue baking until golden brown for 20–25 minutes. Remove the chicken to a warm platter and keep warm. Set the casserole over moderate heat. Add the vermouth and stock. Bring to a boil, stirring to scrape up any drippings. Simmer for 5 minutes. Reduce the heat and whisk in the sour cream. Heat through gently, without boiling. Return the chicken to the casserole. Spoon the sauce over the chicken and heat through.

Chicken Fajitas

SERVES 4

3 fresh long green chiles *or* 4
    ounces canned green chiles cut
    in strips
1/4 teaspoon ground cumin
1/4 teaspoon dried oregano
1/4 teaspoon paprika
1/4 teaspoon chili powder
1/4 teaspoon sugar
2 tablespoons vegetable oil
1 onion, sliced
1 yellow or red bell pepper,
    thinly sliced
1 tablespoon fresh lime juice
1/2 teaspoon salt

1 garlic clove, minced
1 tablespoon minced fresh
    cilantro
1 1/2 pounds chicken, boned,
    skinned, and cut in strips

Condiments Guacamole (below),
    Pico de Gallo (below),
    shredded Cheddar or
    Monterey Jack cheese, sour
    cream, shredded lettuce,
    California black beans,
    steamed tortillas

If you are using fresh long green chiles, they must be roasted before being added to the recipe. Using a long-handled fork, char the fresh chiles over an open flame, turning them for 2–3 minutes, or until the skins are blackened. Or place the chiles on a broiling pan and broil about 2 inches from the heat until the skins are blackened, turning frequently. This will take approximately 15 minutes. Transfer the chiles to a plastic bag. Close tightly and let them steam until they are cool enough to handle. Wash, peel, seed and slice the chiles into thin strips.

Combine the cumin, oregano, paprika, chili powder, and sugar in a small bowl. Set aside. In a 12-inch skillet, heat the oil over low heat. Add the onions, bell pepper, chiles, lime juice, and salt to the pan. Sauté slowly for about 10 minutes or until the vegetables are just tender. Add the garlic and cilantro to skillet and continue sautéing slowly for 2 minutes. Increase to high heat. Add the chicken and spice mixture to the pan and sauté until the chicken is lightly browned. Season to taste with salt. Serve with assorted condiments.

GUACAMOLE

2 medium-size ripe avocados, peeled, pitted (reserving one pit)
2 tablespoons fresh lime juice
1 garlic clove, minced
1/3 cup thinly sliced green onions including 3 inches of the green part

1/8 teaspoon ground cumin
1/8 teaspoon sugar
1 ripe plum tomato, chopped
Salt and pepper to taste

In a small mixing bowl, using a fork, mash the avocados with the lime juice and garlic until creamy. Add the remaining ingredients and combine well. Place the reserved pit in the center of the guacamole and cover tightly to prevent darkening. Remove the pit before serving. This is best if served within 2 hours.

PICO DE GALLO

4 to 6 ripe plum tomatoes, chopped
1 small onion, chopped
1 tablespoon minced fresh cilantro

1/2–1 serrano chile, minced with seeds, or to taste
1 teaspoon fresh lime juice or vinegar
Salt

Combine all ingredients in a small bowl. Season to taste with salt. Allow to stand 1 hour and serve at room temperature.

Orange Rosemary Chicken

SERVES 6–8

This is also excellent with a whole chicken. Stuff the cavity with orange wedges and fresh rosemary and roast on a rotisserie.

I 1/2 cups fresh orange juice
1/4 cup olive oil
1/4 cup chopped fresh chives
3 tablespoons chopped fresh
   rosemary

I tablespoon salt
I tablespoon pepper
8 chicken pieces

Combine the orange juice, olive oil, chives, rosemary, salt, and pepper. Marinate the chicken, refrigerated, in the mixture for at least 4 hours and up to 24 hours. Remove the chicken and pat dry, reserving the marinade for basting. Broil or barbecue chicken pieces, turning and basting frequently. Allow 30–45 minutes cooking time depending on the size of the pieces. The chicken is done when the thickest part of the thigh is pierced with a fork and the juices run clear.

Panko-crusted Sesame Chicken

SERVES 6

Perfect picnic fare.

3 1/2 pounds chicken, cut in
   serving pieces
1/2 cup cornstarch
1/4 cup flour
1/4 cup sugar
2 teaspoons salt
2 eggs, lightly beaten
5 tablespoons soy sauce
1/4 cup sliced green onions,
   including 3 inches of the
   green part

2 garlic cloves, minced
1/4 cup toasted white sesame
   seeds
1/4 cup safflower oil
2 1/2 cups panko (Japanese bread
   crumbs)
Peanut oil for frying

Wash the chicken and pat dry. In a small mixing bowl, combine the cornstarch, flour, sugar, and 1 1/2 teaspoons of the salt. In a large mixing bowl, whisk together the eggs, soy sauce, onions, garlic, sesame seeds, and safflower oil. Whisk in the cornstarch mixture.

Place the chicken pieces in a sealable plastic bag. Pour in the batter and turn to coat. Marinate in the refrigerator for at least 2 hours, or as long as overnight, turning the bag occasionally to keep the marinade combined. Overnight marinating enhances the flavor of the chicken.

Season the panko with the remaining salt and spread on a work surface. Remove the pieces of chicken from the bag, allowing the excess marinade to drip back into the bag. Roll the chicken in the panko, making certain that each piece is well coated.

In a 12–14-inch skillet, heat the peanut oil to 350 degrees. Fry the chicken until golden brown, turning frequently. The chicken is done when the thickest part of the thigh is pierced with a fork and the juices run clear. Drain on paper towels. Serve warm or at room temperature.

Try this also with boned breasts. Slice in strips before serving.

Ginger Chicken with Cracked Wheat

SERVES 4–6

2 tablespoons olive oil
2 tablespoons butter
2–3 pounds chicken, cut in
  serving pieces
4 chopped green onions,
  including 3 inches of green
  part
1/2 cup minced fresh parsley
2 garlic cloves, minced

2 (1/2-inch) slices fresh ginger,
  each the size of a quarter,
  peeled and minced
1 cup cracked wheat (bulgur)
1/4 cup soy sauce
1 cup Chicken Stock
1/2 cup dry white vermouth or
  white wine
1/2 cup water

Preheat the oven to 350 degrees. In a 10–12-inch flameproof casserole, heat the oil and butter over moderately high heat. Add the chicken and sauté for 4 minutes on each side, or until golden brown. Remove to a platter. Pour off all but 1 tablespoon of the fat from the casserole. Add the onions, parsley, garlic, and ginger and sauté over low heat for 2 minutes, or until onions are softened.

Add the cracked wheat and soy sauce. Cook the mixture over moderate heat, stirring for 3 minutes, or until the wheat crackles. In a saucepan heat the stock, vermouth, and water just to boiling. Place the chicken on top of the wheat mixture and pour the heated liquid over the top.

Bake, covered, for 40–45 minutes or until all the liquid is absorbed.

Chicken Chili

SERVES 8

3–4 pounds of chicken, skinned (2 large whole breasts, split, and 6 large thighs)
1 onion, quartered
4 whole cloves
3 garlic cloves, chopped
1 bay leaf
1 jalapeño chili, seeded and chopped
1 tablespoon chili powder
1 carrot, sliced
1 cup chopped celery tops
5 teaspoons instant chicken bouillon or 1 teaspoon for each cup of water
5 cups of water (approximately)
1 tablespoon oil
2 tablespoons butter
2 large onions, chopped
3 garlic cloves, minced
1 red bell pepper, chopped
1 green bell pepper, chopped
5 tablespoons chili powder, or to taste

1 teaspoon dried oregano
1 teaspoon paprika
1 teaspoon ground cumin
1 teaspoon fennel seeds
1 (6-ounce) can whole black olives, drained and coarsely chopped
1 (12-ounce) can tomato paste
1 (28-ounce) can whole, peeled tomatoes with juice
12 ounces beer
1/4 cup chopped fresh parsley
1 jalapeño chili, seeded and diced
1 (27-ounce) can red kidney beans, drained
3 cups reserved stock
4 cups reserved chicken

Condiments Shredded Cheddar cheese, sliced green onions, chopped fresh cilantro, sour cream

In a large stockpot, place the chicken meat side down. Stud each onion quarter with one clove. Top the chicken with the onions, the 3 chopped garlic cloves, bay leaf, the chopped chili, chili powder, carrot, celery tops, and instant bouillon. Poach the chicken and vegetables with just enough water to cover. Bring to a boil, cover, and gently simmer for 20 minutes. Remove the chicken to a work surface to cool. Continue simmering the stock, covered. Remove the chicken meat from the bones and shred. You should have 4 generous cups of shredded chicken. Set aside. Return the carcasses to the stock and continue simmering for 30–45 minutes. Strain the stock through a sieve, pressing vegetables and bones to extract juices. Discard the vegetables and bones. Skim fat off the top and boil over high heat until the stock is reduced to 3 cups.

In a large heavy pot, over moderate flame, heat the oil and butter. Add the chopped onions, the 3 minced garlic cloves, and red and green peppers. Sauté for 3–5 minutes. Add the spices, olives, tomato paste, tomatoes, beer, parsley, the diced chile pepper, beans, stock, and chicken. Simmer, partially covered, for about 2 hours. Serve with condiments. This can be made ahead and frozen.

Grilled Spring Chicken with Caraway Basting Sauce

SERVES 4–6

1 cup dry white wine
1/2 cup olive oil
1/2 cup tomato sauce
2 teaspoons crushed caraway
  seeds
1 teaspoon Worcestershire sauce

2 teaspoons curry powder, or to
  taste
1 garlic clove, mashed with 1 1/2
  teaspoons salt in a mortar
2 (2 1/2–3-pound) spring
  chickens, split or quartered

In a medium saucepan, combine the wine, oil, tomato sauce, caraway seeds, Worcestershire, curry, and garlic-salt mixture. Bring to a boil over low heat and simmer for 5 minutes, stirring frequently.

Prepare the barbecue for grilling the chicken. Wash and dry the chicken. Place on a grill and baste with the sauce. Barbecue over medium to hot coals, turning and basting frequently, for approximately 45 minutes to 1 hour or until the juices run clear when the thickest part of a thigh is pierced with a fork. Heat the remaining basting sauce and serve with the chicken.

Rosemary Chicken with
Italian Sausages and Sweet Peppers

SERVES 8

1/2 cup flour
1 teaspoon salt
1/4 teaspoon pepper
1 teaspoon dry mustard
8 large chicken thighs
1/4 cup vegetable oil
12 Italian sausages, halved
  crosswise
2 onions, thinly sliced
4 red bell peppers, cut in
  1/2-inch strips
4 green bell peppers, cut in
  1/2-inch strips

Cayenne pepper
2 cups dry white wine or dry
  white vermouth
4 cups Chicken Stock
2 tablespoons minced fresh
  rosemary *or* 2 teaspoons dried
  rosemary
1/4 cup fresh lemon juice
Fresh Italian parsley, for
  garnish

Combine the flour, salt, pepper, and mustard. Dip the chicken into the seasoned flour and shake off excess.

Heat the oil in a 12–14-inch skillet. Brown the chicken on all sides until golden but not cooked all the way through. Remove the pieces to a plate. Add the sausage to the same pan and brown thoroughly. Set aside with the chicken. Pour off all but 2 tablespoons of the browning fat. To the same skillet, add the onions, peppers, and a dash of cayenne pepper. Cover and simmer until tender, about 5 minutes.

Add the wine, stock, rosemary, browned chicken, and sausage to the pan. Bring to a boil, cover, and simmer for 25 minutes. Remove the meats and vegetables with a slotted spoon. Skim the excess fat from the surface and boil over high heat, reducing the liquid by half. Add the lemon juice. Season to taste with salt and pepper. Return the meats and vegetables to the pan and heat thoroughly. Garnish with parsley.

Chicken Mendocino

SERVES 4–6

8–10 chicken thighs, boned if
  desired
1/2 cup flour
1/4 teaspoon cinnamon
1/4 teaspoon dried thyme
1 teaspoon salt
1/4 teaspoon white pepper
6 tablespoons clarified butter
2 tablespoons oil
1 large onion, minced
1 1/2 cups raw converted long-
  grain rice

1/2 green apple, finely chopped
3/4 cup golden raisins plumped in
  2 tablespoons sherry
3 ounces dried apricots, chopped
3 ounces pitted prunes,
  moistpack, chopped
4 cups Chicken Stock, heated
Fresh chopped parsley, for
  garnish

Preheat the oven to 350 degrees. Wash and pat the chicken dry. In a small bowl, combine the flour with the seasonings. Dredge the chicken in the flour mixture, coating evenly. Shake off excess.

In a 10–12-inch skillet, heat 4 tablespoons of the clarified butter and the oil over moderately high heat. When the foam subsides, add the chicken and sauté until golden, turning once. Remove the chicken to a platter.

Pour off all but 2 tablespoons of the fat. Sauté the onions until soft but not brown. Add the rice to the onions and cook, stirring frequently, until just golden.

In a small skillet over moderate heat add the remaining 2 tablespoons of the clarified butter. Cook the apples and the raisins until almost tender. Add the apricots and prunes. Sauté briefly.

Combine the fruit and rice mixture. Season to taste with salt and pepper. Pour rice mixture into a large greased casserole dish about 13 inches in diameter and 2 inches deep. Pour the hot stock over the rice mixture and arrange the chicken on top. Bake, uncovered, for about 40 minutes or until the rice is tender. Sprinkle with parsley before serving.

Tandoori Chicken with Punjabi Sauce

SERVES 4–6

This spicy Indian chicken is a perfect company dish. It can be grilled early in the day and then simply finished in the sauce.

6 chicken legs with thighs
  attached
2 teaspoons coarse (kosher) salt
Juice of 1 ½ lemons
3/4 cup plain yogurt
1/2 medium onion, peeled and
  quartered
2 garlic cloves, peeled
3/4-inch piece fresh ginger,
  peeled and quartered

1/2 fresh jalapeño chile, with
  seeds, sliced
2 teaspoons Garam Masala
  (below)
1–1 ½ cups butter, melted
Punjabi Sauce (below)
Cilantro sprigs, for garnish

Make 2 diagonal 2–3-inch slits on the meaty side of each chicken piece. Do not start at the edge of a piece and do not cut all the way through to the bone. Sprinkle the pieces with salt and lemon juice, rubbing the mixture into the slits. Set aside. In a food processor, process the yogurt, onions, garlic, ginger, chile and Garam Masala until well blended. Place the chicken in a sealable plastic bag. Pour in the marinade and coat the chicken well. Marinate, refrigerated, for at least 5 and up to 24 hours.

Prepare hot coals for a barbecue grill. Remove the chicken from the marinade. Grill the chicken 5 inches from the heat for approximately 15 minutes, turning frequently and basting generously with 1/2–1 cup of the butter. Grill until the chicken is browned but not cooked all the way through. Can be made ahead to this point.

In a 10–12-inch skillet, melt the remaining butter. Add the Punjabi Sauce and the grilled chicken and baste well with the sauce. Simmer for 15–20 minutes, basting frequently. The chicken is done when the thickest piece is pierced with a fork and the juices run clear.

To serve, arrange the chicken on a warm platter. Spoon some of the sauce on each piece of the chicken and garnish with the cilantro.

GARAM MASALA

1 tablespoon shelled cardamom
  seeds
1-inch piece cinnamon stick
1/3 whole nutmeg

1 teaspoon whole cloves
1 teaspoon whole black
  peppercorns
1 teaspoon cumin seeds

Place the spices in a blender or coffee grinder and process until powdered.

PUNJABI SAUCE

1 teaspoon cumin seeds, roasted in a skillet and finely ground
1-inch cube fresh ginger peeled and minced
1 cup tomato sauce
1 cup heavy cream
1 teaspoon Garam Masala
1/4 teaspoon salt

1/2–1 fresh jalapeño chile, with seeds, sliced into very thin rounds
1/4 teaspoon cayenne pepper
1/4 teaspoon chopped fresh cilantro leaves
1 tablespoon fresh lemon juice

Combine all ingredients in a medium mixing bowl. Whisk together until well blended.

Orange Chicken Indienne

SERVES 6

2 tablespoons butter
12 chicken thighs, skinned
Salt and pepper
1 1/2 cups fresh orange juice
2 tablespoons fresh lemon juice
1/2 cup seedless raisins
1/4 cup chopped chutney
1/4 cup fresh kumquat skins (optional)
1/2 cup slivered blanched almonds
1/2 teaspoon cinnamon
2 teaspoons curry powder or to taste

3 cups hot steamed rice
2 bananas, for garnish

Condiments Chopped cucumber, chopped crisp bacon, chopped peanuts, crushed pineapple, raisins or currants, shredded coconut, sliced green onions with 3 inches of green, chutney, thinly sliced kumquat skins

Preheat the oven to 325 degrees. In a large skillet, melt the butter. Sauté the chicken pieces until golden, about 4–5 minutes on each side. Sprinkle with salt and pepper. Meanwhile, in a saucepan, combine orange juice, lemon juice, raisins, chutney, kumquat skins, almonds, cinnamon, and curry powder. Bring to a boil, reduce the heat, and simmer slowly for 15 minutes. Place the browned chicken in a large casserole. Pour the sauce over and bake for 40 minutes. Serve on a bed of hot steamed rice. Garnish with slices of banana. Accompany with bowls of assorted condiments.

Hickory Smoked Chicken

MAKES 2–3 CUPS

This is the preferred method for smoking chicken. It is great right off the grill and needs no further embellishment.

2 tablespoons grated onions
1 teaspoon fresh minced oregano
   or 1/4 teaspoon dried oregano
2 tablespoons packed brown
   sugar

2 teaspoons coarse (kosher) salt
1 (3–4-pound) whole chicken

In a blender or food processor purée the onions, oregano, sugar, and salt. Wash the chicken and pat dry. Brush the flavorings over the whole chicken, coating both sides. Smoke over hickory chips in a commercial smoker according to the manufacturer's instructions. This will take 1 1/2–4 hours depending on the smoker. The chicken is done when a meat thermometer inserted in thickest part of the thigh registers 175 degrees.

Baked Smoked Chicken

MAKES 2–3 CUPS

When a smoker is unavailable, try this quick method for a wonderful addition to salads and sandwiches.

2 1/2 pounds chicken parts,
   skinned
1/4 cup chopped onions
1 teaspoon fresh minced oregano
   or 1/4 teaspoon dried oregano

1/4 cup brown sugar
1 tablespoon coarse (kosher) salt
1 1/2 cups canned chicken broth
1 tablespoon Liquid Smoke

Preheat the oven to 375 degrees. Place the chicken in a baking dish. Pour the flavorings over the chicken and bake, covered, for 45 minutes to 1 hour or until the thickest piece is pierced with a fork and the juices run clear. Strip the chicken from the bones and allow to cool in the liquid. Drain well before using.

Roasted Turkey with Confetti Vegetable Dressing

SERVES 8

1 cup pine nuts
2 tablespoons butter
1 tablespoon olive oil
2 large onions, thinly sliced
10 large leeks, washed well and thinly sliced
2 garlic cloves, minced
4 stalks celery, thinly sliced diagonally
1 bell pepper, thinly sliced in 2-inch strips

2 teaspoons grated lemon peel
2 tablespoons fresh lemon juice
2 teaspoons minced fresh tarragon *or* 3/4 teaspoon dried tarragon
4 carrots, grated
1 (10–12-pound) turkey or whole turkey breast
Salt
Lemon slices, for garnish

In a large skillet, sauté the pine nuts in the butter and olive oil over medium heat until golden. Remove with a slotted spoon and set aside. In the same skillet sauté the onions, leeks, and garlic. Add the celery and bell pepper and sauté until the vegetables are limp. Add the lemon peel, lemon juice, tarragon, grated carrots, and pine nuts. Set aside to cool.

Preheat the oven to 350 degrees. Wash the turkey and pat dry. Loosen the breast skin, starting at the neck, by gently sliding the fingers between the meat and skin. Open a pocket on either side of the breastbone, large enough for the stuffing, being careful not to tear the skin or membranes around the edge of the pocket. Spoon a generous layer of the vegetable mixture into the pocket, then gently pat the dressing into place from the outside of the bird. Secure the skin at the opening and use the remaining stuffing in the neck cavity.

Rub the bird with salt. For a whole turkey, roast 4 hours or until a meat thermometer inserted into the thickest part of the thigh registers 175 degrees. For a turkey breast, roast for 2 hours or until a meat thermometer inserted into the thickest part of breast registers 160 degrees. Baste frequently with the drippings. Remove to a warm platter and allow to rest 10 minutes before carving. To carve, slice down along the breastbone releasing each breast in one piece. Slice diagonally through the dressing and the meat. To serve, arrange on a platter and garnish with lemon slices.

Turkey Stuffed with Fruit and Jalapeño Peppers

SERVES 8–10

Although this recipe calls for an unusual combination of ingredients, it just might be the best turkey you will ever taste!

1 (14–16-pound) turkey
Juice of 1 lemon
Salt and pepper

STUFFING

4 slices bacon, diced	**1/2 cup raisins**
1 large onion, chopped	**1/2 cup dried apricots, diced**
3 pounds lean ground pork	**1/4 cup oil**
1/2 cup tomato purée	**1/4 cup white vinegar**
1 cup chopped black olives	**1/2 teaspoon cinnamon**
1 cup pine nuts	**Salt and pepper**
3 bananas, diced	**1/4 cup melted butter**
3 apples, peeled, cored, and diced	**2 cups Beef Stock**
	1 cup apple juice
6 jalapeño chiles, seeded and diced	**3 cups dry white wine**
	1 onion, sliced
3 carrots, diced	**2 whole garlic cloves**

Wash the turkey and pat dry. Rub with the lemon juice, salt, and pepper.

To prepare the stuffing, fry the bacon in a large skillet until the fat is rendered. Add the chopped onions to the bacon and sauté over moderate heat until the onions are tender. Add the pork, tomato purée, olives, pine nuts, bananas, apples, chiles, carrots, raisins, apricots, oil, and vinegar. Combine and sauté over moderate heat for 10 minutes. Lower heat and simmer, covered, for 30 minutes. Add the cinnamon and salt and pepper to taste.

Preheat the oven to 350 degrees. Stuff the turkey with the pork-and-fruit mixture. Truss and place on a rack in a large roasting pan. Brush with the melted butter. Combine the stock, juice, and wine. Place the onion slices, whole garlic cloves, and 1 cup of the wine mixture in the pan with the bird. Roast for 4–5 hours basting frequently using 2 cups of the wine mixture. The turkey is done when a meat thermometer inserted into the thickest part of the thigh registers 170–175 degrees.

Remove the turkey to a heated platter. Add the remaining wine mixture to the roasting pan. Boil rapidly, scraping the brown bits from the bottom of the pan. Strain the liquid and skim off the fat. Boil the remaining liquid until reduced by half. Serve with the turkey.

Turkey and Artichoke Sauté
with Lemon and Rosemary

1 1/2 pounds uncooked turkey
    breast slices, pounded, cut in
    small pieces
1/4 cup flour
1/2 teaspoon salt
1/4 teaspoon white pepper
3 tablespoons olive oil
6 tablespoons unsalted butter
4–6 fresh steamed artichoke
    bottoms, sliced in eighths
    (canned or frozen may be
    substituted)
1/3 cup sliced green onions, with
    3 inches of green
1 garlic clove, minced

1/4 cup fresh lemon juice
1 teaspoon dry mustard
1 teaspoon sugar
1 tablespoon minced fresh
    rosemary *or* 1 teaspoon dried
    rosemary
1 cup Chicken Stock, heated
2 tablespoons freshly grated
    Parmesan cheese
Salt to taste
2 tablespoons minced fresh
    parsley
Sliced green onions and
    Parmesan, for garnish

Wash the turkey pieces and pat dry. Combine the flour, salt, and pepper in a bag. Shake the turkey pieces in the bag a few at a time coating well. Heat the oil and 3 tablespoons of the butter in a 12-inch skillet over moderately high heat. Sauté the turkey in batches 2–3 minutes a side or until springy to the touch. (It is necessary to sauté turkey quickly or it will become tough.) Drain on paper towels.

In the same skillet, sauté the artichokes for 3 minutes. Remove from the skillet and pour off the browning fat. Add the remaining butter to the skillet. Melt over moderately low heat and add the onions and garlic. Sauté until just soft. In a small bowl, whisk together the lemon juice, mustard, sugar, and rosemary. Add along with the heated stock to the onion and garlic. Boil over moderate heat until slightly thickened. Add the Parmesan and stir until it melts. Season to taste with salt. Return the turkey and artichokes to the pan, add the parsley, and heat through.

Top with green onions and Parmesan cheese and serve with buttered rice or thin pasta such as cappellini.

Spicy Grilled Turkey Breast

SERVES 6–8

1 1/2 teaspoons salt
1 1/2 teaspoons dry mustard
1 1/2 teaspoons chili powder
2 1/2 teaspoons tarragon vinegar
5 1/2–6 pounds whole turkey breast, boned
3 tablespoons chopped onions
3 tablespoons oil
2 teaspoons salt
4 teaspoons sugar
1/8 teaspoon dried red pepper flakes

2 teaspoons black pepper
2 teaspoons dry mustard
2 teaspoons chili powder
4 tablespoons tarragon vinegar
1/2 teaspoon Tabasco sauce
2 tablespoons Worcestershire sauce
2 garlic cloves, minced
3 tablespoons butter
1/2 cup water

In a small bowl, combine the salt, 1 1/2 teaspoons mustard, 1 1/2 teaspoons chili powder, and 2 1/2 teaspoons tarragon vinegar, mixing to make a smooth paste. Rub the paste on both sides of the turkey breast. Let stand at room temperature for at least 1 hour, or refrigerate to marinate longer.

Meanwhile, in a 4–6-cup saucepan, sauté the onions in the oil over moderate heat until soft. Add the salt, sugar, red and black peppers, the 2 teaspoons dry mustard, the 2 teaspoons chili powder, the 4 tablespoons vinegar, Tabasco, Worcestershire, garlic, butter, and water. Reduce the heat and simmer slowly for 20 minutes. Set aside.

Prepare the coals for the barbecue. Place the turkey breast, opened flat, on the barbecue. Grill over medium coals, turning frequently and basting generously with the sauce, until a meat thermometer inserted into the thickest part just reaches 160 degrees. This will take from 45 minutes up to 1 hour and 30 minutes depending on the barbecue. Do not overcook or the meat will be dry and tough. Remove to a warm platter, cover loosely with foil, and let rest for 10 minutes before carving.

Roast Duck with Fresh Raspberries

SERVES 6

2 (4–5-pound) ducks, washed and
   dried
Salt and white pepper
2 cups Duck Stock (below)

1/4 cup Framboise or other
   raspberry liqueur
1/2 cup currant jelly
1 cup fresh raspberries

Preheat the oven to 425 degrees. Season the duck cavities with salt and white pepper. Prick the skin around the lower breast, back, and thighs. Truss the ducks and place breast side up on a rack in a shallow roasting pan. Place in the oven for 15 minutes. Reduce the heat to 350 degrees. Roast the ducks 30 minutes on each side. Using a bulb baster, remove some of the accumulated fat as the ducks cook. Turn the ducks breast side up and sprinkle with salt. Continue roasting for another 10–15 minutes for medium rare or until the juices run faintly rosy when the thigh is pierced lightly with a fork. The ducks are well done when the juices run pale yellow.

Remove the trussing and place the ducks on a platter in the oven, which has been turned off, while preparing the sauce. Remove the accumulated fat from the roasting pan. Add 1 cup of the Duck Stock to the drippings and boil rapidly, scraping the brown bits from the bottom of the pan. Strain the enriched stock into the saucepan with the remaining Duck Stock. Add liqueur, jelly, and pepper to taste. Bring to a boil and reduce slightly to thicken. Fold in the raspberries just before serving.

See previous recipe for do-ahead and carving instructions.

DUCK STOCK

Duck giblets including neck and
   scraps (excluding livers)
2 tablespoons unsalted butter
2 carrots, chopped
1 1/2 cups coarsely chopped
   onions
2 garlic cloves, chopped
1 tomato, chopped

1/4 teaspoon black peppercorns
1/2 cup chopped fresh parsley
1 bay leaf
2 tablespoons chopped fresh
   thyme *or* 1 teaspoon dried
   thyme
4 cups canned beef broth

Chop the giblets in small pieces. Heat the butter in a 4-quart saucepan. Sauté the giblets with the carrots and onions over moderate heat until browned. Pour off the browning fat. Add the garlic, tomato, peppercorns, parsley, bay leaf, thyme, beef broth and, if needed, enough water to just cover the giblets. Simmer partially covered for at least 1 1/2 hours.

Strain the stock through a sieve, pressing the vegetables and giblets to extract the juices. Skim off the accumulated fat and return the stock to a saucepan. Boil over high heat until reduced to 2 cups.

Roast Duckling with Black Peppercorn Sauce

SERVES 6

Do not be misled by the length of this recipe. The preparation is quite simple and many steps can be accomplished ahead of time, including roasting the ducks! Shoestring yams are the perfect accompaniment.

1 tablespoon unsalted butter	**2 1/2 cups Duck Stock (below)**
2 shallots, minced	**2 tablespoons arrowroot**
1 vanilla bean, split and scraped	**1/2 cup plus 3 tablespoons**
3 tablespoons unsulfured	** Madeira wine**
** molasses**	**2 (5-pound) ducks**
2 teaspoons freshly crushed	**Salt and pepper**
** black peppercorns**	**2 tablespoons unsalted butter**

In a medium saucepan, melt the butter over moderately low heat. Add the shallots and sauté slowly until soft. Add the vanilla bean, molasses, peppercorns, and Duck Stock. Simmer for 15 minutes. Strain the sauce to remove the shallots. Return the sauce to the pan with the vanilla bean. Blend the arrowroot with 3 tablespoons of the Madeira. Beat the arrowroot mixture into the sauce base and simmer 3–4 minutes or until slightly thickened. Set aside. Can be made ahead to this point.

Preheat the oven to 425 degrees. Season the duck cavities with salt and pepper. Prick the skin around the lower breast, back, and thighs. Truss the ducks and place breast side up on a rack in a shallow roasting pan. Place in the oven for 15 minutes. Reduce the heat to 350 degrees. Roast the ducks 30 minutes on each side. Using a bulb baster, remove some of the accumulated fat as the ducks cook. Turn the ducks breast side up and sprinkle with salt. Continue roasting for another 10–15 minutes for medium rare or until the juices run faintly rosy when the thigh is pierced lightly with a fork. The ducks are well done when the juices run pale yellow. Remove the trussing and place the ducks on a platter and set in the turned-off oven while finishing the sauce. The ducks can be roasted in the morning, and set aside, uncovered, at room temperature. Reheat at 300 degrees for 25 minutes. Place under the broiler for 3–5 minutes for extra-crisp skin.

Remove all but 1 tablespoon of the fat from the roasting pan. Add the 1/2 cup Madeira to the drippings and boil rapidly, scraping the brown bits from the bottom of the pan and reducing the liquid to 3 tablespoons. Strain the wine reduction into the prepared sauce. Simmer for a minute or two and swirl in the 2 tablespoons butter. Remove the vanilla bean before serving. The sauce can be completed earlier in the day and reheated before serving.

To carve the ducks, slice off the thigh with the leg attached. Run a sharp, flexible knife along the breastbone, then down along the carcass, separating the breast from the carcass. Repeat on the other side. Slice the breasts diagonally in ½-inch slices. Carve the meat from the legs and thighs. Arrange on a warm platter. Spoon some of the sauce over the top. Pass the remaining sauce.

DUCK STOCK

Duck giblets including neck and scraps (excluding livers)
3 tablespoons oil or bacon drippings
2 onions, sliced

3 carrots, sliced
5 cups canned beef broth
4 sprigs parsley
1 bay leaf
¼ teaspoon dried thyme

Chop the giblets in small pieces. Heat the oil or fat in a 4-quart saucepan. Sauté the giblets and vegetables over moderate heat until browned. Pour off the browning fat. Add the broth, herbs, and enough water, if needed, to just cover the giblets. Simmer partially covered for at least 1½ hours. Strain the stock through a sieve, pressing the vegetables and giblets to extract the juices. Skim off the accumulated fat and return the stock to a saucepan. Boil over high heat until reduced to 2½ cups. The stock may be prepared the day ahead and refrigerated.

Chinese Roast Duck with Kiwi Sauce

SERVES 3–4

This method of cooking produces a rich mahogany-colored duck that is striking with its Cabbage Chrysanthemum garnish. As part of a Chinese buffet this will serve 6–8.

1 (5-pound) duck
1 teaspoon sugar
1 teaspoon salt
1 teaspoon five spice powder
1 teaspoon oyster sauce
2 tablespoons soy sauce

1 onion, sliced
1 stalk celery, sliced
Kiwi Sauce (below)
Cabbage Chrysanthemum (below)

Place the duck, uncovered, on a rack in a roasting pan in the refrigerator for 2 days to dry out the skin (3 days if duck is frozen). Before roasting, blend together the sugar, salt, five spice powder, oyster sauce, and soy sauce. Rub on the duck skin, coating well.

Preheat the oven to 450 degrees. Fill the duck cavity with the sliced onions and celery. Place breast side up on a rack in a roasting pan. Roast for 25 minutes at 450 degrees. Reduce oven temperature to 350 and continue roasting for about 1 hour and 15 minutes or until the juices run pale yellow when the thigh is pierced lightly with a fork. Place the duck and Kiwi Sauce on a platter using the Cabbage Chrysanthemum as a garnish.

KIWI SAUCE

3 kiwi fruit, peeled and diced
1 tablespoon rice wine vinegar
Juice of half an orange

Grated peel of half an orange
3 tablespoons honey
2–3 dashes Tabasco sauce

Combine all the ingredients in a heavy saucepan. Bring to a boil and simmer for 20 minutes. Serve warm or room temperature. Makes 3/4 cup.

CABBAGE CHRYSANTHEMUM

Take a small, tight head of purple or green cabbage and place it stem down on a cutting board. With a sharp knife, make 8 diagonal cuts through the cabbage, being careful not to cut all the way through to the stem.

Place the cabbage in a large bowl. Pour enough boiling water over the cabbage to cover completely. Let sit for 2–3 minutes to open. Drain and chill. Use the Cabbage Chrysanthemun to garnish the roast duck platter or an hors d'oeuvre tray.

Crisp Cornish Hens Glazed
with Red Pepper and Ginger Butter

SERVES 6

6 small Cornish hens,
   approximately 1 pound each
Red Pepper and Ginger Relish
   (below)
Strained oil from the Red

Pepper and Ginger Relish, for
basting
Red Pepper and Ginger Butter,
   for glazing the hens (below)

Wash and dry the hens. Place on a work surface breast side down. Split the hens with kitchen shears, cutting down one side of backbone and back up along the other side, removing the backbone. Turn the hens breast side up. Press firmly against the breastbone to slightly flatten the hens.

Grill over moderate coals turning frequently and basting with the strained oil. This will take from 25–45 minutes depending on the barbecue. Glaze the hens with the Red Pepper and Ginger Butter the last 15 minutes of grilling. The hens are done when the thickest part of the thigh is pierced with a fork and the juices run clear. The hens can also be placed on a rack and broiled in the oven. Serve with Red Pepper and Ginger Relish on the side.

RED PEPPER AND GINGER RELISH

1/2 cup unsalted butter

1/2 cup olive oil

1/2 cup peeled and minced fresh ginger

3 tablespoons garlic, minced

4 pounds red bell peppers, cut in 1/4-inch strips

Juice of 2 oranges

Grated peel of 2 oranges

3 tablespoons sugar

2 teaspoons black pepper

2 teaspoons salt

In a large covered stockpot, heat the butter and oil over low flame. Add the ginger and garlic and cook slowly for about 5 minutes. Stir in the red peppers, juice, peel, sugar, black pepper, and salt. Simmer covered, for about 25–30 minutes or until the red peppers soften. Uncover and continue simmering over low heat for about 2 hours or until the liquid has evaporated.

Place the relish in a large sieve over a bowl and strain off the oil. Reserve the strained oil for basting the game hens.

Can be made ahead and refrigerated for up to 5 days in advance. Serve warm or at room temperature.

RED PEPPER AND GINGER BUTTER

Place 1 cup of the relish in a food processor. Process until puréed. Use to glaze the hens on the barbecue.

Grilled California Quail with Tomatillo Cream and Cheese Corn Crepes

SERVES 6

This elegant main course combines California native game with subtle flavors of traditional Southwestern cooking.

12 quail

1 cup olive oil

1/2 cup fresh lime juice

1/2 cup minced fresh cilantro

4 garlic cloves, minced

1 teaspoon salt

Tomatillo Cream (below)

Cheese Corn Crepes (below)

Wash and dry the quail. Place on a work surface breast side down. Split the quail with kitchen shears, cutting down one side of the backbone and back up along the other side, removing the backbone. Turn breast side up. Press firmly against the breastbone to slightly flatten the quail.

Combine the oil, lime juice, cilantro, garlic, and salt until well blended. Place the quail in a sealable plastic bag. Pour in the marinade and turn to coat the quail well. Marinate in the refrigerator for at least 2 hours. Longer marinating will enhance the marinade flavor.

Grill over hot coals for 15–20 minutes. Turn and baste frequently with the marinade. Serve with Tomatillo Cream and Cheese Corn Crepes.

TOMATILLO CREAM

4 poblano (pasilla) or 4 fresh long green chiles
3/4 cup dry white wine or vermouth
2 shallots, minced

1 cup heavy cream
1 pound tomatillos, husked
4 tablespoons chilled unsalted butter
Salt

Using a long-handled fork, char the chiles over an open flame, turning them for 2–3 minutes, or until the skins are blackened. Or place the chiles on a broiler pan and broil about 2 inches from the heat until the skins are blackened, turning frequently. This will take approximately 15 minutes. Transfer the chiles to a plastic bag, close tightly, and let them steam until they are cool enough to handle. Wash, peel, and seed. In a medium saucepan, boil the wine and shallots over moderately high flame until the wine is reduced by half. Add the cream, reduce the heat, and simmer until the cream has thickened slightly.

Place the tomatillos and chiles in a food processor and purée. Add to the cream mixture, increase the heat to medium high, and simmer until thickened slightly, about 5–8 minutes.

Strain the sauce through a sieve, discarding the tomatillo mixture. Return the cream sauce to the pan and whisk in the butter, 1 tablespoon at a time, over low heat. Season with the salt. Keep warm in a tepid water bath.

CORN CREPES   MAKES 16

1/2 cup yellow cornmeal
1/2 cup flour
1/2 cup milk
1/2 cup water
3 eggs
2 tablespoons unsalted butter, melted

1/2 teaspoon salt
3 tablespoons minced fresh cilantro
Vegetable oil for cooking crepes

In a blender or food processor, blend together the cornmeal, flour, milk, water, eggs, butter, and salt until well combined. Transfer the batter to a bowl and stir in the cilantro. Cover with plastic wrap and refrigerate for at least 1 hour.

Heat a 5-inch crepe pan or nonstick skillet over moderate heat. When hot, brush with the vegetable oil. Pour a scant 1/4 cup of the batter into the pan and tilt to coat the bottom. Cook the crepe until the underside is browned lightly, turn with a spatula, and slightly brown the other side. Remove to a plate or plastic wrap. Continue making the remaining crepes in the same manner, brushing the pan lightly with the oil as needed. Stack the crepes; wrap them in the plastic when cool. Refrigerate for up to 3 days or freeze for up to 3 months.

CHEESE FILLING FOR CREPES

12 corn crepes

1 1/2 cups shredded Jack cheese

1 1/2 serrano chiles, seeded and minced

2 green onions, thinly sliced with 3 inches of green

1 tomato, seeded, diced, and sprinkled with salt

Melted unsalted butter for brushing the crepes

Preheat the oven to 400 degrees. On each crepe, sprinkle 2 tablespoons of the cheese, some chiles, onions, and tomatoes. Fold the crepes in half and then in quarters. Place on a cookie sheet and brush with the melted butter. Bake for 10–15 minutes. Makes 12 crepes.

Game Pie

SERVES 10–12

For a more authentic version of this traditional country favorite, rabbit and venison can be substituted for the chicken and beef.

2 1/2 pounds top sirloin (or top round), cubed

3 tablespoons vegetable oil

2 cups port wine

1 1/2 cups Brown Sauce (below)

1 1/2 tablespoons Worcestershire sauce

1/2 teaspoon pepper

3/4–1 cup currant jelly

3 tablespoons butter

1 large garlic clove, minced

1 1/2 pounds mushrooms, quartered

1/2 pound pearl onions, parboiled, glazed in butter, and sprinkled with 1 teaspoon sugar

1 (4–5-pound) duck, roasted, cooled, and shredded

2 pounds chicken thighs, roasted, cooled, and shredded

1 recipe Pastry Dough (below)

1 egg white, lightly beaten

In a large kettle, sauté the beef in the oil in small batches until very brown. Set the beef aside and drain the oil. Add the port to the pan and bring to a boil. Add the Brown Sauce and meat and simmer slowly for 1 hour until the meat is very tender. Add the Worcestershire sauce, pepper, and jelly. In a skillet melt the butter and sauté the garlic and mushrooms over moderate heat for 2–3 minutes. Gently combine the mushroom mixture, glazed onions, duck, and chicken with the beef. Pour into a lightly oiled large baking dish, approximately 9 × 13 × 3 inches.

Preheat the oven to 350 degrees. Roll the pastry dough out to a size slightly larger than the top of the baking dish. Place the pastry on top of the dish and press the edges to seal. Trim and flute if desired. Make several slits in the pastry and brush with the egg white. Bake for 30–35 minutes or until the pastry is golden.

BROWN SAUCE

1/3 cup butter

1 cup flour

6 tablespoons tomato paste

2 beef bouillon cubes

2 quarts Beef Stock

In a 3–4-quart saucepan, melt the butter. Add the flour, and cook, stirring constantly, over medium heat for about 10–12 minutes or until the color reaches a rich caramel brown. Add the tomato paste, bouillon cubes, and stock. Simmer, uncovered, for 2 hours or until reduced to 1 quart.

PASTRY DOUGH

2 1/2 cups flour

1/2 teaspoon salt

3/4 cup butter, cut in small
    chunks and frozen

1/4 cup vegetable shortening, cut
    in small chunks and frozen

1/4 cup ice water

In a food processor, process flour, salt, butter, and shortening until crumbly. Add ice water and process just until a ball forms. Pat into a 6-inch circle. Wrap in plastic and chill for 1 hour.

Note   The preparation can be done the day before serving. The duck and chicken can be roasted, the Brown Sauce prepared, and the beef and sauce cooked.

Grilled Squab with Sweet Pungent Sauce

SERVES 4

When squab are unavailable, Cornish game hens are an excellent alternative.

2 cups red wine
1 large garlic clove, crushed
1 teaspoon black peppercorns
1/4 cup currant jelly

1 teaspoon dry mustard
4 squab, cleaned and split (about
  1 pound each)
Salt and pepper

In a small saucepan, combine all ingredients except the squab, salt, and pepper. Heat until the currant jelly has melted. Let cool. With a heavy knife, flatten the squab. Season with salt and pepper on both sides. Place squab in a large baking dish and pour on the marinade. Marinate for 1 hour at room temperature or 4–6 hours, refrigerated.

Grill the squab over medium hot coals, skin side up for 10 minutes, basting frequently with the marinade. Turn the skin side down and cook for 10 minutes more, continuing to baste. Squab will be medium rare. Cook longer if desired.

SWEET PUNGENT SAUCE
1/2 cup currant jelly
3 tablespoons raspberry vinegar

1 tablespoon Dijon mustard
1 tablespoon heavy cream

In a small saucepan, melt the jelly with the vinegar over low heat. Add the mustard and cream and simmer for 5 minutes, stirring occasionally. Serve with the grilled squab.

Grilled Lemon Rabbit with Tarragon and Mustard

SERVES 2–3

2 garlic cloves
2 tablespoons minced fresh
  tarragon *or* 2 teaspoons dried
  tarragon
Zest of 1 lemon
1/2 cup fresh lemon juice
2 teaspoons Dijon mustard

1/2 teaspoon salt
2 teaspoons freshly ground
  pepper
1/2 cup olive oil
1 domestic rabbit, cut in 8
  serving pieces

Place the garlic, tarragon, and lemon zest in a blender or food processor. Process until minced. Add the lemon juice, mustard, salt, pepper, and olive oil. Blend until well combined. Place the rabbit pieces in a sealable plastic bag. Pour in the marinade. Turn to coat. Marinate in the refrigerator for at least 4 and up to 24 hours.

Grill over medium coals, turning and basting frequently with the marinade. The rabbit is done when the thickest part of the leg is pierced with a fork and the juices run clear.

Rabbit with Sweet Sausages, Orange, and Tomato

SERVES 4

This is equally good made with chicken.

1 pound Italian sweet sausages
1 domestic rabbit, cut in 8
  serving pieces
3 garlic cloves, minced
1 medium onion, chopped
2 red bell peppers, thinly sliced
1 (16-ounce) can plum tomatoes,
  undrained
1/2 teaspoon dried red pepper
  flakes

2 tablespoons tomato paste
1/4 cup dry white wine
1 tablespoon minced fresh basil
  or 1 teaspoon dried basil
1 tablespoon minced fresh
  oregano or 1 teaspoon dried
  oregano
Juice of half an orange
Zest of 1 orange
1/2 teaspoon salt

Pierce the sausages to release fat. Simmer in a large covered dry skillet over moderate heat for 10 minutes. Remove the lid and sauté sausages until well browned. Remove the sausages to cool and slice in 1-inch pieces.

In the browning fat from the sausages, sauté the rabbit until golden. Set aside. Pour off all but 1 tablespoon of the fat. Add the garlic, onions, and peppers to the skillet. Sauté over a moderately low flame until the vegetables are tender.

Return the sausage slices to the skillet and add the tomatoes, dried pepper, tomato paste, wine, basil, oregano, orange juice, zest, and salt. Simmer for 10 minutes to blend the flavors.

Return the rabbit to the sauce and simmer, covered, for 20–30 minutes. The rabbit is done when the thickest part of the leg is pierced with a fork and the juices run clear. Serve with buttered pasta or rice.

VIII

Meat

Grilled Beef Tenderloin

SERVES 4–6

1 (3–4-pound) beef tenderloin

MARINADE
1/4 cup olive oil
3/4 cup dry white vermouth or
   dry white wine
1/3 cup Cognac
2 large garlic cloves, minced
2 tablespoons minced shallots
1 teaspoon salt (optional)

2 teaspoons chopped fresh thyme
   or 3/4 teaspoon dried thyme
2 teaspoons fresh rosemary *or*
   3/4 teaspoon dried rosemary
1 bay leaf
1/4 teaspoon cracked black
   pepper, or more, to taste

Place the meat in a shallow dish. Mix the marinade ingredients together in a small bowl. Pour the marinade over the meat, cover, and refrigerate for 24 hours or marinate at room temperature for 4 hours. Turn the meat several times while marinating. Bring the meat to room temperature before cooking.

To barbecue: Sear the meat quickly over glowing coals. Grill, turning frequently, for about 40–55 minutes. The meat will be very rare at 125 degrees on a meat thermometer, and medium rare at 135 degrees. Remove meat to a carving board and let stand for 10 minutes before slicing.

To roast: Preheat the oven to 350 degrees. Place the meat on a rack in a roasting pan and bake in the oven for 40–55 minutes. The meat will register 125 degrees on a meat thermometer for very rare, and 135 degrees for medium rare. Remove to a carving board and let stand for 10 minutes before slicing.

Serve at room temperature with Peach Chutney as an accompaniment.

Beef Tenderloin with Mustard Peppercorn Sauce

SERVES 4–6

1/2 teaspoon salt
1/2 teaspoon cinnamon
1/2 teaspoon ground cumin
2 tablespoons green peppercorns,
   rinsed and drained

1 (3–4-pound) beef tenderloin
1–2 tablespoons oil
Mustard Peppercorn Sauce
   (below)

Preheat the oven to 350 degrees. Mix together the salt, cinnamon, cumin, and peppercorns and spread evenly over both sides of the tenderloin. In a large skillet, heat the oil over medium-high heat. Sear the meat on both sides and then transfer to a rack in a roasting pan. Roast in the oven for 40–55 minutes for rare. The meat will be very rare at 125 degrees on a meat thermometer and medium rare at 135 degrees. Let the meat stand for 10 minutes before carving. Serve with the Mustard Peppercorn Sauce.

MUSTARD PEPPERCORN SAUCE

1 tablespoon sugar
2 tablespoons tarragon vinegar
   (or white wine vinegar)
1/4 cup Dijon mustard
1/2 teaspoon salt

2 egg yolks
2 tablespoons green peppercorns,
   rinsed and drained
1 tablespoon unsalted butter
1/2 cup heavy cream

In the top of a double boiler, combine the sugar, vinegar, mustard, salt, egg yolks, and peppercorns. Whisk over hot water until thickened, about 5 minutes. Remove from the heat and stir in the butter. Set aside. Whip the cream until stiff and gently fold into the mustard base. Cover and refrigerate until serving time. The sauce may be made up to 1 week in advance.

Broiled Flank Steak with Goat Cheese Topping

SERVES 4

This is equally delicious served cold.

1 (2-pound) flank steak
2 tablespoons olive oil
1/2 teaspoon dried rosemary

1/2 teaspoon salt
Topping (below)

Rub each side of the flank steak with the olive oil, rosemary, and salt. Place in a flat dish, cover, and let stand at room temperature for 1–2 hours.

Preheat the broiler. Place the meat on a broiler pan rack. Broil 4 inches from the heat for 3 minutes. Turn the steak over and broil for 1 more minute. Spread the meat with the goat-cheese topping. Broil for an additional 2 minutes or until topping is bubbly. Place on a carving board and slice on the diagonal.

TOPPING

4 ounces Montrachet-type goat cheese (feta may be substituted)

2 tablespoons minced fresh parsley

1 small garlic clove, minced

1/4 teaspoon freshly ground black pepper

4 tablespoons heavy cream

2 teaspoons sherry wine vinegar

In a small bowl, mix the ingredients together and set aside.

Cajun Meat Loaf

SERVES 6

2 pounds lean ground beef

1 cup fresh bread crumbs

1 green bell pepper, chopped

1/2 cup minced green onions, white part only

4 medium garlic cloves, minced

2 1/4 teaspoons ground cumin

2 1/2 teaspoons dried oregano

1 1/2 teaspoons dried thyme

1 1/2 teaspoons paprika

1–2 teaspoons cayenne pepper

1/4 teaspoon ground white pepper

1/4 teaspoon cracked black pepper

1/4 teaspoon dried red pepper flakes (optional)

1 1/2 teaspoons salt

1/2 cup tomato sauce

2 large eggs, lightly beaten

Sour cream and chopped tomatoes, for garnish

Preheat the oven to 350 degrees. In a large bowl, combine the meat, bread crumbs, bell pepper, onions, and garlic. In a small bowl, mix together the cumin, oregano, thyme, paprika, peppers, and salt. Add to the meat mixture. Add the tomato sauce and eggs, mix well, and pat into a loaf pan 5 × 9 × 3 inches, smoothing the top. Bake in the oven for 45–55 minutes. Remove from the oven and let stand 10 minutes before slicing. Garnish with sour cream and chopped tomatoes if desired.

Corned Beef with Apricot Mustard Glaze

SERVES 6

This wonderful glaze puts a traditional favorite in fancy dress. For a truly special presentation substitute baby vegetables for the regular ones.

1 (3–4-pound) end cut corned
  beef
Water
2 tablespoons pickling spice
1 onion
4 large garlic cloves
1/2 cup apricot jam
1/3 cup coarse-grained mustard
  or Dijon mustard

4 large new potatoes, unpeeled,
  cut in half
2 medium rutabagas, peeled and
  cut in quarters
4 carrots, peeled and cut in half
1 medium head green cabbage,
  cut in wedges

Place the corned beef in a large pot and cover it with water. Bring to a boil and then drain. Refill the pan with water to cover and add the pickling spice, onion, and garlic. Again, bring water to a boil, reduce heat, and simmer, partially covered, for 3 hours or until meat is tender. Remove the meat from the broth, reserving liquid, and place in a large baking dish.

Preheat the oven to 325 degrees. Combine jam and mustard in a small saucepan. Stir over medium-low heat until well blended and jam has melted. Spread over the meat and bake in the oven for about 20 minutes or until glazed. Meanwhile, cook the potatoes in the broth for 10 minutes. Add the rutabagas and cook for 10 minutes more. Add the carrots and cook for 10 minutes. When ready to serve add the cabbage and cook until tender, about 10 minutes. Slice the meat and serve with the vegetables and the glaze.

Flank Steak with Red Onions

SERVES 4

1 flank steak, about 2 pounds
1 large red onion, thinly sliced

MARINADE
2/3 cup fresh lemon juice
1/3 cup oil
2 teaspoons salt
1 teaspoon lemon peel
1 teaspoon cracked black pepper

1/2 teaspoon dried oregano
1 teaspoon Worcestershire sauce
2 tablespoons sugar
1 tablespoon unsalted butter

Score the steak on both sides in a diamond pattern 1/8 inch deep. Layer half the onions on the bottom of a shallow glass baking dish. Place the steak on top of the onions and cover with the remaining onions. Combine marinade ingredients together in a small bowl. Pour the marinade over the meat, cover, and marinate 2–3 hours at room temperature or refrigerate overnight. Turn the meat occasionally. When ready to cook, bring the meat to room temperature. Remove the meat from the marinade and pat dry with paper towels. Drain the onions and reserve. Broil the meat 3–5 minutes on each side for rare. While meat is cooking, sauté the onions in butter until soft. Slice the steak and top with the onions.

Beef Fillets with Roquefort Sauce

SERVES 4

A special winter dinner for four good friends.

4 beef fillets, 1 inch thick
Salt
Black pepper
1 medium garlic clove, minced
3 tablespoons unsalted butter
1/2 pound mushrooms, sliced
1 tablespoon vegetable oil

1/2 cup dry sherry
2/3 cup heavy cream
1/2 cup Roquefort cheese
Pinch of cayenne pepper
  (optional)
3 tablespoons minced fresh
  parsley

Season the fillets with salt and pepper. Rub the garlic into both sides of each fillet. Melt 2 tablespoons of the butter in a heavy skillet and sauté the mushrooms in it until tender. Remove the mushrooms and set aside. Pour off any accumulated liquid in the pan. Heat the oil and the remaining tablespoon of butter over medium-high heat. Cook the fillets 2–3 minutes on each side for rare. Remove the fillets from the pan and keep them warm. Again, pour off any liquid in pan. Deglaze the pan with sherry and then add the cream. Reduce sauce until it thickens slightly. Stir in the Roquefort cheese. Add the mushrooms and heat. Adjust seasonings to taste, adding cayenne pepper if desired. Spoon the sauce over fillets and garnish with parsley.

Oriental Steak with Wasabi Butter

SERVES 4

I (I 1/2 –2-pound) tri-tip roast

MARINADE

2 tablespoons soy sauce

I tablespoon honey

I tablespoon rice-wine vinegar

I teaspoon ground ginger

I large garlic clove, minced

2 green onions, minced

I tablespoon dry sherry

1/3 cup vegetable oil

Wasabi Butter (below)

Place the meat in a shallow rectangular dish. Combine the marinade ingredients in a small bowl and whisk to mix thoroughly. Pour over the meat and marinate at room temperature for several hours, turning occasionally. Remove the meat from marinade and pat dry.

To broil the meat: Broil 4 inches from flame for 5–7 minutes on each side for rare.

To barbecue the meat: Grill over medium hot coals 5–7 minutes on each side for rare.

Serve slices of meat topped with Wasabi Butter.

WASABI BUTTER

1/4 cup unsalted butter, softened

2 tablespoons wasabi powder, or to taste

2 tablespoons minced fresh parsley

Mix together the butter and wasabi powder. Stir in the minced parsley. Transfer the mixture to a piece of waxed paper. Roll the paper around the butter to form a cylinder. Chill the butter for at least I hour. May be made several days ahead. To serve, slice in rounds.

Fajitas

Citrus juices and tequila enhance this version of a favorite at Mexican restaurants across California.

1 1/2 **pounds skirt or flank steak**
Marinade (below)
12 **flour tortillas**

Pico de Gallo (below)
2 **cups grated Monterey Jack or**
    Cheddar cheese

MARINADE
1/2 **cup fresh orange juice**
3/4 **cup fresh lime juice**
1/4 **cup tequila**
3 **green onions, minced**
1 **teaspoon salt**

1 **teaspoon Worcestershire sauce**
4 **medium garlic cloves, minced**
1/4 **cup oil**
3/4 **teaspoon paprika**
1/2 **teaspoon black pepper**

Place the meat in a large shallow glass dish. Combine the marinade ingredients in a medium-size bowl. Pour the marinade over the meat and marinate, covered, for 24 hours, turning occasionally. Bring the meat to room temperature before cooking. Grill the meat over hot coals for 2–3 minutes on each side for the skirt steak, or 3–4 minutes on each side for the flank steak, basting frequently with the marinade. Remove the meat to a carving board and let stand for 5 minutes before slicing. Slice the meat thinly across the grain. Place the meat in warmed flour tortillas; topped with Pico de Gallo and cheese. Roll or fold as for a soft taco.

PICO DE GALLO
1 **cup chopped green onions**
2–3 **fresh jalapeño chiles, seeded**
    and finely chopped
4 **large tomatoes, seeded and**
    chopped
1/4 **cup lemon juice**

1 **teaspoon freshly ground black**
    pepper
3 **tablespoons chopped fresh**
    cilantro
Salt to taste
2 **avocados**

In a medium-size bowl combine all ingredients except the avocados. Cover the bowl and refrigerate for at least 6 hours. One hour before serving, peel and chop the avocado and add to chile-tomato mixture.

Pasadena Pot Roast

SERVES 8–10

5 tablespoons oil
1 (6–7-pound) chuck or rump
   roast
1 large onion, minced
2 large carrots, peeled and
   minced
1 celery stalk, minced
2 cups red wine
2 cups Beef Stock

1 cup chopped tomatoes
1/2 teaspoon black peppercorns
2 teaspoons salt
1/2 teaspoon whole cloves
1/2 teaspoon dried tarragon
1/2 teaspoon dried thyme
2 cinnamon sticks
2 bay leaves
2 large garlic cloves, minced

In a large skillet, over moderately high heat, heat 2 tablespoons of the oil. Brown the meat on all sides and set aside. Heat the remaining oil in a large Dutch oven over moderate heat. Sauté the onions, carrots, and celery in the oil until tender. Add the meat, wine, stock, and tomatoes. Stir in the seasonings and garlic. Bring to a simmer, cover, and cook for 3–3 1/2 hours or until the meat is tender, turning the meat several times. Remove the meat to a platter. Remove the cinnamon sticks and bay leaf before serving. If desired, strain the sauce, return to pan and reduce to desired consistency. Serve the meat sliced with the sauce.

Mexican Country Steaks

SERVES 4

1 (2-pound) tenderized round or
   sirloin steak, cut in serving
   pieces
1 large garlic clove, minced
Salt
Freshly ground black pepper
4 tablespoons oil
1 large onion, thinly sliced
4 large tomatoes, chopped, or 1
   (28-ounce) can whole, peeled
   tomatoes, drained and
   coarsely chopped

3/4 teaspoon dried oregano
1/4 teaspoon salt
1/4 teaspoon pepper
1/4 teaspoon ground cumin
10 whole sprigs fresh cilantro
1 pound medium new potatoes,
   peeled and sliced 1/2 inch
   thick
1 (7-ounce) can whole green
   chiles, drained and rinsed
Flour tortillas

Season the steak with garlic, salt, and pepper. Set the meat aside, covered, in a shallow dish for 1 hour, at room temperature. Heat 2 tablespoons of the oil in a large, heavy skillet. Brown the meat on both sides over medium-high heat and place in a large baking dish. Heat the remaining oil and sauté the onions until soft. Add the tomatoes, oregano, 1/4 teaspoon of salt, 1/4 teaspoon of pepper, cumin, and cilantro. Cook quickly over high heat for 5 minutes, stirring constantly to prevent sticking. Remove sauce from heat.

Preheat the oven to 350 degrees. Place the potato slices on top of the meat. Pour the sauce over meat and potatoes. Remove the seeds from chiles. Cut chiles in thin strips and place on top of potatoes. Cover the dish and bake in the oven for 35 minutes. Remove the cover and cook for 55 minutes or until meat is tender and potatoes are done. Serve with warmed flour tortillas.

Beef Brisket with White Beans

SERVES 6

8 ounces dried small white beans	4 plum tomatoes, seeded and chopped
8 slices thick bacon, cut in 2-inch pieces	1 (6-ounce) can tomato paste
1 tablespoon oil	1 teaspoon dried rosemary
1 tablespoon butter	1 teaspoon dried thyme
1 medium onion, chopped	1 teaspoon dry mustard
2 large leeks (tender green and white part), chopped	1 bay leaf
2 medium garlic cloves, minced	2 tablespoons brown sugar
4 carrots, peeled and sliced	3 tablespoons vinegar
1/4 cup chopped fresh parsley	1 teaspoon salt
2 1/2–3 pounds beef brisket	1/2 teaspoon cracked pepper
1 quart water	Chopped fresh parsley, for garnish

Place the beans in a bowl and add water to cover. Soak for 30 minutes. Meanwhile, fry the bacon in a heavy-bottomed skillet over medium-low heat until almost crisp. Remove the bacon from the pan and drain on paper towels. Set aside. In a large skillet, heat the oil and butter over medium heat. Add onions, leeks, garlic, carrots, and parsley. Cook, stirring often, for 10–12 minutes. Place the meat in a 6-quart kettle. Spoon the vegetables and bacon around the meat. Add 1 quart of water, the tomatoes, tomato paste, rosemary, thyme, mustard, bay leaf, brown sugar, vinegar, salt and pepper. Rinse and drain the beans. Add to the kettle. Bring the stew to a boil, reduce heat, and simmer, covered, for about 3 1/2–4 hours or until meat and beans are very tender. (May be prepared ahead to this point. If so, cool, cover, and chill. Remove any fat before proceeding with recipe.) Remove the meat and cut in chunks. Skim any fat from stew.

Remove 3/4 cup of the beans and a little bit of sauce, purée, and return to kettle. Add the meat and stir. Season to taste with salt and pepper. Serve in large soup bowls garnished with chopped parsley.

For a different presentation, serve in hollowed small bread rounds that have been brushed on the inside with rosemary butter.

Autumn Beef in a Pumpkin

SERVES 6–8

BEEF

3 tablespoons oil

2 1/2 pounds beef stew meat, cut in 1 1/2-inch cubes

1 large onion, chopped

2 large garlic cloves, minced

2 large tomatoes, seeded and chopped

2 large red bell peppers, seeded and chopped

1 teaspoon salt

1/2 teaspoon black pepper

1 teaspoon sugar

1 teaspoon cinnamon

1 cup dried apricots

1 cup raisins

2 medium sweet potatoes, peeled and diced

2 cups Beef Stock

1/4 cup dry sherry

1 cup corn kernels, fresh or frozen

Minced fresh parsley, for garnish

Heat 2 tablespoons of the oil over medium-high heat in a 4-quart flameproof casserole. Brown the meat in batches, transferring to a bowl when brown. Add the remaining tablespoon of oil to the pan and sauté the onions and garlic until translucent. Return the meat to the pan and add remaining ingredients except for the sherry, corn, and parsley. Bring the stew to a boil, cover, and simmer over low heat for 1 1/2 hours or until the meat is tender. (Stew may be prepared to this point and frozen. Thaw and continue beginning with pumpkin preparation.)

PUMPKIN

1 large pumpkin

2–3 tablespoons melted butter

While the stew is simmering, prepare the pumpkin. Cut the top of the pumpkin off and remove the seeds and stringy membrane. Brush the inside of the pumpkin with melted butter and set aside.

When the meat is tender, preheat the over to 325 degrees. Stir the sherry and corn into the stew. Carefully pour the stew into the pumpkin shell and place in a shallow baking pan. Bake, uncovered, for 1 hour or until the pumpkin is tender. Remove from the oven and garnish with the parsley. Serve the stew from the pumpkin, scooping out some of the pumpkin with each serving.

Spicy Marinated Chopped Steak

SERVES 6

An excellent steak marinade. Marinate the meat overnight, if possible, and grill according to your preference.

2 pounds lean ground beef	2 teaspoons salt
4 tablespoons olive oil	1 tablespoon dried oregano
Juice of 2 lemons	1 teaspoon dried thyme
2 tablespoons chili powder	1 tablespoon paprika
1 large onion, sliced	1/4 cup brown sugar
2 large garlic cloves, minced	2 tablespoons unsalted butter

Shape the ground beef in 6 patties. Place the patties in a medium-size rectangular glass dish. In a small bowl combine the remaining ingredients, except the butter, and stir to mix well. Pour the marinade over the meat, cover, and refrigerate for 4 hours.

To broil: Preheat the broiler. Remove meat from marinade, reserving onions. Place the meat on a lightly oiled broiler pan and broil 4–5 inches from the flame for 5 minutes on each side for medium rare.

To barbecue: Grill over glowing coals 5 minutes on each side for medium rare.

While the meat is cooking, heat the butter in a small frying pan over moderate heat and lightly sauté the reserved onions from the marinade. To serve, top the meat with the sautéed onions.

People's Choice Chili

SERVES 15–20

1/4 cup olive oil
3 large onions, chopped
2 red bell peppers, coarsely
  chopped
1 green bell pepper, coarsely
  chopped
2 pounds sweet Italian sausage,
  removed from casings and
  crumbled
4 pounds ground beef, crumbled
5 teaspoons minced garlic
1 (12-ounce) can tomato paste
1 tablespoon freshly ground
  black pepper
4 tablespoons ground cumin

7 tablespoons chili powder
2 teaspoons salt
2 tablespoons dried oregano
2 tablespoons dried basil
3 (28-ounce) cans Italian plum
  tomatoes, drained
2 tablespoons fresh lemon juice
1 1/2 cups beer
1 tablespoon ground coriander
1/3 cup chopped fresh cilantro
1/4 cup chopped fresh parsley
3 (16-ounce) cans red kidney
  beans, drained
2 (6-ounce) cans pitted medium
  black olives, drained

In a large kettle, heat the oil over low heat. Sauté the onions and peppers in oil for about 10 minutes or until tender. Add the sausage and beef and brown over moderate heat. Drain any excess fat from pan. Add the garlic, tomato paste, black pepper, cumin, chili powder, salt, oregano, and basil. Stir in the tomatoes, lemon juice, beer, coriander, cilantro, parsley, and beans. Simmer, uncovered, over low heat for 20–30 minutes. Add the olives and continue cooking for an additional 5 minutes. Taste and adjust seasonings if necessary.

Shanghai Beef

SERVES 4

1/4 cup dry sherry
2 teaspoons soy sauce
2 teaspoons cornstarch
1 1/2 pounds flank steak, thinly
  sliced on the diagonal in
  1/4 × 2-inch pieces
1 cup oil
1 tablespoon peeled and minced
  fresh ginger

1/3 cup plum sauce
1 tablespoon hoisin sauce
2 large garlic cloves, minced
Peel of 2 oranges, julienned and
  dried in 325-degree oven for 5
  minutes
1/4–1 teaspoon dried red pepper
  flakes
1 teaspoon sesame seeds

Combine the sherry, soy sauce, and cornstarch. Add the flank steak, stir to coat, and marinate 1 hour. In a large skillet or wok, heat the oil. Quickly sauté the beef in small batches so that it does not steam. Using a slotted spoon, remove to a warm plate. Drain all but 1 tablespoon of the oil. Add ginger and stir-fry 1 minute. Stir in the plum sauce, hoisin sauce, garlic, orange peel, red pepper flakes, and sesame seeds. Mix well. Add the meat, stirring, until hot and glazed, about 2 minutes.

Beef and Peppers in Spicy Garlic Sauce

SERVES 4

1 small flank steak, about 1 1/4 pounds
5 tablespoons soy sauce
2 tablespoons dry sherry
5 teaspoons cornstarch
2 tablespoons water
1 tablespoon red wine vinegar
4 tablespoons sugar
4 tablespoons peanut oil
2 medium green peppers, cut in thin strips

2 medium red peppers, cut in thin strips
1/4 pound mushrooms, sliced
1/4 pound snow peas
1 tablespoon minced garlic
1 tablespoon peeled and minced fresh ginger
1/2 teaspoon dried red pepper flakes, or to taste

Cut the beef across the grain in thin slices. Combine 2 tablespoons of the soy sauce, 1 tablespoon of the sherry, and 2 teaspoons of the cornstarch in a medium-size bowl. Add the beef slices. Mix to coat well. Combine the remaining soy sauce, sherry, the water, vinegar, sugar, and the remaining cornstarch in a small cup. Set aside. Heat 1 tablespoon of the oil in a large skillet or wok until hot over medium-high heat; add the pepper strips, mushrooms, and snow peas. Stir-fry 1–2 minutes. Cover and cook 1 more minute. Remove and set aside. Add 1 more tablespoon of the oil, the garlic, ginger, and red pepper flakes. Stir 1 minute and add the remaining oil. Add the meat and stir until brown. Drain off the excess oil and add the sauce and vegetables to pan. Cook 2 minutes. Serve immediately.

Calf's Liver with Sautéed Apples and Onions

SERVES 4

7 tablespoons butter
2 Golden Delicious apples,
  peeled and cored
1 1/2 cups sliced onions
Flour
1 pound calf's or veal liver

Salt and black pepper
1/4 cup raspberry vinegar
2 tablespoons chopped fresh
  parsley
Additional raspberry vinegar

Melt 3 tablespoons of the butter in a heavy sauté pan. Cut the apples in sixths or eighths and add to the pan. Sauté 2 1/2 minutes on each side, remove, and keep warm.

Add 2 more tablespoons of the butter to the pan and add the sliced onions. Sauté until just starting to brown. Meanwhile, lightly flour the liver and season with salt and pepper. Add more butter to the onions, if necessary. Push the onions aside, add the liver, and sauté for 2 minutes on the first side. Turn the liver and add 1/4 cup raspberry vinegar, the parsley, and the apples. Taste and add 1–2 tablespoons more vinegar if desired. Sauté for 2–3 minutes more.

Glazed Barbecued Lamb

SERVES 6–8

2/3 cup apple jelly
2/3 cup tarragon vinegar
2/3 cup packed brown sugar
2 tablespoons fresh lemon juice
1 teaspoon dried tarragon

1/2 teaspoon salt
1 (6–7-pound) leg of lamb,
  butterflied
2 large garlic cloves, cut in 8
  pieces

Combine the jelly, vinegar, sugar, lemon juice, tarragon, and salt in a small saucepan. Stir over low heat until the jelly is melted. Increase heat to medium and bring just to a boil. Remove from heat and let cool to room temperature.

Score the lamb in crisscrosses at 1-inch intervals. Make 8 small slits at various points in the meat and insert a piece of garlic into each slit. Place the meat in a large shallow baking pan and pour the glaze over it. Turn to coat meat completely. Allow the meat to stand for 2–3 hours at room temperature, turning several times. Remove meat from glaze, reserving liquid. Barbecue the meat over glowing coals for 35–45 minutes or until done. Turn the lamb frequently to prevent burning while cooking. Remove the meat to a platter and let stand for 5 minutes before carving. Heat reserved glaze and serve with lamb.

Rosemary Lamb with Sweet Pepper Relish

SERVES 6–8

1 (6–7-pound) leg of lamb, butterflied
4 tablespoons olive oil
2 teaspoons soy sauce
Grated peel of 1 lemon
2 tablespoons bruised fresh rosemary *or* 2 teaspoons dried rosemary

2 medium garlic cloves, minced
1/2 cup dry red wine
1/4 cup chopped green onion
Sweet Pepper Relish (below)

Place the lamb in a shallow rectangular dish. In a small bowl, combine remaining ingredients, except relish, and pour over the meat. Cover, and refrigerate for 12–24 hours, turning occasionally. Bring to room temperature before cooking.

Barbecue over medium-hot coals 35–45 minutes for medium rare, or longer if desired. Turn several times while cooking. Remove the meat to a carving board and let stand for 5 minutes before slicing. Slice on the diagonal and serve with Sweet Pepper Relish.

SWEET PEPPER RELISH

1/4 cup olive oil
3 red bell peppers, chopped coarsely
3 yellow bell peppers, chopped coarsely
10 large garlic cloves, peeled and cut in half lengthwise
1/4 cup lemon juice

4 teaspoons sugar
3–4 tablespoons bruised fresh rosemary
Dried red pepper flakes, to taste
4 tablespoons finely chopped sun-dried tomatoes
Salt

Heat the oil in a large saucepan. Sauté the peppers and garlic in oil over moderate heat for 15 minutes. Do not brown. Add lemon juice, sugar, rosemary, red pepper flakes and continue cooking for 15 minutes, stirring frequently. Stir in the tomatoes and cook for an additional 10 minutes. Season to taste with salt. Serve at room temperature. May be made in advance.

Leg of Lamb with Pistachio Nut Stuffing

SERVES 8

This impressive roast is surprisingly easy to prepare.

1 (6–7-pound) leg of lamb, boned
Pistachio Nut Stuffing (below)
Salt and black pepper
2 medium garlic cloves, minced

1 1/2 teaspoons dried rosemary
Sherry Glaze (below)
Cumberland Sauce (below)
  (optional)

Preheat the oven to 350 degrees. Roll and tie the lamb, leaving an opening at each end for stuffing. Stuff the lamb with the Pistachio Nut Stuffing. Pack tightly. Place the lamb on rack in a roasting pan. Season with salt and pepper. Make a paste with the garlic and rosemary and rub into the lamb. Bake in the oven for 1–1 1/2 hours (until a meat thermometer registers 135 degrees for medium rare). Roast longer, if desired. Baste frequently with the warm Sherry Glaze. Remove the meat and let stand for 10 minutes before carving. Serve with Cumberland Sauce, if desired.

PISTACHIO NUT STUFFING

2/3 cup golden raisins
1/2 cup dry sherry
1 cup shelled pistachio nuts
4 medium garlic cloves, chopped

1/2 cup chopped fresh flat-leaf
  parsley
2/3 cup fresh bread crumbs
1 large egg, beaten

Plump the raisins in the sherry for 30 minutes. Drain, reserving both raisins and sherry. Coarsely chop 3/4 cup of the pistachio nuts and add the raisins, garlic, parsley, and bread crumbs. Add just enough egg to bind. Stir in the remaining nuts.

SHERRY GLAZE

Sherry reserved from stuffing
  preparation
1/4 cup butter

1 teaspoon dried rosemary
1/4 cup apple jelly

Combine ingredients in a small saucepan. Heat, stirring frequently, until jelly melts.

CUMBERLAND SAUCE

1 large orange
1 cup port
2 tablespoons fresh lemon juice

3/4 cup red currant jelly
1/8 teaspoon cayenne pepper
1/4 teaspoon dry mustard

Remove the zest from the orange and chop finely. Squeeze the juice from orange and reserve. Heat the port and the zest in a small saucepan over moderate heat. Stirring constantly, reduce liquid to about 1/2 cup. Add the juices, jelly, pepper, and mustard. Stir until jelly is melted. Serve warm with the lamb.

Crown Roast of Lamb with Mustard Herb Butter

SERVES 8

3 racks of lamb, about 2 pounds each

3 large garlic cloves, slivered (optional)

Salt and black pepper

Mustard Herb Butter (below)

Have the butcher shape racks into a crown roast. Preheat the oven to 350 degrees. Insert garlic slivers into each chop. Season to taste with salt and pepper. Liberally apply Mustard Herb Butter on the roast, thoroughly coating between chops. Cover the bone tips with foil to prevent burning while cooking. Place the roast on a rack in a large roasting pan and bake in the oven for 1–1 1/2 hours (until a meat thermometer registers 135 degrees, for medium rare). Baste frequently with the Mustard Herb Butter. Remove the roast from the oven and let stand for at least 10 minutes in a warm place. Serve with rice, or pilaf, steamed vegetables, and additional Mustard Herb Butter.

MUSTARD HERB BUTTER

1 cup unsalted butter, softened

1/2 cup Dijon mustard

1 3/4 teaspoons dried thyme

1 3/4 teaspoons dried rosemary

1/2 teaspoon powdered ginger

1/4 cup oriental sesame oil

Salt and black pepper

In a small bowl, cream the butter and add the mustard and spices. Whisk in sesame oil and season to taste with salt and pepper. Divide the butter in half. Refrigerate half to serve with the lamb. Use the remaining butter for preparing the roast.

Skewered Lamb with Peanut Butter Sauce

SERVES 8

3/4 cup salad oil
1/3 cup fresh lime juice
1 tablespoon honey
2 large garlic cloves, minced
5 teaspoons minced shallots
1 bay leaf
1/4 teaspoon cracked black
  pepper
1 teaspoon dry mustard

2 tablespoons chopped fresh
  cilantro
1/2 teaspoon salt
1 (6-pound) leg of lamb, boned
  and cut in 2-inch cubes
10-inch wooden skewers, soaked
  in water 30 minutes before
  threading
Peanut Butter Sauce (below)

Mix the oil, lime juice, honey, garlic, shallots, bay leaf, pepper, mustard, cilantro, and salt in a large bowl. Add the lamb and toss to coat thoroughly. Marinate meat at room temperature, covered, for 4 hours. When ready to cook, thread the lamb on skewers. When cooked, serve with Peanut Butter Sauce.

To prepare in oven: Preheat the oven to 400 degrees. Place the skewers on a rack in a large broiler pan. Bake in the oven for 25–30 minutes, turning several times. Meat should be pink inside.

To barbecue: Place skewers over glowing coals about 6 inches from flame and cook for 20 minutes, turning frequently, or until done.

PEANUT BUTTER SAUCE

1/3 cup coconut milk, preferably
  unsweetened
2/3 cup peanut butter
2 tablespoons honey (omit if
  using sweetened coconut milk)
1/4 teaspoon cayenne pepper, or
  more, to taste
1 tablespoon soy sauce

2 large garlic cloves
3/4 teaspoon dried mustard
1 1/2 teaspoons Worcestershire
  sauce
2 tablespoons fresh lime juice
1/4 teaspoon dried red pepper
  flakes
1/4–1/3 cup half-and-half

Place all of the ingredients except half-and-half in blender. Mix well. With motor running, slowly add half-and-half until desired consistency is achieved. Sauce should be very thick.

Five Spice Racks of Lamb with Peach Chutney

SERVES 4–6

2 racks of lamb, about 1 1/2–2
   pounds each
3/4 teaspoon coarsely ground salt
4 teaspoons five spice powder
2 teaspoons powdered ginger

1/4 teaspoon freshly ground
   black pepper
4 tablespoons oriental sesame oil
1 cup Peach Chutney (below)

Place the lamb fat side down on a cutting board. Slice between chops, without cutting through fat. (Fat side must be intact.) Turn over and carefully score fat in a diamond pattern. In a small bowl combine salt, five spice powder, ginger, pepper, and sesame oil. Thoroughly coat both sides of racks with spice mixture. Let the meat stand at least 1 hour. Before roasting, place the lamb on a rack in a roasting pan. Cover bone tips with aluminum foil to prevent burning. Brush on any remaining spices and juices that have accumulated. Roast in a preheated 400-degree oven for 15 minutes, reduce heat to 375 degrees and cook for an additional 10–15 minutes. The meat will be medium rare. Roast longer if desired. Let the meat stand for 5 minutes before carving. Serve with Peach Chutney

PEACH CHUTNEY   MAKES 6 PINTS

5 pounds ripe peaches, peeled,
   pitted, and sliced
1 1/2 cups loosely packed
   crystallized ginger
2 medium onions, chopped
1/2 lemon, seeded and cut in
   chunks
2 large garlic cloves
2 cups cider vinegar

3 tablespoons mustard seed
1 teaspoon chili powder
1 tablespoon salt
3 1/3 cups packed light brown
   sugar
1–2 teaspoons dried red pepper
   flakes
2 1/2–3 cups currants, raisins, or
   any combination

Place peaches in a heavy-bottomed 8-quart pot. Place the ginger, onions, lemon, garlic, and vinegar in a blender. Blend for 30 seconds or until smooth. Pour over the peaches. Add the remaining ingredients and stir. Bring to a boil over moderate heat. Reduce heat to low and simmer, uncovered, for 1 hour or until thick. Stir frequently to prevent burning. Pour the hot chutney into 6 sterilized pint mason jars with lids and seal according to manufacturer's directions.

Rack of Lamb with Mint Jalapeño Chutney

SERVES 2–3

1 (1 1/2-pound) rack of lamb,
   room temperature
Salt

Freshly ground black pepper
Mint Jalapeño Chutney (below)

Preheat the oven to 400 degrees. Season the lamb with salt and pepper. Place the lamb, fat side up, on a rack in a roasting pan. Cover the bone tips with aluminum foil to prevent burning. Cook the lamb in the oven for 15 minutes. Reduce temperature to 375 degrees and cook for an additional 10–15 minutes. The meat will be medium rare. Roast longer, if desired. Remove the meat from oven and let stand for 5 minutes before carving. At serving time, remove the foil and slice meat into individual servings. Serve with Mint Jalapeño Chutney.

MINT JALAPEÑO CHUTNEY
1 cup fresh mint leaves
1 cup fresh cilantro leaves
1 tablespoon fresh lime juice
3–4 teaspoons apple cider
   vinegar

1–2 fresh jalapeño chiles, seeded
   and chopped
1/4 cup chopped onions
Generous pinch of salt

In a food processor chop the mint and cilantro together. Add the remaining ingredients and chop. Adjust seasonings to taste. Chutney may also be served warm. To do so place ingredients in a small nonaluminum pan. Bring to a simmer and remove from heat. Also delicious with pork. (May be made 1 day in advance.)

Lamb Chops with Blue Cheese Peppercorn Butter

SERVES 4

8 small loin lamb chops, 1 1/2
   inches thick
Salt

Black pepper
Blue Cheese Peppercorn Butter
   (below)

Season the lamb chops with salt and pepper. Using a sharp knife, score the chops on both sides and rub with 4 slices softened Blue Cheese Peppercorn

Butter. Preheat the broiler. Allow the chops to stand for 30 minutes at room temperature. Broil 4 inches from the flame, 5 minutes on each side for medium rare, or longer if desired. Turn the chops several times while broiling to prevent burning. Remove the chops to individual plates and top with slices of Blue Cheese Peppercorn Butter.

BLUE CHEESE PEPPERCORN BUTTER

1/2 cup unsalted butter, softened

2 ounces blue-veined cheese (Roquefort, Maytag, or Danish)

2 tablespoons port

2 teaspoons green peppercorns, rinsed and drained

Mix ingredients together in a small bowl. Transfer butter to a piece of waxed paper and roll paper around butter to form a cylinder. Chill at least 1 hour. Cut the butter into 12 slices. Allow 4 slices to soften and use to rub into chops. Reserve remaining slices to serve on top of the chops.

Lamb Chops with Shiitake Mushrooms and Tarragon

SERVES 4

2 ounces dried shiitake mushrooms or 6 ounces fresh mushrooms

8 small loin lamb chops, 1 1/2 inches thick

Salt and black pepper

1 tablespoon butter

1 tablespoon oil

1/2 cup sherry

1/2 cup Chicken Stock

4 green onions, white part only, minced

1 teaspoon dried tarragon

2 tablespoons minced fresh parsley

1/4 cup chopped prosciutto (optional)

Place the dried shiitake mushrooms in a small bowl. Cover the mushrooms with warm water and soak them for 30 minutes. Remove the mushrooms from the water and squeeze out any liquid. Remove and discard stems. Slice the mushrooms in 1/4-inch strips and set aside. For fresh mushrooms, wash and slice without soaking.

Season the chops with salt and pepper. Heat the butter and oil in a large heavy-bottomed skillet over moderately high heat. Sauté the meat in the butter on each side for 4–6 minutes for medium rare, or longer if desired. Remove the meat from the pan to a plate and keep warm. Pour off any accumulated fat from the pan. Add the sherry, scraping up any meat dripping. Stir in the stock, bring to a boil, and reduce by a third. Add the onions, tarragon, parsley, mushrooms, and prosciutto, and continue cooking for 5 minutes. Add additional sherry and stock if liquid evaporates. Return the meat to pan and heat through. Spoon the sauce on top of the meat and serve.

Hearty Lamb Stew

SERVES 6–8

This delicious stew is best prepared a day ahead, or prepared well in advance and frozen. Just before serving, add the peas.

3 pounds boneless lamb shoulder, trimmed and cut in ¹/₂-inch cubes
Salt and black pepper
2 tablespoons flour
2 tablespoons oil
1 cup dry red wine
3 medium tomatoes, peeled, seeded, and chopped
3 large carrots, peeled and chopped
2 medium onions, peeled and thinly sliced

2 large garlic cloves, minced
1 cup tomato sauce
3 tablespoons brown sugar
1 teaspoon dried dill
¹/₂ teaspoon dried oregano
1 teaspoon dried rosemary
1 teaspoon salt
¹/₄ teaspoon coarsely ground black pepper
8 new potatoes, cut in half
1 cup fresh or frozen peas

Sprinkle the lamb with salt and pepper. Flour it lightly, shaking off any excess. In a large heavy casserole, heat the oil over moderately high heat. In small batches, brown the lamb cubes on all sides. Remove to a bowl and repeat process until all lamb is browned. Add the wine to casserole, scraping up any brown bits when stirring. Return the lamb to the pan and add remaining ingredients excluding peas.

Cover and simmer over low heat for 1–1 ¹/₂ hours or until the meat is tender. Remove cover during last 30 minutes of cooking to allow stew to thicken, if necessary. At serving time, add the peas and cook for an additional 5 minutes to heat through.

Indonesian Lamb Shanks

SERVES 6

A satisfying, flavorful dinner served with couscous and a citrus salad.

6 lamb shanks, cracked in 3
  pieces
Salt and black pepper
1/4 cup flour
3 tablespoons unsalted butter
3 tablespoons olive oil
3 medium onions, chopped
1/3 cup peeled and minced fresh
  ginger
4 large garlic cloves, minced
1 1/2 teaspoons ground turmeric
1 1/4 teaspoons ground cumin
1 1/4 teaspoons ground coriander

1 teaspoon cinnamon
3/4 teaspoon cayenne pepper
1/4 teaspoon ground cloves
3/4 teaspoon salt
2 cups Beef Stock
1 (28-ounce) can whole peeled
  tomatoes, coarsely chopped,
  reserve juice
1 tablespoon tomato paste
1 bay leaf
3/4 cup whipping cream
1/4 cup minced fresh cilantro
  leaves, for garnish

Season the lamb with salt and pepper and sprinkle with the flour, shaking off any excess. In a large flameproof casserole, heat the butter and oil over medium-high heat. Brown the lamb in the butter and oil, transferring to a large dish as cooked. To the same pan add an additional 1 tablespoon oil if necessary and sauté onions over low heat until tender. Add the ginger and garlic to the pan and cook for an additional 5 minutes.

In a small bowl combine spices. Add the spices to the onions and stir to mix well. Stir in the stock, tomatoes, tomato paste, and bay leaf. Add the lamb and bring mixture to a boil. Cover, reduce the heat, and simmer for 2 hours or until lamb is tender. When done, remove shanks to a large bowl and keep warm. Using a spoon, degrease sauce. Add cream and reduce sauce until thick. There should be about 3–4 cups of sauce. Return the lamb to the pan and heat. Serve the lamb garnished with fresh cilantro leaves.

Ham Braised in Port with a Pecan Crust

SERVES 12

Here, port and pecans add variety to a traditional buffet ham. Accompany this with an assortment of mustards.

1/4 cup butter
2 large onions, sliced
2 celery stalks, sliced
2 carrots, sliced
2 sprigs of fresh parsley
6 whole black peppercorns
3 whole cloves
2 1/2 cups ruby port

1 bay leaf
1 (10–12-pound) fully cooked
   ham (with the bone in)
2/3 cup fresh bread crumbs
2/3 cup light brown sugar
1/2 cup ruby port
1/4 cup finely chopped pecans

Preheat the oven to 325 degrees. In a large shallow roasting pan, heat the butter over moderate heat. Add the onions, celery, carrots, and parsley and sauté until tender, about 5 minutes. Stir in peppercorns, cloves, ruby port, and bay leaf. Bring to a boil and remove from heat. Place the ham fat side up in the roasting pan and cover tightly. Bake in the oven for 1 1/2 hours, basting every 20 minutes. Remove cover, and bake an additional 1 1/2 hours or until a meat thermometer registers 130 degrees. Baste frequently and add more port to the pan if it becomes too dry.

Remove the ham from the oven and trim off all but 1/4 inch of fat. Score the ham well and place it on a rack in a baking pan. Combine the bread crumbs and sugar. Cover the ham with the crumb mixture, pressing it onto the surface of the meat. Return to the oven and bake for 10 minutes. Moisten the ham with more port and then sprinkle pecans over top. Bake for an additional 15–20 minutes or until nuts are toast-colored. Be careful that pecans do not burn.

Pork Loin Roast Stuffed with Olives and Garlic

SERVES 6

1 medium head garlic, 6 large
   cloves
1 teaspoon dried oregano
Juice of 2 lemons
1 (3-pound) boneless pork loin
   roast

15 green olives stuffed with
   pimentos
Black pepper
Dried oregano
1–2 cups Chicken Stock

Preheat the oven to 325 degrees. In a small bowl, mash together the garlic and 1 teaspoon oregano. Add enough lemon juice to make a paste. Reserve the remaining juice. Make fifteen 2-inch slits in meat. Insert the garlic paste and an olive into each slit. Season the roast with pepper and more dried oregano. Place the roast on a rack in a roasting pan in the oven. After 30 minutes pour 1/2 cup of the stock into the pan. Continue adding stock to pan as necessary to prevent burning. Pour remaining juice over meat, after meat has cooked 1 hour. Cook an additional 1/2 hour.

When ready to serve, remove meat to a carving board and let stand. Meanwhile, pour any excess fat from roasting pan. Add 1 cup stock to pan and stir over moderate heat. Reduce liquid slightly and serve pan juices with slices of meat.

Pork Medallions with Currants and Scotch

SERVES 4–6

An unusual ingredient in meat preparation, scotch whiskey gives the pork a subtle and delicious flavor.

1/3 cup currants	2 tablespoons unsalted butter
1/2 cup scotch whiskey	1/2 cup Chicken Stock
2 pork tenderloins, about 3/4–1	3 tablespoons Dijon mustard
pound each, visible fat	3 tablespoons brown sugar
removed	1 teaspoon dried thyme
Salt and white pepper	

Combine the currants and scotch in a small bowl. Set aside. Cut the tenderloins in 3/4-inch fillets, reserving pointed ends for another use. Season with salt and white pepper. Heat the butter in a heavy-bottomed skillet over medium-high heat. Brown the fillets quickly for about 1 minute on each side. Lower the heat and cook an additional 5–6 minutes on each side. Remove the fillets and keep warm. Pour off any accumulated fat in the pan. Drain the currants, reserving the scotch. Add the scotch to the skillet, stirring to scrape up drippings. Stir in the stock, mustard, sugar, and thyme.

Whisk until smooth. Bring the mixture to a boil and thicken slightly. Reduce the heat and add the currants and fillets. Cover pan and heat the fillets in the sauce for about 2–3 minutes. Place the fillets on warm plates, spooning sauce over them.

Roast Pork Loin with Apples and Mushrooms

SERVES 6

3 pounds boneless pork loin
  roast
Salt and white pepper
1 teaspoon dried thyme
1/3 cup apple cider
2 tablespoons dry white
  vermouth

1 cup Chicken Stock
1 cup heavy cream
3 tablespoons unsalted butter
3 large Granny Smith apples,
  cored, peeled, and cut in 8
  segments
3/4 pound mushrooms, sliced

Preheat the oven to 450 degrees. Season the roast with salt, white pepper, and thyme. Place the meat on rack in a roasting pan and cook for 20 minutes. Reduce the heat to 325 degrees and continue cooking until a meat thermometer registers 160 degrees. This should take about 30–40 minutes more. Transfer the meat to a platter and keep warm. Pour off any excess fat from the roasting pan. Add the apple cider, stirring to scrape up any drippings. Add the vermouth, Chicken Stock, and cream and boil for approximately 15 minutes or until the sauce thickens.

Meanwhile, in a separate skillet, heat half the butter over moderate heat. Add the apple segments and sauté until golden. Remove the apples from the pan and reserve. Heat remaining butter in the same pan and sauté the mushrooms until tender. Strain the sauce into a saucepan. Add the mushrooms to the sauce and stir. Taste to correct seasonings. Heat briefly over low heat. Spoon sauce onto individual plates and top with meat slices. Garnish with apple slices.

Variation: Pork medallions seasoned with salt, white pepper, and thyme, then sautéed in butter and oil. Proceed with the sauce.

Southwestern Grilled Pork with Cilantro Sauce

SERVES 4

2 pounds boneless pork loin,
  trimmed of all fat and
  butterflied
Salt

Freshly ground black pepper
Marinade (below)
Cilantro Sauce (below)

Place the pork between two pieces of waxed paper. Using a rolling pin, pound the pork until it is about 1/2 inch thick. Season the meat with salt and pepper and put in a large shallow dish. Pour the marinade over the meat, being sure to coat thoroughly. Cover the dish and refrigerate for 24 hours, turning several times. When ready to cook, bring the meat to room temperature. To barbecue, place the meat over hot coals about 6 inches from the flame and grill for 8–10 minutes on each side or until the meat reaches an internal temperature of 155 degrees. Remove the meat from the grill and let it stand for about 5 minutes before slicing. Serve with Cilantro Sauce.

MARINADE
1/4 cup fresh lime juice
1 tablespoon sugar
1 1/2 teaspoons grated lime peel
2 teaspoons peeled and minced
    fresh ginger

3 tablespoons minced fresh
    cilantro
1/3 cup olive oil

With a wire whisk, beat together the lime juice, sugar, lime peel, ginger root, cilantro, and olive oil in a small bowl. Set aside.

CILANTRO SAUCE
1/3 cup unsalted butter
1 tablespoon fresh lime juice
1/2 teaspoon grated lime peel
1 tablespoon minced fresh
    parsley

2 tablespoons minced fresh
    cilantro leaves
Salt to taste

Melt the butter over low heat in a small saucepan. Reserve. When ready to serve, reheat butter, remove from heat, and add the lime juice, lime peel, parsley, cilantro, and salt.

Peking Pork

SERVES 4

2 (1/2–3/4-pound) whole pork
    tenderloins
2 large garlic cloves, peeled
2 tablespoons peeled and
    chopped fresh ginger
1/4 cup Beef Stock
2 tablespoons brown sugar

2 tablespoons soy sauce
3 tablespoons ketchup
1 tablespoon molasses
1/2 teaspoon five spice powder
    (optional)
1/4 cup honey
1 cup sesame seeds

Place the tenderloins in a shallow glass dish. Put the garlic, ginger, stock, sugar, soy sauce, ketchup, molasses, and five spice powder into a blender. Blend thoroughly. Pour the marinade over the meat. Cover and refrigerate for 4–6 hours, turning occasionally. Preheat the oven to 325 degrees. Bring the meat to room temperature and pat dry. Pour the honey on a plate. Roll the tenderloins in the honey. Sprinkle the sesame seeds on the meat, turning to coat evenly. Place the meat in a roasting pan. Bake in the oven for 1 hour or until juices run clear when pricked with a fork. Remove the meat from the oven to a carving board and let stand for several minutes before cutting in thin diagonal slices.

Serve with hot mustard, plum sauce, or Peach Chutney.

Pork with Butternut Squash

SERVES 4

1/4 cup flour
2 pounds boneless pork loin, trimmed and cut into 1-inch fillets (or boneless center-cut pork chops)
Salt and white pepper
2 tablespoons oil
1 tablespoon unsalted butter
1 cup chopped onions
1 carrot, peeled and chopped
1 celery stalk, chopped
3 medium garlic cloves, minced
2 tablespoons flour

2 1/2 cups Beef Stock
1 tablespoon tomato paste
2 tablespoons white wine vinegar
1/2 teaspoon ground allspice
2 cloves
1 bay leaf
1 1/2 pounds butternut squash, peeled, seeded, and cut in 1 1/2-inch pieces
1 1/2 tablespoons Dijon mustard
2 teaspoons brown sugar
Fresh chopped parsley

Flour the pork thoroughly, shaking off any excess. Season the pork with salt and pepper. Heat the oil and butter in a 4 1/2-quart heavy-bottomed casserole. Add the pork and brown over medium-high heat. As the meat browns, transfer it to a large plate. Add the onions, carrots, celery, and garlic to the casserole and cook until the vegetables are tender, about 2–3 minutes. Sprinkle the 2 tablespoons of flour over the vegetables and cook for an additional 2 minutes, stirring frequently. Gradually add stock to the vegetables, whisking until smooth. Add the tomato paste, vinegar, allspice, cloves, and bay leaf. Stir until blended. Return the pork and any accumulated juices to the casserole. Bring the liquid to a boil, cover, and simmer slowly for 35 minutes or until the pork is tender. Remove meat to a platter. Add the squash to the casserole. Return meat to the casserole arranging it on top of the squash. Cover, and simmer for 30 minutes more or until the squash is tender. Using a slotted spoon, transfer the pork and the squash to a serving platter and keep warm. Remove the bay leaf and the cloves from the sauce and skim off any fat. Stir the Dijon mustard and brown sugar into sauce. Bring to a boil and simmer, uncovered, for 5 minutes or until thickened. Strain the sauce over the pork and squash. Garnish with chopped parsley.

Mexicali Meat

SERVES 15

A traditional filling for beef tostados, enchiladas, burritos, and tacos. This freezes beautifully.

1 (3-pound) boneless pork roast, well trimmed of fat
1 pound dried pinto beans (do not presoak)
4 cups water
3 large garlic cloves, minced
2 tablespoons cumin seed
2 tablespoons chili powder
5 teaspoons dried oregano
1 teaspoon ground coriander
1/2–1 teaspoon cayenne pepper
1 (28-ounce) can whole tomatoes, with juice

1 (7-ounce) can diced green chiles, drained
1 tablespoon salt
1/2 teaspoon black pepper
2–3 dozen flour tortillas, warmed

Condiments Grated cheese, chopped onion, olives, salsa, sour cream, guacamole, chopped lettuce, and tomatoes

Preheat the oven to 250 degrees. Place the pork roast in a large Dutch oven. Add the remaining ingredients and stir to mix well. Cover and bake in the oven for 7–8 hours or until beans are tender. Check the roast from time to time during cooking and add more water if mixture gets too dry. When done, remove the meat from pan and shred in bite-size pieces. Return the meat to pan and stir. This should be the consistency of chili and beans. Allow to stand before serving. Correct seasonings.

To assemble, place a warm tortilla on a plate, top with Mexicali meat. Top with choice of condiments, fold in edges, and roll loosely.

Pork Estofado

SERVES 8

This spicy pork stew is inspired by the Latin American cooking influence in California.

3 tablespoons oil
2 1/4 pounds lean boneless pork, cut in 1-inch cubes
3/4 pound smoked pork chops, boned, trimmed, and cut in 1/2-inch cubes (other cuts of smoked pork may be substituted)
2 medium onions, chopped
2 large garlic cloves, minced
3 jalapeño chiles, seeded and minced
2 red bell peppers, seeded and cut in 1/2-inch pieces
2 bay leaves
1 teaspoon dried oregano

1 teaspoon salt
3/4 teaspoon black pepper
1/2 teaspoon ground cumin
2 cups tomatoes, peeled and coarsely chopped *or* 1 (16-ounce) can whole tomatoes with juice, coarsely chopped
1/4 cup fresh lemon juice
3/4 cup raisins
1 cup dry red wine
1 cup Beef Stock
1/2 cup chopped fresh cilantro leaves
1 cup slivered almonds, toasted
Flour tortillas
Steamed white rice

Preheat the oven to 300 degrees. Heat the oil in a large Dutch oven or casserole. Brown the pork in batches in the oil over moderately high heat. As it cooks, remove meat to a bowl. When all the meat is browned, reduce heat and sauté the onions and garlic in browning fat until tender, about 5 minutes. Return the meat to the pan and add the chiles, peppers, bay leaves, oregano, salt, pepper, cumin, and tomatoes. Bring to a boil, reduce the heat, and simmer, uncovered, for 5 minutes. Add the lemon juice, raisins, wine, and stock. Cover, and bake in the oven for 2 hours or until meat is fork tender. Remove the lid during last 30 minutes of cooking to thicken stew, if necessary. Skim any excess fat from stew. Taste for seasonings. Garnish with cilantro and almonds before serving. Serve with warm tortillas or rice. If desired, more chiles may be added to make a spicier stew.

California Moo Shu Pork

SERVES 12

1 ½ pounds pork shoulder or
  loin
1 teaspoon salt
1 teaspoon garlic
1 teaspoon soy sauce
3 tablespoons dried black
  mushrooms (3/4 cup after
  soaking)
½ cup dried golden lilies
  (available in Chinese specialty
  stores)
1 tablespoon cornstarch
8 tablespoons soy sauce
6 tablespoons peanut or
  vegetable oil
¼ pound fresh shiitake or
  domestic mushrooms, sliced

4 green onions, julienned
2 tablespoons peeled and minced
  fresh ginger
4 cups sliced napa cabbage (1/2
  of a small head)
½ cup canned bamboo shoots,
  sliced lengthwise
1 cup diced jícama or water
  chestnuts
½ cup julienned red bell pepper
2 tablespoons sherry
4 eggs, beaten
Flour tortillas or Chinese
  pancakes
Hoisin sauce (available in
  Chinese specialty stores)

Rub pork with salt, garlic and soy sauce. Roast at 350 degrees for 45–60 minutes. Cool and shred or use leftover roast pork.

In a medium bowl, pour boiling water over the dried mushrooms and golden lilies to cover. Soak for 20 minutes. Drain the mushrooms and lilies and remove stems. Slice and set aside. Meanwhile, in another bowl, mix the shredded pork with cornstarch and 6 tablespoons of the soy sauce. Heat 3 tablespoons of the oil in a sauté pan or wok and add the fresh mushrooms, onions, ginger, cabbage, bamboo shoots, jícama, and red peppers. Stir-fry for 3 minutes. Add the other mushrooms and continue cooking for 1–2 minutes. Remove the mixture from the pan and add 1 tablespoon of the oil. When hot, add the pork mixture along with the sherry and 1–2 tablespoons more of the soy. When heated through, remove, and add to the vegetable mixture. Add 1 more tablespoon of oil to the pan. When hot, pour in the eggs, tipping the pan around until all the moisture has disappeared and the eggs resemble a pancake. Slice the eggs in slivers and combine with the pork and vegetables. At this point the mixture may be reheated, refrigerated, or frozen.

To assemble, on a steamed flour tortilla or Chinese Pancake, spread 1 teaspoon of the hoisin sauce and place about ¼ cup pork mixture on top. Fold the pancake over and tuck the ends under.

Chinese Ribs

SERVES 4–6

3 (2-pound) racks of baby pork
  ribs
Salt and black pepper
1/2 cup honey
1 cup soy sauce
1 cup ketchup
1 teaspoon hoisin sauce

4 medium garlic cloves, minced
5 teaspoons peeled and minced
  fresh ginger
1/2–1 teaspoon dried red pepper
  flakes
Sesame seeds, for garnish

Sprinkle the ribs with salt and pepper. Combine the honey, soy sauce, ketchup, hoisin sauce, garlic, ginger, and red pepper in a blender. Blend well. May be made several days in advance.

Oven method: Preheat the oven to 400 degrees. Cut between ribs, leaving them attached. Place the ribs in a foil-lined baking pan and roast in the oven for 45–60 minutes. Cover with the sauce for the last 5–10 minutes of cooking. Sprinkle with the sesame seeds.

Combined method: Preheat the oven to 400 degrees. Bake the ribs in the oven for 30 minutes. Barbecue over medium coals for 15–20 minutes more, turning and basting frequently with the sauce. Cover the barbecue in between bastings. Sprinkle with sesame seeds.

Barbecue: Cook, using the indirect method, for 30 minutes. Begin basting and cook for an additional 15 minutes. Turn the ribs frequently, being sure to thoroughly coat both sides with the sauce. Cover the barbecue in between bastings. Sprinkle with sesame seeds.

Italian Meat Loaf with Tomato Sauce

SERVES 6

1 1/4 pounds lean ground pork
3/4 pound lean ground beef
5 teaspoons minced garlic
1/2 cup pine nuts, toasted
1 cup fresh bread crumbs
1/3 cup chopped fresh parsley

1 cup chopped fresh basil
1/2 cup freshly grated Parmesan
  cheese
1 large egg, lightly beaten
Salt and black pepper
Tomato Sauce (below)

Preheat the oven to 350 degrees. Combine the pork and beef in a large mixing bowl. Add the remaining ingredients. Mix well. Season to taste with salt and pepper. Put the meat loaf into a 5 × 9 × 3-inch loaf pan, smoothing top. Bake in the oven for 1 hour or until juices run clear. Remove from the oven and let sit for 10–15 minutes. Pour off any excess fat. Slice. Serve with Tomato Sauce.

TOMATO SAUCE

2 tablespoons olive oil

1 small onion, chopped

2 large garlic cloves, minced

4 medium tomatoes, peeled, seeded, and chopped

1 bay leaf

1/2 teaspoon dried thyme

1/4 teaspoon salt

1/4 teaspoon black pepper

1/4 teaspoon sugar

1 tablespoon unsalted butter

1/4 cup chopped fresh basil

Heat the oil in a medium-size saucepan over moderate heat. Add the onions and garlic and cook, stirring constantly, until the onions are translucent. Stir in the tomatoes, bay leaf, thyme, salt, pepper, and sugar. Cover and simmer over low heat for 10 minutes. Add the butter and basil and stir to mix well. Remove the bay leaf before serving. May be prepared ahead.

Veal Scallops with Tomatoes and Basil

SERVES 6

12 veal scallops, about 1/8 inch thick

3 tablespoons butter

1 tablespoon oil

2 tablespoons minced shallots

3/4 cup dry white vermouth or dry white wine

3/4 cup Chicken Stock

3/4 cup heavy cream

2 large tomatoes, peeled, seeded, and finely chopped

4 tablespoons fresh chopped basil

Salt and white pepper

Whole basil leaves, for garnish

Pat the veal dry with paper towels. Melt the butter with the oil in a large skillet over medium-high heat. Quickly sauté both sides of the veal scallops in batches until lightly browned. Remove to a warm plate and continue sautéing until all the scallops are browned. Add more oil and butter, as needed.

Pour off all but 2 tablespoons of fat from the pan. Stir in the shallots and cook slowly for 1 minute. Add the vermouth and stock and boil rapidly until the liquid has reduced to about 1/2 cup, 8–10 minutes. Add the cream and boil until slightly thickened, 4–5 minutes more. Stir in the tomatoes and basil.

Season to taste with the salt and pepper. Return the veal scallops to the pan and heat gently until warmed through. Garnish with the whole basil leaves.

This dish may be prepared 1 hour before serving. However, the basil should be chopped and added with the sautéed veal scallops just before reheating.

Veal Chops with Zinfandel Garlic Butter

SERVES 4

The Zinfandel Garlic Butter keeps well in the freezer. It is equally delicious on broiled fish or chicken.

4 veal loin chops (1–1 1/2 inches thick)	**Salt**
1 tablespoon olive oil	**Freshly ground black pepper**
1/2 teaspoon dried thyme	**Zinfandel Garlic Butter (below)**
	Finely chopped fresh parsley

Brush the chops on each side with the olive oil. Rub the thyme, salt, and pepper into the meat. To broil, preheat the broiler and cook 4 inches from the heat for 5–7 minutes on each side for pink. To barbecue, grill over hot coals 5–7 minutes on each side. Cooking time will vary with the thickness of the chops and heat of the flame. The meat should be at 140 degrees for medium rare. Serve with a softened slice of Zinfandel Garlic Butter on top of each chop. Garnish with parsley.

ZINFANDEL GARLIC BUTTER

1 small head garlic, unpeeled	**1/2 teaspoon salt**
1/4 cup olive oil	**1/2 teaspoon dried thyme**
1/4 pound unsalted butter, softened	**1/4 cup Zinfandel wine**

Place the head of garlic in a small saucepan. Cover with olive oil and simmer very gently for 12–15 minutes until soft. Do not allow to boil. With a slotted spoon, remove the garlic to cool. In a small bowl with an electric mixer, blend together the butter, salt and thyme. Squeeze the garlic out of the skins into the butter mixture. Discard the skins. Beat the butter mixture again to blend. Add the wine to the butter mixture 1 tablespoon at a time, beating well. Place the butter mixture on a sheet of waxed paper and roll the paper around the butter to form a cylinder. Chill for 1 hour. Remove the waxed paper and rewrap in plastic wrap. Chill until serving time. Slice in 1-inch slices, soften, and place on top of the grilled chops.

Veal Stew Provençal

4 (1 × 3-inch) strips fresh
   orange peel, julienned
1/4 cup olive oil
2 pounds lean veal stew meat,
   trimmed and cut in 1 1/2-inch
   cubes
2 shallots, minced
1 cup washed and sliced leeks
8 plum tomatoes, peeled and
   chopped *or* 1 (28-ounce) can
   whole plum tomatoes, well
   drained and chopped
Bouquet garni (1 sprig fresh
   thyme, 1 sprig fresh rosemary,
   and 1 sprig fresh tarragon tied
   in cheesecloth) *or* 3/4 teaspoon
   each dried thyme, rosemary,
   and tarragon

1 bay leaf
1 tablespoon tomato paste
1 cup dry white wine
2 large garlic cloves, minced
Salt and black pepper
1/8 teaspoon cayenne pepper
1/2 pound pearl onions, peeled
1 tablespoon unsalted butter
1/2 pound medium mushrooms,
   quartered
Fresh rosemary, for garnish

Preheat the oven to 325 degrees. Place the orange peel on a baking sheet and cook until dry, about 5 minutes. Remove from the oven and set aside. Heat 3 tablespoons of the oil in a 4-quart flameproof casserole over moderate heat. Sauté the meat in the oil, a few pieces at a time. When browned remove to a bowl using a slotted spoon. Reduce the heat to medium low and add remaining oil. Add the shallots, leeks, and orange peel and sauté until tender. Add the tomatoes, bouquet garni, bay leaf, and tomato paste. Stir well and add the wine. Add the meat, garlic, salt and pepper and mix well. Bring to a boil, cover, and simmer for 1 1/2 hours or until the meat is tender. In a medium saucepan, boil the onions until tender. Melt the butter in a small skillet and sauté the mushrooms in it until almost tender. Add the onions and mushrooms to the stew and heat through. Before serving, remove the bouquet garni and the bay leaf and garnish with fresh rosemary. This stew is better when made a day ahead.

Veal Scallops with Lemon Leek Sauce

SERVES 4

4 tablespoons unsalted butter
3 tablespoons olive oil
1 cup thinly sliced leeks,
  carefully rinsed
2 medium garlic cloves, minced
2 teaspoons flour
1 cup Chicken Stock
2 tablespoons fresh lemon juice

Grated peel of 1 lemon
1 tablespoon minced fresh dill *or*
  1/2 teaspoon dried dill
1 pound veal scallops
Salt and white pepper
Flour
Fresh dill, for garnish

Melt 2 tablespoons of the butter and 1 tablespoon of the oil in a saucepan. Add the leeks and garlic and stir to coat thoroughly. Cover the pan and cook gently for 5–6 minutes until the leeks are very soft. Blend in the flour. Stir and add the stock, lemon juice, lemon peel, and dill. Cook for 10–12 minutes, stirring occasionally. Season to taste with more lemon juice and salt if desired. In a large skillet melt the remaining butter and oil. Season the veal with salt and pepper and lightly coat with flour. Sauté quickly over high heat, being careful not to crowd the veal so that a nice brown crust will form. Keep warm until all of the veal is cooked. To serve, top with the sauce and garnish with fresh dill.

IX

Vegetables

Artichoke Bottoms Gratin

SERVES 4

4 cooked artichoke bottoms
3 tablespoons butter

1 cup chopped fresh mushrooms
1/2 cup grated Swiss cheese

Rinse and drain the artichokes and sauté in 2 tablespoons of the butter, 1 minute on each side. Place in a shallow baking dish. Add the remaining tablespoon of butter to the pan. Sauté mushrooms until soft and mound them on the artichoke bottoms. Cover with cheese and place them under the broiler until the cheese melts and turns golden. These can be made a day ahead and kept in the refrigerator.

Ginger Asparagus with Cashews

SERVES 6

1 1/2 pounds asparagus
2 tablespoons peanut oil
2 teaspoons oriental sesame oil
1 tablespoon peeled and finely
   julienned fresh ginger

1 tablespoon finely grated
   orange peel
1 tablespoon soy sauce
1/2 cup coarsely chopped roasted
   cashews

Trim off the tough lower stems of the asparagus and discard. Cut each stalk in 2- to 3-inch pieces. Heat the peanut and sesame oils together in a wok or large frying pan over high heat. Add the asparagus and ginger and stir-fry until tender, about 4–5 minutes. Stir in the orange peel, soy sauce, and cashews. Serve immediately.

Braised Green Beans

SERVES 4

1 pound thin green beans
1/4 cup olive oil
1 dried red chile pepper
5–6 tomatoes, peeled, seeded, and chopped
1 large garlic clove, minced
1 tablespoon chopped fresh basil

1/4 cup minced fresh parsley
1 teaspoon dried thyme
1 teaspoon dried oregano
Salt and pepper
Minced fresh parsley, for garnish

Cut off the ends of the beans, leaving them whole. Rinse them under cold running water and drain well. Bring salted water to a rolling boil in a large pan. Add the beans and cook 5–7 minutes, until they are just tender. Drain in a colander and plunge into cold water to stop the cooking process. Set aside.

Heat the olive oil in a large heavy skillet. Cut the chile pepper in half. Add it to the pan and cook until darkened, then discard. Add the tomatoes, garlic, basil, the 1/4 cup parsley, thyme, oregano, salt and pepper and bring up heat. Cover and simmer for 20–25 minutes until the sauce is thickened.

Stir in the green beans and heat through. Season to taste with additional salt and pepper. Garnish with minced parsley.

Green Beans with Walnuts

SERVES 6

1 tablespoon red wine vinegar
2 large garlic cloves, minced
Salt
White pepper

3 tablespoons walnut oil
1 pound green beans
1/4 cup chopped walnuts, toasted

In a large bowl, blend the vinegar, garlic, salt, and pepper. Whisk in the oil in a thin stream.

Trim the beans and cook them in boiling salted water until they are just tender, about 5 minutes. Drain and toss with the dressing. Top each serving with chopped walnuts.

Hot and Sour Chinese Long Beans

SERVES 3–4

1/2 pound Chinese long beans
  (or, if unavailable, regular
  green beans)
2 small dried red chiles
2 teaspoons cornstarch
2 tablespoons Chinese red or
  white vinegar
2 teaspoons soy sauce
1 tablespoon sugar

2 teaspoons oriental sesame oil
3 tablespoons peanut oil
1 teaspoon Szechuan
  peppercorns
2 teaspoons peeled and minced
  fresh ginger
2 teaspoons finely chopped green
  onions

Cut the beans into 3-inch lengths. If using mature beans, halve them length-wise before cutting into lengths. Cut the stems off the dried red chile peppers and shake out the seeds. Slice peppers into strips. Mix the cornstarch, vinegar, soy sauce, sugar, and sesame oil in a small bowl and set aside.

Heat the peanut oil in a wok until hot. Add Szechuan peppercorns and dried peppers and stir-fry briefly. Add the long beans and stir-fry for 2–3 minutes or until just tender. Add the ginger and onions and toss for 30 seconds. Add the vinegar-soy-sauce mixture and stir-fry for another 30 seconds until beans are coated with sauce. Serve immediately.

California Black Beans

SERVES 8

These beans complement the rich flavor of a Southwestern menu or a California barbecue.

4 cups black beans, washed and
  picked over
3 fresh long green chiles *or* 1
  (4-ounce) can chopped green
  chiles
1 jalapeño chile, roasted, seeded,
  and chopped
2 onions, chopped

1 tablespoon minced garlic
2 cups seeded and chopped
  tomatoes
1 tablespoon dried oregano
2 teaspoons ground cumin
1/2 teaspoon cayenne pepper
1 teaspoon salt
1/4 cup chopped fresh cilantro

Place the beans in a large pot, and add water to cover. Bring to a boil and then cover, reducing heat. Cook for 1 hour, adding more liquid as necessary.

Using a long-handled fork, char the fresh chiles over an open flame, turning them for 2–3 minutes, or until the skins are blackened. Or, place the peppers on a broiler pan and broil about 2 inches from the heat until the skins are blackened, turning frequently. This will take about 15 minutes. Transfer the peppers to a plastic bag, close tightly, and let them steam until they are cool enough to handle and peel. Remove the seeds and chop the chiles.

Add the chiles, onions, garlic, tomatoes, oregano, cumin, cayenne, and salt to the beans, with more liquid if needed to keep moist. Cook, covered, for another 2–2 1/2 hours, until the beans are very soft. Stir in the cilantro when ready to serve. Accompany with grated Jack cheese, sour cream, and chopped red or green onions if desired.

Sautéed Beets and Apples

SERVES 6

6 medium-size fresh beets
2 tablespoons salt
3 tablespoons butter
3 shallots, minced

2 tart apples, peeled, cored, and thinly sliced
1 tablespoon sugar
1/2 teaspoon salt
1/3 cup raspberry vinegar

Scrub the beets well and trim all but 1 inch of the green tops. Bring them to a boil in a large pan of salted water, and simmer, partially covered, for about 45 minutes or until they are tender. Drain the beets. When cool enough to handle, slip off the skins, tops, and roots. Halve each beet and cut in slices about 1/3 inch thick.

Melt the butter in a sauté pan. Add the shallots and cook them gently for 2 minutes. Add the apples, sugar, salt, and vinegar to the pan and simmer, uncovered, for 15 minutes or until the apples are very tender. Add the cooked beets and simmer for an additional 3–4 minutes, stirring gently, until they are warmed through.

Bok Choy Stir-fry with Sherry

SERVES 4

1 head bok choy (1 1/2–2 pounds)
3 tablespoons peanut oil
1 1/2 teaspoons peeled and
   minced fresh ginger
1/2 cup Chicken Stock

1/2 teaspoon salt
1/2 teaspoon sugar
2 tablespoons dry sherry
2 tablespoons soy sauce

Trim off the top of the bok choy leaves and bottom root end. Rinse and pat dry. Slice crosswise in bite-size pieces. Heat a wok or skillet and add the peanut oil. When very hot but not smoking, add the ginger and the bok choy. Stir-fry about 30 seconds. Add the stock, salt, sugar, sherry, and soy sauce. Cook for about 2 minutes. Serve immediately.

Broccoli with Orange-Shallot Butter

SERVES 6

3 pounds broccoli
1/2 cup fresh orange juice
3/4 cup butter
1/3 cup minced shallots

1–1 1/2 teaspoons finely grated
   orange peel
Salt

Cut the broccoli into flowerets. Steam the flowerets until they are just tender. Immerse them in cold water and drain well. (The broccoli can be prepared ahead to this point.)

In a heavy saucepan, boil the orange juice over high heat until it is reduced to 2 tablespoons. At the same time, melt the butter in a large heavy skillet. Add the shallots and orange peel to the skillet. Cover and cook them over moderate heat until the shallots are tender. Stir in the orange juice, broccoli and salt. Increase the heat and toss until the broccoli is heated through. Serve immediately.

Brussels Sprouts with Caraway Seeds

SERVES 6

1 pound small Brussels sprouts, trimmed and washed
1 cup Chicken Stock
1/2 cup dry white wine
3 tablespoons butter, melted

1 1/2 tablespoons fresh lemon juice
1 tablespoon caraway seeds
1/4 teaspoon salt
Freshly ground black pepper

In a heavy covered saucepan, simmer Brussels sprouts in stock and wine for 8–10 minutes, or until just tender. Drain well. Toss the sprouts in melted butter with lemon juice, caraway seeds, salt, and pepper over medium heat until just heated through. Serve immediately.

Orange Glazed Red Cabbage with Black Forest Ham

SERVES 4

1/2 pound Black Forest Ham, cut in 1/2-inch strips
2 tablespoons butter
1 small red cabbage, shredded
2 tablespoons whole-grain mustard

1/2 cup orange marmalade
1/4 cup cider vinegar
Salt and freshly ground pepper to taste

In a large skillet, sauté the ham in 1 tablespoon of the butter for 2 minutes. Remove the ham. In the same skillet, melt the second tablespoon of butter and stir in the cabbage until coated with the ham drippings. Mix the mustard, marmalade, and vinegar together and stir into cabbage. Fold in the ham. Cook until cabbage has softened, about 7–10 minutes.

Carrots with Capers

SERVES 4

1 pound baby carrots, peeled
2 tablespoons butter
2 tablespoons olive oil
1 teaspoon minced garlic

2 tablespoons chopped fresh
   parsley
2 tablespoons capers, drained
   and rinsed

Pat the carrots dry. In a medium skillet, sauté the carrots in the butter and olive oil over medium heat. Add 2 tablespoons of water and cook for 5 minutes. Add 2 more tablespoons of water and the garlic. As the water evaporates, continue adding more, 2 tablespoons at a time until the carrots are just tender, about 10–15 minutes. There should be no water left in the pan when the carrots are done. Allow carrots to brown lightly without scorching. Add the parsley and capers to the carrots and toss. Cook for 1 minute more and serve at once.

Carrots with Port

SERVES 6

1/4 cup olive oil
2 medium garlic cloves, minced
1 onion, cut in 1/4-inch slices
1 1/2 pounds carrots, cut in strips
   2 inches long × 1/4 inch thick

Salt and freshly ground pepper
   to taste
1/4 cup strong Beef Stock
1/4 cup port
Chopped fresh parsley, for
   garnish

In a skillet, heat the oil. Add the garlic and onions and cook over low heat for 5 minutes. Add the carrots, salt and pepper. Mix well.

In a small saucepan, combine the stock and port. Bring to a boil and pour over the carrots. Cook, covered, over moderate heat for about 5 minutes or until the carrots are almost tender.

Remove the cover, and cook over high heat, stirring, until the liquid has evaporated. Sprinkle with the parsley before serving.

Shredded Carrots with Apricots

SERVES 6

1/4 cup unsalted butter
1 cup minced onions
4 cups shredded carrots
1/2 cup slivered dried apricots

1/2 cup Chicken Stock
2 tablespoons sherry vinegar
Salt and fresh ground pepper

Melt the butter in a large skillet. Add the onions and cook until lightly browned. Add the carrots and apricots and stir until well coated. Add the stock and cover, cooking over medium heat until all the liquid has evaporated. Add the vinegar and salt and pepper to taste.

Cauliflower with Broccoli Topping

SERVES 8–10

This is a colorful and unusual buffet dish.

1 medium cauliflower
1 teaspoon salt
6 tablespoons butter, melted
1 cup freshly grated Parmesan
  cheese
3 cups broccoli flowerets with
  small amount of stems

1 cup sour cream
1 large clove garlic, crushed
1 teaspoon curry powder
1/4 cup finely chopped green
  onions

Preheat oven to 325 degrees. Break the cauliflower into flowerets and steam until tender. Toss the cauliflower with the salt, 3 tablespoons of the butter, and 1/3 cup of the Parmesan cheese. Place the cauliflower in a 9 × 11-inch baking dish.

Steam the broccoli. Place the steamed broccoli in a food processor with the remaining butter, the sour cream, garlic, curry, and 1/2 cup of the Parmesan. Process until smooth. Fold in the onions.

Spread the broccoli mixture over the top of the cauliflower. Sprinkle with the remaining Parmesan cheese. (Can be kept in the refrigerator for several hours at this point.) Bake for 15–20 minutes or until heated through. Increase the baking time if the casserole has been refrigerated.

Cauliflower with Hoisin Sauce

SERVES 4–6

This is a distinctive addition to an Oriental-style menu.

6 tablespoons hoisin sauce
1 tablespoon oriental sesame oil
3 tablespoons minced green
onions

1 head cauliflower (about 1 1/2
pounds)

In a saucepan, heat the hoisin sauce, sesame oil, and onions until warm. Separate the cauliflower into flowerets and steam until just tender. Drain. Pour the warm sauce over the cauliflower and serve at once.

Braised Cucumbers and Leeks

SERVES 6

This is particularly good served with seafood or veal.

2 leeks, including 2 inches of
green
3 medium cucumbers, peeled and
seeded
1/2 cup unsalted butter
1/2 teaspoon salt
1/8 teaspoon white pepper

1/4 cup minced fresh parsley
2 tablespoons fresh minced dill
or 1 teaspoon dried thyme
(optional)
1–2 teaspoons fresh lemon juice
(optional)

Cut the leeks in half lengthwise, rinse carefully, and slice in 1/4-inch slices. Cut the cucumbers lengthwise and slice in 1-inch pieces. In a medium skillet, melt 1/4 cup of the butter and sauté the leeks for about 8 minutes or until soft. Remove the leeks and set aside. Sauté the cucumbers in the remaining 1/4 cup of the butter for about 5 minutes. Return the leeks to the pan and season with the salt and pepper. Cover the leeks and cucumbers and cook gently for another 15 minutes. Sprinkle on the parsley and herbs and 1–2 teaspoons of lemon juice, if desired.

Spicy Eggplant and Green Beans

SERVES 6

This spicy vegetable combination reflects the popular Szechuan-style cooking.

1/2 pound green beans, thinly sliced lengthwise

4 Japanese eggplants *or* 1 medium eggplant, cut in 1/2-inch strips

4 tablespoons peanut oil

2 large garlic cloves

1 tablespoon peeled and minced fresh ginger

1 tablespoon Chinese hot bean paste

2 tablespoons soy sauce

1 1/2 teaspoons red wine vinegar

1 teaspoon sugar

1 teaspoon salt

1/2 cup Chicken Stock

1/2 tablespoon oriental sesame oil

1 tablespoon chopped green onions, for garnish

Cook the green beans for 5 minutes in boiling water. Drain and set them aside. Heat the oil in a large skillet and sauté the eggplant until soft, removing with a slotted spoon when done. Add all the remaining ingredients to the pan, including the beans, and cook for 1 minute. Add the eggplant and continue cooking for 1–2 minutes, or until heated through. Sprinkle with onions. Serve warm or at room temperature.

Roasted Japanese Eggplants with Dill

SERVES 6–8

2 1/2 pounds Japanese eggplant, washed and cut in quarters lengthwise

2 large onions, thinly sliced

3 large garlic cloves, minced

1/2 cup olive oil

1 teaspoon salt

Pepper

1/4 cup red wine vinegar

1/4 cup chopped fresh dill

Preheat the oven to 400 degrees. In an oiled shallow baking pan, layer the eggplant, onions, and garlic. Drizzle with the olive oil and season with salt and pepper. Bake for 35–45 minutes, tossing occasionally, until the eggplant is well browned and tender. Turn into a serving dish and let cool 5–10 minutes. Toss with the vinegar and dill. Serve slightly warm or at room temperature.

Sautéed Leeks with Tomato

SERVES 4–6

2 pounds leeks, including ½
  inch green, carefully rinsed
6 tablespoons olive oil
2 large garlic cloves, minced
1 bay leaf

½ teaspoon salt
Pepper
1 cup tomatoes, peeled, seeded,
  and chopped
Juice of 1 lemon

Slice the leeks in half lengthwise and cut in 1-inch slices. In a sauté pan, heat 3 tablespoons of the oil and add the garlic, bay leaf, salt, and pepper to taste. Cover the pan and cook over medium-low heat for 20 minutes, stirring occasionally. Add the tomatoes, the remaining 3 tablespoons of oil, and the lemon juice. Cook for another 5 minutes. Remove the bay leaf before serving.

Leeks au Gratin

SERVES 6

A sophisticated vegetable to serve for a special meal.

3 carefully rinsed leeks,
  including ½ inch of green
3 tablespoons unsalted butter
1 cup cubed Jarlsberg cheese
3/4 cup sour cream

2 teaspoons Dijon mustard
1/4 cup crumbled Boucheron or
  other chèvre (goat cheese)
Salt
6 pattypan squash

Cut the leeks into julienne strips 3 inches long. Heat the butter in a large skillet over moderate heat. Add the leeks and sauté for 5 minutes. Cover the pan and cook for 10–15 minutes more. Remove from the heat and cool. Combine with the cheeses, sour cream, and mustard. Salt to taste.

Cut a thin slice from the bottom of each squash so it will sit level. Slice off the tops of the squash and scoop out enough of the pulp to hold 2–3 tablespoons of the leek mixture. Brush the squash shells with oil inside and out. Stuff with the leek mixture and place in an oiled baking pan. Bake at 350 degrees for 20 minutes or until the squash is tender and the leek mixture is bubbly and lightly browned.

Scallion Pancakes

MAKES 24 4-INCH PANCAKES

Serve with Chinese dishes or as an accompaniment to duck.

2 eggs
1 3/4 cups milk
1 1/2 cups flour
1/3 cup peanut oil

1 teaspoon salt
1/2 cup minced green onions
Additional peanut oil for
  cooking

In a small bowl, combine the eggs and milk. Place the flour in a large bowl and add the egg mixture, the oil, salt, and onions. Mix well. Lightly coat a heavy skillet with additional peanut oil. When very hot, place batter by spoonfuls in pan, spreading as thinly as possible. Brown on both sides. These can be wrapped in foil and reheated in a 350-degree oven for 10–12 minutes.

Onion Mushroom Casserole with Cheese

SERVES 6–8

1 pound small boiling onions
1 pound medium-size mushrooms
8 tablespoons butter
3 tablespoons flour
1 cup milk

1/2 cup shredded sharp Cheddar
  cheese
1/2 teaspoon dried oregano
2 tablespoons chopped fresh
  parsley
1 cup seasoned croutons

Preheat the oven to 350 degrees. In a pot of boiling salted water, cook the onions for 10 minutes, drain, and set aside. Meanwhile, in a heavy skillet, sauté the mushrooms in 4 tablespoons of the butter for about 10 minutes. Transfer the mushrooms to a shallow 1 1/2–2-quart casserole. Add the onions to the mushrooms. Heat 2 more tablespoons of the butter in the same skillet. Add the flour and cook over moderate heat, stirring constantly, until the mixture bubbles. Slowly add the milk, continuing to stir until thickened. Remove from heat and add the cheese, oregano, and parsley. Stir until the cheese melts. Pour the sauce over the mushrooms and onions and mix gently. (The casserole may be refrigerated at this point.)

Melt the remaining 2 tablespoons of butter and mix with the croutons. Sprinkle the croutons over the dish. Bake, uncovered, until heated through, about 25 minutes. Increase cooking time if casserole has been refrigerated.

Onion Marmalade in Onions

SERVES 6

A rich accompaniment for steaks or roast beef.

2 teaspoons olive oil
3 tablespoons sugar
1 1/2 teaspoons salt
1/4 teaspoon freshly ground
  pepper

2 pounds onions, thinly sliced
6 tablespoons sherry wine
  vinegar
6 medium onions *or* 3 large
  yellow onions, halved

In a heavy skillet over low heat, combine the oil, sugar, salt, and pepper. Add the sliced onions. Cover and cook for 30 minutes, stirring frequently with a wooden spoon. After 30 minutes, add the vinegar. Stir, cover, and cook for another 30 minutes, or until the onions are very soft and light brown.

Meanwhile, cut off the top portion of the 6 onions and peel them, leaving the root end intact. Drop into boiling salted water to cover and cook, uncovered, for 25–30 minutes. Drain.

Scoop out the centers, leaving a 3/8–1/2-inch-thick shell. Fill with the marmalade. The onions can be prepared ahead to this point and reheated in a 350-degree oven for 15–20 minutes.

Savory Peas

SERVES 6

1 cup sliced green onions
4 tablespoons butter
3 cups fresh or frozen peas
1 teaspoon sugar
1/2 teaspoon summer savory
1 tablespoon minced fresh basil
  or 1 teaspoon dried basil

2 tablespoons minced fresh
  parsley
3/4 cup water
1 1/2 teaspoons salt
1/2 teaspoon freshly ground
  black pepper
Additional fresh basil leaves, for
  garnish

Over medium heat in a heavy saucepan, sauté the onions in the butter until just soft. Add the peas, sugar, savory, basil, parsley, water, salt, and pepper. Bring the mixture to a boil, lower heat, and simmer gently, covered, for 6–8 minutes or until tender. Drain the excess liquid and serve garnished with basil leaves.

Peas with Prosciutto

SERVES 6

2 tablespoons olive oil
2 large garlic cloves
2 ounces prosciutto, chopped
2 (10-ounce) packages frozen
peas, thawed

1/4 cup minced fresh parsley
1/4 teaspoon salt
1/8 teaspoon freshly ground
pepper

In a medium saucepan, heat the olive oil and sauté the garlic cloves until light brown, 3–5 minutes. Remove and discard the garlic. Add the prosciutto and sauté 1 minute. Add the peas, parsley, salt, and pepper. Cook, covered, over medium heat, stirring occasionally, until the peas are tender, about 5–7 minutes. Add water if necessary to keep the mixture from sticking.

Snow Peas with Cashews

SERVES 4–6

1 pound snow peas, ends
trimmed
1 (10-ounce) package frozen peas
1/4 cup unsalted butter
1 teaspoon minced garlic
2 tablespoons chopped green
onions

1 cup unsalted cashews or
peanuts
1/2 teaspoon salt
1/4 teaspoon freshly ground
pepper
1/4 cup finely chopped fresh
parsley

In a small saucepan, blanch the snow peas and green peas separately until just tender. Drain well and combine in a bowl.

Meanwhile, melt the butter in a medium saucepan. Add the garlic, onions, and nuts, and simmer 1 minute. Add the salt, pepper, and parsley. Combine the butter mixture with the peas and toss gently. Serve immediately.

Florentine Pepper Shells with Orzo and Jarlsberg Cream

SERVES 8–10

Excellent as a main course for a vegetarian luncheon or supper.

2 tablespoons butter
3 tablespoons thinly sliced green
  onions
1 1/4 cups blanched chopped
  spinach *or* 1 (10-ounce)
  package frozen chopped
  spinach*
1/2 teaspoon salt
1/4 teaspoon pepper
1/8 teaspoon nutmeg
4–5 red bell peppers

1 1/2–2 tablespoons olive oil
3/4 cup dry vermouth
1 large garlic clove, minced
1 cup heavy cream
1 tablespoon minced fresh thyme
  or 1 teaspoon dried thyme
2 1/2 cups shredded Jarlsberg
  cheese
1/2 pound orzo (small rice-shaped
  pasta), cooked al dente,
  refreshed in cold water

Preheat the oven to 350 degrees. In an 8-inch skillet, melt the butter over moderate heat. Add the onions and sauté until soft. Stir in the spinach and continue cooking for 2 minutes. Remove from heat. Season with salt, pepper, and nutmeg. Set aside.

Split the red peppers in half lengthwise, leaving the stem halved, but still attached. Scoop out the seeds and ribs. Wash and pat dry. Brush well with olive oil inside and out. Place cut side up in an oiled baking dish.

In a small saucepan, boil the vermouth and garlic over moderately high heat until the vermouth is reduced by half. Add the cream and thyme, reduce heat, and simmer until the cream has thickened slightly to a saucelike consistency. Add 2 cups of the cheese and stir until melted.

In a large mixing bowl, combine the spinach, the well-drained orzo, and the cheese sauce. Blend well and season to taste with more salt, pepper, and nutmeg. Mound the spinach mixture in the pepper shells. Sprinkle each pepper with a portion of the remaining 1/2 cup cheese.

Bake for 30–35 minutes or until the filling is heated through and the peppers are just tender. Can be made ahead up to the point of baking.

Fills 8–10 shells, depending on their size.

Note If using frozen spinach, slightly defrost, cut into 1-inch pieces, and place in a covered 8-inch skillet. Heat over moderate heat. Remove the cover and continue cooking until all the moisture has evaporated. Remove the spinach and set aside.

Crispy Baked Potatoes

SERVES 6

You can never make too many of these.

4 large White Rose potatoes,
  peeled
4 tablespoons butter, melted

Salt and pepper
Summer savory or paprika

Preheat the oven to 425 degrees. Slice the potatoes thinly. Line a jelly-roll pan with foil, and butter the foil with 1 tablespoon of the butter. Arrange the potatoes in rows with the slices overlapping about 1/2 inch. Brush with the remaining butter. Sprinkle with salt, pepper, and summer savory or paprika. Bake for about 40 minutes or until crisp. (The potatoes may be sliced ahead of time, kept in cold water, then drained and patted dry before baking.)

Scalloped Potatoes with Tomatoes

SERVES 6

2 large onions, sliced
2 tablespoons olive oil
1 pound tomatoes peeled and
  seeded *or* 1 (16-ounce) can
  tomatoes, drained
1 red bell pepper (optional)
2 large garlic cloves, minced

1 tablespoon dried basil
2 teaspoons dried oregano
Salt and pepper
8 White Rose potatoes, peeled
1 cup grated mozzarella cheese
1/2 cup freshly grated Parmesan
  cheese

Preheat the oven to 350 degrees. In a medium skillet, sauté the onions in the olive oil until tender. Slice the tomatoes and pepper in strips and add them to the onions. Stir in the garlic, basil, oregano, and salt and pepper. Simmer for 10 minutes.

Thinly slice the potatoes. Pour a third of the tomato mixture in a flat baking dish. Layer half of the potatoes over the sauce. Spread another third of the sauce over the potatoes and cover with half the mozzarella. Add the remaining potatoes, tomato sauce, and mozzarella. Sprinkle with the Parmesan and bake for 1 hour.

Gilroy Potatoes

SERVES 6

1/3–1/2 cup olive oil
12 small new potatoes, peeled
and halved
6–8 bay leaves
2–3 tablespoons fresh thyme
and/or rosemary or 2–3
teaspoons dried

1 head of unpeeled garlic cloves,
separated
Salt and pepper

Preheat the oven to 375 degrees. Thoroughly oil a 9 × 13-inch shallow baking dish. Put the olive oil in a small bowl and dip each potato half in the oil. Place the oiled potatoes in the baking dish and sprinkle with the herbs. Add at least 2 whole unpeeled garlic cloves for each whole potato. Drizzle the remaining oil over the potatoes, herbs, and garlic. Bake for 45 minutes, or until tender.

Garlic Cream Potatoes

SERVES 6–8

Similar to scalloped potatoes, this richly flavored dish is easy to prepare and can be made up to baking ahead of time.

2 cups milk
2 tablespoons butter
1 teaspoon salt
1/4 teaspoon freshly ground
pepper

4 large baking potatoes, peeled
and thinly sliced
6 medium garlic cloves, peeled
1 cup cream
1 cup grated Swiss cheese

Preheat the oven to 325 degrees. In a large saucepan, combine milk, butter, salt, and pepper. Bring to a boil, stirring frequently. Add the potatoes, garlic, and cream and simmer for 15 minutes. Spoon the potato mixture into a buttered 1 1/2–2-quart baking dish and top with the grated cheese. Bake for 10–15 minutes or until bubbly.

Vegetarian Mixed Grill

SERVES 6–8

6 tablespoons unsalted butter
Juice of 1 lemon
Peel of 1 lemon, grated
2 teaspoons dried chicken
    bouillon

2 bunches green onions, chopped
4 carrots, peeled and sliced
3 large baking potatoes, peeled
    and cubed
Salt and pepper

In a small nonaluminum saucepan, melt the butter over low heat. Stir in the lemon juice, peel, and bouillon. Remove from heat and set aside. In a large bowl, combine the green onions, carrots, and potatoes. Add the butter-lemon mixture and toss to mix well. Season to taste with salt and pepper.

Place 2 large pieces of heavy aluminum foil on a work surface. Put half of the vegetable mixture on each piece. Wrap, making sure the packages are flat and even. Cook over hot coals for about 30–45 minutes, turning every 10–15 minutes.

Sauté of Spinach with Chard

SERVES 6

For a variation, substitute walnut oil and walnuts for the olive oil and pine nuts.

2 bunches fresh spinach,
    stemmed
1 bunch fresh Swiss chard,
    stemmed
2 medium garlic cloves, minced
3 leeks, including 1 inch of
    green, well washed and thinly
    sliced

2 tablespoons olive oil
1/3–1/2 cup pine nuts
1/2 teaspoon nutmeg
2 teaspoons finely grated orange
    peel
Salt and pepper
Orange slices, for garnish

Slice the spinach and chard in 1-inch strips. In a large skillet over moderate heat, sauté the garlic and leeks in the olive oil for 5 minutes or until limp. Add the spinach and chard, increase the heat to high, and sauté for 5 minutes longer until slightly wilted. Add the nuts, nutmeg, orange peel, and salt and pepper to taste. Toss and serve immediately garnished with orange slices.

Spinach Stir-fry with Hazelnuts

SERVES 4

3 tablespoons peanut oil
2 bunches fresh spinach,
    stemmed

1 1/2 tablespoons soy sauce
1/2 cup chopped hazelnuts

Heat the oil in a wok. Add the spinach and stir-fry until greens are just beginning to wilt. Add the soy sauce and blend well. Stir in the nuts and serve immediately.

Chile-stuffed Pattypan Squash

SERVES 8

2 tablespoons butter
8 pattypan squash
8 ounces cream cheese, softened
3 tablespoons chopped green
    chiles

2 tablespoons half-and-half
Salt and freshly ground pepper
Dash of hot pepper sauce
1/2 cup grated Monterey Jack
    cheese

Preheat the oven to 400 degrees. Place the butter in a baking dish large enough to hold the squash. Set it in the oven until the butter has melted. Remove the dish from the oven. Meanwhile, add the squash to rapidly boiling water and cook 5–7 minutes or until tender. Drain, rinsing with cold water until cool enough to handle. Scoop out the squash centers and set the shells aside. Combine the cream cheese, chiles, half-and-half, salt and pepper, and hot pepper sauce in a small bowl and beat until well blended. Spoon this mixture into the squash shells. Place the squash in the prepared baking dish and cover it with foil. Bake for about 20 minutes until squash is tender and the filling is heated through. Remove the squash from the oven and discard the foil.

Preheat the broiler. Sprinkle the cheese on the squash. Place dish under the broiler until cheese is golden brown and bubbly.

Autumn Acorn Squash

SERVES 6

3 small acorn squash
2 cups apple juice
I ¼ teaspoons salt

1/8 teaspoon mace
1/4 teaspoon cinnamon

Preheat the oven to 350 degrees. Cut the squash in half and remove seeds. Combine the apple juice and spices in a small bowl. Pour the apple-juice mixture into a baking dish large enough to hold the squash. Place the squash cut side down in the dish. Bake for 45 minutes. Turn cut side up and spoon a few tablespoons of the pan juices into the cavity of each squash. Bake for 10 minutes more, or until tender.

Zucchini Gratin

SERVES 4–6

5 tablespoons butter
4 cups zucchini, sliced in
   ¼-inch rounds
½ teaspoon salt

White pepper
2 tablespoons minced fresh
   parsley
3/4–I cup grated Swiss cheese

Preheat the oven to 350 degrees. In a heavy skillet, melt 3 tablespoons of the butter over moderate heat. Add the zucchini and cook, covered, until soft. Place in a strainer and press to remove any excess moisture. Purée the zucchini in a food processor, adding the salt and pepper to taste. Add the 2 tablespoons of butter and parsley and process for 1–2 seconds.

Place the purée in a shallow gratin dish or baking dish. Top with the cheese. Bake until the cheese is lightly browned.

Tomatoes Stuffed with
Goat Cheese, Shallots, and Mushrooms

SERVES 4

4 medium tomatoes
1/4 cup butter
1/4 cup chopped shallots
1/2 pound mushrooms, sliced

1 tablespoon fresh rosemary or
   tarragon
5 ounces Montrachet cheese,
   crumbled

Preheat the oven to 350 degrees. Cut off the tops of the tomatoes and remove the pulp. Salt and invert the tomatoes to allow to drain. Heat 2 tablespoons of the butter in a medium skillet. Sauté the shallots until softened. Add the remaining 2 tablespoons of butter to the pan. Sauté the mushrooms until soft and the moisture has completely evaporated. Add the rosemary or tarragon and cheese, mixing well. Fill each tomato with a spoonful of the mushroom mixture. Place in a shallow baking dish and bake for 12–15 minutes.

Tomatoes Stuffed with Zucchini Pesto

SERVES 8

8 large tomatoes
16 medium zucchini
1/2 cup Pesto Sauce

1/3–1/2 cup freshly grated
   Parmesan cheese

Preheat the oven to 300 degrees. Cut the tops off the tomatoes and remove the pulp. Invert tomatoes and let them drain for 30 minutes.

Coarsely grate the zucchini. In a medium saucepan filled with water, parboil the zucchini for 3 minutes. Drain well in a colander for 30 minutes. Mix the zucchini with the Pesto Sauce and stuff into the tomatoes. Sprinkle the tomatoes with the cheese. Bake for 30 minutes or until heated through.

Tomatoes Stuffed with Tunisian Rice

SERVES 12

An outstanding side dish for roasted or barbecued lamb.

12 large tomatoes
1 pound onions, minced
1 cup olive oil
1 tablespoon chopped fresh
   parsley
1 tablespoon chopped fresh mint
   or 1 teaspoon dried mint
1 cup uncooked rice

1/2 teaspoon cinnamon
Salt and pepper
1/2 cup currants
1/4 cup pine nuts
1 tablespoon sugar
Additional sugar
Dried bread crumbs
Olive oil

Preheat oven to 350 degrees. Cut a 1/2-inch cap from the top of the tomatoes and remove the pulp. Turn the tomatoes upside down to drain. Reserve the caps. Separate the pulp from the seeds and discard seeds. In a large skillet over moderate heat, sauté the onions in the olive oil with the parsley and mint until the onions are tender. Add the rice, tomato pulp, cinnamon, and salt and pepper. Thin with a little water if necessary. Cook for 5 minutes. Stir in the currants, nuts, and sugar and cook for 10 minutes more. Remove from heat and cool.

Put a pinch of sugar in each tomato. Stuff the tomatoes with the filling, leaving room for swelling. Replace the caps and sprinkle with the crumbs. Pour a little olive oil over each tomato and bake for 25 minutes or until the bread crumbs turn brown.

Oven-dried Tomatoes

MAKES 1–1 1/2 PINTS

A good alternative to sun-dried tomatoes.

3 pounds firm, ripe Roma
   tomatoes
1/4 cup minced fresh basil
2 sprigs fresh rosemary

2 cloves garlic, sliced
3–4 whole black peppercorns
1 1/4 cups olive oil

Preheat the oven to 300 degrees. Wash the tomatoes and remove the stems. Slice lengthwise in halves. Squeeze gently to remove some of the juice and seeds and pat dry.

Arrange the tomatoes in one layer on wire racks placed on a cookie sheet. Bake for 3–5 hours or until dried. Watch carefully not to overdry or they will be tough. Dry them just to the point that all of the moisture is gone. As they start to darken, watch carefully, as they are almost done and will burn quickly.

Place the tomatoes in a 1–1 1/2-pint jar with the rosemary sprigs, garlic, and several black peppercorns. Cover with the olive oil and seal airtight. Store in a cool place.

Lemon Sweet Potatoes

SERVES 8

Lemon lightens these traditional holiday sweet potatoes.

4 pounds fresh sweet potatoes or
   yams
4 tablespoons fresh lemon juice
1 teaspoon salt
1/4 cup butter, softened

2 egg yolks
Salt and pepper
Lemon slices, for garnish
2 tablespoons butter, melted

Preheat the oven to 325 degrees. Cook, peel, and mash the sweet potatoes. Place in a large bowl and beat in the lemon juice, butter, and egg yolks. Season to taste with salt and pepper. Transfer the mixture to a buttered 1 1/2-quart casserole and top with the lemon slices. Brush the top with the melted butter. Bake for 45 minutes, or until heated through.

Bourbon Yams

SERVES 10

2 1/2 cups milk
2 cups sugar
3 eggs
2 teaspoons cinnamon
3–4 medium-sized yams

1/2 cup blanched slivered almonds
2 tablespoons butter
1/2 cup bourbon

Preheat the oven to 350 degrees. In a large bowl, beat the milk, sugar, eggs, and cinnamon until well blended. Peel and grate the yams, adding them to the mixture as you go to prevent them from discoloring. Stir in the almonds. Pour the mixture into a buttered 2-quart casserole. Dot the top with the butter. Bake, uncovered, for 45 minutes. Pour the bourbon over the yams and bake for 30 minutes more.

Shoestring Yams

SERVES 6

A wonderful accompaniment to Roast Duckling with Black Peppercorn Sauce.

Peanut oil for deep-frying
1 1/2 pounds yams, peeled
Salt

In a deep fryer at least 5 inches deep, heat 2 inches of oil to 375 degrees. Using a food processor fitted with the coarse shredding disk, grate the yams. Or, the yams may be cut with a knife in matchstick juliennes.

In the heated oil, fry the potatoes in small batches for about 30 seconds or until they begin to color. Allow oil to return to 375 degrees before adding next batch. Yams will not crisp until they cool. Transfer the fried yams to paper towels to drain and sprinkle with salt.

Yams can be prepared several hours in advance and reheated in a warm 300-degree oven for 10 minutes on a foil-lined cookie sheet.

Broccoli Purée

SERVES 6

1 1/2 pounds broccoli
1 medium onion, chopped
1 garlic clove, minced (optional)
1 cup toasted walnuts
2 teaspoons chopped fresh basil
  (optional)

1 tablespoon chopped fresh
  parsley
1/2 teaspoon salt
1/4 teaspoon white pepper
1/2 cup unsalted butter

Trim and peel the broccoli and cut in 1-inch sections. In a medium saucepan, heat just enough water to cover the broccoli. Add the broccoli and cook just until tender. Drain, reserving the liquid.

Return the reserved liquid to the saucepan and cook the onions and garlic until tender. Remove from heat. In a food processor, purée all of the vegetables until they are smooth, and place in the top of a double boiler. Separately process the walnuts, basil, and parsley and add to the broccoli mixture. Add the salt, pepper, and butter. Heat thoroughly over boiling water.

Carrot Purée

SERVES 6

1 1/2 pounds carrots, peeled and
  thinly sliced
4 tablespoons butter
1/2 teaspoon salt

1/8 teaspoon white pepper
1/4 teaspoon freshly grated
  nutmeg
1/2 teaspoon thyme or tarragon

Place the carrots in a heavy saucepan and barely cover with water. Add 2 tablespoons of the butter and cook over moderate heat for 10–15 minutes until they are very tender.

Drain the carrots well and purée them in a food processor or blender with the remaining 2 tablespoons of butter. Add the salt, pepper, nutmeg, and thyme or tarragon and purée until smooth. Season to taste with additional salt and pepper.

Celery Root Purée

SERVES 4–6

1 1/2 pounds celery root
 (celeriac)
Warm water with fresh lemon
 juice

2 tablespoons butter
1 tablespoon plus 1 teaspoon
 fresh lemon juice
Salt and white pepper

Peel celery root and chop in medium-size chunks. Drop into the water–lemon-juice mixture. Drain and place celery root in a medium saucepan half filled with boiling water. Cover and simmer 15–20 minutes or until tender. Do not overcook.

Purée in a food processor. Add the butter, lemon juice, and salt and pepper to taste. (Can be made a day ahead to this point.) Before serving, reheat in a saucepan over low heat. Garnish with grated nutmeg or chopped parsley.

Grilled Vegetables with Chili Butter

SERVES 6–8

3 medium zucchini
3 medium yellow squash
1/2 teaspoon salt

1/4 teaspoon pepper
Chili Butter (below)

Cut the squash diagonally in 1/2-inch slices. Season with salt and pepper to taste. Place the squash on the grill over medium coals. Brush with the Chili Butter and grill 3–5 minutes, or until tender. Turn the squash midway through the cooking time and brush again with the butter.

CHILI BUTTER
1/2 cup butter, melted
1–2 tablespoons chili powder
Pinch of dried red pepper flakes (optional)

Combine all ingredients.

Sautéed Baby Vegetables with Shallot Butter

SERVES 8

Any baby vegetables of the season will make a colorful addition to your meal.

6 baby carrots
1/2 pound baby turnips
1/2 pound baby green zucchini
1/2 pound baby yellow zucchini

3 tablespoons butter
1 tablespoon minced shallots
Salt and freshly ground pepper
1/4 cup minced fresh parsley

In a 4-quart kettle, bring 2 quarts of water to a boil. Add the carrots and turnips and parboil for 2 minutes. Add the zucchini and boil for an additional 2 minutes. Drain and refresh under cold running water. Vegetables can be refrigerated at this time for later use.

Melt the butter in a large skillet and sauté the shallots until tender. Add the vegetables and sauté until heated through. Season to taste with salt and freshly ground pepper. Sprinkle with parsley.

Baked Vegetables Niçoise

SERVES 8

6 new potatoes
Salt and pepper
1/2 cup olive oil
1 large eggplant
4 small zucchini
1 large sweet red pepper
1 large green pepper

1 large yellow pepper
4 ripe tomatoes
2 onions
1 cup Niçoise or Kalamata
 olives
Oregano and thyme to taste

Preheat oven to 375 degrees. Peel and thinly slice the potatoes. Arrange a layer of potatoes in a 9 × 12-inch glass baking dish. Sprinkle the potatoes lightly with salt and pepper and oil. Cut the eggplant, zucchinis, and peppers in 1/2-inch strips. Thinly slice the tomatoes and onions. Layer each vegetable over the potatoes. Repeat. Distribute the olives over the top of the casserole. Sprinkle the vegetables with more salt, pepper, and oil. Cover the dish tightly with a double thickness of aluminum foil. Place the casserole in the oven for 20–25 minutes or until the juices are bubbling. Remove the foil and reduce the heat to 325 degrees. Continue cooking for 1 hour more, until the vegetables are tender. Brush with a little more oil if the casserole seems dry.

Italian Baked Vegetables

SERVES 4

2 crookneck squash, sliced 1/4 inch thick

2 zucchini squash, sliced 1/4 inch thick

1 small onion, sliced 1/4 inch thick

1 tomato, sliced

8 large basil leaves

1/2 teaspoon dried thyme

Salt and pepper

2 tablespoons Parmesan cheese

Preheat the oven to 350 degrees. Toss all ingredients in a 1 1/2-quart ovenproof casserole. Bake for 20–25 minutes. This can be prepared a day ahead and baked later.

Marinated and Skewered Grilled Vegetables

SERVES 4–6

A colorful and flavorful addition to any grilled dinner.

1/2 cup vegetable oil

1/4 cup soy sauce

1/2 cup red wine

1 teaspoon ground ginger

2 small garlic cloves

1 1/2 teaspoons curry powder

2 tablespoons ketchup

1/4 teaspoon pepper

1/4 teaspoon Tabasco sauce

1 red bell pepper, cut in 3/4-inch slices

1 green bell pepper, cut in 3/4-inch slices

3 Japanese eggplants, cut in 3/4-inch slices

6 boiling onions

1 box cherry tomatoes

1/2 pound small mushrooms, washed and stems trimmed

In a large bowl combine the oil, soy sauce, wine, ginger, garlic, curry, ketchup, pepper and Tabasco. Add the vegetables to the marinade, toss, and let sit for 2–3 hours at room temperature.

Drain and place each type of vegetable on a separate skewer. Cook over hot coals for 10–12 minutes. To serve, empty onto platter and pass.

Stir-fried Vegetables

SERVES 6–8

1/2 cup peanut oil
1 garlic clove, minced
1 1/2 cups broccoli flowerets
1 1/2 cups cauliflower cut in
    small pieces
1 1/2 cups sliced mushrooms

1/2 cup sherry
1 tablespoon peeled and chopped
    fresh ginger or 1 teaspoon
    ground ginger
1 tablespoon soy sauce
Pepper

Heat the oil in a wok. Add the garlic and cook for 1 minute. Stir in the broccoli and cauliflower and cook, stirring, for 3 minutes. Add the remaining ingredients and stir-fry for 5 minutes. Serve immediately.

Summer Baked Vegetables with Herbs

SERVES 6–8

2 medium tomatoes, cut in
    quarters
1 medium crookneck squash,
    thinly sliced
1 zucchini, thinly sliced
1 small onion, cut in chunks
1/2 head cauliflower, cut in
    flowerets
1 cup thinly sliced carrots
1 cup green beans, cut in
    1/2-inch pieces
1 cup White Rose potatoes, cut
    in small pieces

1/2 cup chopped celery
1/4 cup thinly sliced red bell
    pepper
1/2 cup green peas
1 cup Beef Stock or bouillon
1/3 cup olive oil
3 garlic cloves, minced
2 teaspoons salt
1/2 bay leaf
1/2 teaspoon summer savory
1/2 teaspoon tarragon
Freshly grated Parmesan cheese
Monterey Jack cheese

Preheat oven to 350 degrees. Combine all of the vegetables in a shallow baking dish that has a cover. In a small saucepan, combine the stock, oil, garlic, salt, bay leaf, summer savory, and tarragon. Bring to a boil and pour over the vegetables. Cover the casserole tightly. Bake for 1 hour, stirring twice while cooking. At the end of the hour, uncover and sprinkle generously with the Parmesan cheese. Cover the vegetables with slices of Jack cheese. Place under a preheated broiler until the cheese is melted.

Individual Vegetable Strudels

SERVES 12

3 cups coarsely chopped fresh
  broccoli
3 cups chopped fresh cauliflower
2 1/2 cups sliced carrots
2 tablespoons butter
1 large onion, chopped
2 garlic cloves, minced
3 eggs
1 tablespoon minced fresh
  parsley

2 tablespoons minced fresh basil
  or 1/2 teaspoon dried basil
1/4 teaspoon dried tarragon
1 teaspoon salt
1/4 teaspoon pepper
1 pound Gruyère cheese, grated
21 phyllo pastry sheets
3/4 cup butter, melted
Sesame seeds (optional)

Preheat oven to 375 degrees. Combine the broccoli, cauliflower, and carrots in a steamer. Place the steamer over boiling water and steam the vegetables until they are just tender. Set them aside to cool. Melt the 2 tablespoons of butter in a skillet over medium heat. Add the onion and garlic to the butter. Cover the skillet and cook over moderate heat, stirring occasionally, until they are slightly brown, about 10 minutes. In a large bowl, combine the eggs, parsley, basil, tarragon, salt, and pepper. Blend well. Add the vegetables, onion, garlic, and cheese. Mix gently but thoroughly. Can be made ahead to this point.

Lay the phyllo sheets out on a work surface covered with plastic wrap. Using a measuring tape as a guide, cut a 4 × 14-inch strip from the 14 × 18-inch package of phyllo, cutting with kitchen shears through all 21 sheets. There will be a 14-inch square remaining. Cut the square in 4 equal parts so that there are 4 small 7-inch squares, each containing 21 sheets. Cover with a damp (not wet) cloth.

Cover another work surface with plastic. Lay a 7-inch square on the surface and brush with butter. Repeat with 6 more 7-inch sheets, buttering and stacking each. Work very quickly and keep the remainder of the phyllo dough covered with a damp cloth.

Place approximately 1/2 cup of the vegetable filling on the front third of the stacked squares. Tuck in all sides while you roll the pastry as you would a burrito. Brush with butter and place seam side down on a greased cookie sheet. Decorate with rope design (directions follow) or sprinkle with sesame seeds. Repeat with remaining phyllo and vegetables until you have 12 individual strudels.

For the rope design, take 1 or 2 (4 × 14-inch) buttered strips. Roll tightly lengthwise jelly-roll fashion. Twist until evenly corkscrewed. Wrap the pastry rope around the individual strudels like a ribbon around a package and carefully tie. Bake for 20–30 minutes.

Can be made up to 24 hours ahead if the whole cookie sheet is covered tightly with plastic wrap and then covered with a damp cloth and refrigerated.

X

Brunch and Lunch

Balboa Brunch

SERVES 8

3 tablespoons butter
3 cups sliced leeks, white part only
12 slices white bread
1 pound cooked small shrimp

1 pound Swiss cheese, grated
3 tablespoons chopped fresh dill
5 eggs
2 1/2 cups milk
Salt and pepper

Butter a 9 × 13-inch glass casserole dish. In a medium skillet, melt the butter and sauté the leeks until they are tender. Remove the crusts from the bread. In the casserole, layer half of the bread, half of the leeks, half of the shrimp, half of the cheese and half of the dill. Repeat. Beat the eggs with the milk, salt, and pepper, to taste. Pour over the shrimp mixture, cover and refrigerate overnight. The next day, bake, uncovered, in a preheated 350-degree oven for 50–60 minutes.

Three-Cheese Soufflé

SERVES 4

This rich and dense soufflé makes an excellent quick luncheon or supper entree.

4 eggs
2/3 cup heavy cream
2 cups grated sharp Cheddar cheese
1/2 cup grated Swiss or Jarlsberg cheese

1/2 cup grated Parmesan cheese
1/2 teaspoon salt
1/8 teaspoon white pepper
Tomato Coulis (below)

Preheat the oven to 425 degrees. In a medium bowl, whisk the eggs and cream until well mixed. Fold in the cheeses, salt, and pepper. Pour into a lightly buttered 1-quart soufflé dish. Bake for 30–35 minutes or until firm and golden brown. Serve with Tomato Coulis on the side.

TOMATO COULIS

3 cups fresh peeled tomatoes *or*
   1 (28-ounce) can tomatoes, drained
1 tablespoon olive oil

1/2 teaspoon salt
1/2 teaspoon sugar
2 tablespoons chopped fresh basil *or* 1 teaspoon dried basil

In a medium saucepan bring the tomatoes, olive oil, salt, sugar, and basil to a boil. Reduce heat and simmer 15–20 minutes until reduced and thickened.

Corn and Red Pepper Roulade

SERVES 6–8

Serve this spectacular dish with a fresh green salad for a very memorable brunch.

1 red bell pepper	1/2 cup sifted flour
1 cup corn, fresh or canned	2 cups hot milk
1 cup heavy cream	4 eggs, separated
1 cup thinly sliced green onions	Pinch of salt
1 cup plus 1 tablespoon freshly grated Parmesan cheese	1 tablespoon unsalted butter, melted
Salt and cayenne pepper	Roasted Pepper Purée (below)
7 tablespoons butter	

Roast the pepper as directed in Roasted Red Pepper Purée, below. Peel, seed, and chop the pepper. In a medium skillet, combine the corn and 1/2 cup of the cream. Simmer the mixture, stirring occasionally, for 4 minutes. Add the onions and the remaining cream and simmer the mixture, stirring occasionally, for 5 minutes or until it is thick and the cream is absorbed. Stir in the bell pepper, and 1/2 cup of the Parmesan cheese. Season to taste with salt and cayenne pepper. Set aside.

Preheat the oven to 400 degrees. Line a 10 × 15-inch jelly-roll pan with aluminum foil. Grease the pan with 2 tablespoons of the butter and set aside. In a saucepan, melt 4 tablespoons of the butter and add the flour. Cook for 3 minutes, stirring constantly. Gradually add the milk and cook, stirring constantly, until the mixture is thickened and smooth. Continue cooking for 1 minute. Beat in the egg yolks, one at a time, and stir in the second 1/2 cup of Parmesan cheese. Set aside. With an electric mixer, beat the egg whites with the salt until stiff but not dry. Fold into the batter. Pour the batter evenly into the prepared pan. Bake for 20 minutes or until the roulade is golden and firm to the touch. Reduce the oven heat to 350 degrees. Cool slightly and carefully turn the roulade out onto a clean dish towel. Gently remove the foil. Spread the corn-and-red-pepper filling over the warm roulade, leaving a 1-inch border on all sides. Using the dish towel as an aid, roll the roulade jelly-roll fashion, beginning with a long side. Transfer the roulade to an ovenproof platter, spread it with the remaining butter and sprinkle with the remaining tablespoon of Parmesan cheese. The roulade may be prepared ahead to this point, covered with plastic wrap, and refrigerated. At serving time, bring to room temperature and bake in the preheated 350-degree oven for 25–30 minutes or until heated through. Serve with Roasted Red Pepper Purée.

ROASTED RED PEPPER PURÉE
3 red bell peppers
Cayenne pepper

Using a long-handled fork, char the peppers over an open flame, turning them for 2–3 minutes, or until the skins are blackened. Or, place the peppers on a broiler pan and broil about 2 inches from the heat until the skins are blackened, turning frequently. This will take about 15 minutes. Transfer the peppers to a plastic bag, close tightly and let them steam until they are cool enough to handle and peel. In a food processor, purée the peppers and season to taste with cayenne pepper.

Capistrano Quiche

SERVES 6–8

6 corn tortillas
Vegetable oil
Salt
1 pound lean ground beef
1 large onion, chopped
1 garlic clove, minced
1 green bell pepper, chopped
1 (7-ounce) can green chile salsa
1 teaspoon dried oregano
1 teaspoon ground cumin
1 tablespoon chili powder
1/4 cup chopped fresh cilantro

2 cups grated Cheddar cheese
1 (7-ounce) can whole green chiles, seeded and cut in strips
6 eggs
1 1/2 cups milk
1/2 teaspoon salt
1 large or 2 small avocados, sliced
1/4 cup sliced black olives
Sour cream
Fresh salsa, preferably homemade

Cut each tortilla in 8 wedges. In a large skillet, heat 1/4–1/2 inch of oil over medium-high heat. Add 6–8 tortilla pieces and fry until golden brown on both sides. Drain well on paper towels and sprinkle lightly with salt. Repeat with the remaining tortillas.

In another skillet, cook the beef until crumbly. Add the onions, garlic, and green pepper. Cook 5 minutes, then stir in the salsa, oregano, cumin, chili powder, and cilantro.

Preheat the oven to 375 degrees. In a greased shallow 2 1/2–3-quart casserole, place half of the tortilla wedges. Top with half of the meat mixture, half of the cheese, and all of the chile strips. Top with the remaining meat and cheese. Place the remaining tortilla wedges around the edge of the dish, pointed ends up. Beat together the eggs, milk, and the 1/2 teaspoon salt. Pour over the top. Bake for 25–30 minutes or until the quiche is set.

Garnish with the sliced avocados and sliced olives. Pass sour cream and fresh salsa.

Broccoli and Cheddar Pie with Potato Crust

SERVES 6

2 cups grated raw potatoes
Salt
1 egg, beaten
1/4 cup grated onions
2 tablespoons oil
3 tablespoons butter
1 cup chopped onions
1 medium garlic clove, minced

4 cups broccoli flowerets
1 tablespoon minced fresh basil
1/2 teaspoon dried thyme
Salt and pepper to taste
1 1/2 cups grated Cheddar cheese
1/2 cup milk
2 eggs
Paprika

Preheat the oven to 400 degrees. Place the potatoes in a strainer and press with a spoon to remove all moisture. In a bowl, combine potatoes, a dash of salt, the 1 egg, and the grated onions. Pat the mixture into a well-oiled 9-inch pie pan. Bake for 30 minutes. Decrease the oven temperature to 375 degrees, brush the crust with the 2 tablespoons of oil, and continue cooking for 5–10 minutes, or until lightly browned. Leave the oven set at 375 degrees.

In a large skillet, melt the butter and add the chopped onions and the garlic. Sauté for 5 minutes. Add the broccoli, herbs, and salt and pepper to taste. Cook, covered, over low heat for 10 minutes, stirring occasionally. Spread half the cheese over the crust. Top with the vegetables and the remaining cheese. Beat together the milk and eggs and pour over vegetable mixture. Sprinkle with paprika. Bake for 35–40 minutes or until set.

Quiche au Saucisson

SERVES 6–8

PASTRY

1 1/4 cups flour

6 tablespoons cold unsalted butter

2 tablespoons cold vegetable shortening

1/8 teaspoon salt

3 tablespoons cold water

In the bowl of a food processor, process the flour, butter, shortening, and salt until the moisture resembles coarse meal. Add the water, 1 tablespoon at a time, and process just until the dough comes together. Chill for 1 hour. Preheat the oven to 400 degrees. Roll out the dough 1/8 inch thick on a well-floured surface. Place the dough in a 9-inch pie pan and crimp the edges. Line the bottom of the pastry with aluminum foil and fill with pie weights or beans. Bake in the lower third of the oven for 10 minutes. Remove from the oven and reduce the oven temperature to 350 degrees.

FILLING

1 pound Italian sausage, casings removed

1 tablespoon butter

1 tablespoon flour

1 3/4 cups half-and-half

2 cups thinly sliced Red Delicious apples

4 eggs plus 1 egg yolk

1/2 teaspoon salt

Pinch ground nutmeg

1/2 teaspoon dry mustard

2 cups grated Swiss cheese

In a medium skillet, sauté the sausage until brown and crumbly. Drain well on paper towels. In a saucepan melt the butter and stir in the flour. Add the half-and-half, stirring until mixture thickens. Meanwhile, arrange the sausage and apples in the bottom of the prepared quiche shell. Beat eggs and egg yolk with salt, nutmeg, and mustard. Add the cream sauce and blend well. Stir in the Swiss cheese and pour over the sausage and apples. Bake for 45 minutes, or until a knife inserted in the center comes out clean.

San Joaquin Valley Tart

PASTRY

1 1/2 cups flour
1 teaspoon crumbled dried basil
1/2 teaspoon salt
6 tablespoons butter, frozen and cut in 1/2-inch pieces

3 tablespoons vegetable shortening, frozen and cut in 1/2-inch chunks
3–4 tablespoons ice water
1 egg yolk, beaten

Place the flour, basil and salt in a food processor. Distribute the butter and the shortening over the flour. Process for about 8 seconds or until the fat particles look like small peas. Measure the water into a cup with the egg yolk and mix. With the motor running, add the egg mixture slowly through the feed tube. Process until the pastry looks crumbly but does not form a ball. Turn the mixture onto a sheet of waxed paper and pat it into about a 6-inch round. Wrap with the paper and refrigerate for 1–2 hours. This may be made ahead and frozen.

Preheat the oven to 400 degrees. Roll out the dough and line a 10-inch quiche pan or a deep-dish pie pan with the pastry, leaving a 1-inch overlap beyond the edge. Fold the overlap inside to form a double thickness. Prick the bottom with a fork and chill for 30 minutes. Line the pastry with aluminum foil and fill with pie weights or beans. Place in the center of the oven and bake for 8 minutes. Remove the foil and weights and bake for 4 minutes longer. Remove from the oven and set aside. Reset the oven to 375 degrees.

FILLING

2 tablespoons butter
1 onion, chopped
2 garlic cloves, minced
1 red bell pepper, coarsely chopped
1 yellow bell pepper, coarsely chopped
4 medium tomatoes, peeled, seeded, and coarsely chopped

3/4 cup fresh bread crumbs
1/2 cup freshly grated Parmesan cheese
1/4 cup finely chopped fresh basil *or* 1 teaspoon dried basil
Salt and pepper
3 eggs
1 cup heavy cream

In a medium skillet melt the butter over medium heat and sauté the onions and garlic 4–5 minutes until just soft but not browned. Add the bell peppers and cook 3–5 minutes longer.

In a large mixing bowl, combine the tomatoes, bread crumbs, cheese, basil, and onion-pepper mixture. Season to taste with salt and pepper. In a small mixing bowl, beat the eggs with the cream.

To assemble, spoon the filling to within 1/4 inch of the top of the prepared crust. Slowly pour the egg mixture over the filling, making sure that it is evenly distributed. Bake for 50–60 minutes, or until the custard is set. Allow to rest 5–10 minutes before cutting into wedges.

Note Depending on the pan size there may be extra filling or egg mixture.

Sour Cream Enchiladas with Ham

SERVES 4

FILLING

1 cup chopped ham
1/2 pound grated Jack cheese
1/2 cup diced green chiles

1/2 cup sour cream
6 tablespoons chopped fresh
  cilantro

8 small flour tortillas

In a bowl, combine the ham, Jack cheese, chiles, sour cream, and cilantro and mix well.

SAUCE

1/2 cup butter
1/2 cup flour
4 cups milk
1 pound Cheddar cheese, diced

2 teaspoons Dijon mustard
1 teaspoon salt
1/2 medium onion, grated

In a medium saucepan over low heat, melt the butter and add the flour, stirring constantly, for 3–5 minutes. Gradually add the milk and cook, stirring, until the sauce is smooth and thick. Add the cheese and stir until the cheese is melted. Stir in the mustard, salt, and onions. This sauce may be made ahead and refrigerated. Reheat before assembling.

To assemble, preheat the oven to 350 degrees. Place one eighth of the ham mixture near the edge of each tortilla and roll tightly. Place seam side down in an oiled baking dish. Pour the sauce over the enchiladas, covering them thoroughly. Bake for 35–40 minutes.

Spinach Crepes with Tomato Fondue

SERVES 6

Dijon mustard lends distinction to the crepes.

CREPES

2 cups flour
1/2 teaspoon salt
1 cup water
1 cup milk

3 tablespoons Dijon mustard
2 tablespoons minced fresh
   chives
1/4 cup unsalted butter, melted

In a blender or a food processor, blend the flour, salt, water, milk, mustard, and chives until smooth. Add the melted butter and blend for 3 seconds. Let the batter rest for 1 hour.

Oil a crepe pan or small sauté pan and place over high heat until hot. Swirl approximately 1/4 cup of the batter into the pan. Quickly pour out any excess batter so that only a thin layer coats the bottom of the pan. Reduce heat to medium and cook until bottom of crepe is golden brown. Turn the crepe and cook 10–15 seconds more. Repeat with the remaining batter.

SPINACH FILLING

1 egg
4 ounces goat cheese, crumbled
3/4 cup freshly grated Parmesan
   cheese
1/2 teaspoon salt

Freshly ground pepper
6 tablespoons butter
2 pounds fresh spinach, stemmed
   and chopped

In a small bowl, combine the egg, goat cheese, 1/2 cup of the Parmesan cheese, and salt and pepper to taste. Mix well. Melt 3 tablespoons of the butter in a medium skillet and add the spinach. Sauté until wilted. Drain well and press out all the excess moisture. Add to the cheese mixture, blending well. Preheat oven to 350 degrees.

To assemble, place 1–2 tablespoons of the filling on each crepe. Roll up and arrange seam side down in a buttered glass baking dish. Dot with the remaining 3 tablespoons butter and sprinkle with the remaining cheese. Bake about 15 minutes. Serve each crepe with a dollop of Tomato Fondue.

TOMATO FONDUE

2 tablespoons olive oil
2 tablespoons minced shallots
1 large garlic clove, minced
1 bay leaf
1/2 teaspoon sugar

8 ripe tomatoes, peeled and
   chopped *or* 1 (28-ounce) can
   tomatoes, drained and
   chopped
Salt and pepper

Place the oil in a medium saucepan. Add the shallots and garlic and sauté until translucent. Add the bay leaf, sugar, and tomatoes. Simmer the mixture, stirring occasionally, until sauce is fairly thick, about 20–30 minutes. Add salt and pepper to taste. Remove bay leaf. Serve warm or at room temperature.

Corn Cakes

MAKES 18–20 CAKES

These are bound to become a breakfast classic. They are also marvelous as "mini" 2-inch pancakes served in place of potatoes or rice with roast lamb or pork.

1 3/4 cups flour	3 eggs
1/4 cup cornmeal	2 cups milk
2 teaspoons baking powder	1/4 cup butter, melted
2 teaspoons sugar	1 cup corn
1 teaspoon salt	Crème Fraîche (below)

Sift the dry ingredients in a mixing bowl. Make a well in the dry ingredients. Lightly beat the eggs and milk together. Add the mixture to the well in the dry ingredients. Stir in the melted butter and mix lightly. Stir in the corn. Do not overmix.

For each pancake, pour about 1/4 cup of the batter onto a hot, lightly greased griddle. Turn pancakes when bubbles appear and edges are dry. Serve with Crème Fraîche and raspberry jam.

CRÈME FRAÎCHE
1 tablespoon buttermilk or sour cream
1 cup heavy cream

Add the buttermilk or sour cream to cream. Mix and let sit for 6–8 hours at room temperature. Cover and refrigerate for at least 24 hours before serving. This will keep in the refrigerator for 1 week.

Chicken, Spinach, and Gruyère Torta

SERVES 6

1 (10-ounce) package frozen
    chopped spinach
13 tablespoons butter
3 tablespoons minced shallots or
    green onions
1 teaspoon salt
1/4 teaspoon pepper
1/4 teaspoon grated fresh nutmeg
4 large eggs
1 1/2 cups whipping cream

1/8 teaspoon pepper
Pinch of nutmeg
1 cup grated Gruyère cheese
    (other Swiss cheeses may be
    substituted)
2 cups shredded poached chicken
4 tablespoons Dijon mustard
16 sheets phyllo dough, covered
    with a damp cloth

Slightly defrost the spinach. Cut the frozen block in 1-inch pieces. In an 8-inch skillet, sauté the spinach in 2 tablespoons of the butter over moderate heat until the moisture has evaporated. Remove from the skillet and set aside. In the same skillet, melt 1 more tablespoon of the butter over moderate heat. Add the shallots and sauté until just soft. Stir in the spinach and continue cooking for 2 minutes. Remove from heat. Season with 1/2 teaspoon of the salt, the 1/4 teaspoon of pepper, and the 1/4 teaspoon of nutmeg. Set aside and cool to room temperature. Preheat oven to 350 degrees.

In a medium mixing bowl, beat the eggs, cream, the remaining salt, the 1/8 teaspoon of pepper, and the pinch of nutmeg until well blended. Gradually stir in the cooled spinach mixture. Fold in the cheese and chicken. Set aside. In a small saucepan, melt the remaining 10 tablespoons of butter over a low flame. Whisk in the mustard until blended.

Butter a 9-inch springform pan. Place a phyllo sheet in the pan and brush with the melted-butter mixture. Add 9 more sheets of phyllo, buttering each one and overlapping the sheet edges, allowing them to overhang the pan edge in a circular manner. Work quickly, keeping the remaining phyllo covered as you work. Pour the filling into the prepared pan. Fold the overhanging edges of pastry over the top of the filling, toward the center of the pan.

Using a 9-inch pie plate as a guide, cut 6 circles from the remaining phyllo sheets. Top the filled torta with 1 circle and brush with butter mixture. Repeat with the remaining 5 circles. With scissors or a sharp knife, cut through the 6 top phyllo circles to make 6 pie-shaped sections. Brush the top of the torta with the remaining butter mixture. Bake for 45 minutes to 1 hour or until set. Remove to a rack. Cool for 10–15 minutes. Remove sides from pan and serve. May also be served at room temperature.

Breakfast Chimichangas with Fresh Fruit

SERVES 4

Blueberries, raspberries, peaches, or apricots are also delicious when substituted for the strawberries in this simple brunch dish. Use the corresponding fruit preserves.

2/3 cup ricotta cheese
6 ounces cream cheese, softened
1/4 cup sugar
1 teaspoon grated lemon rind
1/2 teaspoon cinnamon
4 flour tortillas

2 teaspoons unsalted butter
2 teaspoons vegetable oil
1/4 cup strawberry preserves
Sour cream
Fresh strawberries

Combine ricotta cheese, cream cheese, sugar, lemon rind, and cinnamon. Mix well and set aside.

Soften the tortillas by placing them in a microwave between damp paper towels for 20–30 seconds or wrapping in foil and heating in the oven at 350 degrees for approximately 10 minutes. Place a quarter of the filling in the center of each tortilla. Fold 2 sides in and fold over to enclose filling.

In a medium skillet heat the butter and oil over medium heat. When hot, place the tortillas seam side down in the pan. Cook for 2–3 minutes or until golden brown, turn, and cook for 2–3 minutes more. Top each with 1 tablespoon of the strawberry preserves and a dollop of sour cream. Garnish with fresh strawberries.

Heavenly Hots

SERVES 4–6

2 cups sour cream
6 tablespoons flour
1 tablespoon sugar

1 teaspoon baking soda
4 eggs, beaten
1 cup blueberries (optional)

Combine the sour cream, flour, sugar, baking soda, and eggs. Mix well. Gently fold in the blueberries, if desired. For each pancake, pour about 1/4 cup of the batter onto a hot, lightly greased griddle. Turn pancakes when bubbles appear and edges are dry. Serve with softened butter and syrup.

Gingerbread Pancakes

MAKES ABOUT 16 PANCAKES

Cranberry Butter, applesauce or the traditional maple syrup are excellent accompaniments to these scrumptious pancakes.

2 1/2 cups flour
1 teaspoon baking powder
1 teaspoon baking soda
1/2 teaspoon salt
1 1/2 teaspoons cinnamon
1 1/2 teaspoons ground ginger
1 1/2 teaspoons ground nutmeg
1/4 teaspoon ground cloves

3 eggs
1/4 cup firmly packed brown
    sugar
1 cup buttermilk
1 cup water
1/4 cup brewed coffee
1/4 cup butter, melted

Combine the flour, baking powder, baking soda, salt, cinnamon, ginger, nutmeg, and cloves and mix well. Combine the eggs and sugar, beating well. Add the buttermilk, water, coffee, and butter to egg mixture. Mix well. Add to the dry ingredients, stirring just until moistened. Batter will be slightly lumpy.

For each pancake, pour about 1/4 cup batter onto a hot, lightly greased griddle. Turn pancakes when bubbles appear and edges are dry.

Hawaiian Pancake

SERVES 6

1/2 cup shredded coconut
3/4 cup orange marmalade
1/2 cup crushed pineapple,
    drained
2 tablespoons light rum
1/2 cup coarsely chopped
    macadamia nuts

2 1/2 tablespoons butter
1 1/4 cups milk
3/4 cup flour
3 eggs
1/3 cup sugar
1/4 teaspoon salt
1/4 teaspoon vanilla

Toast the coconut in the oven at 300 degrees, stirring occasionally, for 10 minutes or until it is light brown. Set aside. Reset the oven to 400 degrees. In a small saucepan, combine the marmalade, pineapple, rum, and macadamia nuts. Heat slowly over low heat. Keep warm but do not allow to boil.

In a 9-inch glass pie plate, melt the butter in the oven. While the butter is melting, place in a blender the milk, flour, eggs, sugar, salt, and vanilla. Blend until smooth. Remove the pie plate from the oven and increase the oven temperature to 425 degrees. Pour the batter into the pie plate and return to the oven. Bake for 20 minutes. Reduce the oven temperature to 325 degrees and bake an additional 8–10 minutes. A well will form in the middle of the pancake.

Spoon the topping into the pancake. Sprinkle with the coconut. Serve immediately or the pancake will flatten and lose its attractive appearance.

Oysters Kilpatrick

SERVES 6–12

3 (8-ounce) jars eastern oysters
1 cup flour
1/4 teaspoon salt
1/2 teaspoon pepper
9 tablespoons butter

1/2 teaspoon cayenne pepper
1 teaspoon Worcestershire sauce
Juice of 1 1/2 lemons
6 large slices sourdough bread

Rinse the oysters and roll in the flour. Season with salt and pepper. In a large skillet, melt 4 tablespoons of the butter. Add the oysters and sprinkle with cayenne. Cook, turning once, for about 10–12 minutes, until the oysters are firm and golden brown. Remove and keep warm. To the pan drippings add the remaining butter, Worcestershire sauce, and lemon juice. Cook, stirring, until thickened. Cut the bread in half and toast. Serve the oysters on toast topped with the sauce.

Breakfast Meats with Apples

SERVES 8

1 fully cooked (6-ounce) ham
   steak
3 red or green apples, peeled,
   cored, and thickly sliced
1/2 cup maple syrup

1 pound spicy bulk sausage
   meat, made into 8 patties
1 pound assorted link sausages
1/2 pound Canadian bacon, sliced

Preheat the oven to 350 degrees. Place the ham and apples in a shallow baking dish and drizzle with the syrup. Bake, uncovered, for 20 minutes or until apples are tender and ham is heated through. Baste frequently with pan juices while baking.

Meanwhile, in a large skillet, fry the sausage patties and link sausages until completely cooked. Drain thoroughly. Set aside in a covered shallow casserole to keep warm. Using the same pan, brown both sides of the Canadian bacon. Add the bacon to the sausages. When ready to serve, arrange the meats with the cooked ham and apples, being sure to drizzle accumulated pan juices over the sausages.

Note Sausages and meat can be browned and cooked ahead of time and reheated in a covered shallow casserole at 350 degrees for 10 minutes.

Sausage Stuffed Baked Apples

SERVES 6

Complete your country breakfast with cornbread and scrambled eggs.

6 large Rome Beauty apples or
   other large baking apples
1 tablespoon butter
1/4 cup chopped onions
1/2 pound bulk sausage
1/4 cup brown sugar
1 teaspoon dried sage

1/2 teaspoon dried thyme
1/2 teaspoon grated orange peel
1 teaspoon salt
1/4 teaspoon pepper
1/4 cup chopped walnuts
1/2 cup fresh orange juice

Preheat the oven to 350 degrees. Core the apples and peel each about a quarter of the way down. Carefully scoop out the centers to make hollow shells. Chop the apple pulp from the center of the apples and set aside. Melt the butter in a large skillet, add the onions, and cook until tender but not browned. Add the sausage and cook until browned, stirring to keep meat crumbly. Add the reserved apple pulp, brown sugar, sage, thyme, orange peel, salt, pepper, and nuts. Cook 2 minutes. Stuff into the prepared apples, packing mixture down. Place the apples in a shallow baking dish and pour the orange juice over the apples. Bake, uncovered, for 50–60 minutes, or until tender.

SANDWICHES

Aram Sandwiches with Roast Beef

SERVES 4

Perfect picnic fare. The roast beef, chicken, and turkey fillings may also be used on tortillas as in the Imperial Valley Sandwiches.

1 large white or wheat lahvosh, cracker bread
3 ounces cream cheese, softened
1/3 cup mayonnaise
1 tablespoon prepared horseradish, or more to taste

8 ounces thinly sliced roast beef
1 medium tomato, sliced thinly
3/4 cup thinly sliced red onions
2/3 cup shredded lettuce or alfalfa sprouts

Soften the lahvosh by holding it under cold running water for 10 seconds per side. Place the lahvosh between 2 damp terry-cloth towels for 45 minutes. Remove the towels and carefully place the lahvosh sesame-seed-side down on a large cutting board.

In a small bowl, combine the cream cheese, mayonnaise, and horseradish. Stir to mix well. Spread the mixture onto the lahvosh leaving a 1/2-inch border around the edges. Cover with the slices of roast beef. Arrange the sliced tomatoes and red onions in a single layer over the beef. Sprinkle with shredded lettuce or alfalfa sprouts. Roll the sandwich tightly, jelly-roll fashion. Wrap securely in plastic wrap and refrigerate for several hours. When ready to serve, slice crosswise into 3/4-inch slices with a serrated knife.

Curried Chicken Filling (for Aram Sandwiches)

SERVES 4

1 large white or wheat lahvosh, cracker bread
3/4 cup mayonnaise
1 1/2 tablespoons fresh lemon juice
1 1/2 teaspoons curry powder
1/2 teaspoon salt
1/4 teaspoon pepper

2 cups coarsely chopped cooked chicken breast
1/2 cup chopped green onions
1/2 cup chopped green bell peppers
1/2 cup golden raisins
1/2 cup chopped peanuts
1 cup alfalfa sprouts

Prepare lahvosh as for Aram Sandwiches with Roast Beef.

In a medium bowl, combine the mayonnaise, lemon juice, curry powder, salt and pepper. Add the chicken, onions, bell peppers, and raisins. Mix well. Spread the mixture over the softened lahvosh, leaving a 1/2-inch border around the edges. Sprinkle with the chopped peanuts and then with the alfalfa sprouts. Roll tightly, jelly-roll fashion. Wrap securely in plastic wrap and refrigerate for several hours. When ready to serve, slice crosswise into 3/4-inch slices with a serrated knife.

Turkey and Cilantro Filling (for Aram Sandwiches)

SERVES 4

1 large white or wheat lahvosh, cracker bread
1/2 cup mayonnaise
3 ounces cream cheese, softened
1/2 teaspoon salt
1/4 teaspoon pepper

2 tablespoons finely chopped fresh cilantro
2 tablespoons minced onions
1/2 pound thinly sliced turkey breast
1 medium tomato, thinly sliced
1 cup shredded iceberg lettuce

Prepare lahvosh as for Aram Sandwiches with Roast Beef.

In a small bowl combine the mayonnaise, cream cheese, salt, pepper, cilantro, and onions. Mix until smooth. Spread the mixture on the lahvosh, leaving a 1/2-inch border around the edges. Top with the turkey and tomato slices. Sprinkle with the shredded lettuce. Roll tightly jelly-roll fashion. Wrap securely in plastic wrap and refrigerate several hours. When ready to serve, slice crosswise into 3/4-inch slices with a serrated knife.

Imperial Valley Sandwiches

MAKES 6

2 (8–10-inch) flour tortillas
8 ounces cream cheese
1 tablespoon milk
1/4 cup chopped fresh parsley
3 tablespoons chopped fresh dill
2 large tomatoes, thinly sliced

1 cucumber, peeled and thinly
    sliced
1/2 cup thinly sliced red onions
1/4 cup sunflower seeds
1/2 cup alfalfa sprouts
12 large spinach leaves

Lightly moisten both sides of 1 tortilla with warm water. In a small bowl, mix
the cream cheese with the milk. Add the parsley and dill. This may be done in
a food processor.

Spread half of the cheese mixture on the tortilla. Evenly layer half of the
tomatoes, cucumbers, onions, sunflower seeds, and sprouts. Cover with about
6 of the spinach leaves. Roll up jelly-roll fashion and wrap in a damp paper
towel, then in plastic wrap. Repeat with remaining tortilla, cheese, and vegetables. Refrigerate until serving time. Slice each tortilla roll in 3 sandwiches.

Note   Neufchâtel cheese or cottage cheese may be substituted for the cream
cheese. If cottage cheese is used, omit the milk.

Note   This filling can also be used for Aram Sandwiches.

Wagon Wheel Loaf

SERVES 8

1 (8-inch) round loaf sourdough
    bread, unsliced
1 tablespoon prepared
    horseradish
1/4 pound thinly sliced roast beef
2 tablespoons mayonnaise
4 slices Swiss cheese, about
    4 × 4 inches
1 tablespoon Dijon mustard
1/4 pound thinly sliced ham

1 medium tomato, thinly sliced
8 thin round slices salami
4 thin slices Cheddar cheese,
    approximately 4 × 4 inches
1/2 medium-size red onion, thinly
    sliced
4 tablespoons unsalted butter,
    softened
1/2 teaspoon onion salt
1/2 teaspoon dried dill

Slice the bread horizontally in 6 equal slices, preferably using an electric knife.
Spread the bottom layer with the horseradish and top with the roast beef and

the second bread slice. Spread the bread with mayonnaise and top with the Swiss cheese. Top with a third bread slice. Spread with the mustard and top with ham. Top with bread, tomato slices, salami, and a bread layer. Top with Cheddar, onions, and the last slice of bread.

Combine the butter, onion salt, and dill. Spread over top and sides of loaf. Place loaf on a baking sheet and bake, uncovered, at 400 degrees for 15–20 minutes. Slice in wedges.

Pizza Loaf

SERVES 4 FOR LUNCH
SERVES 8 AS A SNACK

1/2 pound Italian sausage
2 garlic cloves, minced
1 medium brown onion, chopped
1 (1-pound) can crushed Italian
   tomatoes
1–2 tablespoons tomato paste
1 tablespoon dried basil

1 teaspoon dried oregano
Salt and pepper to taste
1/2 pound mozzarella cheese,
   grated
1/4 pound Cheddar cheese, grated
1 long loaf French bread,
   unsliced

Cook the Italian sausage in a heavy skillet over medium heat until brown and crumbly. Remove with a slotted spoon and drain well. In the same skillet, sauté the garlic and onions until soft. Add the tomatoes, tomato paste, and herbs. Simmer for 10–15 minutes. The sauce should be fairly thick. Add more tomato paste if necessary.

Preheat the oven to 300 degrees. Slice the top off of the bread lengthwise, and set aside. Scoop out the center of the bread, leaving a 1-inch shell. Spread the tomato sauce on bottom and sides of the loaf. Layer with the sausage and cheeses, pressing down firmly for a compact filling. Replace the top of the loaf. Wrap the loaf twice in sturdy aluminum foil. Bake for 1 1/2 hours. Remove from oven and let set for 20–25 minutes. Cut in 2-inch slices.

Optional additions: Sautéed mushrooms, sautéed peppers, chopped olives.

Sausage-filled Baguettes

SERVES 6–8

4 (10–12-inch) French bread
  baguettes
1 1/2 pounds Italian sausage,
  casings removed
1/2 pound pork sausage
1 medium onion, chopped
1/4 cup water

1/4 cup heavy cream
2 eggs, slightly beaten
4 tablespoons Dijon mustard
1/2 cup chopped fresh parsley
Freshly ground pepper
Herbes de Provence
4 tablespoons melted butter

Preheat the oven to 350 degrees. Cut off the ends of the baguettes. Scoop out the centers of the loaves and place in a blender or a food processor. Process until fine bread crumbs have formed. Bake the crumbs in the oven for 10–15 minutes or until golden. Set aside. Reset the oven to 450 degrees. In a large skillet over medium heat, fry the Italian sausage, the pork sausage, and the onions until the sausage is brown and crumbly and the onions are soft. Remove from the heat and drain off all but 1 tablespoon of fat. Add the water, cream, eggs, mustard, parsley, pepper, and Herbes de Provence to taste. Stuff the mixture into the baguettes. Brush with melted butter, wrap in foil, and bake for 15 minutes. Remove the foil and continue to bake for 2–3 minutes longer until the bread is crisp. With a serrated knife, cut in slices.

Smoked Turkey Sandwiches on Rosemary Raisin Bread

SERVES 4

8 thin slices Rosemary Raisin
  Bread
1/4 cup unsalted butter, softened
1/3 cup mayonnaise
1 medium cucumber, peeled and
  thinly sliced

8 ounces smoked turkey breast,
  thinly sliced
2 teaspoons minced fresh
  rosemary

Spread one side of each bread slice with the butter and then the mayonnaise. Divide cucumber and turkey among 4 slices of bread. Sprinkle 1/2 teaspoon rosemary over each. Top with the remaining bread. Cut in half.

XI

Breads

Beer Bread

An easy, great-tasting bread.

3 cups self-rising flour
3 tablespoons sugar
1 1/2 cups beer

Sesame seeds (optional)
1/4 cup unsalted butter, melted

Preheat the oven to 350 degrees. In a large bowl, combine flour, sugar, and beer. Place the dough in a 5 × 9 × 3-inch buttered loaf pan. Top with sesame seeds, if desired. Bake for 1 hour. Remove bread from oven and pour melted butter over the top. Let bread cool before slicing.

Corn Sticks

MAKES 14

For a traditional Southwestern menu, make these with blue cornmeal.

1 cup yellow cornmeal
3/4 cup flour
2 teaspoons baking powder
2 teaspoons sugar
1 teaspoon salt

1 large egg, slightly beaten
1 1/4 cups heavy cream
1/2–1 jalapeño pepper, seeded
and finely chopped (optional)

Preheat oven to 425 degrees. Generously grease 2 seven-stick heavy cast-iron corn-stick molds with vegetable shortening. Preheat them in the oven for 7–10 minutes. While molds are heating, stir together the cornmeal, flour, baking powder, sugar, and salt in a large bowl. In a separate bowl, whisk together the egg and cream and stir into the cornmeal mixture. Mix until the batter is just combined. Add jalapeño pepper if desired. Remove molds from the oven and spoon batter into them, spreading evenly. Bake 15 minutes, or until golden. Invert on racks and serve immediately.

Note   For an alternate elegant presentation, use madeleine molds instead of corn-stick molds. Press batter evenly into greased molds, being careful not to overfill. These molds do not have to be preheated. Yield: 24 madeleines

Garlic Bread Sticks

Serve this simple and delicious accompaniment with soups and salads.

1 loaf unsliced day-old French
  bread
1/2 cup unsalted butter, melted
1 teaspoon paprika

2 teaspoons garlic salt
1/2 cup milk
4–6 ounces Parmesan cheese

Preheat oven to 400 degrees. Remove crust from bread. Cut bread in 1 × 3-inch sticks. Mix melted butter with paprika, garlic salt, and milk. Finely grate Parmesan cheese. Dip bread sticks in butter mixture, then roll in Parmesan. Place on greased cookie sheet. Bake about 10–15 minutes or until golden brown.

Parmesan Pretzels

MAKES 16

Serve these as an accompaniment to any soup or salad.

1–1 1/2 cups flour
1/2 teaspoon yeast
1/3 cup plus 1 tablespoon hot
  water
1/2 teaspoon olive oil
1 large egg

3 1/2 tablespoons freshly grated
  Parmesan cheese
1/3 cup thinly sliced green onions
1 large egg
Kosher salt

Combine 1/2 cup of the flour with the yeast in a food processor. With the motor running, add 1/3 cup hot water. Turn the motor off and add another 1/2 cup of flour, the olive oil, egg, Parmesan cheese, onions, and remaining tablespoon water. Process until the mixture just forms a ball. Let the dough rise in the processor bowl in a warm place for 15 minutes. On a floured surface, knead in enough of the remaining flour to make a smooth and elastic dough.

Preheat the oven to 400 degrees. Roll the dough in a 12 × 4-inch rectangle. Using a sharp knife, cut lengthwise in 16 strips. Roll the strips in ropes, then form them in pretzel shapes and place on a buttered baking sheet. Brush the pretzels with lightly beaten egg. Sprinkle generously with salt. Bake for 12–15 minutes.

Currant and Caraway Bread

MAKES 1 LOAF

This excellent quick bread is particularly delicious for breakfast.

3 cups flour
2/3 cup sugar
1 teaspoon baking soda
2 teaspoons baking powder
1 teaspoon salt
1 1/2 cups currants

2 tablespoons caraway seeds
1 3/4 cups buttermilk
2 large eggs, beaten
2 tablespoons unsalted butter, melted

Preheat the oven to 350 degrees. Sift together the flour, sugar, baking soda, baking powder, and salt into a large bowl. Stir in the currants and caraway seeds. In a small bowl, combine the buttermilk, eggs, and melted butter. Add to the dry ingredients, stirring, until the flour is barely moistened. Pour the batter into a buttered 9 × 5 × 3-inch pan and bake for 50–55 minutes. Remove the bread from the pan immediately and cool on a rack.

Ginger Cornmeal Muffins

MAKES 12 MUFFINS OR 24 MINIATURE MUFFINS

1 cup yellow cornmeal
1 cup flour
2 teaspoons sugar
1/2 teaspoon salt
3 teaspoons baking powder

1/2 cup crystallized ginger
2 large eggs
1 cup milk
1/4 cup unsalted butter, melted

Preheat the oven to 425 degrees. Sift together the cornmeal, flour, sugar, salt, and baking powder into a large bowl. Place the ginger in a food processor and process until minced. Add the eggs and milk and process until eggs are just beaten (2–3 seconds). Pour the egg mixture over the cornmeal mixture, add the butter, and stir gently until just combined. Spoon into buttered muffin tins filling them three-quarters full. Bake for 12–15 minutes or until tops begin to crack.

Rosemary Raisin Bread

MAKES 2 LOAVES
MAKES 24 ROLLS

1 1/2 cups buttermilk
1 package dry yeast
1/4 cup sugar
2 large eggs, slightly beaten
1/2 cup plus 3 tablespoons
    unsalted butter, melted

5–5 1/2 cups unbleached white
    flour
1 1/2 teaspoons salt
1/2 teaspoon baking soda
1 cup golden raisins
2 tablespoons chopped fresh
    rosemary

Heat buttermilk to warm (105–110 degrees), add yeast and sugar, and stir until yeast is dissolved. Mix together the eggs and 1/2 cup of cooled butter. Stir into the yeast mixture. Sift dry ingredients together. Add by thirds to the yeast-egg mixture, beating well after each addition. Remove to a well-floured board and knead until dough is smooth and elastic, about 8–10 minutes. Knead in raisins and rosemary at the last. Place dough in oiled bowl, brush with remaining melted butter, cover, and let rise in a warm place until double, about 1 hour. Punch down, divide in half, and place halves on floured board to rest for 15 minutes. Shape into loaves and place in buttered loaf pans. Or, to make rolls, divide dough in 24 equal pieces. Form each piece into a ball and place in a buttered muffin tin. Cover loaves or rolls and let rise until double, about 1 hour. Bake in a preheated 400-degree oven for 30–35 minutes for loaves or 20–25 minutes for rolls.

Sheepherder's Bread

YIELD: 1 LARGE LOAF

3 cups hot water
1/2 cup unsalted butter, softened
1/2 cup sugar
2 1/2 teaspoons salt

2 packages dry yeast
9 1/2 cups flour
Salad oil

In a large bowl, combine the water, butter, sugar, and salt. Stir until butter melts. Cool to 110 degrees. Stir in the yeast, cover, and let rest for 15 minutes.

(Mixture should be foamy.) Beat in 5 cups of the flour. Add about 3 1/2 cups more flour. Put remaining flour on a board and turn out dough. Knead for 10 minutes, incorporating the remaining flour as needed to prevent sticking. Oil a large bowl and add the kneaded dough, turning once. Cover with plastic wrap. Let the dough rise in a warm place until doubled in size, about 1 1/2 hours. Punch down the dough and knead on a floured board. Line a 3-quart Dutch oven or cast-iron pot with foil. Oil the foil, the Dutch oven, and the oven lid with salad oil. Place the dough in the Dutch oven and let rise with the lid on until the dough rises 1/2–1 inch above the pan rim, about 1 hour. Bake, covered, in a preheated 375-degree oven for 12 minutes. Remove lid and bake uncovered for 30–35 minutes longer. Turn out on a rack to cool. Best served warm.

Whole Wheat Bread

MAKES 2 LOAVES

1 package dry yeast
1 1/2 cups warm water (110 degrees)
3/4 cup milk
1/2 cup molasses
2 teaspoons salt

2 tablespoons vegetable shortening
1/2 cup wheat germ
2 cups whole wheat flour
5 cups sifted white flour
1 tablespoon vegetable oil
1/2 cup unsalted butter, melted

Dissolve yeast in warm water for 5 minutes. Scald milk and cool to 110 degrees. Add to yeast, along with molasses, salt, shortening, and wheat germ. Stir in whole wheat flour and 1 cup of the white flour. Gradually add remaining flour and knead 8 minutes. Place dough in an oiled bowl. Cover with a damp cloth and let rise in warm place until double, about 1 1/2–2 hours. Punch down, turn dough over, and let rise again for 30–45 minutes. Divide in half. Place halves on a floured board to rest for 10 minutes, and then knead each dough portion until free of bubbles. Shape into 2 loaves and brush with vegetable oil. Place on a greased cookie sheet and let loaves rise until rounded and loaf size. Bake in a preheated 375-degree oven for 25 minutes. Remove immediately and brush crusts with melted butter.

Cranberry Raisin Bread

MAKES 2 LOAVES

Serve this bread warm topped with Cranberry Butter (below) on Christmas morning.

4 cups flour
1 3/4 cups sugar
1 tablespoon baking powder
1 1/2 teaspoons salt
1 teaspoon baking soda
1/2 cup unsalted butter
2 large eggs
1 1/2 cups orange juice

1 tablespoon finely grated
   orange peel
2 cups fresh cranberries,
   washed, stemmed, and
   chopped (or frozen
   cranberries, thawed and patted
   dry)
1 cup raisins

Preheat the oven to 350 degrees. In a large bowl, combine flour, sugar, baking powder, salt, and baking soda. With a pastry blender or fork, cut in butter until the mixture makes coarse crumbs. In another bowl beat eggs, orange juice, and orange peel until well blended. Stir in flour mixture. Gently fold in cranberries and raisins. Pour batter into 2 buttered 9-inch × 5-inch × 3-inch loaf pans and bake for 1 hour and 10 minutes, or until a toothpick inserted in the center comes out clean. Cool in pans on rack for 10–15 minutes before removing from pans.

CRANBERRY BUTTER

1 cup fresh cranberries, washed
   and stemmed (or frozen
   cranberries, thawed and patted
   dry)

1 1/2 cups powdered sugar
1/2 cup unsalted butter, softened
1 tablespoon lemon juice

In a food processor, purée the cranberries with the sugar. Add the butter and lemon juice, and blend until smooth. Transfer to a serving bowl and chill, covered, until firm.

Strawberry Nut Bread

MAKES 2 LOAVES

4 large eggs
I cup vegetable oil
2 cups sugar
2 (10-ounce) packages frozen
  sliced strawberries, defrosted,
  reserving I tablespoon of the
  juice

3 cups flour
I tablespoon cinnamon
I teaspoon baking soda
I teaspoon salt
I 1/2 cups coarsely chopped
  walnuts
3 ounces cream cheese

Preheat the oven to 350 degrees. In a large bowl beat eggs until fluffy. Add oil, sugar, and strawberries and mix well. Sift together flour, cinnamon, baking soda, and salt into a separate mixing bowl. Add strawberry mixture and mix until well blended. Stir in nuts. Pour batter into 2 buttered and floured 9 × 5 × 3-inch loaf pans. Bake 1 hour or until a toothpick inserted in the middle comes out clean. Cool in pans for 10 minutes. Turn out onto racks and cool before slicing. Serve with softened cream cheese sweetened with 1 tablespoon juice from the frozen strawberries.

Glazed Orange Muffins

MAKES 24 MUFFINS OR 48 MINIATURE MUFFINS

I cup butter
I cup sugar
2 large eggs
I teaspoon baking soda
I cup buttermilk
2 cups sifted flour

1/2 cup golden raisins
Peel from 2 oranges, finely
  grated
Juice from 2 oranges
I cup firmly packed brown sugar

Preheat the oven to 400 degrees. In a large mixing bowl, beat the butter until light. Gradually add the sugar, and continue beating until well blended. Add the eggs one at a time, beating after each addition. Dissolve baking soda in the buttermilk. Alternately add flour and milk mixtures to the sugar mixture, beginning and ending with the flour. Fold the raisins and grated orange peel into the batter, being careful not to overmix. Pour batter into buttered muffin tins, filling them three-quarters full. Bake for 20–25 minutes (15 minutes for small muffins). Meanwhile, to make a glaze, heat the orange juice and brown sugar in a small saucepan over low heat just until sugar has melted. Remove the muffins from oven. Pour the glaze over the muffins and let it soak in before serving.

Cinnamon Crunch Coffeecake

SERVES 10–12

2 1/4 cups flour
1 cup firmly packed brown sugar
3/4 cup granulated sugar
2 teaspoons cinnamon
1/2 teaspoon salt
1/2 teaspoon powdered ginger
3/4 cup vegetable oil

1 cup sliced and lightly toasted
   almonds
1 teaspoon baking powder
1 teaspoon baking soda
1 large egg
1 cup buttermilk

Preheat the oven to 350 degrees. In a large bowl, mix flour, sugars, 1 teaspoon of the cinnamon, salt, and ginger. Add oil and blend until well combined. Remove 3/4 cup of this mixture to a small bowl, add the almonds and remaining cinnamon, and set aside. To the mixture remaining in the large bowl add the baking powder, baking soda, egg, and buttermilk. Mix until just blended. Pour batter into a buttered 9 × 13-inch baking pan. Top with almond mixture. Bake 30–35 minutes, or until a wooden pick inserted in center comes out clean. Cut in squares and serve warm.

Raisin Cinnamon Scones

MAKES 14–16

Serve this traditional British teatime favorite with butter and preserves.

2 cups flour
2 tablespoons sugar
1 tablespoon baking powder
1 teaspoon cinnamon
3/4 teaspoon salt

1/4 cup unsalted butter, chilled
   and cut in bits
1 large egg
1/2 cup milk
1/3 cup raisins

Preheat the oven to 425 degrees. Sift together the flour, sugar, baking powder, cinnamon, and salt into a large bowl. Add the butter and, using a fork or pastry blender, blend the mixture until it resembles coarse meal. In a small bowl, beat together the egg and milk. Reserve 1 tablespoon of this mixture for brushing the scones and stir the remaining mixture into the flour. Add the raisins and mix just until dough holds together. On a floured surface, roll or pat the dough until 1/2 inch thick. Using a pastry cutter, cut out 2-inch rounds. Arrange the scones on a buttered cookie sheet and brush with reserved milk-and-egg mixture. Bake in the middle of the oven 12–15 minutes or until tops are golden brown. Best served warm from the oven with butter and fresh jam.

Herbed Potato Bread

MAKES 2 LOAVES

1 medium potato, peeled and
  coarsely chopped
2 packages dry yeast
5 tablespoons unsalted butter,
  softened
2 tablespoons sugar
2 teaspoons salt
1 cup warm milk
6 1/2 cups flour
1 garlic clove, minced

1 tablespoon chopped fresh
  marjoram leaves *or* 1 1/2
  teaspoons dried marjoram
1 tablespoon chopped fresh
  rosemary leaves *or* 1 1/2
  teaspoons dried rosemary
1 tablespoon chopped fresh sage
  leaves *or* 1 1/2 teaspoons dried
  sage
1 egg
Dried rosemary, for garnish

Place the potato in a saucepan, cover with water, and cook over medium heat 20 minutes. Drain, reserving liquid. Add hot water to potato water to make 1 cup. Pour warm potato water in warm mixing bowl and cool to 110 degrees. Sprinkle yeast over liquid and stir until dissolved. Mash potato and measure out 3/4 cup. Add the 3/4 cup potato, 2 tablespoons of the butter, the sugar, and salt to yeast mixture. Add warm milk and 3 cups of the flour, beating until smooth. Stir in about 3 more cups flour to make a stiff dough. Turn out onto lightly floured board and knead until smooth and elastic, about 8–10 minutes. Place dough in oiled bowl, turning dough to oil all surfaces. Cover with a damp cloth and let rise in a warm place until double in bulk, about 1 hour.

Meanwhile, make herb filling by combining the garlic, marjoram, rosemary, and sage with the remaining butter. Punch dough down. On lightly floured board, divide dough in half. Roll each half to a 14 × 9-inch rectangle and spread with half the herb butter. Beginning with a 9-inch side, roll the dough tightly jelly-roll fashion. Seal and fold ends under. Place seam sides down in 2 buttered 9 × 5-inch loaf pans. Cover and let rise in a warm place until dough reaches top of pans. Brush loaves with lightly beaten egg. Sprinkle with dried rosemary and bake in a preheated 400-degree oven for 35–40 minutes. Remove from pans and cool on racks.

Pumpkin Doughnut Drops

MAKES ABOUT 4 DOZEN

Unusual and absolutely wonderful!

3 cups flour
1/3 cup nonfat dry milk powder
3 teaspoons baking powder
3/4 teaspoon cinnamon
1/2 teaspoon powdered ginger
1/4 teaspoon nutmeg
1/4 teaspoon salt
2 tablespoons vegetable shortening

1 1/4 cups sugar
2 large eggs
1 cup canned pumpkin
1 teaspoon vanilla
1 1/2 cups ginger ale
Oil for frying
1/2 cup sugar
1 teaspoon cinnamon

Sift together the flour, dry milk, baking powder, cinnamon, ginger, nutmeg, and salt. In a large bowl, cream together the shortening and sugar; then beat in the eggs. Mix in the pumpkin and vanilla. Add the dry ingredients alternately with ginger ale, mixing well after each addition. In a large heavy pan, heat 3 inches of oil to 375 degrees. Drop batter 1 tablespoon at a time for each doughnut into hot oil. Cook 4–5 doughnuts at a time for about 2 minutes, turning to brown evenly. Remove with a slotted spoon and drain. Combine sugar and cinnamon in a paper bag and shake doughnuts in the bag to coat. These are best served immediately, though they may be made a day ahead and reheated in a 450-degree oven for 5–6 minutes.

XII

Desserts

Almond Pound Cake

SERVES 12–16

Topped with a mélange of fresh berries or served beside a dish of sorbets, this is excellent for dessert or tea.

I cup unsalted butter, softened
2 1/2 cups sugar
4 large eggs
3 cups sifted flour
1/4 teaspoon baking soda
I cup buttermilk

1/2 teaspoon vanilla
2 teaspoons almond extract
I 1/2–2 tablespoons butter, softened
1/2 cup sliced almonds
1/8–1/4 cup powdered sugar

Preheat the oven to 350 degrees. In a large bowl, blend together butter and sugar. Add eggs one at a time, beating well after each addition. Sift together dry ingredients. Add to the butter mixture, alternating with the buttermilk. Stir in the extracts and beat until smooth. Butter the sides and bottom of a bundt pan. Press almonds against sides. Pour batter into the pan. Bake I hour or until toothpick inserted in center comes out clean. Let cake cool in pan 10 minutes then remove from pan and cool on a rack. Dust with powdered sugar.

Coconut Pound Cake

SERVES 8–10

4 large eggs, separated
I cup unsalted butter, softened
2 cups sugar
I cup milk
2 teaspoons baking powder
I teaspoon vanilla

2 1/2 cups flour
I cup shredded fresh coconut, lightly toasted (or I cup packaged shredded unsweetened coconut, toasted)*

Preheat the oven to 350 degrees. In a medium bowl beat egg whites until stiff peaks form. Set aside. In a large bowl blend together the egg yolks, butter, and sugar, beating until fluffy. Add the milk, baking powder, vanilla, and flour. Beat on medium-high speed for 5 minutes. Stir in the coconut; then carefully fold in egg whites. Pour the batter into a buttered and floured 9-inch tube pan. Bake I hour or until a wooden toothpick inserted in the center comes out clean. Cool in the pan 10 minutes; then turn out onto a serving plate to continue cooling.

Note   Unsweetened coconut is available in health-food or other specialty shops. However, sweetened coconut may be "unsweetened" by the following method:

MAKES ABOUT 5 CUPS

1 1/2 cups milk
1 1/2 cups water
2 (7-ounce) packages sweetened coconut

In a 2 1/2-quart shallow baking dish, combine the milk and water. Add the coconut and let the mixture stand, covered, for 2 hours. Stir occasionally. Drain the mixture in a large sieve and pat with paper towels until it is almost dry. The coconut can be kept covered and chilled for up to 2 days.

Lemon Coconut Cake

SERVES 10–12

FILLING

Peel of 6 lemons, finely grated
1 cup fresh lemon juice
2 cups sugar
3/4 cup unsalted butter, cut in 12 pieces
6 large eggs, well beaten

In a double boiler, mix the lemon peel, juice, sugar, and butter and simmer over hot water until the sugar dissolves and the butter melts. Pour the eggs into the mixture and cook, stirring constantly, for about 20 minutes until the mixture thickens. Do not allow it to boil.

Pour into a bowl and cover the top with plastic wrap. Chill in the refrigerator for 6 hours or overnight. Mixture will be very thick.

BATTER

3/4 cup vegetable shortening
1 1/2 cups sugar
3 large eggs, separated
1 teaspoon coconut extract
2 1/4 cups cake flour
2 teaspoons baking powder
1/2 teaspoon salt
1 cup milk
3 cups grated fresh coconut or unsweetened packaged coconut (see note regarding coconut in previous recipe)
Coconut Frosting (below)

Preheat the oven to 350 degrees. In a large mixing bowl, cream together the shortening and sugar, beating until light and smooth. Add the egg yolks one at a time, beating well after each addition. Stir in the coconut extract. Sift together the flour, baking powder, and salt. Add the dry ingredients alternately with the milk to the sugar mixture in 3 equal parts, beating until well blended. Stir in 1 cup of the coconut. In another large mixing bowl, beat the egg whites until stiff but not dry. Stir a third of the whites into the batter and gently fold in the remainder. Spoon the batter into 2 buttered and floured 9-inch cake pans. Bake for 25 minutes or until a wooden toothpick inserted in the center comes out clean. Let the cakes cool for 10 minutes in the pan. Remove to a cake rack and let cool completely.

Spread half of the filling on one of the cake layers. Top with the second layer. Spread the remaining filling on the top of the cake. Frost the sides of the cake with the coconut frosting. With a fine-tipped pastry tube, decorate the top of the cake with the frosting in a lattice pattern. Put the remaining coconut along the sides of the cake. Chill before serving.

COCONUT FROSTING

2 large egg whites	1/2 cup unsalted butter, softened
4 tablespoons vegetable shortening	2 cups sifted powdered sugar
	1/4 teaspoon coconut extract

In a mixing bowl, combine the egg whites, shortening, and butter and beat until smooth. Gradually add the sugar and extract, beating until light.

Blackberry Jam Cake

SERVES 10–12

BATTER

1 cup unsalted butter, softened	1 teaspoon ground cloves
1 1/2 cups sugar	1 teaspoon ground allspice
4 large eggs	1 cup raisins dusted with 1/4 cup flour
1 cup buttermilk	1 1/2 cups seedless blackberry jam
3 cups flour	
1 teaspoon baking soda	1 1/2 cups chopped pecans
1 teaspoon baking powder	Icing (below)
1 teaspoon cinnamon	

Preheat the oven to 350 degrees. In a large bowl, cream the butter and sugar. Stir in eggs, buttermilk, and dry ingredients. Beat until smooth. Gently stir in the raisins, jam, and pecans. Pour batter into a well-buttered bundt or 10-inch tube pan. Bake 50–60 minutes, or until wooden toothpick inserted in center comes out clean. Place the pan on a rack and cool for 10–15 minutes. Loosen edges of pan and turn cake out on a plate. Pierce the top with a toothpick in several places.

ICING
1/2 cup sour cream
1/2 cup unsalted butter
I cup sugar

While the cake is baking, in a small saucepan combine sour cream, butter, and sugar and bring to a boil. Continue boiling until sugar is completely dissolved. Pour the icing on the cake a little at a time every 10 minutes while the cake is cooling.

Chocolate Sour Cream Cake

SERVES 8

This rich, dense cake is best when made with Dutch process cocoa.

1/2 cup unsweetened cocoa	I teaspoon baking soda
3/4 cup boiling water	I 1/2 cups sifted flour
1/2 cup unsalted butter	I cup sour cream
I 1/2 cups sugar	Chocolate Sour Cream Frosting
I teaspoon vanilla extract	(below)
1/2 teaspoon salt	1/2–3/4 cup chopped walnuts
2 large eggs	

Preheat the oven to 350 degrees. In a small bowl mix the cocoa and boiling water until smooth. Set aside. In a large bowl, cream the butter and sugar together. Mix in the vanilla and salt. Add the eggs, one at a time, beating well after each addition. Combine the baking soda, flour, and sour cream. Add the flour-and-sour-cream mixture alternately to the butter mixture. Stir in the cocoa until just blended. Do not overmix. Pour the batter into 2 buttered and floured 9-inch cake pans. Bake 30 minutes, or until a wooden toothpick inserted in the center comes out clean. Cool in pans 15 minutes before transferring to racks. Frost with Chocolate Sour Cream Frosting and sprinkle walnuts on the top.

CHOCOLATE SOUR CREAM FROSTING

3 ounces unsweetened chocolate
2 tablespoons unsalted butter
3/4 cup sour cream

I teaspoon vanilla extract
1/4 teaspoon salt
3 cups powdered sugar

In a small, heavy saucepan melt chocolate and butter over low heat. Stir until smooth and remove from heat. In a medium bowl, beat together the sour cream, vanilla, and salt. Gradually add sugar, mixing until smooth. Add chocolate mixture and beat until smooth.

Orange Ring Cake

SERVES 10

I cup unsalted butter
I cup sugar
3 large eggs, separated
I cup sour cream

I heaping tablespoon grated
    orange peel
I 3/4 cups flour
I teaspoon baking powder
I teaspoon baking soda

Preheat the oven to 350 degrees. In a large bowl, cream the butter and sugar, beating until fluffy. Add the egg yolks to the butter and sugar and beat until light and fluffy. Add the sour cream and orange peel. Sift together the flour, baking powder, and baking soda, and add to the butter mixture. Beat the egg whites until stiff but not dry. Fold into the batter. Pour into a buttered and floured 10-inch tube or bundt pan. Bake for 50–60 minutes, or until a toothpick inserted in the center comes out clean. Turn out on a rimmed plate and prick the top of the cake with a fork. Pour the glaze over the cake while it is still hot.

ORANGE GLAZE
1/2 cup orange juice
I tablespoon lemon juice
1/3 cup sugar

In a small saucepan bring the orange and lemon juices and sugar to a boil and cook for 4 minutes.

Grand Marnier Walnut Cake

SERVES 10–12

This simple but elegant cake is a lovely addition to your brunch or supper table.

2 cups sugar
1 cup unsalted butter, softened
2 large eggs
2 cups flour
1/2 teaspoon salt
1 teaspoon baking powder
1/2 teaspoon cinnamon
1 cup sour cream

1 teaspoon vanilla
2 tablespoons Grand Marnier or
other orange-flavored liqueur
1 1/2 cups coarsely chopped
walnuts
1 tablespoon grated orange peel
1 tablespoon powdered sugar, for
garnish

Preheat the oven to 350 degrees. In a large bowl, cream together the sugar and butter until fluffy. Add eggs one at a time, beating well after each addition. Sift together the dry ingredients. In a small bowl, combine the sour cream, vanilla, and liqueur. To the butter mixture, add the dry ingredients alternately with the sour-cream mixture, beating well after each addition. Stir in the walnuts and the orange peel. Spoon the batter into a buttered and floured 10-inch bundt or tube pan. Bake for 1 hour or until a wooden toothpick inserted at the center comes out clean. Cool the cake in the pan for 20 minutes. Turn out onto a rack, and cool completely. Sift powdered sugar over the top.

Palm Springs Date Nut Cake

SERVES 6

1/2 cup unsalted butter, melted
3/4 cup hot water
1/2 pound pitted dates, finely
chopped
1 cup firmly packed brown sugar

1 1/2 cups flour
1 teaspoon baking soda
1 cup coarsely chopped walnuts
Smooth Butter Frosting (below)

Preheat the oven to 375 degrees. In a large bowl, combine the butter and hot water and add dates. Let stand 10 minutes. In another bowl, combine the sugar, flour, and baking soda. Stir into date mixture; then fold in walnuts. Pour into an 8-inch square buttered and floured pan. Bake for 30 minutes. Cool in the pan for 10 minutes. Remove to a rack and cool. Spread frosting over the top of the cake. Cut into squares.

SMOOTH BUTTER FROSTING

3 tablespoons unsalted butter, softened

1 cup sifted powdered sugar

1 teaspoon vanilla

1 tablespoon heavy cream

Cream together the butter and sugar until smooth. Beat in vanilla and cream.

Soft Gingerbread with Apricot Walnut Sauce

SERVES 8

Always a family favorite.

1/2 cup vegetable shortening, melted

1/2 cup molasses

1 cup sugar

3/4 teaspoon powdered ginger

1 teaspoon cinnamon

1 large egg

1 teaspoon baking soda

1 cup hot water

2 1/2 cups flour

2 teaspoons baking powder

Apricot Walnut Sauce (below)

Preheat the oven to 350 degrees. In a large bowl, combine the shortening, molasses, sugar, ginger, cinnamon, and egg. Dissolve baking soda in the hot water and add to the sugar mixture. Add the flour and baking powder, beat well, and pour into a buttered and floured 9-inch square pan. Bake for 40 minutes or until a wooden toothpick inserted in the center comes out clean. Cut into squares and serve with Apricot Walnut Sauce.

APRICOT WALNUT SAUCE

1 1/2 cups apricot jam

1/2 cup water

1 tablespoon sugar

1 teaspoon grated orange peel

1 tablespoon rum

1/2 cup chopped walnuts

Combine the jam, water, sugar, and orange peel in a small saucepan. Over high heat, bring to a boil and simmer for 5 minutes, stirring constantly. Remove from heat and stir in the rum and walnuts. Serve warm over gingerbread.

Pumpkin Cake Roll

SERVES 8–10

3 large eggs
1 cup sugar
2/3 cup canned pumpkin
1 teaspoon lemon juice
3/4 cup flour
1 teaspoon baking powder
2 teaspoons cinnamon

1 teaspoon powdered ginger
1/2 teaspoon nutmeg
1/2 teaspoon salt
1 cup powdered sugar
1 cup finely chopped walnuts
Cream Cheese Filling (below)

Preheat the oven to 375 degrees. In a large bowl, beat the eggs for 5 minutes. Gradually add the sugar and stir in pumpkin and lemon juice. Sift together the flour, baking powder, cinnamon, ginger, nutmeg, and salt, and fold into the pumpkin mixture. Mix gently until well blended. Spread in a buttered 15 × 10-inch jelly-roll pan. Bake for 15 minutes. Turn cake onto a tea towel sprinkled with the powdered sugar and walnuts. Roll the towel and cake together and cool for 2 hours. Spread with the filling. Reroll, and refrigerate until serving. May be made the day before serving.

CREAM CHEESE FILLING
1 cup powdered sugar
6 ounces cream cheese, softened

1/4 cup unsalted butter, softened
1/2 teaspoon vanilla

Combine the sugar, cream cheese, butter, and vanilla. Beat until smooth.

Amaretto Cheesecake

SERVES 8–10

CRUST
1 cup blanched slivered almonds,
   lightly toasted
1/3 cup sugar

1 1/2 cups chocolate wafer
   crumbs
6 tablespoons butter, softened

Finely chop the almonds and combine with the sugar, chocolate crumbs, and butter. Pat the mixture into the bottom and sides of a 9-inch springform pan and chill for 30 minutes.

FILLING

1 1/2 pounds cream cheese, softened

1 cup sugar

4 large eggs

1/3 cup heavy cream

1/4 cup Amaretto or other almond-flavored liqueur

1 teaspoon vanilla

Preheat the oven to 375 degrees. In a large bowl, blend the cream cheese and sugar. Add the eggs one at a time, beating well after each addition. Add the cream, Amaretto, and vanilla and beat until mixture is light. Pour the batter in prepared chocolate crumb crust and bake the cake in the middle of the oven for 30 minutes. Transfer the cake to a rack and let stand for 5 minutes. (The cake will not be set.)

TOPPING

2 cups sour cream

1 tablespoon sugar

1 teaspoon vanilla

1/3 cup blanched slivered almonds, lightly toasted, for garnish

Combine the sour cream, sugar, and vanilla. Spread evenly over the cake and bake 5 minutes longer. Transfer the cake to a rack and cool completely. Chill cheesecake, lightly covered, overnight. To serve, remove the sides of the pan and press the almonds around the top edge of the cake.

Pumpkin Cheesecake

SERVES 10–12

A superb ending to a traditional Thanksgiving dinner.

PASTRY

1/4 cup sugar

3/4 cup unsalted butter, softened

1 1/4 cups flour

1 large egg yolk

1/2 cup finely chopped pecans

Preheat the oven to 350 degrees. In a large bowl, combine the sugar and butter. Blend well. Add the flour, egg yolk, and pecans and mix well. Press the dough on the bottom and sides of a 10-inch springform pan. Bake for 10 minutes. Cool in pan.

FILLING

I 1/2 pounds cream cheese,
    softened
I 3/4 cups sugar
I (16-ounce) can pumpkin
3 tablespoons flour
I teaspoon vanilla

5 large eggs
2 large egg yolks
1/4 cup heavy cream
I teaspoon cinnamon
1/2 teaspoon powdered ginger
1/4 teaspoon ground cloves

In a large bowl, beat together the cream cheese and sugar until smooth. Blend
in the pumpkin, flour, and vanilla. Beat the eggs and yolks into the mixture
one at a time, beating well after each addition. Add the cream and spices and
beat well. Pour the mixture into the prepared crust. Bake for I hour and 40
minutes, or until firm in the center. Remove the cake from the oven and cool I
hour. Loosely cover, and refrigerate overnight before serving.

Apricot Almond Tea Cookies

MAKES 3 DOZEN

These exceptional cookies are well worth the time.

I cup blanched almonds, lightly
    toasted
1/2 cup sugar
I 1/2 cups sifted flour
I 1/4 teaspoons grated orange
    peel
1/4 teaspoon baking powder
1/2 teaspoon salt

3/4 cup unsalted butter, well
    chilled
I large egg
1 teaspoon vanilla
3/4 teaspoon almond extract
Apricot Filling (below)
Glaze (below)

In a food processor, combine the almonds and sugar and process until almonds are finely chopped. Set the mixture aside. Again using the food processor, combine the flour, orange peel, baking powder, and salt. Add the butter
and process until mixture resembles coarse meal. Blend in the egg, vanilla, and
almond extract. Add the almond mixture and process just until mixed. Shape
the dough into a roll about 9 inches long and 2 inches in diameter. Refrigerate
for at least I 1/2 hours or up to 2 days.

Preheat the oven to 350 degrees. Cut roll into 36 slices. For each cookie
place I slice of the dough in the center of a 6-inch square piece of plastic wrap.
Press the round dough until it is 3 inches in diameter. Top with I teaspoon of

Apricot Filling. Using plastic wrap as an aid, gently form the dough around the filling into a ball. Place cookie balls on a buttered cookie sheet. Bake for 20 minutes and cool on racks. When the cookies are cool, dip them in the Glaze.

APRICOT FILLING

6 ounces dried apricots

1/3 cup apricot preserves

1 tablespoon orange liqueur

1 teaspoon lemon juice

Finely chop the dried apricots in a food processor. Add the preserves, liqueur, and lemon juice and mix. This filling may be made up to 2 days in advance.

GLAZE

1 cup powdered sugar, sifted

2 tablespoons almond liqueur

2 teaspoons milk

Blend together the powdered sugar, almond liqueur, and milk until smooth. Use additional milk if necessary.

Chocolate Chip Brownies

MAKES 9–16

4 ounces unsweetened chocolate

1 cup unsalted butter

2 cups sugar

4 large eggs

1/2 cup flour

1/2 teaspoon salt

1 1/4 teaspoons vanilla

3/4 cup chopped walnuts

1 (6-ounce) package semisweet
   chocolate chips

1/4 cup powdered sugar

Preheat the oven to 350 degrees. Melt the chocolate and butter together in a heavy saucepan over low heat. Remove from heat and stir in the sugar. Add the eggs one at a time, beating well after each addition. Stir in the flour, salt, and vanilla. Add nuts and chocolate chips. Pour into a buttered 9-inch square pan. Bake for 35 minutes. Do not overbake. Brownies should be very moist. Cool in the pan. Dust the cooled brownies with powdered sugar and cut into squares.

Chocolate Brownies with Mocha Icing

MAKES 24–28

4 large eggs
2 cups sugar
1/2 cup plus 3 tablespoons
  unsalted butter, softened
1 1/3 cups sifted flour

1/2 cup unsweetened cocoa
1/8 teaspoon salt
2 teaspoons vanilla
1 cup coarsely chopped pecans
Mocha Icing (below)

Preheat the oven to 350 degrees. In a large bowl, beat the eggs, adding the sugar a little at a time. Beat the mixture until it is thick and pale. Add the butter and beat until smooth. Sift the flour, cocoa, and salt, blending the batter well. Stir in the vanilla and pecans.

Pour the batter into a buttered and floured 9 × 13-inch baking pan. Bake in the middle of the oven for 25–30 minutes, or until it pulls away slightly from the sides of the pan and a wooden toothpick inserted in the center comes out clean. Cool. Spread with Mocha Icing. Chill for at least 30 minutes or until icing is set. Cut in squares before serving.

MOCHA ICING

2 1/4 cups sifted powdered sugar
2 tablespoons unsweetened cocoa
2 tablespoons unsalted butter,
  softened

2 teaspoons vanilla
6–8 tablespoons hot strong
  coffee

Cream together the sugar, cocoa, butter, and vanilla. Add the coffee, 1 tablespoon at a time, beating until the mixture is spreading consistency.

Double Chocolate Rum Bars

MAKES 28–32

BARS

4 ounces unsweetened chocolate
1 cup unsalted butter
4 large eggs
2 cups sugar
1/4 teaspoon salt

1 teaspoon vanilla
1 cup sifted flour
Filling (below)
Topping (below)

Preheat the oven to 325 degrees. In a medium-size heavy saucepan, melt chocolate and butter over low heat. Cool slightly. In a large bowl, beat eggs until light, then add sugar gradually. Add chocolate mixture, salt, vanilla, and flour. Beat until fluffy. Pour into a buttered 9 × 13-inch pan. Bake in the oven for 25 minutes. Cool in pan. Spread Filling over bars and chill well. Add hot Topping and chill well before cutting in squares. Store in refrigerator.

FILLING

1/2 cup unsalted butter, softened
4 cups powdered sugar
1/4 cup heavy cream

4 tablespoons rum
1 cup chopped walnuts

Beat the butter and sugar together, adding the cream and rum gradually. When light and fluffy add walnuts.

TOPPING

1 (6-ounce) package chocolate chips
3 tablespoons water
4 tablespoons unsalted butter

In a small heavy saucepan, melt the chocolate, water, and butter together over low heat and mix well. While still hot, drizzle over the bars and spread.

Chocolate Chocolate Chip Butterball Cookies

MAKES 4–5 DOZEN

1 cup unsalted butter, softened
2/3 cup firmly packed brown
  sugar
1 teaspoon vanilla
1 large egg
2 cups flour
1/8 teaspoon salt

1/2 cup unsweetened cocoa
1 (12-ounce) package semisweet
  chocolate chips
3/4 cup chopped walnuts or
  pecans
1 cup powdered sugar

In a large bowl, cream together the butter and brown sugar. Continue beating until mixture is light and fluffy. Beat in the vanilla and egg. Combine the flour, salt, and cocoa and blend into butter mixture. Stir in the chocolate chips and nuts. Chill dough for 20–30 minutes. Preheat the oven to 350 degrees. Form dough in 1-inch balls and place an inch apart on buttered cookie sheets. Bake in the oven for 10–12 minutes. Remove to a wire rack to cool. Roll cooled cookies in powdered sugar until well coated. Must be stored in airtight container.

Domino Chip Cookies

MAKES ABOUT 4 DOZEN

1 cup unsalted butter, softened
1 3/4 cups sugar
2 large eggs
2 teaspoons vanilla
1 ounce unsweetened baking
  chocolate, melted
1/4 cup sour cream
2 cups flour

3/4 cup unsweetened cocoa
1/2 teaspoon baking soda
1/4 teaspoon baking powder
1/2 teaspoon salt
1 (12-ounce) package white
  chocolate chips
1 cup coarsely chopped pecans

Preheat the oven to 350 degrees. In a large bowl, cream the butter and sugar together until fluffy. Beat in the eggs, one at a time. Add the vanilla, chocolate, and sour cream, mixing until well combined. Sift together the flour, cocoa, baking soda, baking powder, and salt. Gradually add to the chocolate mixture. Stir in the chocolate chips and pecans.

Drop the batter by teaspoonfuls onto buttered cookie sheets. Bake for approximately 8–10 minutes. Remove to wire rack and cool.

Millionaire Shortbread

MAKES 16–20

3/4 cup flour
1/4 cup sugar
3/4 cup unsalted butter
2 tablespoons corn syrup

1 (14-ounce) can sweetened
  condensed milk
1 teaspoon vanilla extract
3 ounces sweet dark chocolate

Preheat the oven to 350 degrees. In a food processor, blend together the flour, sugar, and 1/4 cup of the butter. Press into a buttered 8-inch square baking pan. Bake for 10–15 minutes or until golden. Cool.

In a medium saucepan, melt the remaining butter. Add the corn syrup and condensed milk. Bring to a boil and cook for 12–15 minutes, stirring constantly, until the mixture turns a medium caramel color. Be careful not to let the mixture burn. Remove from the heat and stir in the vanilla. Pour over the shortbread layer. Cool until firm.

In a small heavy saucepan, melt the chocolate over low heat. Spread over the caramel layer. Cover and chill. When firm, cut into small squares.

Ginger Cream Snaps

MAKES ABOUT 4 DOZEN

This dough is best prepared twenty-four hours in advance. The cookies are good with or without the Ginger Cream.

3/4 cup unsalted butter
I cup sugar
1/4 cup dark molasses
I large egg
2 cups flour
2 teaspoons baking soda

1/2 teaspoon salt
1/2 teaspoon powdered ginger
1/2 teaspoon ground cloves
I teaspoon cinnamon
Ginger Cream (below)

In a large heavy saucepan, melt the butter. Add the sugar and molasses and mix well. Cool the mixture to lukewarm. Add the egg and beat well. Sift the dry ingredients together and combine thoroughly with the butter mixture. Cover and chill overnight or up to 3 days in advance of baking.

Preheat the oven to 375 degrees. Form dough in 1-inch balls and place 1 inch apart on a greased cookie sheet. Bake for 8–10 minutes. Gently press each cookie with a spatula to flatten slightly. Cool thoroughly. Spread 1 tablespoon of the Ginger Cream on half of the cookies. Sandwich the remaining cookies on top of the cream.

GINGER CREAM
2 1/4 cups powdered sugar
3 tablespoons chopped
   crystallized ginger

4 tablespoons cold unsalted
   butter, cut in small pieces
3 tablespoons ginger marmalade

Blend the sugar and the ginger in a food processor until the ginger is minced, about 2 minutes. Add the butter and marmalade to the ginger mixture and process until thick and well blended.

Lemon Pistachio Bars

MAKES 16 LARGE SQUARES OR 24 MEDIUM SQUARES

PASTRY

1 1/2 cups flour

2 tablespoons sugar

6 tablespoons unsalted butter,
  cut in pieces

2 egg yolks, lightly beaten

2 teaspoons vanilla

Preheat the oven to 350 degrees. Into the bowl of a food processor, sift the flour and sugar. Blend in the butter until the mixture resembles coarse meal. Add the egg yolks and vanilla and process until well mixed. Press into an 11 × 7-inch baking dish. Prick with a fork. Bake for 15 minutes and let cool. Leave the oven set at 350 degrees.

FILLING

1/4 cup unsalted butter

1/2 cup sugar

3 eggs

1/4 cup lemon juice

2 teaspoons grated lemon peel

1 tablespoon flour

1/2 cup sweetened coconut

In a large bowl, cream together butter and sugar. Add the eggs one at a time, beating well after each addition. Add the lemon juice, peel, flour, and coconut. Mix well. Pour into the partially baked pastry shell and bake 30 minutes.

LEMON ICING

1 1/2 cups powdered sugar

1 teaspoon unsalted butter,
  softened

1 1/2 tablespoons lemon juice

1/3 cup coarsely chopped
  pistachio nuts*

Sift the sugar into the top of a double boiler. Add the butter and lemon juice, mixing until smooth. Stir over simmering water until the icing reaches spreading consistency. Spread the icing over the warm bars. Sprinkle the top with chopped pistachio nuts. Cut into squares.

Note To remove the skin from the pistachio nuts, place in a 300-degree oven for 5 minutes. Remove immediately and wrap in a kitchen towel. Let sit for 2–3 minutes and then rub the nuts briskly with the towel, removing as much skin as possible.

Orange Anise Madeleines

MAKES 24

The orange flower water and anise extract are available at most gourmet specialty shops.

2 large eggs
3/4 cup sugar
1 tablespoon grated orange peel
2 teaspoons orange flower water
1 cup flour

1 teaspoon anise extract
1/2 cup unsalted butter, melted and cooled
1/2 cup powdered sugar

Preheat the oven to 425 degrees. In a small saucepan, whisk together the eggs and the sugar over moderate heat until the eggs are warm to the touch. Turn the mixture into a bowl. Beat until eggs are tripled in bulk. Beat in the orange peel and orange flower water. Sift 1/2 cup of the flour over the egg mixture and fold in. Repeat with the remaining flour. Fold in the anise extract and the butter.

Fill buttered and floured madeleine pans two-thirds full. Bake in the oven for 8 minutes or until golden. Turn out onto a rack and sift the powdered sugar over the madeleines while they are still warm. Wipe the molds clean, butter and flour again, and bake the remaining cookies.

Orange Chocolate Chip Cookies

MAKES 4–6 DOZEN

Vegetable shortening in this recipe is the key to the soft texture of this cookie.

2 1/4 cups flour
1 teaspoon baking soda
1/2 teaspoon salt
1 1/4 cups granulated sugar
1 1/4 cups firmly packed brown sugar
1/2 cup vegetable shortening
1/2 cup unsalted butter, softened

1 teaspoon vanilla
1 teaspoon orange juice
2 large eggs
1 (12-ounce) package chocolate chips
1 cup coarsely chopped walnuts
Peel of one orange, finely grated

Combine the flour, baking soda, and salt and set aside. In a separate mixing bowl, cream the sugars, shortening, butter, vanilla, and orange juice. Beat in the eggs one at a time. Add the flour mixture 1/2 cup at a time, mixing well after each addition. Stir in the chocolate chips, nuts, and grated orange peel. Chill at least 1 hour.

Preheat the oven to 350 degrees. Drop the dough by teaspoonfuls onto a lightly buttered cookie sheet. Bake for 8–10 minutes. Remove to a wire rack to cool.

Golden Nut Cookies

MAKES ABOUT 3 DOZEN

This makes an untraditional but perfect ending to an oriental meal.

1 cup unsalted butter
1/2 cup firmly packed brown
   sugar
1/2 cup sifted powdered sugar
1 teaspoon vanilla extract

1 cup cornmeal
1 1/3 cups flour
1/4 teaspoon salt
1/2 cup slivered almonds, lightly
   toasted

In a large bowl, cream together the butter and sugars. Add the vanilla, 2/3 cup of the cornmeal, flour, and salt. Blend well. Shape dough in a ball and wrap with waxed paper. Chill 1 hour.

Preheat the oven to 350 degrees. Using about 1 tablespoon of the dough for each cookie, shape the dough in balls. Roll in the remaining cornmeal and place 2 inches apart on a lightly buttered cookie sheet. Using a spatula, flatten each cookie to 1/4-inch thickness. Sprinkle each cookie with toasted almonds, pressing the nuts into the dough. Bake for 10–12 minutes, or until browned. Cool slightly and then remove to wire racks to finish cooling.

Hazelnut Cookies

MAKES 2–3 DOZEN

1 1/4 cups flour
3/4 cup powdered sugar
1/2 teaspoon cinnamon
1/2 cup cold unsalted butter, cut
   in small pieces

1/2 cup ground hazelnuts
1 teaspoon grated lemon rind
1 large egg yolk
6 ounces sweet dark chocolate

Preheat the oven to 350 degrees. Sift the flour, powdered sugar, and cinnamon into the bowl of a food processor. Add the butter to the flour mixture. Process until the mixture resembles coarse meal. Add the hazelnuts, lemon rind, and egg yolk, and mix until the mixture begins to blend. Turn onto a lightly floured board and knead gently until smooth. Roll out the dough to a 1/8-inch thickness. Cut in rounds with a 2 1/2-inch scalloped cookie cutter. Place on a lightly buttered cookie sheet and bake for 10–15 minutes. Remove to wire racks and cool.

In a heavy saucepan, melt the chocolate over low heat. Dip half of each cookie in the chocolate, place on waxed paper, and chill until set.

Pine Nut Puffs

MAKES ABOUT 7 DOZEN

1 1/2 cups pine nuts
2 cups flour
1/4 teaspoon baking powder
1/8 teaspoon salt

1 cup unsalted butter, melted and cooled
1 cup powdered sugar
2 teaspoons vanilla

Preheat the oven to 350 degrees. Toast 1/2 cup of the pine nuts until golden, about 8–10 minutes. Cool, then finely chop and set aside. Chop the remaining cup of pine nuts and set aside.

Sift together the flour, baking powder, and salt. In a large bowl, cream together the butter and 1/2 cup of the powdered sugar. Blend in the vanilla. Add the flour mixture gradually, until combined. Stir in the 1/2 cup of toasted pine nuts. Cover the dough and chill for at least 2 hours.

Preheat the oven to 350 degrees. Using approximately 1 teaspoon of the dough for each, form in balls. Roll the balls in the reserved pine nuts, gently pressing in the nuts. Arrange the balls 2 inches apart on cookie sheets lined with parchment. Bake for 10–12 minutes or until set and lightly golden around the edges. Remove the cookies to wire racks to cool, for about 5 minutes. Sift the remaining powdered sugar over the cookies. When completely cooled, store in layers, separated by waxed paper in airtight containers.

Pistachio Macaroons

MAKES 4 DOZEN

I (14-ounce) package sweetened coconut
I 1/2 cups powdered sugar
2/3 cup chopped pistachios

1/4 cup flour
1/8 teaspoon salt
4 egg whites
I 1/2 teaspoons vanilla

Preheat oven to 350 degrees. In a medium bowl, combine coconut, sugar, pistachios, flour, and salt. Beat egg whites and vanilla until foamy. Add to coconut mixture and mix thoroughly. Drop by teaspoonfuls onto a buttered cookie sheet.

Bake for 15–17 minutes or until lightly browned. Cool on a wire rack and store in a covered container.

Raspberry Cheesecake Bars

MAKES 16

1/4 cup unsalted butter
1/3 cup firmly packed brown sugar
I cup flour
1/2 cup chopped pecans
1/2 cup seedless raspberry jam
8 ounces cream cheese, softened

1/4 cup sugar
I large egg
2 tablespoons milk
2 tablespoons fresh lemon juice
I teaspoon vanilla
16 pecan halves

Preheat the oven to 350 degrees. In the bowl of a food processor, cream the butter. Add the brown sugar and flour and blend until it resembles coarse meal. Stir in the chopped pecans. Press the mixture into the bottom of a buttered 9-inch square pan. Bake for 15 minutes. Remove from the oven and cool. Spread with jam. Leave the oven set at 350 degrees.

In a medium mixing bowl, beat the cream cheese and sugar together until the mixture is smooth. Beat in the egg, milk, lemon juice, and vanilla. Pour over the crust and bake for 30 minutes. Remove from the oven and cool. Cut into 16 squares and top each square with a pecan half.

Almond and Pine Nut Tart

SERVES 8

PASTRY

1 cup flour

6 tablespoons cold unsalted
   butter

2 tablespoons sugar

1 large egg, lightly beaten

In the bowl of a food processor, blend the flour, butter, and sugar until the mixture resembles coarse meal. Add the egg and mix well. Form the dough into a flat round and wrap in waxed paper. Chill for at least 30 minutes. On a floured surface, roll out into an 1/8-inch thick round, large enough to fit an 11-inch tart pan. Fit the pastry into the tart pan, cutting off excess dough. Prick the bottom of the shell with a fork and chill for 30 minutes.

Preheat the oven to 375 degrees. Line the tart shell with aluminum foil, fill with raw rice or beans and bake in the bottom third of the oven for 10 minutes. Remove the rice or beans and foil and bake for 10 minutes longer. Cool for 15 minutes.

FILLING

3/4 cup apricot preserves

8 ounces almond paste, room
   temperature

1/4 cup unsalted butter, room
   temperature

1/3 cup sugar

1/4 teaspoon almond extract

4 large eggs

1/4 cup flour

1/2 teaspoon baking powder

3/4 cup pine nuts

In a small saucepan, melt the apricot preserves. Brush the tart shell with the preserves. In a medium mixing bowl, beat the almond paste, butter, and sugar together until smooth. Beat in the almond extract and the eggs, one at a time, mixing well after each addition. Add the flour and baking powder. Beat until smooth. Gently stir in the pine nuts. Pour the mixture into the shell and bake for 30–45 minutes or until set.

Apple Almond Tart

SERVES 8

PASTRY

1 cup flour
1/8 teaspoon salt
6 tablespoons cold unsalted
   butter, cut in pieces

2–3 tablespoons ice water

In the bowl of a food processor, combine the flour and salt. Add the butter and blend until the mixture resembles coarse meal. With the machine running, gradually add the ice water and process just until the dough comes together. Remove the dough from the bowl and press into a round shape. Wrap the dough in waxed paper and chill for about 20 minutes. Transfer to a floured board and roll into a round, large enough to fit into a 9-inch tart pan. Fit the pastry into the tart pan, cutting off excess dough.

FILLING

1 1/2 cups blanched almonds
3/4 cup plus 3 tablespoons sugar
7 tablespoons unsalted butter
2 tablespoons flour

1/4 cup almond liqueur
2 large eggs
6 medium apples, peeled and
   cored

Grind the almonds in a food processor until fine. Add 3/4 cup of the sugar, 4 tablespoons of the butter, the flour, liqueur, and eggs and process 15 seconds. Spread the mixture in an even layer over the unbaked tart shell.

Preheat the oven to 400 degrees. Cut the apples in uniform 1/4-inch slices. Arrange the slices, tightly packed, in overlapping concentric circles on top of the almond filling. Dot with the remaining butter and sprinkle with the 3 tablespoons of sugar. Bake the tart for approximately 1 hour until golden brown. Remove from the oven and cool.

GLAZE

1 (6-ounce) jar apricot preserves
1 tablespoon lemon juice
1/4 cup chopped pistachios

In a small saucepan, bring the preserves and lemon juice to a boil, stirring until smooth. Strain and brush over the cooled tart. Sprinkle with pistachios.

Lemon Blueberry Tart

SERVES 8

The use of cake flour makes a delicious, cookielike crust.

PASTRY

1/2 cup sugar

3/4 cup unsalted butter

1 large egg yolk

2 cups unsifted cake flour

In a food processor, cream together the sugar and butter. Thoroughly mix in the egg yolk and cake flour. (At this point, the dough may be covered and stored in the refrigerator for up to 3 days. Bring to room temperature before using.) Preheat the oven to 325 degrees. If the dough is too sticky to handle, chill briefly. Press the dough on the bottom and sides of an 11-inch tart pan. Prick the crust all over with a fork. Bake for 25–30 minutes or until lightly browned. Cool before filling.

FILLING

1/2 cup unsalted butter

1 cup sugar

4 tablespoons lemon juice

Peel of 1 lemon, grated

4 large egg yolks, lightly beaten

In a heavy medium saucepan, melt the butter. Mix in the sugar, lemon juice, and lemon peel. Whisk in the egg yolks and cook over medium heat, stirring constantly. Cook until very thick, about 10–12 minutes. Remove from heat and let cool. Pour into the baked pastry shell.

TOPPING

4–5 cups blueberries

6 tablespoons sugar

1/2 teaspoon grated lemon peel

1 tablespoon lemon juice

Powdered sugar (optional)

In a medium saucepan, combine 2 cups of the blueberries, sugar, lemon peel, and juice. Bring to a boil. Cook over medium heat, stirring frequently, until the berries are as thick as soft jam, about 8–10 minutes. Cool to room temperature. Spread evenly on top of the lemon mixture. Neatly arrange the remaining blueberries on the top of the tart. Sprinkle with powdered sugar, if desired.

Blueberry Cheese Tart

SERVES 6

With the assistance of a food processor, this can be an extremely quick and easy dessert.

PASTRY

1/2 cup unsalted butter

1/3 cup sugar

1/4 teaspoon vanilla

1 cup flour

In a food processor, cream together the butter and sugar. Add the vanilla and flour and process just until the dough comes together. Press the crust on the bottom and 1 inch up the sides of an 8-inch springform pan.

FILLING

8 ounces cream cheese, softened

1/4 cup sugar

1 large egg

1 teaspoon vanilla

1/4 cup apricot preserves, melted

Preheat the oven to 400 degrees. In a food processor, cream together the cream cheese and the sugar. Add the egg and vanilla. Mix well and pour into the unbaked shell. Bake for 10 minutes. Pour the melted apricot preserves over the top. Bake 15 minutes more.

TOPPING

1/3 cup sugar

1/2 teaspoon cinnamon

1/4 cup sliced, toasted almonds

1 pint blueberries

Mix together all ingredients. Sprinkle on top of the tart. Bake 15 minutes more.

Raspberry Tart with Mascarpone Cheese

SERVES 8

Mascarpone cheese is an Italian cream cheese found in gourmet specialty shops and Italian markets. Use only very fresh cheese. The filling can also be used as a sauce over mixed berries or other fresh fruit. Just add 1 teaspoon of vanilla and enough heavy cream to achieve the desired consistency.

PASTRY

1 1/4 cups flour

6 tablespoons cold unsalted butter

2 tablespoons cold vegetable shortening

1/8 teaspoon salt

1/2 teaspoon sugar

3 tablespoons cold water

In the bowl of a food processor, process the flour, butter, shortening, salt, and sugar until the mixture resembles coarse meal. Add the water 1 tablespoon at a time and process just until the dough comes together. Chill 1 hour. Preheat the oven to 400 degrees. Roll out the dough on a well-floured surface, to fit an 11-inch tart pan. Place in the pan and line with aluminum foil. Fill with rice or beans. Bake in the bottom third of the oven for 10–12 minutes. Remove the rice or beans and aluminum foil and bake 5 minutes more or until the pastry is light brown.

FILLING

1 1/2 cups mascarpone cheese (about 3/4 pound)

3 tablespoons sugar

1/2 cup well chilled heavy cream

1 1/2–2 cups fresh raspberries

1/3 cup melted raspberry or red currant jelly

In a medium bowl, mix the cheese and sugar together with a fork until well blended. Mix in the cream 1 tablespoon at a time, stirring until smooth. Do not overmix or the filling will become too liquid.

Spread the cream mixture in the cooled pie shell. Arrange the raspberries over the top, completely covering the cream. Brush the berries with jelly. Chill in the refrigerator for 3–4 hours before serving.

Cranberry-Pear Cobbler

SERVES 8

This colorful autumn dessert may be made up to a day in advance. Keep loosely covered in a cool dry place. Reheat in a 350-degree oven for 10–15 minutes.

PASTRY

I 1/2 cups flour
1/4 teaspoon salt
5 tablespoons frozen, unsalted
  butter, cut in small pieces

4 tablespoons frozen vegetable
  shortening
4–5 tablespoons ice water

Place the flour and the salt in a food processor. Blend well and add the butter and vegetable shortening and process until the mixture resembles coarse meal. With the machine running, add the ice water a tablespoon at a time, and process just until the dough comes together. Wrap the dough in waxed paper and chill for at least 1 hour.

FILLING

3 cups (12-ounce bag) fresh or
  frozen cranberries, washed
  and stemmed
5 large pears, peeled, cored, and
  sliced
I cup maple syrup

I teaspoon cinnamon
1/2 teaspoon ground allspice
4 1/2 teaspoons cornstarch
  dissolved in 2 tablespoons cold
  water
I large egg yolk, lightly beaten

In a saucepan, combine the cranberries, pears, maple syrup, cinnamon, and allspice. Bring the mixture to a boil and simmer, stirring occasionally, for 3–4 minutes or until the cranberries pop. Add the cornstarch mixture to the cranberry mixture, stirring, and simmer 1 minute or until it thickens. Transfer the mixture to a bowl and cool. Turn the fruit mixture into a well-buttered 2-quart shallow baking dish.

Preheat the oven to 425 degrees. On a well-floured surface, roll out the dough 1/8 inch thick. With a fluted pastry wheel or a knife, cut out 1/2-inch strips of the dough. Weave the pie-crust strips in a lattice pattern over the fruit. Moisten the ends of each strip to attach to the edge of the baking dish. Brush with the beaten egg yolk. Bake for 10 minutes, reduce heat to 350 degrees and continue baking for 35–40 minutes. Serve warm with a dollop of Whipped Cream Topping (below).

WHIPPED CREAM TOPPING

I 1/2 cups heavy cream
I tablespoon sugar

1/2 teaspoon vanilla
1/2 teaspoon cinnamon

In a small bowl, beat the cream, sugar, and vanilla until lightly whipped. Sprinkle with cinnamon.

Strawberry-Nectarine Cobbler

SERVES 8

PASTRY

2 cups flour
3 tablespoons sugar
1 tablespoon baking powder
1/2 teaspoon salt

6 tablespoons unsalted butter, cut in 6 pieces
2 large egg yolks
1/3 cup half-and-half

In the bowl of a food processor, or in a mixing bowl, combine the flour, sugar, baking powder, and salt. Add the butter and process until the mixture resembles coarse meal. Combine the egg yolks and half-and-half in a small bowl. Add to the flour mixture all at one time. Process only until the mixture just comes together. Shape the dough into a flat round and wrap in plastic wrap. Chill for 30 minutes. (The dough may be refrigerated for up to 3 days.)

FILLING

8 nectarines, peeled and sliced in 1/2-inch slices
2 cups sliced strawberries
3/4 cup firmly packed brown sugar
1 1/2 tablespoons cornstarch

2 tablespoons orange juice
1 tablespoon grated orange peel
2 tablespoons unsalted butter, cut in pieces
1 egg beaten with 1 teaspoon water

In a large bowl, combine the nectarines and strawberries. Add the brown sugar, cornstarch, orange juice, and orange peel. Toss until well combined. Pour into a buttered 11 × 7-inch baking dish or a 4–5-cup oval gratin dish. Top with the butter.

Preheat the oven to 400 degrees. Roll out the dough into a shape 1 inch smaller than the diameter of the dish, about 1/2 inch thick. Flute the edges. Place over the fruit. Cut slashes in the pastry about 2 inches long. Decorate with remaining dough, if desired. Brush the pastry with the egg-and-water mixture. Bake 30–35 minutes or until the pastry is golden and the filling is bubbly.

Gingered Pecan Peach Pie

SERVES 6–8

PASTRY

1 1/4 cups flour

6 tablespoons cold unsalted butter

2 tablespoons cold vegetable shortening

1/8 teaspoon salt

1/2 teaspoon sugar

3 tablespoons cold water

In the bowl of a food processor, process the flour, butter, shortening, salt and sugar until the mixture resembles coarse meal. Add the water, 1 tablespoon at a time, and process just until the dough comes together. Chill for 1 hour. Preheat the oven to 400 degrees. Roll out the dough 1/8 inch thick on a well-floured surface. Place the dough in a 10-inch pie pan and crimp the edges. Line the bottom of the pastry with aluminum foil and fill with beans or raw rice. Bake in the lower third of the oven for 10 minutes. Remove from the oven. Lower the oven temperature to 375 degrees.

FILLING

3 pounds peaches, peeled, pitted and sliced

1/4 cup firmly packed light brown sugar

1/4 cup minced crystallized ginger

2 tablespoons unsalted butter, cut in pieces

2 tablespoons fresh lemon juice

1 tablespoon flour

1/4 teaspoon freshly grated nutmeg

In a large bowl, toss the peaches with the brown sugar, ginger, butter, lemon juice, and flour. Add the nutmeg and place the mixture in the prepared crust.

TOPPING

1/2 cup flour

1/2 cup sugar

1/2 cup chopped pecans

4 tablespoons cold unsalted butter, cut in pieces

1/8 teaspoon salt

In the bowl of a food processor, combine the flour, sugar, pecans, butter, and salt and blend the mixture until it resembles coarse meal. Spread the topping over the peach mixture. Bake in the lower third of the oven for 50–60 minutes or until the top is golden and the filling is bubbly.

Pear Torte

SERVES 8–10

PASTRY

1 1/4 cups flour
6 tablespoons cold unsalted
   butter
2 tablespoons cold vegetable
   shortening

1/8 teaspoon salt
1/2 teaspoon sugar
3 tablespoons cold water

In the bowl of a food processor, process the flour, butter, shortening, salt and sugar until the mixture resembles coarse meal. Add the water, 1 tablespoon at a time, and process just until the dough comes together. Chill for 1 hour.

Preheat the oven to 400 degrees. Roll out the dough 1/8 inch thick on a well-floured surface. Place the dough in an 11-inch springform pan with a removable bottom. Line the bottom of the pastry with aluminum foil and fill with beans or raw rice. Bake in the lower third of the oven for 10–15 minutes or until lightly golden. Remove and cool.

FILLING

Juice of 1 lemon
4–6 ripe pears, peeled, cored,
   and halved
3/4 cup sugar
2 large eggs

1/2 cup flour
1/4 teaspoon salt
1/2 cup unsalted butter, melted
1 teaspoon vanilla

Reduce the oven temperature to 350 degrees. Mix lemon juice in a bowl with enough water to cover pears and set aside. In a mixing bowl, combine the sugar, eggs, flour, and salt, beating until pale yellow and thick. Beat the butter into the sugar mixture and add the vanilla. Set aside. Drain the pear halves. Score the pears by making thin vertical cuts through only the top third of each one. This ensures even cooking and gives a decorative appearance. Arrange the pears in the pastry shell. Pour the egg mixture over the pears. Bake for 50–60 minutes in the lower third of the oven. This dessert is best served slightly warm.

Walnut Torte

SERVES 8–10

PASTRY
1 cup unsalted butter, room
    temperature
1/2 cup sugar

1 large egg, beaten
2 3/4 cups flour
1 egg white, slightly beaten

In a food processor, cream the butter and sugar until smooth. Beat in the egg and flour. Process until the dough is crumbly, stopping just before dough forms a large ball. Pat two thirds of the dough into a 9-inch springform pan, extending it approximately 2 inches up the sides. Refrigerate 30 minutes. Roll out the remaining third of the dough between 2 pieces of waxed paper, to a circle approximately 10–11 inches in diameter, and refrigerate 30 minutes.

FILLING
2 cups sugar
1 cup heavy cream
2 1/2 cups coarsely chopped walnuts

In a heavy skillet, melt the sugar over medium heat. Stir with a wooden spoon to prevent burning. Sugar will become firm and crumbly and turn brown gradually. When completely melted, lower the heat and add the cream very slowly, 1 tablespoon at a time, stirring constantly. If the cream is added too quickly, the mixture will turn into caramel candy. Remove from heat and stir in the walnuts. Let stand at room temperature for 15 minutes. Then spoon the filling into the chilled crust. Preheat the oven to 325 degrees. Peel off the waxed paper from one side of the top crust. Cut the crust into a 9-inch circle and place very carefully on top of the filling. Peel off the top piece of waxed paper and seal the edges of the crust by folding the side edges of the crust over the top and crimping. Prick holes on top and brush with egg white. Bake for 1 1/2 hours or until the crust is golden brown. Cool 3 hours. Before serving, remove the sides of the springform pan.

Country Baked Apples

SERVES 6

For a striking presentation, serve these in oversized wineglasses surrounded by the pan juices and garnished with Orange Whipped Cream (below).

6 large Golden Delicious apples, peeled and cored
6 small pieces crystallized ginger
6 large pitted dates (apricots or prunes may be substituted)
1/2 cup flour
1 cup sugar

1/4 teaspoon cinnamon
1/4 teaspoon freshly grated nutmeg
6 tablespoons unsalted butter, softened
3/4 cup orange juice
1/2 cup orange-flavored liqueur

Preheat the oven to 350 degrees. Place the apples in a buttered 9 × 13-inch baking dish. Fill each apple with a small piece of ginger. Stuff the center of the apple with the date.

In the bowl of a food processor, combine the flour, sugar, cinnamon, and nutmeg. Mix in the butter until the dough just comes together. Divide the dough into 6 equal portions. Pat over the top of each apple, mounding it slightly in the center.

Combine the orange juice and liqueur and pour into the bottom of the baking dish. Bake in the oven for 45 minutes to 1 hour, basting 2–3 times, until the apples are just tender when pierced through the side with a sharp knife. Cool 1 hour.

ORANGE WHIPPED CREAM
1/2 cup heavy cream
2 tablespoons powdered sugar
1 tablespoon orange-flavored liqueur

In a medium bowl, whip the cream and sugar together until soft peaks form. Fold in the liqueur. Spoon over the apples.

Pears en Croute

SERVES 4

SWEET PASTRY

1 2/3 cups flour

2 tablespoons sugar

1/8 teaspoon salt

1/2 cup plus 1 tablespoon cold
  unsalted butter, cut in pieces

1 large egg yolk

3–4 tablespoons cold water

In a food processor, combine the flour, sugar, and salt. Add the butter and process until the mixture resembles coarse meal. Combine the egg yolk and water and with the machine running, slowly pour the mixture into the bowl, processing just until the dough comes together. Wrap the dough in waxed paper and refrigerate for 20 minutes. On a well-floured board, roll out the dough in a circle and cut it in 4 wedges.

FILLING

3 tablespoons sugar

1/4 teaspoon cinnamon

2 slightly ripe pears, Bosc
  preferred, peeled, halved, and
  cored

1 large egg, beaten

Combine the sugar and cinnamon in a plastic bag. Shake each pear half in the sugar mixture until evenly coated. Place a pear half on each section of dough and wrap, cutting off excess dough. Roll out excess dough and make decorative shapes, such as leaves, to place on pears as desired. Refrigerate the wrapped pears for 1–2 hours. Before baking, brush each pear with the beaten egg. Place on a buttered cookie sheet and bake in a preheated 375-degree oven for 20–25 minutes or until the pastry is golden. To serve, ladle a spoonful of hot Caramel Sauce (below) on each plate and top with a pear.

CARAMEL SAUCE

1 1/2 cups heavy cream

2/3 cup sugar

2 tablespoons water

1 tablespoon unsalted butter

Heat cream over low heat. In a large heavy-bottomed saucepan, cook the sugar and water over medium heat. Cook, stirring constantly with a wooden spoon, until the sugar melts and turns a light caramel color. The water will evaporate completely before the sugar melts. Remove from the heat and stir in the hot cream. Add the butter, stirring until the mixture thickens slightly. Sauce can stand for several hours and be reheated over low heat.

Cream Puff Ring with Strawberries and Blueberries

SERVES 8

A delicious summertime dessert that may be prepared early in the day.

PASTRY
1 cup water
6 tablespoons unsalted butter, softened
1 cup flour
4 large eggs
1/2 teaspoon vanilla
1/2 teaspoon almond extract
1 egg, lightly beaten with 1 teaspoon water
1/4 cup sliced almonds
2 teaspoons sugar

Preheat oven to 375 degrees. Draw an 8-inch circle with the tip of a knife on a buttered and lightly floured baking sheet. In a medium-size saucepan, bring the water and butter to a boil, stirring, until the butter melts. Reduce the heat and add the flour all at once, stirring vigorously with wooden spoon until mixture pulls away from the pan. Cook, stirring, 1–2 minutes, or until mixture is dry. Transfer to a mixing bowl and beat in the eggs one at a time. Mix in the vanilla and almond extract. The mixture will be thick and glossy. Drop the pastry from a spoon around the circle to make a large ring. Brush the surface with the egg mixture and sprinkle with sliced almonds and sugar. Bake for 35–40 minutes or until well puffed and golden brown. Turn the oven off. Remove the pastry and carefully cut in half horizontally with a serrated knife. Place both halves cut side up on baking sheet and return to oven for 10 minutes or until pastry is dry. Remove from the oven and cool. Pastry may be stored overnight at room temperature, well covered, or frozen, wrapped in tin foil for up to 1 month.

FILLING
1 cup heavy cream
3 tablespoons powdered sugar
2 tablespoons almond liqueur or dark rum
1 pint strawberries, sliced
1 pint blueberries, stemmed

In a mixing bowl, beat the cream until it begins to thicken. Gradually add the powdered sugar and beat until soft peaks form. Mix in the liqueur.

To assemble, spread the whipped-cream filling over the bottom of the pastry ring. Combine the strawberries and blueberries. Arrange them on top of the cream and place top of ring over the berries. Dust top with powdered sugar. May be refrigerated up to 8 hours.

California Custard with Fresh Berries

SERVES 6–8

This combination of blueberries, strawberries, and raspberries is delicious as well as very colorful.

5 large egg yolks	**1 tablespoon vanilla**
1/2 cup sugar	**1 cup heavy cream**
1 tablespoon gelatin	**2 pints fresh berries**
3 tablespoons Kirsch	**Berry Sauce (below)**

In the top of a double boiler, mix the egg yolks and sugar, until the mixture is thick and pale. Dissolve the gelatin in the Kirsch and add to the yolk mixture. Cook over simmering water, stirring constantly, until mixture thickens and lightly coats the back of a spoon. Remove from the heat and blend in the vanilla. Pour into a bowl, let cool, and refrigerate until mounds form when custard is dropped from a spoon. Whip the cream and gently fold into the chilled custard. Spoon into a 1 1/2–2-quart serving bowl. Before serving, top with the 2 pints of fresh berries. Spoon the Berry Sauce over the top.

BERRY SAUCE
1 pint fresh berries
2 tablespoons Kirsch
6 tablespoons currant jelly

In a food processor, purée the berries and Kirsch. Strain through a sieve to remove seeds. Melt the jelly over low heat and add to the berry purée. Cover and chill.

Raspberry Zabaglione

SERVES 10–12

6 large egg yolks	**1 3/4 cups heavy cream**
7 tablespoons sugar	**1 pint raspberries (set aside 12**
1/2–3/4 cup sweet Marsala (to	**berries for garnish)**
taste)	

In a mixing bowl, beat the egg yolks and the sugar until thick and pale. Add the Marsala and put in the top of a double boiler. Continue to beat with a wire whisk over water at medium boil. Cook until thick enough to hold a small mound when the whisk is withdrawn. Cool in the refrigerator. Whip the cream and gently fold in the raspberries. Carefully fold the raspberry-whipped-cream mixture into the Marsala-egg mixture. Chill. Garnish with the remaining raspberries before serving.

Orange Custard

SERVES 12

4 large eggs	1 quart half-and-half
5 large egg yolks	1 cup sugar
Peel of 2 oranges, finely grated	3 tablespoons Grand Marnier

Preheat oven to 350 degrees. In a bowl, lightly beat the eggs, egg yolks, and orange peel. In a saucepan, heat the half-and-half with the sugar until the mixture is warm to touch. Gradually add to the egg mixture in a thin stream, beating constantly. Stir in the Grand Marnier. Strain through a fine sieve.

Pour into eight 3/4-cup ramekins and put into a large pan. Fill with water about halfway up the side of the ramekins. Cover the pan with aluminum foil and bake until custard is set, about 30 minutes. Chill thoroughly before serving.

Layered Lemon Crème

SERVES 8

2 envelopes unflavored gelatin	2/3 cup fresh lemon juice
1/2 cup water	1 1/2 cups heavy cream
6 large eggs	2 cups fresh fruit, such as
1 1/2 cups sugar	strawberries, kiwis, or
1 tablespoon grated lemon peel	blueberries

In a small saucepan, sprinkle the gelatin over the water. Let stand for 10 minutes and place over low heat until gelatin is dissolved. Cool. In a large mixing bowl, combine the eggs and sugar, beating until thick and pale. Combine the lemon peel and juice with the cooled gelatin. Add to the egg mixture and continue beating until well blended. Refrigerate, stirring occasionally, until mixture is thick enough to mound when dropped from a spoon, about 10 minutes. Whip the cream until thick. Fold into the lemon mixture until no white streaks remain.

In a 2-quart glass bowl or 8 large wineglasses, place a layer of sliced fruit, a layer of lemon crème, a second layer of fruit, and top with the lemon crème. Chill 2–3 hours before serving.

Cold Peach Soufflé

SERVES 6

2 tablespoons unflavored gelatin
1 cup sugar
Pinch salt
5 medium peaches, peeled and
  sliced
1/2 cup lemon juice

6 large eggs, separated
1 tablespoon grated lemon peel
1/4 teaspoon almond extract
Raspberry Sauce (optional)
Fresh berries and peaches
  (optional)

Mix the gelatin, 1/4 cup of the sugar, and salt in a saucepan. In a food processor, place the peaches and 1/4 cup of the lemon juice and purée. Beat together the egg yolks and 1 cup of the peach purée. Stir into the saucepan with the gelatin and cook over low heat until the gelatin is dissolved, about 5 minutes. Remove from the heat and stir in the remaining purée, remaining lemon juice, lemon peel and almond extract. Chill, stirring occasionally, until mixture mounds slightly when dropped from a spoon.

Beat the egg whites until soft peaks form. Add the remaining sugar and continue to beat until stiff but not dry. Fold into the peach mixture. Pour the peach soufflé into a 1 1/2-quart soufflé dish with a waxed-paper collar 2–3 inches high. Chill for 3–4 hours. Serve soufflé on plates masked with Raspberry Sauce or garnish with fresh berries and sliced peaches.

Raspberry Meringue Bread Pudding

SERVES 6

1 1/2 cups milk
1 1/2 cups heavy cream
1/3 cup sugar
2 teaspoons grated lemon peel
12 slices homemade-style white
   bread, crusts removed

1/4 cup unsalted butter, softened
4 large eggs, separated
1 teaspoon vanilla
1/2 cup seedless raspberry jam

In a saucepan, combine the milk, cream, 1 1/2 tablespoons of the sugar, and lemon peel and bring to a boil, stirring to dissolve sugar. Cool. Spread the bread with the butter and arrange in 3 layers in a buttered 8-inch square baking dish. Beat the egg yolks and vanilla. Add the milk mixture all at once and blend well. Pour over the bread and let stand at least 1 hour or as long as overnight. Preheat oven to 350 degrees. Place dish of pudding in a large baking pan. Pour in enough hot water to reach halfway up the sides of the dish. Bake for 20–30 minutes. Let cool 10 minutes. Spread with the jam. Beat the egg whites to form soft peaks. Gradually add remaining sugar and beat until stiff but not dry. Swirl on top of pudding. Bake for 15 minutes at 350 degrees or until golden.

Steamed Chocolate Pudding with Bittersweet Chocolate Sauce

SERVES 10

3/4 cup unsalted butter, softened
3/4 cup sugar
8 large eggs, separated
4 ounces sweet dark chocolate
1/4 cup strong coffee
2 tablespoons almond liqueur

2 tablespoons dark rum
3/4 cup soft white bread crumbs
3/4 cup ground almonds
Bittersweet Chocolate Sauce
   (below)

In a large bowl, cream the butter and sugar. Add the egg yolks one at a time, beating after each addition. Continue beating until light and fluffy. In a small saucepan, over low heat, melt the chocolate with the coffee. Add the almond liqueur and rum and stir into the egg mixture. Blend in bread crumbs and almonds.

Beat the egg whites until stiff but not dry. Fold the beaten whites into the chocolate mixture and pour into a well-buttered 1 1/2-quart pudding mold or bundt pan. Cover tightly with the buttered lid or with buttered foil. Place the mold in a heavy pot. Add enough hot water to reach halfway up the sides of the mold. Cover the pot and steam for 1 hour over medium heat. When the pudding is done, remove from the water and cool for 20 minutes. Remove the lid and invert on a serving plate. Chill. Serve with Bittersweet Chocolate Sauce.

BITTERSWEET CHOCOLATE SAUCE

1/2 cup heavy cream	1/2 cup unsalted butter
1 cup sugar	2 large egg yolks
2 squares unsweetened chocolate	1 teaspoon vanilla
2 ounces Swiss semisweet	1–2 tablespoons dark rum
chocolate	1–2 tablespoons almond liqueur

In a heavy saucepan, combine the cream and sugar. Cook over medium heat, stirring, just until the mixture starts to simmer. Add the chocolates and butter. Cook over low heat, stirring, until smooth, about 5 minutes. Remove from the heat.

In a small bowl, lightly beat the egg yolks. Stir in a few spoonfuls of the hot chocolate mixture. Add the egg mixture to the chocolate in the saucepan, stirring constantly. Cook gently over low heat for 3 minutes, stirring continuously. Remove from the heat.

Stir in the vanilla, rum, and almond liqueur until well blended. Store in the refrigerator. Reheat when ready to serve. Makes about 2 cups.

Chocolate Pâté with Pistachio Sauce

SERVES 6–8

PÂTÉ

9 ounces bittersweet Swiss	5 large eggs, separated
chocolate	1/2 cup chopped pistachio nuts,
3/4 cup powdered sugar	toasted
3/4 cup unsalted butter, softened	Pistachio Sauce (below)

In a heavy saucepan over very low heat, melt the chocolate. Whisk in 1/2 cup of the sugar and the butter. Add the egg yolks, mixing well. Remove from the heat. In a mixing bowl, beat the egg whites until soft peaks form. Add the remaining sugar and beat until stiff but not dry. Fold a third of the egg-white mixture into the chocolate. Gently fold the mixture into the remaining egg whites.

Rinse a 9 × 5 × 3-inch loaf pan with water and line with plastic wrap. Pour in the chocolate mixture and refrigerate 24 hours. Unmold on a serving plate and sprinkle with the chopped toasted pistachios. To serve, pour several spoonfuls of Pistachio Sauce in the center of a plate and top with a slice of pâté.

PISTACHIO SAUCE

1/2 cup raw, shelled, unsalted pistachio nuts

1/3 cup sugar

1 small egg white

2 cups milk

4 large egg yolks

1/2 cup sugar

2 teaspoons cornstarch

1/2 teaspoon vanilla

1/2 teaspoon almond extract

To remove the skins from the raw pistachio nuts, place them in a 300-degree oven for 5 minutes. Remove immediately and wrap in a kitchen towel. Let sit for 2–3 minutes, then rub the nuts briskly, removing as much skin as possible. Place the nuts in a food processor and grind them to a paste. Blend in the 1/3 cup of sugar and the egg white. Paste will keep in refrigerator for 1 week.

In a medium saucepan, combine the pistachio paste with the milk and bring to a boil over medium heat. Remove from the heat and allow to steep for 10 minutes. Strain through cheesecloth and set aside. In a mixing bowl, beat the 4 egg yolks and the 1/2 cup of sugar until thick and pale. Mix in the cornstarch. Gradually add the milk mixture in a thin stream, beating constantly. Pour the mixture into a saucepan and cook over medium heat, stirring continuously, until the sauce thickens and coats a spoon lightly, about 10–15 minutes. Do not allow to boil. Remove from the heat and beat 2–3 minutes. Strain through a fine sieve and add the vanilla and the almond extract. Chill before serving.

Chocolate Meringue with Raspberry Crème Anglaise

SERVES 10–12

CHOCOLATE MERINGUE

5 large egg whites
3/4 cup granulated sugar

I 3/4 cups powdered sugar
1/3 cup unsweetened cocoa

Preheat the oven to 300 degrees. In a large bowl, beat the egg whites until they form soft peaks. Beat in the granulated sugar 2 tablespoons at a time. Continue to beat until stiff peaks form. Sift together the powdered sugar and cocoa and fold into the egg-white mixture. Using an inverted 8-inch square cake pan as a guide, trace 3 squares on sheets of parchment paper and set on the baking sheets. Divide the meringue among the squares, spreading it evenly to the edges. Bake for 1 hour and 15 minutes. Alternate baking sheets if necessary for even baking. Transfer the meringues to a rack and let cool.

CHOCOLATE MOUSSE

12 ounces semisweet chocolate
7 large egg whites
3 cups heavy cream, well chilled

I 1/2 teaspoons vanilla
3 tablespoons raspberry-flavored
   liqueur

Melt the chocolate in a heavy saucepan over low heat. Cool until it is lukewarm. In a large bowl, beat the egg whites until they hold stiff peaks. In another bowl, beat the cream with the vanilla until it holds soft peaks. Add the liqueur to the whipped cream and beat until it holds stiff peaks. Fold the chocolate carefully into the egg whites and then fold in the whipped cream until no white streaks remain.

RASPBERRY PURÉE

3 cups fresh raspberries (reserve 1 cup for garnish)
2 tablespoons raspberry liqueur

Purée 2 cups of the raspberries and press through a sieve. Set aside 1 cup of the purée and reserve for Raspberry Crème Anglaise. Mix the remaining purée with the 2 tablespoons of the liqueur.

To assemble, place the meringue on a serving dish and spread it with 1/2 cup of the Raspberry Purée. Then spread it thickly with about a third of the mousse. Top with the second meringue and spread with 1/2 cup purée followed by another third of the mousse. Top with remaining meringue and frost with remaining mousse. May be refrigerated at this point for up to 4–6 hours before serving. Garnish with reserved raspberries and serve with Raspberry Crème Anglaise.

RASPBERRY CRÈME ANGLAISE

4 large egg yolks

1/2 cup sugar

2 cups milk, scalded

1 cup Raspberry Purée

In a mixing bowl, beat the egg yolks and sugar, until thick and pale. Gradually beat in the milk. Pour into a heavy saucepan and stir constantly, over low heat until the custard coats the back of a spoon, about 10–15 minutes. Do not allow to boil. Remove from the heat and cool to room temperature. Stir in the Raspberry Purée. Refrigerate until ready to serve.

Frozen Strawberry Cream Cake

SERVES 10

This frozen dessert can be made up to a month in advance. We recommend using commercially prepared sherbet or frozen yogurt, as they will give the best results.

1 1/2 quarts strawberry sherbet or frozen yogurt, softened

3/4 cup almond macaroons, crumbled and toasted

1/4 cup Grand Marnier

1 cup heavy cream

3 ounces semisweet chocolate

1/2 cup blanched almonds, toasted and chopped

1 1/2 pints vanilla ice cream, softened

1 cup strawberries

Mint leaves or whipped cream, for garnish

Lightly oil a 10-inch springform pan or a 2-quart plastic mold. Line the entire pan with 1 quart of the sherbet. Freeze until firm.

Sprinkle the macaroon crumbs with 2 tablespoons of the Grand Marnier and set aside. Whip the cream with the remaining Grand Marnier and beat until it forms peaks. In a heavy saucepan over medium heat, melt the chocolate with the almonds and the macaroon mixture. Let cool 10 minutes. Fold the melted chocolate mixture into the softened ice cream. Chunks of chocolate will form. Fold in the whipped cream.

Remove the sherbet from the freezer and pour in the ice cream mixture. Freeze until firm, then spread the remaining sherbet over the top. Freeze for several hours or overnight. One hour before serving, place in the refrigerator. To serve, remove the bottom and sides of a springform pan and invert on a serving dish. Garnish with strawberries and mint leaves or rosettes of whipped cream, if desired.

Chocolate Mousse Cake with Coffee Whipped Cream

SERVES 10

12 ounces bittersweet chocolate
1/2 cup strong coffee
12 large eggs, separated
1 cup plus 1 tablespoon sugar

1 tablespoon coffee liqueur
Coffee Whipped Cream (below)
Chocolate Leaves (below)

Preheat oven to 375 degrees. In a heavy saucepan over low heat, melt the chocolate with the coffee and cool slightly. In a large mixing bowl, beat the egg yolks with the cup of sugar until thick and pale. Mix the coffee liqueur into the chocolate.

In a large mixing bowl, beat the egg whites until soft peaks form. Add the remaining sugar and beat until stiff but not dry. Fold about a quarter of the egg whites into the chocolate. Gently fold this mixture back into the remaining egg whites. Streaks of egg white may still be visible.

Pour half of the mixture into a buttered and sugared 10-inch springform pan, refrigerating the remaining half. Bake 30–35 minutes, or until the cake is set around the edges but is still soft in the center. Remove from oven and cool for 20 minutes. Fill the center of the cake with the remaining chocolate mixture. Refrigerate for 4–5 hours. Remove from the pan and frost the top and sides with the Coffee Whipped Cream. Refrigerate 1–2 hours and garnish with Chocolate Leaves or shaved chocolate.

COFFEE WHIPPED CREAM
1 cup heavy cream
1/4 cup powdered sugar
1 tablespoon coffee liqueur

In a large bowl, whip the cream with the powdered sugar until soft peaks form. Fold in the coffee liqueur.

CHOCOLATE LEAVES
24 nonpoisonous leaves, such as camellia or lemon
4 ounces semisweet chocolate

Wash and thoroughly dry the leaves. Line a baking sheet with waxed paper. In a heavy saucepan over low heat, melt the chocolate. With a table knife or small spatula, spread the leaves with the chocolate. Place the leaves chocolate side up on the baking sheet. Refrigerate until the chocolate is firm. Leaves may be frozen. To remove the chocolate, grasp the stem and pull gently. The chocolate and leaf will separate.

Chocolate Almond Ice Cream Torte

SERVES 8

CRUST

1/3 cup chopped toasted almonds
1/2 cup graham cracker crumbs
1 tablespoon sugar

3 tablespoons unsalted butter, melted

Preheat the oven to 350 degrees. Mix together the almonds, crumbs, sugar, and butter. Press in the bottom of a buttered 8-inch springform pan. Bake for 10 minutes. Cool, then chill in freezer.

FILLING

2 cups vanilla ice cream, softened
1 (6-ounce) package semisweet chocolate chips
2 large eggs, separated

1 tablespoon rum
2 tablespoons strong coffee
1/2 cup heavy cream
1/4 cup chopped toasted almonds

Spread the ice cream in an even layer over the crust. Return to the freezer until firm. Melt the chocolate chips in a heavy saucepan over low heat and set aside. In a large mixing bowl, beat the egg yolks until pale yellow. Add the rum, coffee, and chocolate. Beat until smooth. Beat the egg whites until they form soft peaks. Gently fold into the chocolate mixture. Whip the cream and gently fold into the mixture. Spread over the ice cream layer and sprinkle with the almonds. Return to the freezer until serving time.

Frozen Chocolate Decadence

SERVES 8–10

An elegant dessert for chocolate lovers only!

CRUST

1 1/2 cups chocolate wafer crumbs
1/3 cup unsalted butter, melted

Preheat the oven to 325 degrees. In a small bowl, combine the crumbs and butter. Press into a 9-inch springform pan and bake for 10 minutes. Remove from the oven and cool.

FILLING

8 ounces cream cheese, softened
1/2 cup sugar
1/8 teaspoon almond extract
1 teaspoon vanilla
2 large eggs, separated
6 ounces semisweet chocolate
   chips, melted

1 cup heavy cream, whipped
3/4 cup chopped walnuts
Chocolate Leaves, for garnish
1/2 cup heavy cream, whipped
   (optional)

In a large mixing bowl, combine the cream cheese, 1/4 cup of the sugar, and the almond and vanilla extracts. Mix until well blended. Stir in the slightly beaten egg yolks and melted chocolate. Mix well. In another mixing bowl, beat the egg whites until soft peaks form, and gradually beat in the remaining sugar until stiff but not dry. Fold into the chocolate mixture. Fold in the whipped cream and walnuts. Pour over the crumb mixture. Place in the freezer for several hours or overnight. Remove from the freezer and place in refrigerator 1 hour before serving. Garnish with Chocolate Leaves and extra whipped cream, if desired.

Rum Raisin Ice Cream

MAKES 1 QUART

3 cups heavy cream
1 cup milk
3/4 cup sugar
4 large egg yolks, slightly beaten

3/4 cup raisins
2 tablespoons dark rum
1/2 cup toasted pecans, coarsely
   chopped

In a medium saucepan, heat the cream, milk, and sugar, stirring occasionally until the sugar is dissolved and the mixture is hot. Whisk about 1/4 cup of the hot cream mixture into the egg yolks. Add the eggs to the cream mixture in the saucepan, stirring constantly. Cook over medium heat, continuing to stir, until mixture thickens and coats the back of a spoon. Do not allow to boil. Strain the mixture into a bowl and cool thoroughly.

Soak the raisins in the rum at least 1 1/2 hours. Fold the raisin-rum mixture and the pecans into the cooled ice-cream mixture. Pour into an ice-cream maker and freeze according to the manufacturer's instructions.

Chocolate Hazelnut Ice Cream

MAKES I QUART

I cup hazelnuts, shelled
12 ounces semisweet chocolate
I ounce unsweetened chocolate
1/3 cup water
2 cups heavy cream

4 teaspoons powdered instant
    coffee (for a richer flavor, use
    powdered instant espresso)
4 egg yolks
I cup sugar

Place the hazelnuts in a 300-degree oven for 10–15 minutes until the skins are dry and loose. Wrap in a towel and let steam for a minute. Rub hard to remove the skins. Some small bits of skin will remain on the nuts. Chop coarsely.

In a medium-size saucepan, melt the chocolates with the water over low heat. In another saucepan, scald the cream and then add the coffee.

In a large bowl, beat the egg yolks with the sugar until the mixture is thick and pale. Slowly add the cream and the chocolate mixture in a stream, beating continuously until well blended. Pour the mixture into a medium saucepan and cook it over moderate heat. Continue stirring until mixture thickens, about 3–4 minutes. Do not let boil. Transfer mixture to a bowl, set in ice, and stir until custard is almost cold. Add the nuts. Pour into an ice-cream maker and freeze according to manufacturer's directions.

White Chocolate Ice Cream

MAKES I QUART

I pound white chocolate
12 large egg yolks
I 1/4 cups sugar

I quart whole milk
3 tablespoons Kirsch
Raspberry Sauce (below)

In a heavy saucepan, melt the chocolate over low heat. Set aside. In a mixing bowl, beat the egg yolks and sugar together. Bring the milk to a boil. Whisk in the egg mixture. Cook over low heat, stirring constantly, until the mixture is thick enough to coat a spoon, about 8 minutes. Do not allow mixture to boil. Stir in the melted chocolate. Remove from the heat and add the liqueur. Pour into ice-cream maker and freeze according to manufacturer's directions. Serve with Raspberry Sauce.

RASPBERRY SAUCE   MAKES ABOUT 2 CUPS

I pint fresh raspberries *or* I (10-   3 tablespoons sugar, or to taste
  ounce) package frozen   I tablespoon Kirsch
  raspberries, thawed

In a blender or food processor, purée the berries and strain through a fine
sieve. Add the sugar and Kirsch and mix well. Serve over ice cream.

Orange Sherbet with Blackberry Sauce

MAKES ABOUT I QUART

2 cups orange juice   I cup half-and-half
3/4 cup sugar   I cup sour cream
1/2 cup domestic orange   Blackberry Sauce (below)
  marmalade

In a medium bowl, combine the orange juice, sugar, and marmalade. Stir in
the half-and-half and sour cream. Pour into an ice-cream maker and freeze
according to manufacturer's directions.

Alternate method: Pour into 9 × 5 × 3-inch loaf pan. Cover with foil and
freeze until almost firm, 1–3 hours. Remove from the freezer and beat with an
electric mixer until light and fluffy but not thawed. Return to freezer for 1–3
hours more.

BLACKBERRY SAUCE   MAKES ABOUT 2 CUPS

I pint fresh blackberries *or* I   3–6 tablespoons sugar
  (10-ounce) package frozen   I tablespoon crème de cassis
  blackberries, thawed

Purée blackberries and strain through a fine sieve. Add 3–6 tablespoons sugar,
or to taste, and the liqueur and mix well. Serve over sherbet.

FRUIT SORBETS

A wonderful variety of fruit sorbets can be made using the following Simple Syrup.

SIMPLE SYRUP
4 cups sugar
4 cups water

In a saucepan, cook the sugar and water over low heat until the sugar is dissolved. Cool to room temperature and refrigerate in a covered jar. This syrup is the basis for all of the following sorbets.

Kiwi Sorbet

MAKES I QUART

8 kiwi fruits, peeled and puréed
1 1/3 cups Simple Syrup
4 teaspoons fresh lemon juice

In a bowl, combine the kiwi purée, syrup, and lemon juice. Pour the mixture into an ice-cream maker and freeze according to manufacturer's directions.

Lemon Sorbet

MAKES I QUART

1 1/2 cups fresh lemon juice
1 tablespoon grated lemon peel
3 cups Simple Syrup

In a bowl, combine the lemon juice, peel, and syrup. Pour the mixture into an ice-cream maker and freeze according to manufacturer's directions.

Blueberry Sorbet

MAKES I QUART

4 cups blueberries, puréed*
I ¹/₂ cups Simple Syrup
Juice of 2 lemons

In a bowl, combine the blueberry purée, syrup, and lemon juice. Pour the mixture into an ice-cream maker and freeze according to manufacturer's directions.

Note   Blueberry purée may be pressed through a fine sieve to remove skins if a smoother texture is desired.

Mango Sorbet

MAKES I QUART

I cup Simple Syrup
2 cups mango purée (approximately 4–6 ripe mangos)
2 tablespoons lime juice

In a bowl, combine the syrup and mango purée and stir in lime juice to taste. Pour the mixture into an ice-cream maker and freeze according to manufacturer's directions.

Raspberry Sorbet

MAKES I QUART

3 pints fresh raspberries, puréed
  ***or* 2 (10-ounce) packages**
  frozen raspberries

I ¹/₂ cups Simple Syrup
Juice of I lemon

In a bowl, combine the raspberry purée, syrup, and lemon juice. Pour the mixture into an ice-cream maker and freeze according to manufacturer's directions.

Alternate method of freezing for all sorbets: Pour the mixture into a 1 1/2-quart pan or bowl. Freeze until solid around the edges but still soft in the center. Remove from the bowl and beat until smooth. Return to the freezer until solid around the edges. Beat until smooth again. Return to freezer until solid. Remove from the freezer and place in the refrigerator for 30 minutes before serving.

Pear and Zinfandel Sorbet

MAKES 1 1/2 QUARTS

3 cups Zinfandel wine
1 2/3 cups sugar
1 1/2 pounds ripe pears, such as

Anjou or Comice, peeled, quartered, and cored

In a large saucepan, combine the wine and sugar. Cook the mixture over low heat until the sugar is dissolved. Add the pears to the wine-and-sugar mixture. Poach the pears over moderate heat for 15–20 minutes or until they are tender. Transfer the pears to a blender or a food processor and purée. Combine 2 cups of the syrup with the purée and chill. Pour the mixture into an ice-cream maker and freeze according to manufacturer's directions. Keeps well in the freezer for 4–5 days.

Strawberry Champagne Sorbet

MAKES ABOUT 1 1/2 QUARTS

1 cup heavy cream
3/4 cup sugar
1 1/2 cups champagne
1 (10-ounce) package frozen strawberries, thawed

2 egg whites
12 fresh strawberries, for garnish
12 fresh mint sprigs, for garnish

In a medium saucepan, combine the cream and 1/2 cup of the sugar and stir over medium heat until sugar dissolves. Cool to room temperature. Stir in the champagne and undrained strawberries. In a large bowl, beat the egg whites to soft peaks. Slowly add the remaining sugar, beating to form peaks that are stiff but not dry. Fold the egg whites into the strawberry mixture. Pour mixture into an ice-cream maker and freeze according to manufacturer's directions. Garnish with strawberries and mint sprigs.

Alternate method: Pour the strawberries, cream, and champagne mixture into an 8-inch square pan. Cover and freeze until firm. Break up the frozen mixture and turn into a chilled mixing bowl. Beat until smooth. Fold in the beaten egg whites. Return to the pan. Cover and freeze until firm.

Spiced Blueberry Sauce

MAKES I CUP

3 tablespoons sugar
I ¹/₂ teaspoons cornstarch
I ¹/₂ cups fresh or frozen
   blueberries
3 tablespoons water

I ¹/₂ tablespoons fresh lemon
   juice
¹/₄ teaspoon cinnamon
¹/₂ teaspoon nutmeg

In a medium saucepan, combine the sugar and cornstarch. Add the remaining ingredients and cook, stirring constantly, until the mixture boils. Reduce the heat and simmer for 5 minutes, stirring constantly. Serve warm over ice cream. Store, covered, in the refrigerator.

Brandied Ginger Sauce

MAKES I ¹/₂ CUPS

Try this sauce on gingerbread as well as vanilla ice cream.

8 ounces crystallized ginger
¹/₂ cup sugar

I cup pear nectar
¹/₂ cup brandy

In a blender or food processor, mince the ginger. In a medium saucepan, over high heat, combine the sugar, pear nectar, and brandy. Add the ginger and bring to a boil. Reduce the heat and simmer for 20 minutes, stirring occasionally.

Lemon Curd

MAKES ABOUT 5 CUPS

6 large eggs	3 cups sugar
Peel from 6 lemons, grated	1 1/2 cups unsalted butter, cut in
Juice from 6 lemons	pieces

Lightly beat the eggs and place them in the top of a double boiler. Add the lemon peel, lemon juice, sugar, and butter. Cook over low heat, stirring constantly, until thick and creamy. Remove from the heat. The mixture will thicken more as it cools. Store in the refrigerator in airtight jars.

Praline Sauce

MAKES 1 CUP

1/4 cup unsalted butter	1/4 cup water
1/2 cup powdered sugar	1 teaspoon rum
2 tablespoons maple syrup	1/2 cup chopped pecans

In a saucepan, melt the butter over medium heat and cook until just starting to brown. Cool, and then gradually add the sugar. Stir in the syrup and water and heat to boiling. Boil for 1 minute, stirring constantly. Stir in the rum and nuts. Serve over ice cream.

Mango Cream

MAKES 1 CUP

2 mangos, peeled and pitted
1/2 cup heavy cream
1 tablespoon Grand Marnier

In a blender or food processor, purée mangos until smooth. With the machine running, slowly add the cream. Process until thick and smooth. Blend in the Grand Marnier.

Serve over a fruit compote of kiwi, green grapes, and strawberries.

Grand Marnier Sauce

MAKES 1 1/2 CUPS

5 large egg yolks
1/2 cup sugar
1/4 cup Grand Marnier

1 cup heavy cream
2 tablespoons sugar

Place the egg yolks and the 1/2 cup sugar in top of double boiler. Beat the mixture over boiling water. Remove from the heat and stir in 1/8 cup of the Grand Marnier. Allow the sauce to cool, then refrigerate until cold.

Beat the cream with 2 tablespoons of sugar until stiff peaks form. Fold into the sauce and add the remaining Grand Marnier.

Mint Truffles

MAKES ABOUT 5 DOZEN

6–8 ounces semisweet Swiss
   chocolate
1/2 cup unsalted butter, softened
1/2 cup powdered sugar
2 large eggs

1 (12-ounce) package chocolate
   chips, melted
2 teaspoons vanilla
1/2 teaspoon peppermint extract

In a small heavy saucepan, melt the Swiss chocolate over low heat. Spread it evenly in a foil-lined 8-inch square pan. Refrigerate until set. Blend the butter and sugar in a food processor. Add the eggs and blend well. Add the melted chocolate chips, vanilla, and peppermint extract. Spread over the hardened chocolate layer and refrigerate again until firm, about 1 hour. Lift the truffle from the pan, remove foil, and cut in small squares. Serve immediately or return to the refrigerator. Truffles will keep 2 weeks in the refrigerator, covered with plastic wrap.

Chocolate Truffles

MAKES 2–3 DOZEN

1 (12-ounce) package chocolate
  chips
1/2 cup plus 2 tablespoons heavy
  cream
2 tablespoons Grand Marnier or
  brandy

1/2 pound semisweet Swiss
  chocolate
Cocoa, finely chopped nuts, or
  powdered sugar, for coating

In a small saucepan melt the chocolate chips over low heat. In another pan, boil the cream for 1 minute, remove from the heat, and cool until just warm. Add the cream to the melted chocolate chips and whisk until well blended. Add the Grand Marnier and chill 1–2 hours or until the mixture can be formed into balls. Roll into walnut-size balls. Place on waxed paper and refrigerate for 10–15 minutes more. Meanwhile, in a small saucepan, melt the chocolate over low heat. Dip the truffles in the melted chocolate, then roll in desired coating. Allow finished candies to stand at room temperature for 10–15 minutes.

Truffles freeze well in an airtight container for up to 1 month.

Mocha Truffles

MAKES ABOUT 2 DOZEN

1 (6-ounce) package chocolate
  chips
2/3 cup unsalted butter, softened
1 large egg yolk

1 1/4 cups powdered sugar
1 tablespoon rum
1 teaspoon instant coffee
1/2 cup finely chopped pecans

In a small heavy saucepan, melt the chocolate chips over low heat. Set aside. In a large bowl, cream the butter, egg yolk, and sugar. Add the rum, coffee, and the melted chocolate chips and beat well. Chill 1–2 hours or until the mixture can be formed into balls. Form into 1-inch balls and roll in the pecans. Refrigerate 1–2 hours before serving.

Holiday Eggnog

SERVES 10–12

12 large eggs, separated
1 1/2 cups sugar
1 1/2 pints bourbon
2 ounces rum

1 quart heavy cream, whipped
1 quart whole milk
Freshly grated nutmeg

In a large mixing bowl, beat the egg yolks, 1 cup of the sugar, bourbon, and rum. Refrigerate the yolk mixture several hours or overnight. Beat the egg whites until stiff and add the remaining sugar to the beaten whites. Combine the whites with the yolk mixture and whisk in the cream and milk. Refrigerate at least 1 hour. Serve with nutmeg on top.

XIII

Menus

A BLACK TIE DINNER

Dilled Shrimp on Cucumbers
Wild Mushroom Soup
Breast of Chicken with Pears, Port,
  and Stilton
Crispy Baked Potatoes
Julienned Carrots and Zucchini,
  sautéed

Boston Lettuce with Champagne
  Vinaigrette
Raspberry Tart with Mascarpone
  Cheese

A FORMAL DINNER

Layered Salmon Mold with Melba
  Hearts
Elegant Leek Soup
Leg of Lamb with Pistachio Nut
  Stuffing and Cumberland Sauce

Wild, Wild Rice
Carrot Purée
Gruyère Walnut Salad
Steamed Chocolate Pudding with
  Chocolate Sauce

A CALIFORNIA THANKSGIVING DINNER

Tortilla Rolls with Mustard
Cold Clam Bisque
Turkey Stuffed with Fruit and
  Jalapeño Peppers
Lemon Sweet Potatoes

Chile-stuffed Pattypan Squash
Green Beans with Walnuts
Corn Sticks
Pumpkin Cheesecake

AN ORIENTAL DINNER

Chinese Wontons
Chinese Ginger-Meatball and
  Watercress Soup
Thai Shrimp with Peppers
Asparagus with Cashews

Sushi
Mango Cream with Kiwi, Grapes,
  and Strawberries
Golden Nut Cookies

ST. PATRICK'S DAY DINNER

Herb Cheese with Soufflé Crackers
Apple Broccoli Soup (chilled)
Corned Beef with Apricot Mustard
  Glaze

Beer Bread
Cranberry-Pear Cobbler

A SPRING DINNER

Gruyère Puffs
Boston Lettuce with Avocado,
    Hazelnuts, and Raspberry
    Vinaigrette
Salmon with Tomato Basil Beurre
    Blanc

Braised Cucumbers and Leeks
Parsley Potatoes
California Custard with Fresh
    Berries

SEASHORE DINNER

Chile Bites
Mexican Vegetable Soup
Steamed broccoli
Southwest Snapper with Cilantro
    Cream

Corn Cakes
Frozen Strawberry Cream Cake

ELEGANT BUT EASY DINNER

Baked Oysters with Lime and
    Shallots
Swordfish with Wasabi Marinade

Sauté of Spinach with Chard
Steamed Brown Rice
Strawberry Nectarine Cobbler

A CALIFORNIA BARBECUE

Tomato Cheese Crostini
Chilled Curried Pea Soup
Rosemary Lamb with Sweet Pepper
    Relish

Summer Baked Vegetables with
    Herbs
Gingered Peach Pie

BIG GAME SUPPER

Quesadilla
Crudités with Lemon Sour Cream
    Dressing for Dipping
Tossed Green Salad

Chicken Chili
Hot Crusty Rolls
Chocolate Chip Brownies

AN AUTUMN SUPPER

Moroccan Dip
Assorted Greens with Oranges, Red
   Onions, and Walnut Dressing
Indonesian Lamb Shanks
Savory Peas

Couscous
Orange Sherbet with Blackberry
   Sauce
Pistachio Macaroons

HOLLYWOOD BOWL PICNIC

Cold Tomato Yogurt Soup
Feta Crisps
Grilled Beef Tenderloin
Cold Asparagus with Mustard
   Vinaigrette

Wild Rice Salad with Peas
Lemon Blueberry Tart

FOURTH OF JULY PICNIC

Layered California Guacamole
Napa Cabbage Salad
Pepper and Tomato Salad
Panko-crusted Sesame Chicken

White Chocolate Ice Cream,
   Raspberry Sauce, and Fresh
   Blueberries

AN ITALIAN LUNCH

Carpaccio
Red Pepper Soup
Lemon Pasta with Mussels
Assorted Greens with Parmesan
   Vinaigrette

Crusty Italian Bread
Raspberry Zabaglione

LUNCH AL FRESCO

Foccacio with Eggplant and Pepper
   Topping
Rosemary Chicken
Italian Marinated Vegetable Salad

Pasta Salad with Tomatoes, Basil,
   and Sherry Vinegar
Layered Lemon Crème

LUNCHEON FOR THE LADIES

Sunshine Soup

Chicken Pasta Salad

Miniature Croissants

Chocolate Almond Ice Cream Torte

BEST-EVER BRUNCH

Sliced Melon Platter

California Greek Salad

Corn and Red Pepper Roulade

Ginger Cornmeal Muffins

Orange Ring Cake

BREAKFAST WITH SANTA

Freshly Squeezed Orange Juice

Gingerbread Pancakes with
  Cranberry Butter

Breakfast Meats with Apples

Coffee and Hot Chocolate

BREAKFAST ON THE TERRACE

Mimosas or Freshly Squeezed
  Orange Juice

Breakfast Chimichangas with Fresh
  Fruit

Assorted Morning Meats

Cinnamon Crunch Coffeecake

HOLIDAY BUFFET

Goat Cheese Mold

Pâté with Green Peppercorns

Stuffed Cherry Tomatoes

Gravlax with Mustard Sauce

Green Bean, Walnut, and Feta
  Salad

Shrimp and Pasta Salad

Ham Braised in Port with a Pecan
  Crust

Assorted Dinner Rolls

Amaretto Cheesecake

Chocolate, Mint, and Mocha
  Truffles

MEETING DAY BUFFET

Aram Sandwiches with Curried
  Chicken Filling
Green Pea and Apple Salad
Spinach Salad with Chutney
  Mustard Dressing

Lemon Pistachio Bars
Raspberry Cheesecake Bars

CHINATOWN FEAST

Minced Chicken in Lettuce
Oriental Soup with Shrimp and
  Pineapple
Peking Pork
Scallion Pancakes

Spicy Eggplant and Green Beans
Cauliflower with Hoisin Sauce
Scallop Sausage Fried Rice
Apple Almond Tart

FIESTA BRUNCH BUFFET

Tequila Sunrises
Fresh Fruit Platter
Capistrano Quiche
Salad of Mixed Greens with Red
  Wine Vinaigrette

Glazed Orange Muffins
Chocolate Brownies with Mocha
  Icing

ROSE QUEEN® AND COURT TEA

Dilled Shrimp on Cucumbers
Smoked Turkey Sandwiches on
  Rosemary Raisin Bread
Gingered Kumquats
Crab and Asparagus Dijonnaise

Raisin Cinnamon Scones with
  Lemon Curd
Almond Pound Cake
Orange Anise Madeleines
Millionaire Shortbread

Index

Acorn Squash, Autumn, 264
Albacore with Red Pepper Sauce, Barbecued,
  133
Almond(s)
  -Chocolate Ice Cream Torte, 353
  Cookies
    Golden Nut, 328
    Tea, 320
  Pound Cake, 311
  Tart
    Apple, 332
    Pine Nut and, 331
Amaretto Cheesecake, 318
Anchovy Mayonnaise, Cauliflower and Olive
      Salad with, 79
Anderson, Carol, 8
Anderson, Stanley, 8
Andouille Sausage, Grilled Oysters with, 13
Angel Hair Pasta with Lemon Lime, 107
Anise Orange Madeleines, 327
Antipasto Salad, Spinach, 85
Appetizers, 11–48
  Beef
    Carpaccio, 27
    Satay, 31
  Belgian Endive with Two Fillings, 42
  California Rolls, 38
  Cheese
    Ball, Red Pepper, 17
    Bread Round with Melted Brie, 18
    Brie with Apricot Sauce, 18
    Brioche with Tomatoes and Brie, 43
    Feta Crisps, 48
    Focaccio with Ricotta, Feta, and Spinach
        Topping, 41
    Gorgonzola-Pistachio Loaf, 29
    Gorgonzola Walnut Rounds, 19
    Gruyère Puffs, 20
    Herb, 25
    Mexican Sandwiches, 39
    Mold, Goat, 19
    Parmesan French Toast, 16
    Puffs, Stilton, 21
    Quesadilla, 36
    Ricotta, Sliced Figs with, 40

    Sesame Cheese Twists, 48
    Spread, Solvang Caraway, 16
    Stilton Puffs, 21
    Tomato Crostini, 17
  Cherry Tomatoes, Stuffed, 39
  Chicken
    in Lettuce, Minced, 35
    Smoked, Radicchio Cups with, 37
    Wings, Spicy, 30
  Chile Bites, 36
  Crab
    and Asparagus Dijonnaise, 11
    California Rolls, 38
  Crackers, Soufflé, 47
  Dip
    Beet, 25
    Indian, 26
    Moroccan, 24
    Mustard, Tortilla Rolls with, 38
  Figs, Sliced, with Ricotta, 40
  Focaccio, 41
  Gravlax with Mustard Sauce, 22
  Guacamole, Layered California, 23
  Kumquats, Gingered, 41
  Lamb
    in Lettuce Leaves, Thai, 35
    Meatballs with Mint Chutney, Indian, 34
  Melba Hearts, 47
  Mushrooms
    Escargot and Prosciutto Stuffed, 32
    Stuffed with Smoked Oysters, 32
  Mussels with Red Pepper Relish, Cold, 12
  Oysters, Grilled, 13
  Pâté with Green Peppercorns, 26
  Potatoes
    Baked, 45
    San Diego Spuds, 46
    New, with Wasabi Mayonnaise, 45
  Salmon
    Mold, Layered, 20
    with Wild Rice Pancakes, Smoked, 21
  Salsa, 24
  Sausage in Brioche, 30
  Scallops, Tangerine, 14

Shrimp
  on Cucumbers, Dilled, 14
  Rémoulade, 15
Spread
  Roasted Pepper, 23
  Solvang Caraway Cheese, 16
Tarte Provençale, 44
Tortellini with Sour Cream Gorgonzola Sauce,
  44
Tortilla Rolls with Mustard Dip, 38
Veal and Pork Terrine, 28
Wontons
  Chinese, 33
  Indian, 34
Apple(s)
  Almond Tart, 332
  Baked
    Country, 341
    Sausage Stuffed, 290
  and Beets, Sautéed, 248
  Breakfast Meats with, 290
  Brie Salad with Pecans and, 80
  -Broccoli Soup, 65
  Calf's Liver with Onions and, 220
  Cheddar-crusted Chicken Pie with Sausage
    and, 178
  -Cider Steamed Mussels, 154
  and Green Pea Salad, 74
  Roast Pork Loin with Mushrooms and, 232
Apricot(s)
  Almond Tea Cookies, 320
  Carrots, Shredded, with, 252
  -Mustard Glaze, Corned Beef with, 210
  Sauce
    Brie with, 18
    Walnut-, Soft Gingerbread with, 317
Artichoke
  Bottoms
    Gratin, 245
    and Turkey Sauté with Lemon and
      Rosemary, 193
  Hearts
    and Beef Salad, Cold, 87
    California Riviera Salad with, 96
    Green Salad with Hearts of Palm and, 82
    Linguine, 106
Asparagus
  with Cashews, Ginger, 245
  and Crab Dijonnaise, 11
  with Mustard Vinaigrette, Cold, 73
  with Raspberry Cream, 73
  in Spring Seafood Salad, 93
Avocado(s)
  Boston Lettuce with Hazelnuts, Raspberry
    Vinaigrette, and, 84
  California Greek Salad with, 82
  California Riviera Salad with, 96
  Guacamole
    Chicken Fajitas with, 181
    Layered California, 23
  Spring Green Salad with Strawberries, Kiwi,
    and, 101

Bacon
  Appetizer Baked Potatoes with, 45

  Canadian, Breakfast Meats and Apples with,
    290
  Cherry Tomatoes Stuffed with, 45
  Creamy Leek Soup with Shallots and, 62
  Dressing, Spinach Salad with, 86
Balsamic Vinegar
  Orange Roughy with Capers and, 145
  Vinaigrette
    Cajun Chicken Salad with, 90
    Thyme and, 81
Banana Soup Indienne, Chilled, 55
Bars
  Double Chocolate Rum, 322
  Lemon Pistachio, 326
  Raspberry Cheesecake, 330
  See also Brownies, Chocolate
Basil
  Butter, Chicken Breasts with, 168
  Capellini with Sauce of Fresh Tomato and,
    107
  Chicken with Lemon and, 174
  Dressing, Creamy, Spring Seafood Salad with,
    93
  Fettucine with Gorgonzola, Bell Peppers, and,
    114
  Pasta Salad with Tomatoes, Sherry Vinegar,
    and, 94
  Shells with Peas and, 115
  Tomato Cream with Linguine, 108
  Torta Cheese, Tomato Crostini with, 17
  Veal Scallops with Tomatoes and, 239
Bass, in Cioppino, 140
Bean(s)
  Moroccan Dip, 24
  See also Black Bean(s); Chinese Long Beans;
    Great Northern Beans; Green Beans;
    White Bean(s)
Beef, 207–19
  and Artichoke Salad, Cold, 87
  Brisket with White Beans, 215
  Carpaccio, 27
  Corned, with Apricot Mustard Glaze, 210
  Fajitas, 213
  Fillets with Roquefort Sauce, 211
  Flank Steak
    Fajitas, 213
    with Goat Cheese Topping, Broiled, 208
    and Peppers in Spicy Garlic Sauce, 219
    with Red Onions, 211
    Shanghai, 218
  in Game Pie, 201
  Ground
    Cajun Meat Loaf, 209
    Capistrano Quiche with, 279
    Italian Meat Loaf with Tomato Sauce, 238
    People's Choice Chili, 218
    Spicy Marinated Steak, 217
  Horseradish Filling, Chile Bites with, 36
  Pasadena Pot Roast, 214
  in a Pumpkin, Autumn, 216
  Roast
    Aram Sandwiches with, 291
    Wagon Wheel Loaf with, 293
  Satay, 31
  Steak. *See also* Flank Steak *above*
    Mexican Country, 214

with Wasabi Butter, Oriental, 212
Stock, 68
Tenderloin
  Grilled, 207
  with Mustard Peppercorn Sauce, 208
Beet(s)
  and Apples, Sautéed, 248
  Dip, 25
Belgian Endive with Two Fillings, 42
Berry(-ies)
  California Custard with Fresh, 344
  Sauce, California Custard with Fresh Berries
    and, 344
  See also Blackberry; Blueberry(-ies);
    Raspberry(-ies); Strawberry(-ies)
Bibb Lettuce
  Leaves, Thai Lamb in, 35
  Minced Chicken in, 35
Bisque, Cold Clam, 54
Bittersweet Chocolate Sauce, Steamed Chocolate
    Pudding with, 347
Black Bean(s)
  California, 247
  Soup, Cajun, 60
Blackberry
  Jam Cake, 313
  Sauce, Orange Sherbet with, 356
Black Forest Ham, Orange Glazed Red Cabbage
    with, 250
Blueberry(-ies)
  in California Custard with Fresh Berries, 344
  Cream Puff Ring with Strawberries and, 343
  Layered Lemon Crème with, 345
  Sauce, Spiced, 360
  Sorbet, 358
  Tart, Lemon, 333
Blue Cheese
  and Nectarine Salad, 100
  Peppercorn Butter, Lamb Chops with, 226
  Winter Ham Soup with, 65
Bok Choy Stir-fry with Sherry, 249
Boston Lettuce
  with Avocado, Hazelnuts, and Raspberry
    Vinaigrette, 84
  Center Stage Salad, 77
  in Green Salad
    with Artichoke Heart and Hearts of Palm,
      82
    with Fennel, 83
  in Gruyère and Walnut Salad, 83
  Leaves, Thai Lamb in, 35
  Minced Chicken in, 35
Bourbon Yams, 268
Brandied Ginger Sauce, 360
Bread(s), 299–308
  Balboa Brunch, 277
  Beer, 299
  Brioche
    Sausage in, 30
    with Tomatoes and Brie, 43
  Corn Sticks, 299
  Currant and Caraway, 301
  Curried Cracker, 26
  Foccacio, 40
  Gorgonzola Walnut Rounds, 19
  Herbed Potato, 307

Melba Hearts, 47
Parmesan French Toast, 16
Pizza Loaf, 294
Pudding, Raspberry Meringue, 347
Pumpkin Doughnut Drops, 308
Raisin
  Cinnamon Scones, 306
  Cranberry, 304
  Rosemary, 302
  Rosemary, Smoked Turkey on, 295
Round with Melted Brie, 18
Sheepherder's, 302
Sticks, Garlic, 300
Strawberry Nut, 305
Wagon Wheel Loaf, 293
Whole Wheat, 303
See also Muffin(s)
Brie
  with Apricot Sauce, 18
  Bread Round with Melted, 18
  Brioche with Tomatoes and, 43
  Salad with Pecans, 80
Brioche
  Sausage in, 30
  with Tomatoes and Brie, 43
Broccoli
  -Apple Soup, 65
  and Cheddar Pie with Potato Crust, 280
  Individual Vegetable Strudels with, 274
  with Orange-Shallot Butter, 249
  Purée, 269
  Stir-fried, 273
  Topping, Cauliflower with, 252
Brownies, Chocolate
  with Mocha Icing, 322
  Chocolate Chip, 321
Brown Sauce, for Game Pie, 202
Brussels Sprouts with Caraway Seeds, 250
Bulgur, Ginger Chicken with, 183
Bulk technique (Charmat process), 7
Butter
  Basil, Chicken Breasts with, 168
  Blue Cheese Peppercorn, Lamb Chops with,
    227
  Capellini with Spices and, 106
  Chili, Grilled Vegetables with, 270
  Cranberry, Cranberry Raisin Bread with, 304
  Frosting, Smooth, Palm Springs Date Nut
    Cake with, 317
  Mustard Herb, Crown Roast of Lamb with,
    223
  Pine Nut, Grilled Halibut with, 141
  Sauce
    Cayenne, Lobster with, 164
    Macadamia, Baked Crab Stuffed Trout
      with, 156
    Sherry, Lobster with, 163
  Tomato Basil, Salmon with, 146
  Wasabi, Oriental Steak with, 212
  Zinfandel Garlic, Veal Chops with, 240
Butternut Squash, Pork with, 234

Cabbage
  Bok Choy Stir-fry with Sherry, 249
  Chrysanthemum, Chinese Roast Duck with
    Kiwi Sauce and, 198

Red, with Black Forest Ham, Orange Glazed,
    250
Salad, Napa, 79
Sautéed, Noodles with Caraway Seeds, 117
Cajun Barbecued Shrimp, 160
Cajun Bean Soup, 60
Cajun Chicken Salad, 90
Cajun Meat Loaf, 209
Cajun Seasoning, 90
Cakes, 311–20
    Blackberry Jam, 313
    Cheesecake
        Amaretto, 318
        Bars, Raspberry, 330
        Pumpkin, 319
    Chocolate
        Mousse, with Coffee Whipped Cream, 352
        Sour Cream, 314
    Date Nut, Palm Springs, 316
    Gingerbread with Apricot Walnut Sauce, Soft,
        317
    Grand Marnier Walnut, 316
    Lemon Coconut, 312
    Orange Ring, 315
    Pound
        Almond, 311
        Coconut, 311
    Pumpkin Roll, 318
    Strawberry Cream, Frozen, 351
Calf's Liver with Sautéed Apples and Onions,
    220
California Black Beans, 247
California Cucumber Soup, 53
California Custard with Fresh Berries, 344
California Greek Salad, 82
California Moo Shu Pork, 237
California Niçoise Salad, 99
California Riviera Salad, 96
California Rolls, 38
Calzone
    with Black Forest Ham and Ricotta, 121
    Pizza Dough, 119
    with Smoked Chicken and Goat Cheese, 122
Capers
    Carrots with, 251
    Orange Roughy with Balsamic Vinegar and,
        145
Capistrano Quiche, 279
Capellini
    with Butter and Spices, 106
    with Fresh Tomato and Basil Sauce, 107
    with Smoked Salmon and Black Caviar, 117
Caramel Sauce, Pears en Croute with, 342
Caraway (Seeds)
    Basting Sauce, Grilled Spring Chicken with,
        185
    Brussels Sprouts with, 250
    Cheese Spread, Solvang, 16
    and Currant Bread, 301
    Noodles with Sautéed Cabbage and, 117
Carpaccio, 27
Carrot(s)
    with Apricots, Shredded, 252
    with Capers, 251
    Individual Vegetable Strudels with, 274
    with Port, 251

Purée, 269
Sautéed with Shallot Butter, 271
Sunshine Soup, 51
in Vegetarian Mixed Grill, 262
Cashews
    Ginger Asparagus with, 245
    Snow Peas with, 258
Cauliflower
    with Broccoli Topping, 252
    with Hoisin Sauce, 253
    Individual Vegetable Strudels with, 274
    and Olive Salad, 79
    Stir-fried, 273
Caviar, Black, Capellini with Smoked Salmon
        and, 117
Cayenne
    Butter Sauce, Lobster with, 164
    Nuts, 77
Celery Root Purée, 270
Center Stage Salad, 77
Center Stage Vinaigrette, 77
Champagne
    Strawberry Sorbet, 359
    Vinaigrette, 75
Chanterelle Mushrooms, Pricey Rice with, 126
Charmat process (bulk technique), 7
Cheddar Cheese
    and Broccoli Pie with Potato Crust, 280
    Capistrano Quiche with, 279
    -Crusted Chicken Pie with Sausage and
        Apple, 178
    Onion Mushroom Casserole with, 256
    Three-Cheese Soufflé with, 277
    Wagon Wheel Loaf with, 293
Cheese(s)
    appetizers
        Ball, Red Pepper, 17
        Bread Round with Melted Brie, 18
        Brie with Apricot Sauce, 18
        Brioche with Tomatoes and Brie, 43
        Feta Crisps, 48
        Focaccio with Ricotta, Feta, and Spinach
            Topping, 41
        Gorgonzola-Pistachio Loaf, 29
        Gorgonzola Walnut Rounds, 19
        Gruyère Puffs, 20
        Herb, 25
        Mexican Sandwiches, 39
        Mold, Goat, 19
        Parmesan French Toast, 16
        Puffs, Stilton, 21
        Quesadilla, 36
        Ricotta, Sliced Figs with, 40
        Sesame Cheese Twists, 48
        Spread, Solvang Caraway, 16
        Stilton Puffs, 21
        Tomato Crostini, 17
    Corn Crepes, Grilled California Quail with
        Tomatillo Cream and, 199
    Onion Mushroom Casserole with, 256
    Rigatoni with Four, 112
    Salad
        Blue, and Nectarine, 100
        Brie with Pecans, 80
        Goat, Baked, 81
        Gruyère and Walnut, 83

Soufflé, Three-, 277
Tart
  Blueberry, 334
  Mascarpone and Raspberry, 335
  See also Blue Cheese; Brie; Cheddar Cheese;
    Cheesecake; Cream Cheese; Feta; Goat
    Cheese; Gorgonzola; Gruyère;
    Mascarpone; Parmesan; Ricotta;
    Roquefort; Stilton; Swiss Cheese
Cheesecake
  Amaretto, 318
  Bars, Raspberry, 330
  Pumpkin, 319
Chèvre. See Goat Cheese
Chicken
  Breasts
    with Basil Butter, 168
    Chile Relleno, 176
    Cilantro with Tomatillo Sauce, 172
    Coronado, 167
    Garlic, 170
    with Lemon and Basil, 174
    Mediterranean, 170
    in Parmesan Cream, 169
    with Peanuts, Szechuan, 171
    and Pear Slices with Port and Stilton
      Cream, 174
    Piccata, 168
    and Plum Tomatoes in Port, 167
    with Raspberry Vinegar, 175
    Southwestern Grilled, 177
    Stuffed with Goat Cheese, Glazed, 173
  with Caraway Basting Sauce, Grilled Spring,
    185
  Chili, 184
  Fajitas, 180
  Filling, Curried (for Aram Sandwiches), 292
  in Game Pie, 201
  with Honey and Mustard, Curry Glazed, 180
  Indienne, Orange, 189
  with Italian Sausages and Sweet Peppers,
    Rosemary, 186
  in Lettuce, Minced, 35
  Liver Pâté with Green Peppercorns, 26
  Mendocino, 187
  Orange Rosemary, 182
  Panko-crusted Sesame, 182
  Pie with Sausage and Apple, Cheddar-crusted,
    178
  Salad
    Cajun, 90
    Mandarin, 91
    Pasta, 95
    Sonoran, 89
    with Stilton Cheese, 88
    with Wild Rice, 99
  Smoked
    Baked, 190
    Calzone with Goat Cheese and, 122
    Hickory, 190
    Radicchio Cups with, 37
  and Spinach, and Gruyère Torta, 286
  Stock, 69
  Tandoori with Punjabi Sauce, 188
  Wings, Spicy, 30

Chile(s)
  Green
    Bites, 36
    Chicken Relleno, 176
    in Mexican Sandwiches, 39
    Salsa, 24
    -stuffed Pattypan Squash, 263
  Red, Mayonnaise, 37
Chili
  Butter, Vegetables with, 270
  Chicken, 184
  People's Choice, 218
Chimichangas with Fresh Fruit, Breakfast, 287
Chinatown Snapper, 150
Chinese Cabbage Salad, Napa, 79
Chinese Ginger-Meatball and Watercress Soup,
  57
Chinese Long Beans, Hot and Sour, 247
Chinese Ribs, 238
Chinese Roast Duck with Kiwi Sauce, 197
Chinese Wontons, 33
Chocolate
  -Almond Ice Cream Torte, 353
  Brownies
    Chocolate Chip, 321
    with Mocha Icing, 322
  Cake
    Mousse, with Coffee Whipped Cream, 352
    Sour Cream, 314
  Cookies, Chocolate Chip
    Butterball, 323
    Domino, 324
    Orange, 327
  Decadence, Frozen, 353
  Ice Cream
    Hazelnut, 355
    White, 355
  Meringue with Raspberry Crème Anglaise,
    350
  Millionaire Shortbread with, 324
  Pâté with Pistachio Sauce, 348
  Pudding, Steamed, with Bittersweet Chocolate
    Sauce, 347
  Rum Bars, Double, 322
  Sauce, Bittersweet, Steamed Chocolate
    Pudding with, 347
  Sour Cream Frosting, Chocolate Sour Cream
    Cake with, 315
  Truffles, 363
  See also Mocha
Chowder, Corn
  Country, 62
  Mexican, 58
Chutney
  Dip, Indian, 26
  Mint
    Indian Meatballs with, 29
    Jalapeño, Rack of Lamb with, 226
    Mustard Dressing, Spinach Salad with, 85
    Peach, Five Spice Rack of Lamb with, 225
Cilantro
  Chicken with Tomatillo Sauce, 172
  Cream, Southwest Snapper with, 148
  Dressing
    Creamy, Sonoran Chicken Salad with, 89

Vinaigrette, Shrimp and Jícama Salad with, 93
Sauce, Southwestern Grilled Pork with, 233
and Turkey Filling for Aram Sandwiches, 292
Cinnamon
  Crunch Coffeecake, 306
  Raisin Scones, 306
Clam(s)
  Bisque, Cold, 54
  in Cioppino, 140
  Fish Stew Normande with, 137
  Provençale, 154
Cobbler
  Cranberry-Pear, 336
  Strawberry-Nectarine, 337
Coconut
  Cake
    Lemon, 312
    Pound, 311
  Frosting, Lemon Coconut Cake with, 313
Cod
  with Chèvre, Sonoma Style, 134
  with Pickled Red Ginger, Thai style, 143
  Poisson Printemps with, 136
Coffee Whipped Cream, Chocolate Mousse Cake with, 352
Coffeecake, Cinnamon Crunch, 306
Confetti Pasta, 115
Cookies
  Apricot Almond Tea, 320
  Chocolate Chip
    Orange, 327
    Domino, 324
    Chocolate Butterball, 323
  Ginger Cream Snaps, 325
  Madeleines, Orange Anise, 327
  Nut
    Golden, 328
    Hazelnut, 328
    Pine Nut Puffs, 329
    Pistachio Macaroons, 330
  Shortbread, Millionaire, 324
  See also Bars
Coriander
  and Red Wine Vinaigrette, California Niçoise Salad with, 99
  See also Cilantro
Corn
  Cheese Crepes, Grilled California Quail with Tomatillo Cream and, 199
  Chowder
    Country, 62
    Mexican, 58
  in Confetti Pasta, 115
  and Red Pepper Roulade, 278
Corned Beef with Apricot Mustard Glaze, 210
Cornish Hens, Glazed with Red Pepper and Ginger Butter, Crisp, 198
Cornmeal
  Cakes, 285
  Ginger Muffins, 301
  Gorgonzola Polenta, 124
  Sticks, 299
Cottage Cheese, Herb, 25
Country Corn Chowder, 62
Couscous, 123

Crab(meat)
  and Asparagus Dijonnaise, 11
  California Rolls, 38
  with Cold Cucumber Relish, Punjab, 155
  in Spring Seafood Salad, 93
  Stuffed Trout with Macadamia Butter Sauce, Baked, 156
Cracked Wheat (Bulgur), Ginger Chicken with, 183
Cracker(s)
  Bread (Lahvosh), Curried, 26
  Soufflé, 47
Cranberry(-ies)
  Butter, Cranberry Raisin Bread with, 304
  -Pear Cobblers, 336
  Raisin Bread, 304
Cream
  Garlic Potatoes, 261
  Ginger Snaps, 325
  Jarlsberg, Florentine Pepper Shells with Orzo and, 259
  Orange Ginger, Fish Fillets with, 134
  Sauce
    Cilantro, 148
    Mango, 361
    Parmesan, Breasts of Chicken in, 169
    Porcini, Pasta Twists with, 108
    Raspberry, Asparagus with, 30
    Stilton, Breast of Chicken and Pear Slices with Port and, 174
    Tomato-Basil, with Linguine, 108
    Watercress, Seafood Boudin with Lobster and, 139
    Wild Mushroom, Poached Fillets with, 136
  Scallops with Kiwi in, 157
  Tomatillo, Grilled California Quail with Cheese Corn Crepes and, 200
  Whipped
    Coffee, Chocolate Mousse Cake with, 352
    Orange, Country Baked Apples with, 341
  See also Crème
Cream Cheese
  Breakfast Chimichangas with Fresh Fruit and, 287
  Filling, Pumpkin Cake Roll with, 318
  -Gorgonzola-Pistachio Loaf, 29
  in Tortilla Rolls with Mustard Dip, 38
Cream Puff Ring with Strawberries and Blueberries, 343
Creamy Leek Soup with Shallots and Bacon, 62
Crème
  Anglaise, Chocolate Meringue with, 350
  Fraîche, Corn Cakes with, 285
  Lemon, Layered, 345
Crepes
  Cheese Corn, Grilled California Quail with Tomatillo Cream and, 200
  Cheese Filling for, 201
  Spinach, with Tomato Fondue, 284
Crookneck Squash, Italian Baked, 272
Crostini, Tomato Cheese, 17
Croustades, 163
  Parmesan, Scallops with, 158
Cucumber(s)
  Dilled Shrimp on, 14
  and Leeks, Braised, 253

Relish, Punjab Crab with, 155
Salad, Japanese, Sake Swordfish with, 152
Soup
   California, 53
   Classic, 53
Currant(s)
  and Caraway Bread, 301
  Mustard Sauce, 33
  Pork Medallions with Scotch and, 231
Curry(-ied)
  Chicken
   Filling (for Aram Sandwiches), 292
   Glazed with Honey and Mustard, 180
  Cracker Bread, 26
  Dressing
   Cream, Chicken Salad with Stilton Cheese
    and, 89
   Spinach Salad with, 86
   Wild Rice and Shrimp Salad with, 98
  Pea Soup, Cold, 55
  Shrimp, 161
  Sole, 151
Custard
  with Fresh Berries, California, 344
  Orange, 345
  Raspberry Crème Anglaise, Chocolate
   Meringue with, 350

Date Nut Cake, Palm Springs, 316
Dessert(s), 311–64
  Apples, Country Baked, 341
  Bread Pudding, Raspberry Meringue, 347
  Chocolate
   Decadence, Frozen, 353
   Meringue with Raspberry Crème Anglaise,
    350
   Pâté with Pistachio Sauce, 348
   Pudding, Steamed, with Bittersweet
    Chocolate Sauce, 347
  Cobbler
   Cranberry-Pear, 336
   Strawberry-Nectarine, 337
  Cream Puff Ring with Strawberries and
   Blueberries, 343
  Eggnog, Holiday, 364
  Gingered Pecan Peach Pie, 338
  Lemon Crème, Layered, 345
  Peach Soufflé, Cold, 346
  Pears en Croute, 342
  Sauce
   Brandied Ginger, 360
   Grand Marnier, 362
   Lemon Curd, 361
   Mango, 361
   Praline, 361
   Spiced Blueberry, 360
  Torte
   Pear, 339
   Walnut, 340
  Truffles
   Chocolate, 363
   Mint, 362
   Mocha, 363
  See also Cakes; Cookies; Custard; Ice Cream;
   Sorbet; Tarts
Dijon Sauce, 11

Dill(ed)
  Mustard Dressing, 102
  Roasted Japanese Eggplants with, 254
  Shrimp on Cucumbers, 14
  Tomato Soup in Puff Pastry, 66
Dips
  Beet, 25
  Indian, 26
  Moroccan, 24
  Mustard, Tortilla Rolls with, 38
Domino Chip Cookies, 324
Doughnut Drops, Pumpkin, 308
Dressings. *See* Salad Dressings
Duck (Duckling), Roast
  with Black Peppercorn Sauce, 196
  with Fresh Raspberries, 195
  in Game Pie, 201
  with Kiwi Sauce, Chinese, 197
  Salade de, 88
  Stock, 195, 197

Egg(s)
  Balboa Brunch, 277
  Custard. *See* Custard
  Garlic Salad Dressing, 102
  Lemon Curd, 361
  Meringue
   Bread Pudding, Raspberry, 347
   Chocolate, with Raspberry Crème Anglaise,
    350
  Quiche
   au Saucisson, 281
   Capistrano, 279
  Soufflé
   Crackers, 47
   Peach, Cold, 346
   Three-Cheese, 277
  Zabaglione, Raspberry, 344
Eggnog, Holiday, 364
Eggplant
  with Dill, Roasted Japanese, 254
  and Green Beans, Spicy, 254
  Marinated and Skewered Grilled, 272
  Niçoise, Baked, 271
  and Pepper Topping, Foccacio with, 41
  Salad, Mediterranean, 75
Enchiladas with Ham, Sour Cream, 283
Endive, Belgian, with Two Fillings, 42
Escargot and Prosciutto Stuffed Mushrooms, 32
"Estate bottled" notation, 4

Fajitas, 213
  Chicken, 180
Fennel, Green Salad with, 83
Feta
  California Greek Salad with, 82
  Crisps, 48
  Foccacio with topping of Spinach, Ricotta,
   and, 41
  Green Bean, and Walnut Salad, 74
  Tarte Provençale, 44
  Topping, Broiled Flank Steak with, 208
Fettucine
  California Riviera Salad with, 96
  Chicken Salad, 95
  with Gorgonzola, Bell Peppers, and Basil, 114

with Gruyère Cheese, 112
with Mussels, Lemon, 118
Figs, with Ricotta, Sliced, 40
Fish, 133–64
  Albacore with Red Pepper Sauce, Barbecued, 133
  Fillets
    with Orange Ginger Cream, 134
    Poached, with Wild Mushroom Cream Sauce, 136
    Sonoma Style, with Chèvre, 134
  Lotte (Monkfish) with Red Pepper Cream, Poached, 144
  Orange Roughy with Balsamic Vinegar and Capers, 145
  with Pickled Red Ginger, Thai, 143
  Poisson Printemps, 136
  Spicy Baked, 145
  Stew
    Cioppino, 139
    Normande, 137
  Stock, 69
    Quick, 70
  See also Cod; Halibut; Orange Roughy; Salmon; Snapper; Sole; Swordfish; Tuna
Flamiche, 43
Florentine Pepper Shells with Orzo and Jarlsberg Cream, 259
Foccacio, 40
French Toast, Parmesan, 16
Frosting
  Chocolate Sour Cream, Chocolate Sour Cream Cake with, 315
  Coconut, Lemon Coconut Cake with, 313
  Smooth Butter, Palm Springs Date Nut Cake with, 317
  See also Icing
Fruit(s).
  Breakfast Chimichangas with, 287
  Chicken Mendocino with, 187
  Layered Lemon Crème with, 345
  Sorbet
    alternate method for freezing, 359
    Blueberry, 358
    Kiwi, 357
    Lemon, 357
    Mango, 358
    Pear and Zinfandel, 359
    Raspberry, 358
    Simple Syrup for, 357
    Strawberry Champagne, 359
  Turkey Stuffed with Jalapeño Peppers and, 192
  See also specific fruits

Game
  Pie, 201
  See also Quail; Rabbit; Squab
Garam Masala, 34, 188
Garbanzo Bean Dip, Moroccan, 24
Garlic
  Bread Sticks, 300
  Chicken Breasts, 170
  Cream Potatoes, 261
  Egg Salad Dressing, 102
  Pork Loin Roast Stuffed with Olives and, 230

Sauce, Spicy, Beef and Peppers in, 219
  Zinfandel Butter, Veal Chops with, 240
Gazpacho, Yellow Pepper, 51
Gilroy Potatoes, 261
Ginger(ed)
  Asparagus with Cashews, 245
  Butter, Crisp Cornish Hen Glazed with Red Pepper and, 198
  Chicken with Cracked Wheat, 183
  Cornmeal Muffins, 301
  Cream Snaps, 325
  Kumquats, 41
  -Meatball and Watercress Soup, Chinese, 57
  Orange Cream, Fish Fillets with, 134
  Pecan Peach Pie, 338
  Pumpkin Soup with, 67
  and Red Pepper Relish, 199
  Sauce, Brandied, 360
  Tomato Soup, 64
Gingerbread
  with Apricot Walnut Sauce, Soft, 317
  Pancakes, 288
Goat Cheese (Chèvre)
  Calzone with Smoked Chicken and, 122
  Chicken Breasts Stuffed with, Glazed, 173
  Fish Fillets with, Sonoma Style, 134
  Mold, 19
  Salad, Baked, 81
  Seafood Risotto with Sun-dried Tomatoes and, 140
  Shrimp Baked with, 159
  Tomato Crostini, 17
  Tomatoes Stuffed with Shallots, Mushrooms, and, 265
  Topping, Broiled Flank Steak with, 208
Gorgonzola
  Chicken Salad with, 88
  Fettucine with Bell Peppers, Basil, and, 114
  in Pasta with Four Cheeses, 112
  -Pistachio Loaf, 29
  Polenta, 124
  -Sour Cream Sauce, Tortellini with, 44
  Walnut Rounds, 19
Grand Marnier
  Sauce, 362
  Walnut Cake, 316
Grapefruit, Pink, Sautéed Shrimp with Vodka Glaze and, 161
Gravlax with Mustard Sauce, 22
Great Northern Beans, California Niçoise Salad with, 99
Greek Salad, California, 82
Greek Spinach Rice, 125
Green Bean(s)
  Braised, 246
  and Eggplant, Spicy, 254
  Hot and Sour, 247
  Walnut, and Feta Salad, 74
  with Walnuts, 246
Gruyère
  Chicken, and Spinach Torta, 286
  Pasta with, 112
  Puffs, 20
  in Solvang Caraway Cheese Spread, 16
  and Walnut Salad, 83

Guacamole
  Chicken Fajitas with, 181
  Layered California, 23

Halibut
  Steaks
    Oriental Style, 142
    with Pine Nut Butter, Grilled, 141
    Scandinavian Baked, 142
  in Cioppino, 140
  in Fish Stew Normande, 137
Ham
  Black Forest
    Calzone with Ricotta and, 121
    Orange Glazed Red Cabbage with, 250
  Braised in Port with a Pecan Crust, 230
  Breakfast Meats and Apples with, 290
  Shells Genovese with, 116
  Soup with Blue Cheese, Winter, 65
  Sour Cream Enchiladas with, 283
  and Tomato Sauce, Linguine with, 116
  Tortilla Rolls with Mustard Dip, 38
  in Wagon Wheel Loaf, 293
  Wild Rice and Raisin Salad with, 97
  See also Prosciutto
Hawaiian Pancake, 288
Hazelnut(s) (Filberts)
  Boston Lettuce with Avocado, Raspberry
    Vinaigrette and, 84
  Chocolate Ice Cream, 355
  Cookies, 328
  Spinach Stir-fry with, 263
Hearts of Palm, Green Salad with Artichoke
    Hearts and, 82
Heavenly Hots, 287
Herb(s,-ed)
  Cheese, 25
  Mustard Butter, Crown Roast of Lamb with,
    223
  Potato Bread, 307
  Rice with Tomatoes and Onions, 124
  Summer Baked Vegetables with, 273
  See also specific herbs
Hoisin Sauce, Cauliflower with, 253
Honey, Curry Glazed Chicken with Mustard
    and, 180
Horseradish
  Beef Filling for Chile Bites, 36
  Cream Dressing, 74
  Wasabi Mayonnaise, New Potatoes with, 45

Ice Cream
  Chocolate
    Hazelnut, 355
    White, 355
  Rum Raisin, 354
  Sauce for
    Brandied Ginger, 360
    Praline, 361
    Spiced Blueberry, 360
  Torte, Chocolate Almond, 353
Icing
  Lemon, Lemon Pistachio Bars with, 326
  Mocha, Chocolate Brownies with, 322
  See also Frosting
Imperial Valley Sandwiches, 293

Indian-style dishes
  Dip, 26
  Meatballs with Mint Chutney, 29
  Orange Chicken Indienne, 189
  Punjab Crab with Cold Cucumber Relish, 155
  Tandoori Chicken with Punjabi Sauce, 188
  Wontons, 34
  See also Curry
Indonesian-style dishes
  Beef Satay, 31
  Dipping Sauce, 31
  Lamb Shanks, 229
Italian-style dishes
  Antipasto Salad, Spinach, 85
  Baked Vegetables, 272
  Carpaccio, 27
  Cioppino, 140
  Focaccio, 41
  Marinated Vegetable Salad, 80
  Polenta, 124
  Tomato Crostini, 17
  Vegetable Soup, 56
  Zabaglione, Raspberry, 344
  See also Pasta; Pizza
Italian Sausage
  Pizza Loaf with, 294
  Pizza with Olives, Peppers, Three Cheeses
    and, 121
  Quiche with, 281
  Rabbit with Orange, Tomato, and, 204
  Rosemary Chicken with Sweet Peppers and,
    186

Jalapeño (Peppers)
  Dressing, Shrimp Salad Guadalajara, 92
  Mint Chutney, Rack of Lamb with, 226
  Red Pepper Sauce, Barbecued Albacore with,
    133
  Turkey Stuffed with Fruit and, 192
Japanese Cucumber Salad, Sake Swordfish with,
    152
Japanese Eggplants with Dill, Roasted, 254
Jarlsberg Cheese
  Cream, Florentine Pepper Shells with Orzo
    and, 259
  Leeks au Gratin with, 255
  in Solvang Caraway Cheese Spread, 16
  Three-Cheese Soufflé with, 277
Jícama
  California Greek Salad with, 82
  and Shrimp Salad, 92

Kielbasa Sausage in Brioche, 30
Kiwi(s)
  Layered Lemon Crème with, 345
  Sauce, Chinese Roast Duck with, 197
  Scallops in Cream with, 157
  Sorbet, 357
  Spring Green Salad with Strawberries,
    Avocado, and, 101
Kumquats, Gingered, 41

Lamb, 220–29
  Chops
    with Blue Cheese Peppercorn Butter, 226

with Shiitake Mushrooms and Tarragon, 227
Crown Roast of, with Mustard Herb Butter, 223
Leg of
  Glazed Barbecued, 220
  with Pistachio Nut Stuffing, 222
  Skewered Lamb with Peanut Butter Sauce, 224
  with Sweet Pepper Relish, Rosemary, 221
  in Lettuce Leaves, Thai, 35
Meatballs with Mint Chutney, Indian, 29
with Peach Chutney, Five Spice, 225
Rack of
  with Mint Jalapeño Chutney, 226
  with Peach Chutney, Five Spice, 225
Shanks, Indonesian, 229
Stew, Hearty, 228
Wontons, Indian, 34
Layered Lemon Crème, 345
Leek(s)
au Gratin, 255
and Cucumbers, Braised, 253
Lemon Sauce, Veal Scallops with, 242
Sautéed with Tomato, 255
Soup with Shallots and Bacon, Creamy, 62
Lemon(s)
Blueberry Tart, 333
Chicken with Basil and, 174
Coconut Cake, 312
Crème, Layered, 345
Curd, 361
Icing, Lemon Pistachio Bars with, 326
Leek Sauce, Veal Scallops with, 242
-Lime Pasta, 107
Mustard Vinaigrette, Green Salad with Artichoke Hearts and Hearts of Palm and, 82
Pasta with Mussels, 118
Pesto, Orzo with, 123
Pistachio Bars, 326
Rabbit with Tarragon and Mustard, Grilled, 203
Sorbet, 357
Sweet Potatoes, 267
Tomato Sauce, Pasta with, 113
Turkey and Artichoke Sauté with Rosemary and, 193
Lettuce
in Green Salad
  with Artichoke Hearts and Hearts of Palm, 82
  with Fennel, 83
See also Bibb Lettuce; Boston Lettuce; Red Leaf Lettuce; Romaine Lettuce
Lime
Baked Oysters with Shallots and, 156
-Lemon Pasta, 107
and Red Wine Vinegar Dressing, Cold Beef and Artichoke Salad with, 87
Linguine
Artichoke, 106
with Ham and Tomato Sauce, 116
Sweet Red Pepper Sauce with, 110
Tomato Basil Cream with, 108

Liver(s)
Calf's, with Sautéed Apples and Onions, 220
Chicken, Pâté with Green Peppercorns, 26
Lobster
with Flavored Butters, 163
Ragoût, 164
in Seafood Boudin with Watercress Cream Sauce, 138
Lo Mein Noodles, Oriental Salad with Dried Mushrooms and, 94
Lotte (Monkfish)
with Orange Ginger Cream, 134
with Red Pepper Cream, Poached, 144

Macadamia Butter Sauce, Baked Crab Stuffed Trout with, 156
Macaroons, Pistachio, 330
Madeleines, Orange Anise, 327
Mandarin Chicken Salad, 91
Mango
Cream, 361
Sorbet, 358
Manicotti with Lemon Tomato Sauce, 113
Marmalade, Onion, in Onions, 257
Martini Scallops, 158
Mascarpone
Raspberry Tart with, 335
Tomato Crostini, 17
Mayonnaise
Anchovy, Cauliflower and Olive Salad with, 79
Red Chile, 37
Tarragon, Shrimp and Pasta Salad with, 97
Wasabi, New Potatoes with, 45
Meat, 207–42
with Apples, Breakfast, 290
Loaf
  Cajun, 209
  with Tomato Sauce, Italian, 238
  Mexicali, 235
See also Beef; Lamb; Pork; Veal
Meatball(s)
with Mint Chutney, Indian, 29
and Watercress Soup, Chinese Ginger-, 57
Mediterranean Eggplant Salad, 75
Melba Hearts, 47
Menus, 365–71
Meringue
Chocolate, with Raspberry Crème Anglaise, 350
Raspberry, Bread Pudding, 347
Méthode champenoise technique, 7
Mexican-style dishes
Chicken Fajitas, 180
Corn Chowder, 58
Country Steaks, 214
Guacamole, Layered California, 23
Quesadilla, 36
Salsa, 24
Sandwiches, 39
Vegetable Soup, 59
See also Chile(s); Chili; Tortillas
Millionaire Shortbread, 324
Mint
Brown Rice with Raisins and, 125
Chutney, Indian Meatballs with, 29

Dressing, 75
Jalapeño Chutney, Rack of Lamb with, 226
Spinach Sauce, Grilled Whole Salmon with, 146
Truffles, 362
Mocha
    Icing, Chocolate Brownies with, 322
    Truffles, 363
Monkfish (Lotte)
    with Orange Ginger Cream, 134
    with Red Pepper Cream, Poached, 144
Montrachet Cheese, Tomatoes Stuffed with Shallots, Mushrooms, and, 265
Moroccan Dip, 24
Mousse Cake, Chocolate, with Coffee Whipped Cream, 352
Mozzarella, Pizza Loaf with, 294
Muffin(s)
    Ginger Cornmeal, 301
    Glazed Orange, 305
Mushroom(s)
    Marinated and Skewered Grilled, 272
    -Onion Casserole with Cheese, 256
    Pasta Salad with Dried, Oriental, 94
    Porcini and Cream Sauce, Pasta Twists with, 108
    Pricey Rice with, 126
    Roast Pork Loin with Apples and, 232
    Stir-fried, 273
    Stuffed
        Escargot and Prosciutto, 32
        with Smoked Oysters, 32
    Tomatoes Stuffed with Shallots, Goat Cheese, and, 265
    Wild
        Cream Sauce, Poached Fillets with, 136
        Soup, 56
        and Wild Rice Soup, 64
    See also Oyster Mushrooms; Shiitake Mushrooms
Mussel(s)
    Apple Cider Steamed, 154
    in Cioppino, 140
    Lemon Pasta with, 118
    Provençale, 154
    with Red Pepper Relish, Cold, 12
    Seafood Risotto with Goat Cheese, Sun-dried Tomatoes and, 140
Mustard
    Apricot Glaze, Corned Beef with, 210
    Sauce
        Currant, 33
        Dijon, 11
        Gravlax with, 22
        Peppercorn, Beef Tenderloin with, 208
    Vinaigrette
        Cold Asparagus with, 73
        Lemon, Green Salad with Artichoke Hearts and Hearts of Palm and, 82

Nectarine(s)
    and Blue Cheese Salad, 100
    -Strawberry Cobbler, 337
New Orleans Shrimp Boil, 15
Niçoise Salad, California, 99

Noodles
    Lo Mein, Oriental Salad with Dried Mushrooms and, 94
    with Sautéed Cabbage and Caraway Seeds, 117
Nori, California Rolls with, 38
Nuts
    Cayenne, 77
    Macadamia Butter Sauce, Baked Crab Stuffed Trout with, 156
    Peanut Sauce, Spicy Chicken Wings with, 31
    See also Almond(s); Cashews; Hazelnut(s); Pecan(s); Pine Nut(s); Pistachio; Walnut(s)

Olive(s)
    and Cauliflower Salad, 79
    Pizza with Sausage, Peppers, Three Cheeses and, 121
    Pork Loin Roast Stuffed with Garlic and, 230
Onion(s)
    Calf's Liver with Sautéed Apples and, 220
    Herbed Rice with Tomato and, 124
    Marmalade in Onions, 257
    Mushroom Casserole with Cheese, 256
    Soup, 66
Orange(s)
    Anise Madeleines, 327
    Chicken
        Indienne, 189
        Rosemary, 182
    Chocolate Chip Cookies, 327
    Custard, 345
    Dressing. See also Vinaigrette below
        Spring Green Salad with Strawberries, Avocado, Kiwi and, 101
    Ginger Cream, Fish Fillets with, 134
    Glaze, Orange Ring Cake with, 315
    Glazed Red Cabbage with Black Forest Ham, 250
    Muffins, Glazed, 305
    Rabbit with Sweet Sausages, Tomato, and, 204
    Ring Cake, 315
    Shallot Butter, Broccoli with, 249
    Sherbet with Blackberry Sauce, 356
    Szechuan Shrimp with Spinach, 162
    Vinaigrette
        Brie Salad with Pecans and, 81
        Raspberry, Pear and Raspberry Salad with, 100
    Whipped Cream, Country Baked Apples with, 341
Orange Roughy
    with Balsamic Vinegar and Capers, 145
    with Chèvre, Sonoma Style, 134
    with Orange Ginger Cream, 134
    with Pickled Red Ginger, Thai style, 143
    Poached with Wild Mushroom Cream Sauce, 136
    with Red Pepper Cream, Poached, 144
Oriental Halibut Steaks, Baked, 142
Oriental Pasta Salad with Dried Mushrooms, 94
Oriental Soup with Shrimp and Pineapple, 57
Oriental Steak with Wasabi Butter, 212

Orzo
　Florentine Pepper Shells with Jarlsberg Cream
　　and, 259
　with Lemon Pesto, 123
　Vegetable Soup with Pesto and, 61
Oyster Mushrooms
　Oriental Pasta Salad with, 94
　in Wild, Wild Rice, 129
Oysters
　Baked with Lime and Shallots, 156
　Grilled, 13
　Kilpatrick, 289
　Smoked, Mushrooms Stuffed with, 32

Palm Springs Date Nut Cake, 316
Pancake(s)
　Corn, 285
　Gingerbread, 288
　Hawaiian, 288
　Heavenly Hots, 287
　Scallion, 256
　Wild Rice, Smoked Salmon with, 21
　See also Crepes
Panko-crusted Sesame Chicken, 182
Paprika Dressing, Pepper and Tomato Salad
　　with, 78
Parmesan
　Cream, Breasts of Chicken in, 169
　Croustades, Scallops with, 158
　French Toast, 16
　Pasta with, 112
　Pretzels, 300
　Rice with Walnuts, 129
　Sesame Twists, 48
　Three-Cheese Soufflé with, 277
Parsley and Tomato Salad, 78
Pasta, 105–19
　with Baked Tomato Sauce, 111
　Basic Cooking Directions for, 105
　Confetti, 115
　with Four Cheeses, 112
　Fresh, 105
　with Gruyère Cheese, 112
　with Lemon Lime, 107
　Manicotti with Lemon Tomato Sauce, 113
　with Mussels, Lemon, 118
　Noodles with Sautéed Cabbage and Caraway
　　Seeds, 117
　Sage, Rosemary, and Thyme, 109
　Salad
　　California Riviera, 96
　　Chicken, 95
　　with Dried Mushrooms, Oriental, 94
　　Shrimp, 97
　　with Tomatoes, Basil, and Sherry Vinegar,
　　　94
　Shrimp Vermicelli, 119
　Spaghettini, Summer Tomato Sauce with, 109
　Tortellini with Sour Cream Gorgonzola Sauce,
　　44
　Twists with Porcini and Cream Sauce, 108
　See also Capellini; Fettucine; Linguine; Orzo;
　　Shells; Spaghetti
Pastry
　Cheddar Crust, 179
　Dough, for Game Pie, 202

　for Quiche au Saucisson, 281
　for San Joaquin Valley Tart, 282
Pâté, Chocolate, with Pistachio Sauce, 348
Pâté with Green Peppercorns, 26
Pattypan Squash, Chile-stuffed, 263
Pea(s)
　and Apple Salad, Green, 74
　California Riviera Salad with, 96
　with Prosciutto, 258
　Savoy, 257
　Shells with Basil and, 115
　Snow, with Cashews, 258
　Soup, Chilled Curried, 55
Peach(es)
　Chutney, Five Spice Rack of Lamb with, 225
　Pecan Pie, Gingered, 338
　Soufflé, Cold, 346
Peanut(s)
　Sauce, Spicy Chicken Wings with, 31
　Szechuan Chicken with, 171
Peanut Butter
　Indian Dip with, 26
　Sauce Skewered Lamb with, 224
Pear(s)
　Breast of Chicken with Port, Stilton Cream
　　and slices of, 174
　-Cranberry Cobblers, 336
　en Croute, 342
　and Raspberry Salad, 100
　Sorbet, Zinfandel and, 359
　Torte, 339
Pecan(s)
　Brie Salad with, 80
　Cayenne Nuts, 77
　Chocolate Brownies with Mocha Icing and,
　　322
　Chocolate Chocolate Chip Butterball Cookies
　　with, 323
　Crust, Ham Braised in Port with a, 230
　Domino Chip Cookies, 324
　Peach Pie, Gingered, 338
　Praline Sauce, 361
　Wild Rice and Raisin Salad with, 97
Peking Pork, 233
Penne with Four Cheeses, 112
Pepper(s), Sweet Bell (Green, Red, Yellow)
　and Beef in Spicy Garlic Sauce, 219
　Cheese Ball, Red, 17
　and Corn Roulade, 278
　and Eggplant Topping, Foccacio with, 41
　Fettucine with Gorgonzola, Basil, and, 114
　Gazpacho, Yellow, 51
　and Ginger Butter, Crisp Cornish Hen Glazed
　　with, 198
　and Ginger Relish, 199
　Marinated and Skewered Grilled, 272
　Niçoise, Baked, 271
　Pizza with Sausage, Olives, Three Cheeses
　　and, 121
　Purée, Red, Poached Lotte (Monkfish) with,
　　144
Relish, Red
　Cold Mussels with, 12
　Rosemary Lamb with, 221
Roasted, Pilaf with Snow Peas, Pine Nuts,
　　and, 127

Rosemary Chicken with Italian Sausages and, 186
San Joaquin Valley Tart with, 282
Sauce, Red
  Barbecued Albacore with, 133
  Linguine with, 110
  Tomato, Summer Salmon with, 147
Shells with Orzo and Jarlsberg Cream, Florentine, 259
Soup, Purée of, 52
Spread, Toasted Red, 23
and Tomato Salad, 78
Peppercorn(s)
  Black, Sauce, Roast Duckling with, 196
  Green
    Blue Cheese Butter, Lamb Chops with, 227
    Mustard Sauce, Beef Tenderloin with, 208
    Pâté with, 26
Pesto, 61
  Lemon, Orzo with, 123
  Vegetable Soup with Orzo and, 61
  Zucchini, Tomatoes Stuffed with, 265
Pico de Gallo
  Chicken Fajitas with, 181
  Fajitas with, 213
Pie
  Broccoli Cheddar with Potato Crust, 280
  Chicken with Sausage and Apple, Cheddar-crusted, 178
  Game, 201
  Gingered Pecan Peach, 338
Pilaf with Snow Peas, Pine Nuts, and Roasted Peppers, 127
Pineapple, Oriental Soup with Shrimp and, 57
Pine Nut(s)
  and Almond Tarts, 331
  Butter, Grilled Halibut with, 141
  Pilaf with Snow Peas, Roasted Peppers, and, 127
  Puffs, 329
  Tart, Cheese, 334
Pistachio
  -Gorgonzola Loaf, 29
  Lemon Bars, 326
  Macaroons, 330
  Nut Stuffing, Leg of Lamb with, 222
  Sauce, Chocolate Pâté with, 348
Pizza
  Dough
    Calzone, 119
    Food-Processor Method, 120
  Loaf, 294
  with Sausage, Olives, Peppers and Three Cheeses, 121
Polenta, Gorgonzola, 124
Porcini Mushrooms
  Pasta Twists with Sauce of Cream and, 108
  Pricey Rice with, 126
Pork, 230–39
  Chinese Ginger-Meatball and Watercress Soup, 57
  Estofado, 236
  Fruit, and Jalapeño Peppers, Turkey Stuffed with, 192
  in Italian Meat Loaf with Tomato Sauce, 238
  Loin

  with Butternut Squash, 234
  California Moo Shu, 237
  with Cilantro Sauce, Southwestern Grilled, 232
  Roast Stuffed with Olives and Garlic, 230
  Roast with Apples and Mushrooms, 232
  Mexicali Meat, 235
  Moo Shu, California, 237
  Ribs, Chinese, 238
  Tenderloin
    Medallions with Currants and Scotch, 231
    Peking, 233
  and Veal Terrine, 28
  Wontons, Chinese, 33
  See also Bacon; Ham; Prosciutto; Sausage
Port
  Breast of Chicken and Pear Slices with Stilton Cream and, 174
  Carrots with, 251
  Chicken and Plum Tomatoes in, 167
  Ham in a Pecan Crust Braised in, 230
Potato(es)
  Bread, Herbed, 307
  Crispy Baked, 260
  Crust, Broccoli Cheddar Pie with, 280
  Garlic Cream, 261
  Gilroy, 261
  Niçoise, Baked, 271
  with Tomatoes, Scalloped, 260
  in Vegetarian Mixed Grill, 262
  New
    Salad with Roquefort, 76
    with Wasabi Mayonnaise, 45
  Red
    Appetizer Baked, 45
    San Diego Spuds, 46
Poultry. See Chicken; Cornish Hens; Duck; Turkey
Praline Sauce, 361
Pretzels, Parmesan, 300
Prosciutto
  and Escargot Stuffed Mushrooms, 32
  Peas with, 258
  Shells Genovese with, 116
  in Sliced Figs with Ricotta, 40
Pudding
  Bread, Raspberry Meringue, 347
  Chocolate, Steamed, with Bittersweet Chocolate Sauce, 347
Puff Pastry
  Sesame Cheese Twists, 48
  Tarte Provençale, 44
  Tomato Dill Soup in, 66
Pumpkin
  Autumn Beef in a, 216
  Cake Roll, 318
  Cheesecake, 319
  Doughnut Drops, 308
  Soup with Ginger, 67
Punjab Crab with Cold Cucumber Relish, 155
Punjabi Sauce, Tandoori Chicken with, 188

Quail with Tomatillo Cream and Cheese Corn Crepes, Grilled California, 199
Quesadilla, 36
Quiche

au Saucisson, 281
Capistrano, 279

Rabbit
  with Sweet Sausages, Orange, and Tomato,
    204
  with Tarragon and Mustard, Grilled Lemon,
    203
Radicchio Cups with Smoked Chicken, 37
Raisin(s)
  Bread
    Cinnamon Scones, 306
    Cranberry, 304
    Rosemary, 302
    Rosemary, Smoked Turkey on, 295
  Brown Rice with Mint and, 125
  Rum Ice Cream, 354
  and Wild Rice Salad, 97
Raspberry(ies)
  in California Custard with Fresh Berries, 344
  Cheesecake Bars, 330
  Cream, Asparagus with, 73
  Crème Anglaise, Chocolate Meringue with,
    350
  Duck (Duckling), Roast, with Fresh, 195
  Meringue Bread Pudding, 347
  and Pear Salad, 100
  Sauce, White Chocolate Ice Cream with, 355
  Sorbet, 358
  Tart with Mascarpone Cheese, 335
  Vinaigrette
    Blue Cheese and Nectarine Salad with, 100
    Creamy, Boston Lettuce with Avocado,
      Hazelnuts, and, 84
    Orange, Pear and Raspberry Salad with,
      100
  Vinegar, Chicken with, 175
  Zabaglione, 344
Red Cabbage with Black Forest Ham, Orange
    Glazed, 250
Red Chile Mayonnaise, 37
Red Leaf Lettuce, in Green Salad with Fennel,
    83
Red Snapper. *See* Snapper
Relish
  Red Pepper
    Cold Mussels with, 12
    and Ginger, 199
  Sweet Pepper, Rosemary Lamb with, 221
Rice, 124–29
  Brown, with Raisins and Mint, 125
  Chicken Mendocino with, 187
  Greek Spinach, 125
  Parmesan Walnut, 129
  Pilaf with Snow Peas, Pine Nuts, and Roasted
    Peppers, 127
  Pricey, 126
  Scallop and Sausage Fried, 128
  Seafood Risotto with Goat Cheese and Sun-
    dried Tomatoes, 140
  Sushi, 126
  with Tomatoes and Onions, Herbed, 124
  Tunisian, Tomatoes Stuffed with, 266
  Wild, Wild, 129
  Wine Vinaigrette, Wild Rice and Raisin Salad
    with, 98

Ricotta
  Breakfast Chimichangas with Fresh Fruit and,
    287
  Calzone with Black Forest Ham and, 121
  Foccacio with topping of Spinach, Feta, and,
    41
  in Pasta with Four Cheeses, 112
  Sliced Figs with, 40
  Tomato Crostini, 17
Rigatoni with Four Cheeses, 112
Riviera Dressing, California Salad with, 96
Romaine Lettuce
  in Green Salad with Artichoke Heart and
    Heart of Palm, 82
  in Green Salad with Fennel, 83
Roquefort
  Center Stage Salad, 77
  Dressing, 101
  Potato Salad with, 76
  Sauce, Beef Fillets with, 211
Rosemary
  Chicken with Italian Sausages and Sweet
    Peppers, 186
  Lamb with Sweet Pepper Relish, 221
  Marinade, Chicken Pasta Salad with, 95
  Orange Chicken, 182
  Pasta, Sage, and Thyme, 109
  Raisin Bread, 302
    Smoked Turkey on, 295
  Turkey and Artichoke Sauté with Lemon and,
    193
Rotelle
  with Baked Tomato Sauce, 111
  Salad with Tomatoes, Basil, and Sherry
    Vinegar, 94
Rum
  Bars, Double Chocolate, 322
  Raisin Ice Cream, 354

Sage
  Pasta, Rosemary, and Thyme, 109
Sake, Swordfish with Japanese Cucumber Salad,
    152
Salad, 73–100
  Asparagus
    with Mustard Vinaigrette, Cold, 73
    with Raspberry Cream, 73
  Beef and Artichoke, Cold, 87
  Boston Lettuce, with Avocado, Hazelnuts, and
    Raspberry Vinaigrette, 84
  Cabbage, Napa, 79
  Cauliflower and Olive, 79
  Center Stage, 77
  Cheese
    Blue, and Nectarine, 100
    Brie with Pecans, 80
    Goat, Baked, 81
    Gruyère and Walnut Salad, 83
  Chicken
    Cajun, 90
    Mandarin, 91
    Pasta, 95
    Sonoran, 89
    with Stilton Cheese, 88
    with Wild Rice, 99
  de Canard, 88

Greek, California, 82
Green
    with Artichoke Hearts and Hearts of Palm,
        82
    with Fennel, 83
    with Strawberries, Avocado, and Kisi,
        Spring, 101
Green Bean, Walnut, and Feta, 74
Green Pea and Apple, 74
Italian Marinated Vegetable, 80
Mediterranean Eggplant, 75
Mushroom, Warm, 76
Niçoise, California, 99
Pasta
    California Riviera Salad, 96
    Chicken, 95
    with Dried Mushrooms, Oriental, 94
    Shrimp, 97
    with Tomatoes, Basil, and Sherry Vinegar,
        94
Pears and Raspberry, 100
Pepper and Tomato, 78
Potato, with Roquefort, 76
Seafood, Spring, 93
Shrimp
    Guadalajara, 92
    Jícama, 92
    Pasta, 97
    Wild Rice, 99
Spinach
    Antipasto, 85
    with Chutney Mustard Dressing, 85
    with Three Dressings, 86
Tomato
    Parsley and, 78
    Pepper and, 78
Wild Rice
    and Chicken, 99
    and Raisin, 97
    and Shrimp, 98
See also Dressings; Salad Dressings
Salad Dressings
    Antipasto, Spinach Salad with, 86
    Bacon, Spinach Salad with, 86
    Basil, Creamy, Spring Seafood Salad with, 93
    Chutney Mustard, Spinach Salad with, 85
    Cilantro, Creamy, Sonoran Chicken Salad
        with, 89
    Curry(-ied)
        Cream, Chicken Salad with Stilton Cheese
            and, 89
        Spinach Salad with, 86
        Wild Rice and Shrimp Salad with, 98
    Garlic Egg Salad, 102
    Horseradish Cream, Green Pea and Apple
        Salad with, 74
    Jalapeño, Shrimp Salad Guadalajara with, 92
    Mandarin, Chicken Salad with, 91
    Mint, Green Bean, Walnut, and Feta Salad
        with, 75
    Mustard
        Creamy, Spinach Salad with, 87
        Dill, 102
        Sour Cream, Green Salad with Fennel and,
            83

Orange, Spring Green Salad with
    Strawberries, Avocado, Kiwi and, 101
Paprika, Pepper and Tomato Salad with, 78
Red Wine Vinegar and Lime, Cold Beef and
    Artichoke Salad with, 87
Riviera, California Salad with, 96
Roquefort or Stilton, 101
Tarragon, 102
Walnut, Napa Valley Cabbage Salad with, 79
See also Vinaigrette
Salami, Wagon Wheel Loaf with, 293
Salmon
    Gravlax with Mustard Sauce, 22
    Mold, Layered, 20
    Smoked
        Capellini with Black Caviar and, 117
        Filling for Chile Bites, 37
        with Wild Rice Pancakes, 21
    with Spinach Mint Sauce, Grilled Whole, 146
    Summer, 147
    Tartare, Belgian Endive with, 42
    with Tomato Basil Beurre Blanc, 146
Salsa, 24
    Fresh, Marathon Snapper with, 135
    Tomatillo, 13
Sandwich(es), 291–95
    Aram
        Curried Chicken Filling for, 292
        with Roast Beef, 291
        Turkey and Cilantro Filling for, 292
    Imperial Valley, 293
    Mexican, 39
    Pizza Loaf, 294
    Sausage-filled Baguettes, 295
    Smoked Turkey on Rosemary Raisin Bread,
        295
    Wagon Wheel Loaf, 293
San Joaquin Valley Tart, 282
Sauce(s)
    Apricot
        Brie with, 18
        Walnut, Soft Gingerbread with, 317
    Berry, California Custard with Fresh Berries
        and, 344
    Bittersweet Chocolate, Steamed Chocolate
        Pudding with, 347
    Blackberry, Orange Sherbet with, 356
    Black Peppercorn, Roast Duckling with, 196
    Blueberry, Spiced, 360
    Brandied Ginger, 360
    Brown, for Game Pie, 202
    Butter
        Cayenne, Lobster with, 164
        Macadamia, Baked Crab Stuffed Trout
            with, 156
        Sherry, Lobster with, 163
    Caramel, Pears en Croute with, 342
    Caraway Basting, Grilled Spring Chicken
        with, 185
    Cilantro, Southwestern Grilled Pork with, 233
    Cream
        Cilantro, 148
        Mango, 361
        Parmesan, Breasts of Chicken in, 169
        Porcini, Pasta Twists with, 108
        Raspberry, Asparagus with, 30

Stilton, Breast of Chicken and Pear Slices
with Port and, 174
Tomato-Basil, with Linguine, 108
Watercress, Seafood Boudin with Lobster
and, 139
Wild Mushroom, Poached Fillets with, 136
Cumberland, for Leg of Lamb with Pistachio
Nut Stuffing, 222
Grand Marnier, 362
Hoisin, Cauliflower with, 253
Indonesian Dipping, 31
Kiwi, Chinese Roast Duck with, 197
Lemon
Curd, 361
Leek, Veal Scallops with, 242
Mango Cream, 361
Mustard
Currant, 33
Dijon, 11
Gravlax with, 22
Peppercorn, Beef Tenderloin with, 208
Peanut, Spicy Chicken Wings with, 31
Peanut Butter, Skewered Lamb with, 224
Pistachio, Chocolate Pâté with, 348
Praline, 361
Punjabi, Tandoori Chicken with, 188
Raspberry, White Chocolate Ice Cream with,
355
Red Pepper, Barbecued Albacore with, 133
Roquefort, Beef Fillets with, 211
Sour Cream Gorgonzola, Tortellini with, 44
Spicy Garlic, Beef and Peppers in, 219
Spinach Mint, Grilled Whole Salmon with,
146
Sweet Pungent, Grilled Squab with, 203
Sweet Red Pepper, Linguine with, 110
Tomatillo, Cilantro Chicken with, 172
Tomato
Baked, Pasta with, 111
and Basil, Cappellini with, 107
Double, Shells with, 111
and Ham, Linguine with, 116
Italian Meat Loaf with, 238
Lemon, Manicotti with, 113
Red Pepper, Summer Salmon with, 147
Summer, Spaghettini with, 109
See also Salsa
Sausage
in Brioche, 30
Cheddar-crusted Chicken Pie with Apple and,
178
-filled Baguettes, 295
Grilled Oysters with, 13
Italian
Pizza Loaf with, 294
Pizza with Olives, Peppers, Three Cheeses
and, 121
Quiche with, 281
Rabbit with Orange, Tomato, and, 204
Rosemary Chicken with Sweet Peppers and,
186
and Scallop Fried Rice, 128
Stuffed Baked Apples, 290
Scallion Pancakes, 256
Scallop(s)
in Cioppino, 140

in Cream with Kiwi, 157
Martini, 158
with Parmesan Croustades, 157
and Sausage Fried Rice, 128
in Seafood Boudin with Lobster and
Watercress Cream Sauce, 138
Seafood Risotto with Goat Cheese, Sun-dried
Tomatoes and, 140
in Spring Seafood Salad, 93
Tangerine, 14
Scandinavian Baked Halibut Steaks, 142
Scones, Raisin Cinnamon, 306
Seafood
Boudin with Lobster and Watercress Cream
Sauce, 138
Salad, Spring, 93
See also Fish
Seaweed, California Rolls with, 38
Serra, Father Junipero, 3
Sesame
Cheese Twists, 48
Panko-crusted Chicken, 182
Shallot(s)
Baked Oysters with Lime and, 156
Butter, Sautéed Baby Vegetables with, 271
Creamy Leek Soup with Bacon and, 62
Orange Butter, Broccoli with, 249
Tomatoes Stuffed with Goat Cheese,
Mushrooms, and, 265
Shanghai Beef, 218
Shellfish. See Clam(s); Lobster; Mussel(s);
Oysters; Scallop(s); Shrimp
Shells
Confetti, 115
with Double Tomato Sauce, 111
with Four Cheeses, 112
Genovese, 116
with Peas and Basil, 115
and Shrimp Salad, 97
Sherbet, Orange, with Blackberry Sauce, 356
Sherry
Bok Choy Stir-fry with, 249
Butter Sauce, Lobster with, 163
Glaze for Leg of Lamb with Pistachio Nut
Stuffing, 222
Vinegar, Pasta Salad with Tomatoes, Basil,
and, 94
Shiitake Mushrooms
Lamb Chops with Tarragon and, 227
Oriental Pasta Salad with, 94
Pricey Rice with, 126
in Wild, Wild Rice, 129
Shrimp, 159–63
Baked with Goat Cheese, 159
Balboa Brunch with, 277
Cajun Barbecued, 160
California Riviera Salad with, 96
in Cioppino, 140
on Cucumbers, Dilled, 14
Oriental Soup with Pineapples and, 57
Rémoulade, 15
Salad
Guadalajara, 92
Jícama, 92
Pasta, 97
Wild Rice, 99

Sautéed with Pink Grapefruit and Vodka
Glaze, 161
Seafood Risotto with Goat Cheese, Sun-dried
Tomatoes and, 140
with Spinach, Orange Szechwan, 162
Stock, 160
Summer Curry, 161
with Tarragon, 162
Thai, 159
Vermicelli, 119
Snails and Prosciutto Stuffed Mushrooms, 32
Snapper
with Chèvre, Sonoma Style, 134
Chinatown, 150
with Cilantro Cream, Southwest, 148
Marathon, 135
with Orange Ginger Cream, 134
Pacific, 149
Piccata, 149
with Pickled Red Ginger, Thai style, 143
Poached with Wild Mushroom Cream Sauce, ·
136
Poisson Printemps with, 136
with Red Pepper Cream, Poached, 144
Spicy Baked, 145
Snow Peas
with Cashews, 258
Pilaf with Pine Nuts, Roasted Peppers, and,
127
Sole
Curry, 151
with Jade Butter, 150
Poached with Wild Mushroom Cream Sauce,
136
Poisson Printemps with, 136
in Seafood Boudin with Lobster and
Watercress Cream Sauce, 138
Solvang Caraway Cheese Spread, 16
Sonoran Chicken Salad, 89
Sorbet
alternate method for freezing, 359
Blueberry, 358
Kiwi, 357
Lemon, 357
Mango, 358
Pear and Zinfandel, 359
Raspberry, 358
Simple Syrup for, 357
Strawberry Champagne, 359
Soufflé
Crackers, 47
Peach, Cold, 346
Three-Cheese, 277
Soup, 51–70
Apple Broccoli, 65
Banana Indienne, Chilled, 55
Bean
Cajun, 60
White, with Swiss Chard, 63
Clam Bisque, Cold, 54
Corn Chowder
Country, 62
Mexican, 58
Cucumber
California, 53
Classic, 53

Gazpacho, Yellow Pepper, 51
Ginger-Meatball and Watercress Soup,
Chinese, 57
Leek with Shallots and Bacon, Creamy, 62
Mexican Vegetable, 58
Mushroom
Wild, 56
and Wild Rice, 64
Onion, 66
Pea, Chilled Curried, 55
Pepper, Sweet
Purée of, 52
Yellow, Gazpacho, 52
Pumpkin with Ginger, 67
with Shrimp and Pineapple, Oriental, 57
Stock
Beef, 68
Chicken, 69
Fish, 69
Fish, Quick, 70
Vegetable, 70
Sunshine, 51
Tomato
Dill in Puff Pastry, 66
Ginger, 64
-Yogurt, Cold, 52
Tortilla, 59
Vegetable
Italian, 56
Mexican, 59
with Orzo and Pesto, 61
Vichyssoise, Sweet Potato, 54
Wild Rice and Mushroom, 64
Winter Ham with Blue Cheese, 65
Sour Cream
Chocolate Cake, 314
Chocolate Frosting, Chocolate Sour Cream
Cake with, 315
Enchiladas with Ham, 283
Gorgonzola Sauce, Tortellini with, 44
Mustard Dressing, Green Salad with Fennel
and, 83
Southwestern Grilled Chicken, 177
Southwestern Grilled Pork with Cilantro Sauce,
232
Spaghetti
Sage, Rosemary, and Thyme, 109
Salad with Dried Mushrooms, Oriental, 94
Spaghettini, Summer Tomato Sauce with, 109
Spinach
Chicken, and Gruyère Torta, 286
Crepes with Tomato Fondue, 284
Florentine Pepper Shells with Orzo, Jarlsberg
Cream, and, 259
Focaccio with topping of Ricotta, Feta, and,
41
Mint Sauce, Grilled Whole Salmon with, 146
Orange Szechuan Shrimp with, 162
Rice, Greek, 125
Salad
Antipasto, 85
with Chutney Mustard Dressing, 85
with Three Dressings, 86
Sauté of Chard with, 262
in Spring Seafood Salad, 93
Stir-fry with Hazelnuts, 263

Spread(s)
  Roasted Pepper, 23
  Solvang Caraway Cheese, 16
Squab with Sweet Pungent Sauce, Grilled, 203
Squash
  Acorn, Autumn, 264
  Butternut, Pork with, 234
  Pattypan, Chile-stuffed, 263
  Yellow, Grilled with Chili Butter, 270
  See also Zucchini
Stew(s)
  Beef in a Pumpkin, Autumn, 216
  Fish
    Cioppino, 139
    Normande, 137
  Lamb, Hearty, 228
  Pork Estofado, 236
  Veal Provençal, 241
Stilton Cheese
  Chicken Salad with, 88
  Cream, Breast of Chicken and Pear Slices
    with Port and, 174
  Dressing, 101
  Puffs, 21
Stock
  Beef, 68
  Chicken, 69
  Duck, 195, 197
  Fish, 69
  Shrimp, 160
  Vegetable, 70
Strawberry(-ies)
  in California Custard with Fresh Berries, 344
  Champagne Sorbet, 359
  Cream Cake, Frozen, 351
  Cream Puff Ring with Blueberries and, 343
  Layered Lemon Crème with, 345
  -Nectarine Cobbler, 337
  Nut Bread, 305
  Spring Green Salad with Avocado, Kiwi, and,
    101
Summer Baked Vegetables with Herbs, 273
Sunshine Soup, 51
Sushi Rice, 126
  in California Rolls, 38
Sweet Potato(es)
  Lemon, 267
  Vichyssoise, 54
Swiss Chard
  Sauté of Spinach with, 262
  White Bean Soup with, 63
Swiss Cheese
  Balboa Brunch with, 277
  Three-Cheese Soufflé with, 277
  Wagon Wheel Loaf with, 293
  Zucchini Gratin with, 264
Swordfish
  au Poivre Rose, 151
  Grilled, 153
    with Wasabi Marinade, 153
  with Japanese Cucumber Salad, Sake, 152
Szechuan Chicken with Peanuts, 171

Tandoori Chicken with Punjabi Sauce, 188
Tangerine Scallops, 14
Tarragon

Dressing, 102
Grilled Lemon Rabbit with Mustard and, 203
Lamb Chops with Shiitake Mushrooms and,
  227
Mayonnaise, Shrimp and Pasta Salad with, 97
Shrimp with, 162
Vinaigrette, 76
Tart(s)
  Almond and Pine Nut, 331
  Apple Almond, 332
  Blueberry
    Cheese, 334
    Lemon, 333
  Cheese
    Blueberry, 334
    Mascarpone and Raspberry, 335
  San Joaquin Valley, 282
Tarte Provençale, 44
Terrine, Veal and Pork, 28
Thai Fish with Pickled Red Ginger, 143
Thai Lamb in Lettuce Leaves, 35
Thai Shrimp, 159
Thyme
  and Balsamic Vinaigrette, Baked Goat Cheese
    Salad with, 81
  Pasta, Sage, and Rosemary, 109
Tomatillo
  Cream, Grilled California Quail with Cheese
    Corn Crepes and, 199
  Salsa
    Grilled Oysters with, 13
    in San Diego Spuds, 46
  Sauce, Cilantro Chicken with, 172
Tomato(es)
  Basil Beurre Blanc, Salmon with, 146
  Brioche with Brie and, 43
  California Riviera Salad with, 96
  Cheese Crostini, 17
  Cherry
    Marinated and Skewered Grilled, 272
    Stuffed Cherry, 39
  and Chicken in Port, 167
  Coulis, Three-Cheese Soufflé with, 277
  Fondue, Spinach Crepes with, 284
  Herbed Rice with Onion and, 124
  Leeks Sautéed with, 255
  Oven-dried, 266
  Pasta Salad with Basil, Sherry Vinegar and,
    94
  Rabbit with Sweet Sausages, Orange and, 204
  Salad
    Parsley and, 78
    Pepper and, 78
  San Joaquin Valley Tart with, 282
  Sauce
    Baked, Pasta with, 111
    and Basil, Capellini with, 107
    Double, Shells with, 111
    and Ham, Linguine with, 116
    Italian Meat Loaf with, 238
    Lemon, Manicotti with, 113
    Red Pepper, Summer Salmon with, 147
    Summer, Spaghettini with, 109
  Scalloped Potatoes with, 260
  Soup
    Ginger, 64

in Puff Pastry, Dill, 66
Stuffed
  with Goat Cheese, Shallots, and
    Mushrooms, 265
  with Tunisian Rice, 266
  with Zucchini Pesto, 265
Sun-dried, Seafood Risotto with Goat Cheese
  and, 140
Tarte Provençale, 44
Veal Scallops with Basil and, 239
Yogurt Soup, Cold, 52
Torta, Chicken, Spinach, and Gruyère, 286
Torta Cheese Tomato Crostini, 17
Torte
  Pear, 339
  Walnut, 340
Tortellini with Sour Cream Gorgonzola Sauce,
  44
Tortilla(s)
  Capistrano Quiche with, 279
  Chimichangas with Fresh Fruit, Breakfast,
    287
  Imperial Valley Sandwiches with, 293
  Rolls with Mustard Dip, 38
  Soup, 59
  Sour Cream Enchiladas with Ham, 283
Trout
  with Crab Stuffing and Macadamia Butter
    Sauce, Baked, 156
  Spicy Baked, 145
Truffles
  Chocolate, 363
  Mint, 362
  Mocha, 363
Tuna
  California Niçoise Salad with, 99
  Chile Bites with, 36
Tunisian Rice, Tomatoes Stuffed with, 266
Turbot, in Fish Stew Normande, 137
Turkey, 191–94
  and Artichoke Sauté with Lemon and
    Rosemary, 193
  and Cilantro Filling (for Aram Sandwiches),
    292
  with Confetti Vegetable Dressing, Roasted,
    191
  Smoked
    Rémoulade Belgian Endive with, 42
    on Rosemary Raisin Bread, 295
  Spicy Grilled Breast, 194
  Stuffed with Fruit and Jalapeño Peppers, 192
Turnips Sautéed with Shallot Butter, 271

Veal, 239–42
  Chops with Zinfandel Garlic Butter, 240
  Liver with Sautéed Apples and Onions, 220
  and Pork Terrine, 28
  Scallops
    with Lemon Leek Sauce, 242
    with Tomatoes and Basil, 239
  Stew Povençal, 241
Vegetable(s), 245–74
  Baked
    with Herbs, Summer, 273
    Italian, 272
    Niçoise, 271

Dressing, Confetti, Roasted Turkey with, 191
Filling, for Imperial Valley Sandwiches, 293
Grilled with Chili Butter, 270
Marinated and Skewered Grilled, 272
Salad, Italian Marinated, 80
with Shallot Butter, Sautéed Baby, 271
Soup
  Italian, 56
  Mexican, 59
  with Orzo and Pesto, 61
Stir-fried, 273
Stock, 70
Strudels, Individual, 274
See also specific vegetables
Vermicelli
  Sage, Rosemary, and Thyme, 109
  Shrimp, 119
Vichyssoise, Sweet Potato, 54
Vinaigrette
  Balsamic
    Cajun Chicken Salad with, 90
    and Thyme, Baked Goat Cheese Salad with,
      81
  Center Stage, 77
  Champagne, 75
  Cilantro, Shrimp and Jícama Salad with, 93
  Creamy Raspberry, Boston Lettuce with
    Avocado, Hazelnuts and, 84
  Lemon Mustard, Green Salad with Artichoke
    Hearts and Hearts of Palm and, 82
  Mustard, Cold Asparagus with, 73
  Orange, Brie Salad with Pecans and, 81
  Raspberry, Blue Cheese and Nectarine Salad
    with, 100
  Raspberry Orange, Pear and Raspberry Salad
    with, 100
  Red Wine, Gruyère and Walnut Salad with,
    84
  Rice Wine, Wild Rice and Raisin Salad with,
    98
  Tarragon, 76
Vinegar
  Balsamic, Orange Roughy with, 145
  Raspberry, Chicken with, 175
  See also Vinaigrette
Vintage dating, 4
Vitus vinifera, 3
Vodka Glaze, Sautéed Shrimp with Pink
  Grapefruit and, 161

Walnut(s)
  Apricot Sauce, Soft Gingerbread with, 317
  Chocolate Chip Brownies with, 321
  Chocolate Chocolate Chip Butterball Cookies
    with, 323
  Date Cake, Palm Springs, 316
  Double Chocolate Rum Bars with, 323
  Dressing, Napa Cabbage Salad with, 79
  Gorgonzola Rounds, 19
  Grand Marnier Cake, 316
  Green Bean, and Feta Salad, 74
  Green Beans with, 246
  and Gruyère Salad, 83
  Parmesan Rice with, 129
  Strawberry Bread, 305
  Torte, 340

Warm Mushroom Salad, 76
Wasabi
  Butter, Oriental Steak with, 212
  Marinade, Grilled Swordfish with, 153
  Mayonnaise, New Potatoes with, 45
Watercress
  Cream Sauce, Seafood Boudin with Lobster
    and, 139
  and Ginger-Meatball Soup, Chinese, 57
White Bean(s)
  Beef Brisket with, 215
  Soup with Swiss Chard, 63
White Chocolate Ice Cream, 355
Whole Wheat Bread, 303
Wild, Wild Rice, 129
Wild Mushroom Soup, 56
Wild Rice
  and Mushroom Soup, 64
  Pancakes, Smoked Salmon with, 21
  Salad
    Chicken and, 99
    Shrimp and, 98
    Raisin and, 97
Wine, 3–8
  Cabernet Sauvignon, 6
  Chardonnay, 5
  labeling laws for, 4
  Pinot Noir, 6
  Port. *See* Port

Riesling, 5–6
Sauvignon Blanc, 5
sparkling, 7
Vinaigrette. *See* Vinaigrette
Vinegar and Lime Dressing, Red
  Cold Beef and Artichoke Salad with, 87
Zinfandel, 6–7. *See also* Zinfandel
Winter Ham Soup with Blue Cheese, 65
Wontons
  Chinese, 33
  Indian, 34

Yams
  Bourbon, 268
  Shoestring, 268
Yogurt
  Tomato Soup, Cold, 52

Zabaglione, Raspberry, 344
Zinfandel
  Garlic Butter, Veal Chops with, 240
  and Pear Sorbet, 359
Zucchini
  Gratin, 264
  Grilled with Chili Butter, 270
  Italian Baked, 272
  Niçoise, Baked, 271
  Pesto, Tomatoes Stuffed with, 265
  Sautéed with Shallot Butter, 271